Family transformation through divorce and remarriage

One marriage in three is likely to end in divorce.
One in seven families is likely to be a single-parent household.
One in eight families is probably a stepfamily.

These are the present estimates. Many of the children of these families will be referred to child and family guidance clinics with divorce-related problems, while others, whose parent(s) are often living near the poverty line, may be considered to be seriously at risk through neglect or abuse.

The past twenty years have seen the emergence of family therapy, as well as the development of family research, some of it related to divorce, stepfamilies and the effects of divorce on children. Socio-legal studies have also been a recent, though separate, development. In *Family Transformation Through Divorce and Remarriage*, Margaret Robinson integrates these two strands of research with the application of systems theory, the basis of family therapy.

This book is the first to look so thoroughly at the complete divorce–remarriage–stepfamily cycle in the context of the demographic data, the legal processes and the systemic theoretical framework. For each phase of the cycle, the author describes the stages of development, summarises the relevant research and illustrates the effects on family members with case examples. In doing so, she discusses the various ways of intervening with families during the divorce process and the differing orientations of the professionals involved. In the last phase of the cycle, she introduces the concept of the 'good enough' post-divorce and remarried family, attempting to define it and provide appropriate guidelines for families and practitioners. Finally, she outlines some of the present research proposals which are likely to change both attitude and practice in relation to families during divorce.

Family Transformation Through Divorce and Remarriage will be an essential source of reference for counsellors, conciliators, marital and family therapists, social workers and other professionals in the area.

Margaret Robinson has been involved in therapeutic work with families for over thirty years, and in mediation for ten years. She is Consultant Conciliator to the Institute of Family Therapy, London, a marital and family therapist in private practice, and a guardian *ad litem*.

Family transformation through divorce and remarriage

A systemic approach

Margaret Robinson

Tavistock/Routledge
London and New York

First published in 1991
by Routledge
11 New Fetter Lane, London EC4P 4EE

Simultaneously published in the USA and Canada
by Routledge
a division of Routledge, Chapman and Hall Inc.
29 West 35th Street, New York, NY 10001

© 1991 Margaret Robinson

Typeset from Author's disks by J&L Composition Ltd,
Filey, North Yorkshire

Printed and bound in Great Britain by Mackays of Chatham PLC, Kent

British Library Cataloguing in Publication Data
Robinson, Margaret, *1927–*
   Family transformation through divorce and remarriage: a
   systemic approach.
   1. Families. Effects of divorce
   I. Title
   306.89

Library of Congress Cataloging in Publication Data
Robinson, Margaret, 1927–
   Family transformation through divorce and remarriage: a systemic
   approach/Margaret Robinson.
   p.   cm.
   1. Remarriage—Great Britain.   2. Stepfamilies—Great Britain.
   3. Divorce—Great Britain.   4. Family—Great Britain.   I. Title.
   HQ1019.G7R63   1990
   306.87—dc20   90–36325
                                                                  CIP

ISBN 0–415–05227–0

For Sue, Barry and Max
who were at the heart of it

Contents

Illustrations

Family case examples

Foreword

There can be few people with as distinguished a professional pedigree as Margaret Robinson. She was Psychiatric Social Worker and Tutor at the Tavistock Clinic in the great days when Henry Dicks was in charge of its Marital Unit, undertaking the research on couples therapy which led to his seminal book 'Marital Tensions'; and when John Bowlby was heading the Department of Children and Parents, developing the ideas for his books on attachment theory. She also worked during this time in what is now known as the Tavistock Institute of Marital Studies.

Though Margaret and I have since become close friends, I can recall a certain sense of awe that I felt towards her, with her august Tavistock connections, when she enrolled in the mid-1960s for the Introductory Course in Group Work I had designed, on behalf of the Group Analytic Society, for members of the Association of Psychiatric Social Workers. The course was later opened to all the mental health professions and became part of the programme of the Institute of Group Analysis. She then took further training in group analysis, and has been influential in carrying its approach to the understanding of systems into the field of family and marital therapy.

Our next meeting was at the first Day-Conference on Family Therapy in 1967, which took place at the Woodberry Down Child Guidance Unit where I was then Director. This was the first coming together of professionals experimenting with the new techniques of family therapy in London, where she represented the Tavistock Clinic and the work being done there.

In the years that followed, our professional contact and personal friendship grew as we met at the increasing number of conferences on family and marital therapy. Margaret was a natural choice when I invited colleagues to join me in staffing the first Introductory Course in Family Therapy, set up in 1973, within the Institute of Group

Analysis. In 1975 she joined with us in founding the Association of Family Therapy, and in founding the Institute of Family Therapy the following year, as the increasing demand for our family therapy courses made it necessary to create an organisation able to cater for the wide range of professional orientations involved in the field.

Throughout the life of this new institute, her wide experience, wisdom, and the respect and affection in which she is held have made her a central and crucial influence on its development in a general sense, as well as in specific areas including her special contribution towards the formation of its Conciliation Service. She set up the telephone advice service for the Stepfamily Association; she has played a leading part in the development of the mediation movement in this country; and, as this book now clearly establishes, she is one of the principal authorities on divorce and stepfamilies at an international level. Academic posts, *inter alia*, have included the post of Senior Lecturer in Social Work at the Universities of London and (later) Southampton.

One reason for our close association is our shared belief that the personal and professional lives of therapists deeply affect each other – whether one believes or wishes that to be the case or not – and that ideally this connection between the personal and professional worlds should be conscious and explicit, so that growth and learning in one can facilitate development in the other.

Her own experience of being a parent in a reconstituted family has thus had a deep influence on her understanding. This has ensured that her theories about divorce and stepparenting are scrutinised against the day-to-day reality of these experiences, and that her own ideas and advice are firmly grounded in the practical knowledge of ordinary family life. She and her husband have been among my and my late wife's closest friends for over fifteen years, and their lively and loving relationship with each other, their capacity to consult and cooperate in their dealings with their children, and their warmth, humour and generosity towards their friends and colleagues all testify to the validity and usefulness of the ideas and information this book contains.

No doubt this is one reason for her choice of title, which expresses a new attitude, and affirms the strength and special potential of reconstituted families, instead of viewing them as a second-best arrangement through the lens of a deficit model. Seeing this title, I immediately thought of an experience in Dallas, Texas, where I had been asked to give a foundation lecture at a prestigious private school for senior girls. After it was concluded I was asked to talk with groups of pupils, and found so many of their questions connected with the effects of divorce on children that it was clear – though their questions were impersonal – that they were talking about their own anxieties. I said they probably knew more about the subject than I did, by direct experience, and invited them to teach me. I was then fascinated, and greatly heartened, to learn that those girls whose parents had divorced acknowledged that this loss, though painful, had made them more confident and self-reliant; while the girls from intact families were quite rueful that their better fortune had left them feeling less resilient and less ready to cope with the outside world. Margaret Robinson helps us to be more aware of such strengths and advantages that members of reconstituted families may gain.

Although her background in the Tavistock Clinic has given her a particularly strong foundation in psychoanalytic ideas and techniques (both orthodox Freudian and Kleinian), and in attachment theory – to all of which her connection with the Institute of Group Analysis has added the group dimension – her work stands upon an unusually wide theoretical base. More recently she has been influenced by 'constructivist' ideas, particularly those of Hoffmann, Anderson and Goolishian, and White. Seventeen years of work within the Institute of Family Therapy, however, and the courses from which it grew (that were set up with the express aim of bringing together all the main schools of family therapy) have enabled her to draw from the whole range of methods. No other colleague I know is more questioning towards existing ideas, or more open to new ones. Yet as the reader will find, she is eminently commonsensical and her knowledge is expressed in clear and simple language, illustrated by good case examples.

Two further merits that should be pointed out, particularly for those in the legal profession, are the very full treatment of the new conciliation and mediation movements, and the use of systems theory not only for the practice of therapy, but also for better understanding and management of the legal process. And finally, Chapter 12 explores the implications of current developments for the future.

I am sure this book will be influential towards the development of more positive, realistic attitudes and more successful approaches among professionals dealing with cases of divorce and stepfamilies. Its broad and solid theoretical base, its grounding in practical everyday experience, and the clarity of its writing also make it an ideal general text on these subjects for mental health professionals and members of the legal profession at all levels of experience.

Robin Skynner,
July 1990

Preface

The origins of this book really began nearly forty years ago when I met and later married a man who had previously been married and divorced. Although he continued to see his two young sons and to maintain them and their mother, we had not envisaged that he either could or would become a custodial father. As things turned out, on the day prior to the birth of our daughter, my husband became the custodial parent of his sons, primarily because their mother had remarried and gone to live in France. Subsequently, and for the remaining years of their childhood, they lived with us, regularly visiting their 'other' family which consisted of their mother, step-father and half-brother.

In my early attempts to become a good stepmother I found myself isolated and without guidelines as to how I should feel or behave. Mistakenly, we tried to pass as if we were a nuclear family, and when my stepmother status was revealed, it seemed me that I was either treated as the object of a somewhat erotic interest, or stigmatised by the social network within which we lived. Within two years of marriage, I had two stepchildren, a young baby, a husband whose occupation took him away a great deal, and a developing sense of guilt and failure. Looking back, it is hardly surprising that I became what is known as mildly depressed and this led me to seek help in the form of psychoanalysis – which, thanks to my analyst, somewhat restored my self-esteem and enabled me to recover some ability to manage the demanding family life which, as well as each other, my husband and I had unwittingly chosen.

Later, as a mental health practitioner, I began to see that many of my attempts to make sense of what was making life difficult for many stepfamilies, as it had done for us, and for those who became my clients, were based on the nuclear family model. When I became a teacher of social work, and subsequently as a family therapist and mediator as well as a teacher in both fields, I gradually came to realise that many of my ideas about stepfamilies were also based on the somewhat skewed sample of those who came to seek help because someone considered that the stepfamily had a problem for which 'treatment' was necessary, and that many of them were struggling with the same confused and complex issues as we had done so many years earlier.

During my time as a Senior Lecturer at London University, I was part of a group of family researchers who met together to share ideas with one another, and I began to give up some of my unrealistic expectations with regard to families in transition from divorce to remarriage. A key member of this 'Chelsea Group' was the late Jackie Burgoyne, and it was she who originally asked me to write this book and who, despite her own terminal illness, encouraged me in the early stages of writing, as she did so many others in the field of family studies.

The book would not have been written at all but for my clients, who not only generously shared their experiences with me but also from whom I learned much of what is in the book. I found their courage and openness both challenging and humbling, their ability to change rewarding and at times almost incredible. While those whose stories I have included will recognise themselves, I have changed certain facts so as to ensure their privacy, and I would like to thank them for their goodwill and trust in my therapeutic endeavours.

Becoming involved in a field of considerable family stress takes its toll on the practitioner, and were it not for my colleagues and friends I could not continue to do so. I especially want to express my gratitude to my colleagues in the Conciliation Team at the Institute of Family Therapy, Irene Gee, Margaret Adcock and Alan Morris, whose support and encouragement has both guided and enabled me to stay with the pain of the couples who come to us for mediation during their separation and divorce. Several of my close friends, notably Margaret Adcock, Ros Draper, Phyllida Parsloe and Donna Smith, as well as engaging in extensive discussions, also kindly read parts or the whole of the manuscript, giving me both useful feedback which I have tried to incorporate in the final manuscript and the encouragement to continue writing. Some twenty years ago, my friend and colleague Robin Skynner introduced me to the field of family therapy; he and his late wife Prue, together with my husband and myself, subsequently spent many hours discussing how to help couples with their marital difficulties.

I am grateful to a number of colleagues and teachers – in

particular, John Haynes, Florrie Kaslow, Joan Kelly, John and Emily Visher and Michael White – for sharing their ideas with me, thus influencing my own thinking and for allowing me to draw so freely on their own work. A course I attended in Williamstown, USA, in the summer of 1988, organised by Carlos Sluzki, led to my rewriting the theoretical chapter on family systems and I am (now!) glad that I was thus forced to re-examine my own beliefs and theoretical framework.

To the National Stepfamily Association (founded by Elizabeth and Dick Hodder in 1983) I want to convey my very good wishes for providing much of the information and support for stepfamilies, which I lacked all those years ago. My years as a member of the Executive and, together with Donna Smith, in the setting up of the Telephone Counselling Service, gave me some opportunity to repay the experience and the help which I felt I had eventually received. I also want to express my admiration and gratitude to the National Family Conciliation Council, especially to the Director, Thelma Fisher, my co-consultant Jan Walker, and many other conciliators, with whom I shared the struggle to distinguish between the differences and similarities in therapy and mediation. Similarly, I would like to say thank you to Judy Cunnington, Deputy Director of London Marriage Guidance and to the counsellors who are or were members of my case discussion group. I want to express my appreciation to one of my legal colleagues, Helen Garlick, who read earlier drafts of the section on lawyers and helped me to correct some of the inevitable mistakes.

I would also like to thank my editor, Edwina Welham, for her supportive assistance during the process of transition from manuscript to publication.

By far my greatest debt is to my husband, Denis, who really ought to be credited with the co-authorship, for had we not spent the last forty years together, I would never have become interested in the subject in the first place. Indeed, during the writing of the book he consistently encouraged me to 'sit down and get on with it', gave up much of his retirement leisure time to listen to interminable discussions, and also ensured that the word processor became not only 'user friendly', but through him, almost human and 'user cherishing'! To my daughter and stepsons, to whom this book is dedicated, I can only say with deep affection that had I known then what I do today, there are many things that I would do differently, but I would not change the composition of my stepfamily.

During the three years which I have taken to write this book there has developed a considerable interest in families during divorce and remarriage. The final responsibility for what I have written remains mine, and I can only hope that it will prove useful to the many 'interventionist practitioners' in this developing field.

Winchester
July 1990

ACKNOWLEDGEMENTS

To Faber & Faber and Random House for permission to use extracts from the work of W. H. Auden.

To Faber & Faber for permission to use extracts from the work of T. S. Eliot and Philip Larkin.

To the editors of *Family Process*, Lyman Wynne and Jurg Willi, for allowing me to use the diagrams from articles published by them.

Every effort has been made to obtain permission to reproduce copyright material throughout this book. If any proper acknowledgement has not been made the copyright holder should contact the publishers.

1 Introduction
The post nuclear family

Each venture
Is a new beginning, a raid on the inarticulate
With shabby equipment always deteriorating
In the general mess of imprecision of feeling.

T. S. Eliot (1888–1965), 'East Coker'

That dear octopus we call the family, from whose tentacles we can never quite escape.

Dodie Smith, *Dear Octopus*

They f—— you up your Mum and Dad,
They may not mean to but they do.

Philip Larkin, 'This be the Verse'

The family, it seems, is here to stay. In modern times some kind of family unit remains as popular as ever, though the shape and beliefs about its purpose appear to be changing. While many families experience changes in the membership of their households, as couples they cohabit, marry, remarry and (apart from a small number of the voluntarily childless) procreate children or endeavour to do so, with apparent passion and determination. The present tendency to marry, divorce and, for one if not both the formerly married spouses, then to remarry or to cohabit, leads to a subsequent proliferation of networks of families connected through the 'one-time married couple', their children and subsequent children with further partners. According to Chester (1983), 'historians, such as Shorter (1975) and Stone (1977) describe a complex and curvilinear process which includes the dissolution of a collective way of life and the extrusion of the nuclear family' from its previous context of kin and community. Such a process has led to the rise of privacy and domesticity, the ideologies of romantic and eroticised love and marriage and felicific parenthood. Indeed Stone's (1977) picture of the contemporary family as 'intensely self centred, inward turned, emotionally bonded, sexually liberated, child oriented' also accords closely enough with that of many social scientists (Chester 1983). However, the wide-ranging and sometimes passionate arguments about the emergence of the modern nuclear family amount to what have been described as 'the war over the family' (Berger and Berger 1983). Some of these battles range from feminist arguments relating to the oppression of women in the family – see, for instance, Smart (1984), *The Ties that Bind* – and for the availability of alternative choices to the prevailing and favoured patterns of family life – Barrett and McIntosh (1982), *The Anti-social Family* – to those 'for popular marriage, a relationship sealed by a vow of lifelong fidelity between adults' evinced by Mount (1982), *The Subversive Family.*

There are also other well-rehearsed arguments, as, for instance, that the family is a 'haven in a heartless capitalist world' (Lasch 1977) or that the modification of modern family law has led to the therapeutic tutelage of the family by the welfare state, which has invaded the space between the 'intrafamilial' and the 'extrafamilial' and thus undermined the autonomy of the family (Donzelot 1979). According to the Bergers' spirited defence of the bourgeois family, the modern family is perceived with a kind of double vision. In one vision

> the bourgeois family is a natural unit of parents and children, united by love, mutual respect, trust, and fidelity, based on religiously inspired values and giving a distinct moral quality to this basic unit of social life. In the other vision ... [it] is a narrowly constraining cage, turning its members into mere instruments of production, profoundly destructive of the personalities of women and children (and perhaps to a lesser degree of men) and generally cutting off its members from participation in the larger concerns of society.

During the fifties and sixties Talcott Parsons (1964), one of the pioneers in the field and one of the most respected family sociologists, argued that the family had been stripped to its essential functions, that of the socialisation of children and the stabilisation of the adult personality; these processes taking place in the privacy of the home, where the family conducts its emotional life and meets its emotional needs. While Talcott Parsons has been considerably criticised by subsequent sociologists, Poster (1978) has argued similarly that it is necessary to 'redefine the family structure away from issues of family size towards issues relating to emotional patterns'. It is on such attempts to develop theories of family interaction through which these emotional patterns can be both conceptualised and understood that this book is based, although it is specificially focused on those aspects of family life relating to marital breakdown, separation, divorce and remarriage.

DIVORCE

One of the issues relating to emotional patterns of this kind of family breakdown is that of the divorce process, which leads on to families living in single-parent households and ultimately to remarriage of one, if not both, parents and the creation of stepfamilies. This process, now considered likely to occur to one marriage in every three, also results in one in five children experiencing the divorce of their parents and the subsequent remarriage of at least one of them (perhaps more than once) during childhood. The subsequent emergence of binuclear families (Ahrons 1980), it will be argued, could appropriately be described as *re-formed extended families*. These post-nuclear families, whose members are not all biologically related to one another, and which form approximately a third of families in the United Kingdom, now take their place in society alongside the more traditional nuclear families.

Demographic trends: couples who divorce

The number of couples who seek a divorce to end their marriage has steadily been increasing since 1971, following the implementation of the 1969 Divorce Reform Act. Until that time, the divorce rate, though steadily increasing, rose to a sudden peak after the war. The number of divorces rose sharply from 51,594 during the years 1941–45 to 199,507 between 1946 and 1950.

As well as the substantial increase in the number of divorces (in 1985 these rose to 175,000, a rise of 24,000 on 1984, though by 1987

Table 1.1 Divorces granted in the United Kingdom, 1951–87 (in thousands)

1951	1961	1966	1971	1976	1980	1981	1982	1983	1984	1985	1986	1987
31	27	43	80	136	160	157	159	162	158	175	168	165

Note: These figures are based on the OPCS definitions which include dissolutions and nullity proceedings. The figures are rounded up to the nearest thousand.
Source: Social Trends 18 (1988), HMSO and OPCS

the numbers had dropped again to 165,000), men and women are getting divorced at a younger age. However, the particularly sharp rise in the number of divorces in 1985 is at least partially accounted for by the Matrimonial and Family Proceedings Act (1984), which permitted divorce after one year of marriage. Nevertheless, according to the briefing paper prepared by the Family Policy Studies Centre (1983), the rates of divorce are highest after three years of marriage and between the ages of 25 and 29, when nearly one in thirty couples divorces. Divorce rates among couples who have been married seven years have fallen to about two-thirds and one-half respectively, and they continue to decline the longer the duration of the marriage. The length of marriage is also becoming shorter; in 1979 the median duration for couples *with children* under 16 was 11.2 years, this showing a slow decline until 1982, when it was 11 years. In 1985 there was a sharp decrease to 8.4 years, but by 1987 the median length of marriage was 9.3 years. As the paper subsequently comments,

> In any year the total number of couples divorcing will be affected by three factors: (i) The number of couples 'at risk'. (ii) The numbers in particular age groups. (iii) The numbers of those in particular high risk groups. It is therefore important to consider the divorce rates rather than simply the numbers of divorces, which can give a misleading impression on underlying trends.

> In 1981 the United Kingdom had the second highest divorce rate in the EEC, 11.9 per thousand existing marriages, Denmark having the highest of 12.1, and Italy the lowest at 0.8. By 1986 the United Kingdom had the highest divorce rate, 12.9. However, these figures must be set within the context of different legislative, social and cultural histories of the countries concerned.

THE LEGAL FRAMEWORK: GROUNDS FOR THE DISSOLUTION OF MARRIAGE

According to Chester (1983),

> family law inevitably both embodies policy and expresses social values, and concern to preserve marital stability. ... Evidence suggests that many older values and typifications of marriage are deeply rooted in individual consciousness as well as institutional expressions of historical culture and thus contribute to the shaping of attitudes and behaviour. The 1969 Divorce Reform Act attempted

to hold the balance between divorce by consent which would legitimise current behavioural reality, and the traditional morality in the community interest.

As Chester states,

> [the] solution adopted ... was to take a positive but symbolic stance on the stability of marriage, while diminishing the capacity of the State by introducing the principle of breakdown without inquest. The result was a system of easy divorce, with some provision for divorce by consent, and thus a transfer of effective discretion over divorce to married persons.

The dissonance between the concept of matrimonial fault and the current behavioural realities was thus still implicitly retained. Since the 1969 Divorce Reform Act, which was implemented in 1971 and consolidated within Section 1 of the Matrimonial Proceedings Act (1973), the sole ground for granting a divorce is that of irretrievable breakdown of the marriage, which must be established by alleging and proving one or more of the five 'facts' set out below.

1 That the respondent has committed adultery and the petitioner therefore finds it intolerable to live with the respondent (usually referred to as 'adultery').
2 That the respondent has behaved in such a way that the petitioner cannot reasonably be expected to live with the respondent (usually referred to as 'behaviour').
3 That the respondent has deserted the petitioner for a continuous period of at least two years immediately preceding the presentation of the petition (usually referred to as 'desertion').
4 That the parties have lived separately and apart continuously for two years immediately preceding the petition and that the respondent agrees to the granting of a decree (usually referred to as 'two years' separation').
5 That the parties have lived separately and apart continuously for a period of five years immediately preceding the presentation of a petition (usually referred to as 'five years' separation').

There has also been a trend towards the separation of the adjudication of ancillary matters (that is, those related to children, finance and property) from the issues raised in the divorce petition itself. There was a continuing controversy over the matter of conduct, which culminated in the perhaps infamous Wachtel judgement – Mr Justice Ormerod (1973), who ruled that marital conduct should not be taken into account as regards the spouses' share of the assets, unless it was both 'obvious and gross'. This dissonance between current realities of behaviour, in particular the changing role of women, and the law as it now stood, eventually, and amid considerable opposition, led to the Matrimonial Proceedings Act (1984) (see also the section on page 16 entitled 'The increase in households headed by a lone parent'). This allowed for divorce after one year of marriage; hitherto it had been necessary for a couple to have been married for three years prior to the lodging of a petition for divorce. The Act also ended what was known as the wife's 'meal ticket for life', and some women who have mid- to higher-range incomes may be required to pay cash settlements to their husbands, as was demonstrated in *Browne* v. *Browne* (Court of Appeal, November 1988). The first consideration must now be for the courts to consider the needs of the children. While they are now expected to put more emphasis on encouraging the ex-spouses to become independent of each other and self-sufficient, each case is still considered on its merits. However, there is the implication that factors such as the length of the marriage and the former wife's ability to look after herself, are to be taken into consideration. The courts now only take behaviour of the spouses into account where it 'would be inequitable to disregard it'.

The great majority of petitioners for divorce are wives; in 1987, 73 per cent of all decrees were awarded to wives; in 1986, 131,000 out of a total of 180,000 (Law Commission 1988). According to Haskey (1986), the trends of the decrees granted to wives (in England and Wales) on the grounds of their husbands' behaviour are rising – decrees absolute granted have risen from under 20 per cent in 1971 to over 50 per cent in 1987, while those granted for adultery have remained consistently at just under 20 per cent. Wives' petitions for two years' separation remained at around 20 per cent, while those for desertion fell from approximately 8 per cent in 1971 to virtually nil in 1985. Petitions on the grounds of five years' separation, after a sharp rise in 1971 (a 'backlog effect' of the Matrimonial Proceedings Act, which allowed divorce after five years without the consent of the respondent) have since steadily declined to less than 5 per cent of the total in 1985. The husbands who were granted a divorce petitioned mainly on the grounds of their wives' adultery – for instance, in 1986 30 per cent (that is, 19,019) of all the decrees absolute granted – petitions rising from about 25 per cent in 1971 to 45 per cent in 1987. Those for desertion declined from about 15 per cent in 1971 to virtually nil in 1985, while those for two years' separation rose from just under 20 per cent to about 30 per cent and for five years' separation fell sharply from 40 per cent in 1971 to approximately 15 per cent in 1985. On the other hand, petitions by husbands on the grounds of their wives' behaviour rose from virtually nil in 1971 to about 16 per cent in 1985.

By far the greatest number of petitions for divorce are based on allegations of fault, which as Eekelaar, Clive et al. (1977) – and others, such as Parkinson (1986) and Davis and Murch (1988) – conclude from their research findings of divorcing couples in England and Scotland, have not only aroused strong reactions in the respondents, but also made it less likely that mutual agreements regarding arrangements about custody and access for their children would be possible.

THE LEGAL PROCESS OF DIVORCE

The majority of petitioners for divorce do seek the advice of a solicitor, and most petitioners are eligible for what is known as the 'Green Form' Legal Advice Scheme. This entitles them to a certain, if limited, amount of time with a solicitor, who receives a modest fee for the service. A divorce is obtained in two separate stages. The first stage involves a review of the petition and the supportive documentation (such as affidavits) which is usually undertaken by the registrar. Matters relating to finance and the matrimonial home and arrangements regarding the children are dealt with separately and may not be concluded before the decree nisi is granted. Six weeks after the decree nisi the petitioner may apply for the decree absolute which, when granted, is pronounced by a judge in open court (see Chapters 3, 8 and 10).

Until the introduction of the Special Procedure during the midseventies, the grounds on which divorce petitions were based had to be proved in open court, a complicated and expensive ritual, which was often humiliating to the participants (see Davis and Murch 1988). Initially this was introduced for couples without children, who were divorcing by consent, but was later extended to all undefended divorce petitions. In effect this Special Procedure led to the virtual abolition of court hearings, and after scrutiny of the affidavits by the registrar a list of decree nisi petitions was read out in so called 'open court'. As a corollary to this procedure in cases involving children a system of judicial appointments was introduced, in which the parents were interviewed in chambers regarding their proposed arrangements

for the care of their children. This allowed the courts to discharge
their duties under Section 41 of the Matrimonial Causes Act (1973)
(see Chapter 5, 'The legal process', page 93).

THE STRUCTURE OF THE COURTS

The findings of the Finer Committee Report (1974) convincingly and
eloquently revealed the plight of one-parent families and recommended the establishment of a unified Family Court. These proposals
were subsequently supported by considerable evidence of the need
for it – see, for example, the Law Society, *A Better Way Out* (1979);
Murch, *Justice and Welfare in Divorce* (1980); the Justices' Clerks
Society, *Resolving Family Conflict in the Eighties: a Unified Family
Court* (1982); British Association of Social Workers, *Family Courts*
(1985); Association of Directors of Social Services, *Children Still in
Trouble* (1985); British Agencies for Adoption and Fostering, *Family
Justice: a Structure for the Family Court* (1986). For a number of years
there was an active Family Courts Forum which pressed for major
restructuring and the setting up of Family Courts, and was only
disbanded very recently (May 1989) following many changes, albeit
in a piecemeal fashion and the declared intention of the Lord
Chancellor to move gradually to a Family Court. The Children Act
(1989), which is perhaps the cornerstone of this new legislation and
which is to be implemented in 1991, will be discussed in Chapter 12.

In 1982 the Government set up a committee under Mrs Justice
Booth to review the Matrimonial Causes Procedure. This was a
complementary committee to several others, including the 1981
Financial Consequences of Divorce (see page 38, 'The marital
system') and the Interdepartmental Review of Family and Domestic
Jurisdiction. The Booth Committee Report (1985) made no major
recommendations for change as to the grounds on which there might
be an application for divorce; and has generally been regarded as a
disappointment in that it did nothing to halt the growing tide of quick
and cheap divorces. However, the report did suggest the possibility of
joint petitions and an initial hearing before a Registrar, which the
applicant should attend, and proposed various changes in terminology and many other recommendations, some of which will be
discussed later. The Consultation Paper from the *Interdepartmental
Review of Family and Domestic Jurisdiction* (1986) acknowledges the
present state of fragmentation and overlapping jurisdiction of the
present system in which Magistrates' Courts, County Courts and the
Family Division of the High Court can each or all become involved.

The Children Act (1989) proposes moving towards uniformity of procedure, which will allow rationalisation and reorganisation as between the different courts.

Table 1.2 Summary of applications for divorce made in Great Britain, 1984*

	High Court and County Courts	Magistrates' Courts	
		Domestic Courts	Juvenile Courts
1 Divorces, nullity and judicial separation (petitions presented)	186,000	–	–
2 Financial and property matters			
(a) maintenance orders or variations sought	93,000	88,000	–
(b) enforcement actions	3,000	104,000	–
3 Matters affecting children	124,000	37,000	5,000 (105,000 juveniles proceeded against)
4 Personal protection	22,000	11,000	–
Total	428,000	239,000	110,000

* These figures do not concur with those in the next section, which are those of divorce decrees granted and for England and Wales only.
Source: 'Interdepartmental Review of Family and Domestic Jurisdiction', consultation paper.

In addition to the volume of business, there is also the issue of the costs of administering matrimonial matters in the courts, not only those of salaries of the courts; in 1984, for instance, they amounted to a total of £167 million (excluding the judicial salaries) but also an additional £114 million on legal aid.

The Interdepartmental Committee Consultation document acknowledged the Family Court proposals by Finer (those referred to above, plus others), and drew particular attention to the Scottish system, where criminal and civil matters are combined.

CHILDREN IN FAMILIES AND DIVORCE

From 1980 to 1983 the number of children under 16 whose parents divorced showed a downward trend, more or less in line with the declining number of children in the population. Fifteen out of every

1,000 children aged under 16 experienced their parents' divorce in 1983. There was a further decline in 1984, when 58 per cent of divorcing couples had a child under the age of 16, of whom 24 per cent had only one such child. By 1985 only 24 per cent of the couples who divorced had only one child, a further 23 per cent had two and only 8 per cent had three or more children under 16 and 9 per cent three or more. However, because of the trend for couples to divorce at a younger age, the number of children aged under 5 increased by 14 per cent between 1984 and 1985, though the numbers of children between 5 and 16 remained similar.

Table 1.3   Divorcing couples and their children, England and Wales, 1979–86

	1979	1980	1981	1982	1983	1984	1985	1986
Couples with children under 16	83,176	88,202	86,838	87,253	86,695	83,530	88,955	86,286
No. of children under 16	155,425	163,221	159,403	158,168	155,562	148,600	155,740	151,964

Source: Compiled from *OPCS Bulletins*

THE CUSTODY OF CHILDREN

A recent (1986) publication (Law Commission, *150,000 Children Divorced a Year: Who Cares?*) draws stark attention to the plight of those children who are affected by the divorce of their parents. As they point out,

> there are presently two types of order which are commonly made by the courts after divorce. (i) Sole custody to one or other parent (the mother in 77 per cent of cases and the father in 9 per cent) usually with access to the other; (ii) custody to mother and father jointly (13 per cent of cases) usually with care and control to one and access to the other.

Although such joint custody orders are becoming increasingly common and are intended to promote cooperation between the parents, they usually only imply that the parents share the legal responsibilities for decision-making about the child, rather than 'shared care' (sometimes even sharing the physical care), as is the presumption in many states in the USA. Although the main benefit of joint custody is therefore symbolic, and tends to emphasise the parents' rights rather than their responsibilities, there are many arguments in favour of its meaning for the divorced family (see Chapter 5, 'Custody matters', page 96; Chapter 11, 'Custody', page 258).

The paper, which now forms the main basis of the 1989 Children Act (see introduction to Chapter 12, page 282) stressed again that the present system needs simplifying, and states unequivocally that we need a system which will promote and safeguard the interests of the children involved. The Law Commission invited responses on the views expressed. The authors considered that, as far as possible, the law ought to:

1 Separate the issues relating to the children from those of the parents and other adults and give priority to them.
2 Recognise and maintain the beneficial relationships already established between the child, parents and other adults and to encourage their continuation.
3 Promote a secure and certain environment for the child while growing up.
4 Protect the child from the risk of harm to physical or mental health and to ensure proper physical intellectual, social and emotional development.
5 Recognise and ascertain, where practicable, the child's own point of view and wishes, and to give them due consideration.
6 Ensure that where parental responsibility is divided or shared, the people concerned understand what the legal responsibilities are and the powers they can and should exercise in relation to the child.
7 Secure the legal allocation of powers and responsibilities which are workable in every day life.

MARRIAGE MATTERS

A working party was set up in 1975 by the Home Office in consultation with the Department of Health and Social Security with the terms of reference being 'to improve the services for helping with problems of personal relationships in marriage'. The membership was predominantly composed of members who could be said to have vested interests in maintaining marriages, and while this was entirely understandable, a broader representation might have produced some more controversial findings on the possible reasons for the state of modern marriage and the high rate of breakdown.

The working party unfortunately had no opportunity to build in a research component, nor did they sufficiently take into account such research as was available at the time. It is at least possible that more weight might have been given to their recommendations had they had done so. Their subsequent report, *Marriage Matters* (1979), offers two theories of the causes of social problems, 'on the one hand that these problems are solely or mainly due to emotional factors within individuals due to their genetic structure, upbringing, and personal relationships; or on the other, that the root cause lies in the physical and wider social environment'. The working party argued that

> the most likely explanation is highly complex and that factors both internal and external to the individual are intertwined ... though the physical and social environment is often one factor in the causing or exacerbation of marital disharmony, the influence of underlying problems of personal relationships requires equal attention.

However, the report does not discuss the possibility of combining both these causal explanations; as would be possible by taking the perspective of a circular causation which results from the interaction between the transactions both within the family network and between the family and the environment or context within which it is located. Such a conceptual framework is the basis for the ideas contained in this book (see Chapter 2).

Marriage Matters contains a brief account of the (then) current state of marriage and family life. In a discussion on the expectations of marriage, the working party explain that expectations cannot be measured and are not necessarily reflected in what people do. As they stated, the

> gap between expectations and aspirations in marriage and the actual experience is a critical factor in causing stress. People vary in their ability to tolerate frustration of hopes and expectations in marriage, but the wider the gap between expectation and experience the more likely is conflict to occur.

They also point out that there are generational differences, as there are different sectors of society, all strongly influenced by the changing cultural values of rapidly changing society. As the report stated, 'our [present] difficulty is the more deeply rooted and lies in the fact that we are in a period of transition' moving towards a society in which there is an attempt to control social processes ... by new concepts of social justice and community participation. Interdependence rather than independence has become increasingly important; more and more adaptation depends on ecological regulation. These factors affect marriage and the family directly and profoundly.

During the ten years since the report the considerable rise in unemployment has further complicated the social fabric of present-day society. This has led to an increasing divide between North and South, as well as a rise in the number of families where the woman is the major breadwinner.

The *Marriage Matters* report also noted the central importance of primary personal relationships, and identified a trend towards the requirement that 'marriage is increasingly required to serve the partners' own personal development, thereby throwing into relief the level of their capacity for close and intimate relationships. What constitutes need and sustains development varies' according to marriage, age group, and social class. Although the working party commented that 'there have been radical changes in the relationship between men and women', they did not outline the complexity and comprehensiveness of these. Some examples of these radical changes are particularly related to the changing role of women and include the easy availability of oral contraception, the possibilities for abortion, the increasing employment of women (including mothers of young children) outside the home, a total 45.7 per cent in 1987. These changes, together with other factors, have led to a reduction in the child-bearing years. For instance, according to Dominian (1985), the global factors which influence marital breakdown are the progressive change in the nature of marriage to a companionate rather than an institutional marriage, the gradual emancipation of women and the rise in material standards against a background of the diminishing influence of religion. As *Marriage Matters* concluded,

> marriage has been 'never more popular, never more risky'. Marital disharmony is a major social problem, and the State should exercise a reponsibility – shared with caring individuals and independent initiatives – for relieving private misery and exercising social concern by the provision of services through statutory and other public agencies to help with marital problems.

The working party also drew attention to the paucity of research related to marital problems and marital work, and indicated some areas in which research would be most likely to promote effective work in this field – case studies, development studies, policy studies, epidemiological, sociological and organisational studies. Some such studies, largely financed from charitable trusts, have subsequently been carried out. Their conclusions contained proposals which, they suggested, should be funded from central government. These included a Central Development Unit for Marital Work and local Marital Training and Development Groups. However, for the next decade, even these relatively modest proposals were largely ignored.

CHARACTERISTICS OF COUPLES WHO DIVORCE

Much of our present knowledge regarding marital relationships has come from clinical studies of marital breakdown; see, for instance, Dicks (1967) and Skynner (1976), which attempt to explore the factors which lead couples either to continue with their marriage or to seek a divorce. Dominian (1985) pointed out that research distinguishes three peaks of marital difficulties: first, that 30–40 per cent of those who ultimately divorce have ceased to live together by the time they reach the fifth anniversary of their marriage. A second peak of marital problems arises during the years between 30 and 40, when couples are preoccupied with child-rearing, pressures at work and above all personal growth and maturity. The third peak is when the adolescent children have left and an underlying emptiness is revealed in the marriage.

Whereas it is predominantly wives who seek to end their marriage by petitioning for a divorce, according to Goode (1956) it is often the husbands who first desire to leave the marriage and 'engage in behaviour, whose function, if not intent, whose result, if not aim, is to force the other spouse to ask for it first'. There is some evidence from practitioners in the field of divorce which indicate support for this view. However, we do not know how many couples remain in an unhappy marriage, rather than seek to end it by divorce. Nor do we know how many couples resolve their difficulties only through separation (in essence, a *de facto* divorce) which they do not pursue to the conclusion of a *de jure* divorce, perhaps in order to remarry.

A careful and comprehensive study carried out in the Midlands by Thornes and Collard (1979), compared 520 couples who continued their marriage with 570 who divorced. Their tentative conclusions stress the importance of communication within marriage, which they define broadly as 'the total process whereby husbands and wives learn to understand the needs and expectations of each other; the process

... makes use of both verbal and nonverbal cues, and as such would be relevant to both companionate and instrumental models of marriage'.

Although poor communication can arise from a number of different sources and levels, and is a component of many of the other factors, its impairment is particularly significant, perhaps especially for wives. A particular component of communication includes the role expectations which the couple have of each other. Their cautious findings also show that couples who are dissimilar in culture, social background or religion, or too disparate in age, are more prone to divorce. 'Dissatisfaction with the sexual side of the marital relationship', particularly from the beginning of the marriage, seemed to suggest that 'many marriages from the outset lacked at least one important source of affirmation and reassurance'. The model of their parents' marital relationship was another and important factor – as, for instance, if the parents themselves had been divorced. Also significant were marriages in which one or both partners married in order to escape from home, as with teenage marriages which were found to be 'divorce-prone', as were those which involved premarital pregnancy. A further correlate was the couples' low level of education. Then there were external factors also, such as low income, or sub-standard housing or frequent moves of household. While Thornes and Collard did not regard their study as conclusive, their findings are nevertheless important and they also give some guidelines for future research.

Table 1.4 Families headed by type and lone mothers by marital status, Great Britain, 1971–87 (percentages)

Family type	1971	1975	1977	1979	1981	1983	1985	1986	1987
Married couple	92	90	90	88	87	86	86	86	85
Lone mother	7	9	9	10	11	12	12	13	12
Single	1	1	2	2	2	3	3	3	4
Widowed	2	2	2	2	2	2	1	1	1
Divorced	2	3	3	4	4	5	5	6	5
Separated	1	1	1	2	2	2	3	3	2
Lone father	1	1	1	2	2	1	2	1	1
All lone parents	8	10	10	12	13	14	14	14	14
Base 100 %	4,864	4,776	4,481	4,203	4,445	3,538	3,348	3,337	3,361

Source: Family Policy Studies Centre Fact Sheet (1986) updated

THE INCREASE IN HOUSEHOLDS HEADED BY A LONE PARENT

The number of families headed by a lone parent is now one in seven, about two-thirds of whom are women who are separated or divorced. There is a small but growing number of households headed by single fathers, 14 per cent of the total. The 1981 Census revealed a total of 900,000 one-parent families, an increase of 58 per cent since the census of 1971, with a figure of 1.5 million one-parent families projected by the year 2005.

The Family Policy Studies Centre point out that nearly a fifth of the lone mothers work full-time, though there appears to be little difference between two-parent or lone-parent families as to the proportion of children receiving day care. However, housing figures show that only 19 per cent of lone parents are owner occupiers as compared with 67 per cent of married couple families. Haskey (1989) provides a succinct summary of the sharp rise in the proportion of all dependent children who live in one-parent families, which has increased by more than 50 per cent since the seventies; while 'the proportion of children who live with a divorced lone mother has trebled'.

Households headed by a single parent are only part of the broken family jigsaw which results from separation and divorce. A study of custody carried out in England and Scotland (Eekelaar and Clive et al. 1977) found that over half the children of divorced parents in their study had lost contact with one of their parents within a few months of their parents' separation. According to Toynbee (1987), after a divorce, one father in three never sees his children again. But this is not all: research carried out by Ambrose, Harper and Pemberton (1983) on a survey of ninety-two men beyond marriage in the South of England showed that 32 per cent of them suffered physical health problems, and 22 per cent mental health problems of varying severity. Half of the fifty-six non-custodial fathers had not had any contact with their children during the month prior to the survey, though most would have liked more. Eight fathers who had re-married and were not in contact gave the following reasons as to why they felt unable to play the expected paternal role: 'obstruction by previous wife'; 'geographical distance' (in all cases children living overseas); 'second wife of father objects'; 'access stopped by court'; 'children's resentment of father's new partner' and 'the child was disturbed by access'.

FINANCIAL CONSEQUENCES OF DIVORCE

It will already be apparent from the previous section that the financial consequences of divorce are considerable for the families involved. No two households can live as cheaply as one, whatever their previous lifestyle, so that there is always a reduction in the family's standard of living subsequent to divorce. For the custodial parent (usually, though not always, the mother) living with their children in single-parent households, as well as the psychological effects of the separation and divorce there are considerable financial burdens.

The Law Commission's report (1981) on this subject pointed out these realities and recommended that the first consideration should be the needs of the children. But the report also recognised that in some cases second wives are in effect supporting their husband's first wife, who was neither caring for young children nor supporting herself. The report essentially recommended a 'clean break' following divorce but drew attention to the need for the ex-wife to re-establish herself.

The Matrimonial and Family Proceedings Act (1984) which followed, while removing the previous persisting obligation principle whereby previous spouses and children were awarded post-divorce support, required the court to have regard to all the circumstances of the case giving the first consideration to the welfare of the minor children of the family. According to the Family Policy Studies Centre (1986), over half of such families are 'poor', 52 per cent of them either receiving Supplementary Benefit or on incomes below that level. Of those families with incomes just above the level of Supplementary Benefit, six out of ten are living in or on the margins of poverty, as compared with only two out of ten families with two parents. A recent article (Field 1989) pointed out that more than 1 million children have fathers who do not contribute to their keep. Only a proportion of these are the children of divorce, but current figures show that of the £3.4 billion paid out in Social Security payments to families with children, £43 out of every £100 is paid to lone parents.

In this country Eekelaar and Maclean's (1986) study of 276 individuals, (92 men and 184 women) considered the impact of divorce on the household as an economic unit. They argue that the dependency ratio of each household alters throughout the family life cycle, as family members 'enter or leave the labour market according to their age, health and child care responsibilities'; this dependency ratio is suddenly and fundamentally altered by the advent of a divorce. While the change in dependency ratio may be altered by remarriage or cohabitation, by the addition of a potential second income, it may also introduce new dependents such as stepchildren and the subsequent children of the new partnership. They therefore constructed two different categories of divorces, those which they described as childless and those families with dependent children.

In this country Eekelaar and Maclean found that the disposable income of divorced parents with dependent children living alone was lower than that of parents without children, while that of the reconstituted families lay somewhere between. Where maintenance was paid to the woman in female lone-parent households, it only made a difference to the total household income if the woman worked full-time. The amounts paid in maintenance were low, in half the cases ranging from 11 to 30 per cent, but for many families this merely went to offset Supplementary Benefit. The maintenance paid by fathers formed a low percentage of their own household income, and, in reconstituted families with children, any increase in such payments would have reduced their standard of living below that of the average family. A major cause of the inability to pay maintenance is unemployment; and while it is suggested that such men use unemployment to avoid paying maintenance, it is also likely that marital problems and unemployment problems are interlinked (see Mattinson 1988).

As the result of their study Eekelaar and Maclean were particularly concerned about the position of women with older children, whose child-rearing responsibilities had altered their position in the labour market, and yet who would shortly reach the stage in which they would lose their entitlement to support.

With regard to the housing following divorce, they found that where the family were living in local authority housing at the time of the separation, in most cases the custodial parent remained in the accommodation (79 per cent of the women and 30 per cent of the men).

In divorcing families of owner-occupiers the outcome was more complex, though in almost half the cases in both categories, the house was sold. In some such situations, the recent fall in the housing market has resulted in a housing stalemate in which, although the former partners have agreed that the house is sold in order to provide them each with accommodation, the house cannot fetch the required price. As it is the policy of the courts that one of the primary goals of divorce settlements is to secure the accommodation for the children, usually through keeping them in the matrimonial home, this seems to imply that the children of divorce in the owner-occupier sector may suffer greater disruption than those of the public sector. Nevertheless, Eekelaar and Maclean found that about three quarters of the divorced mothers with dependent children who had not remarried were still living in the private sector when interviewed. There were also a few cases involving a 'Mesher' agreement (*Mesher* v. *Mesher* 1980) – that is, where the house is settled on trust for sale by both parents, but the sale is postponed until the education of the youngest child is completed, or by court order. Such agreements are no longer considered advantageous as they are generally too difficult to change, even if subsequent events make it advantageous to both parties to do so (1989).

Eekelaar and Maclean conclude by evaluating the principles which they propose should govern post-divorce maintenance, which they consider confront fundamental questions relating to the ideology of family responsibility, including the boundaries between the individual and the state, and the roles of the legislature and the judiciary.

Weitzman's (1985) meticulously researched US study shows that the so-called 'enlightened' Californian legal reform of 'no fault divorce', which ended the previous practice whereby the 'innocent party' gained economic advantage because of the linking of financial awards to fault, has in practice left women, and especially mothers, even more impoverished. Men have been freed from many of the financial responsibilities which they had under the old laws but women have lost much of the security to which they were previously entitled.

REMARRIAGE AND STEPFAMILIES

Since 1961, while the total marriage rate has remained remarkably stable, the rate of first marriages has declined while the remarriage rate has increased. The remarriage rate for both men and women increased substantially between 1961 and 1983, the remarriage rate for men being nearly three times as high as for women. This is in contrast to just below 50 per cent of eligible men who marry for the first time. On the other hand, the figures for remarriage of women, per thousand women who are eligible, rose very slowly, reaching a peak in 1977 and falling again to just below 25 per cent in 1983. Marriages in which *both* partners were remarrying rose from 9 per cent of all marriages in 1961 to 32 per cent in 1987.

Second or subsequent unions are more likely to take the form of cohabitation; one factor which apparently influences the proportion of women who remarry being the age of their youngest child at the time of the divorce (Rimmer 1981). The General Household Survey estimated that the proportion of women aged 18–49 who were cohabiting more than doubled between 1979 and 1987. Indeed, the 1986 figures indicate that the proportion of divorced women aged 16–59 who were cohabiting was 24 per cent while that of divorced men between the same ages was 28 per cent. A study by Leete and Anthony (1979) found that by five years after divorce over half of all custodial parents had remarried. The figures for a second or even subsequent divorce have also been rising; in 1984, of 21 per cent of every thousand couples who divorce, either one or both partners had been previously divorced.

Table 1.5   Marriages, United Kingdom, 1961–87 (thousands and percentages)

	1961	1971	1976	1981	1984	1987
Marriages (000s)						
First marriage for both partners	340	369	282	263	259	260
First marriage for one partner only						
Bachelor/divorced woman	11	21	30	32	32	34
Bachelor/widow	5	4	4	3	2	2
Spinster/divorced man	12	24	32	36	38	39
Spinster/widower	8	5	4	3	2	2
Second (or later) marriage for both partners						
Both divorced	5	17	34	44	46	47
Both widowed	10	10	10	7	6	5
Divorced man/widow	3	4	5	5	5	4
Divorced man/widower	3	5	5	5	5	5
Total marriages	397	459	406	398	395	398
Remarriages						
Remarriages[a] as a % of all marriages	14	20	31	34	35	35
Remarriages[a] of the divorced as a % of all marriages	9	15	26	31	32	32(a)

Note: [a] Remarriages for one or both partners.
Source: Office of Population Censuses and Surveys and Government Statistical Service

The Family Formation Survey (1976) indicated that 7 per cent of all children under 16 were living with a stepparent (a total of 928,000); and the National Child Development Study of 16,000 children born in 1958 found that over 5 per cent at the age of 16 were living with their natural parent and an adoptive stepparent or cohabitee. On current trends, therefore, it is likely that more than 1 million children are living in stepfamilies and that a further 1.5 million are currently living with a separated or divorced parent who may remarry (Stepfamily Information Sheet).

2 The family as a system

And the new philosophy calls all in doubt.

> John Donne (1571–1631), 'Anatomie of the World,
> The First Anniversary'

All theory, dear friend is grey, but the golden tree of actual life springs ever green.

> Johann Wolfgang von Goethe (1749–1832)

There are many theories, frameworks and models which seek to describe 'the family'. Indeed, there have been as many, if not more, which seek to develop such theories and their application towards understanding the family and the relationships within it. The aim of this chapter is to present a selective review of some of those most associated with families who may be in difficulty and which have been found to be useful as a basis for understanding family development, interaction and communication.

In recent years many of the practitioners whose task is to intervene in such families have found that a *systems approach* not only allows them to gain an understanding of the families who become their clients, but also to develop frameworks or to build practice models of intervention based upon it. What follows is an an attempt to develop a theoretical framework within which families where the parents divorce, as well as those who subsequently remarry, can provide both a focus and some understanding as a system passing through time, and also to develop practice models for interventions based upon it.

Such a family systems framework and the models of intervention both provide the theoretical basis for the subsequent chapters and underpin the practice described therein. It is hoped also that such a framework may provide some guidance for those who, because of their professional roles, become closely involved with families during divorce and remarriage – as, for instance, doctors, health visitors, lawyers, marriage guidance counsellors, psychologists, psychotherapists, social workers, teachers and others – who, when referred to collectively, will be described as interventionist practitioners.

MARRIAGE AS A RELATIONSHIP

In a wide-ranging examination of politics and social theory in relation to the family, Morgan (1985) argues that there is a wide and shared acceptance of marriage as more than a legal contract, or an institution defined in terms of its reproductive or economic functions. This is amply demonstrated by a shift towards an emphasis on relationship, which implies that the 'main points of reference come from within, from the parties themselves'. If the marriage relationship is thus perceived in terms of personal growth and fulfilment in which sexuality is a crucial element, then it follows that marital disharmony can be seen in terms of interpersonal emotional costs. As Morgan points out,

> the medical model implies that there exists some class of problems called 'marital problems', that is a class of problems related to the marital relationship in some strong sense and which can, therefore be relatively isolated for examination and treatment. . . . To treat a class of problems called 'marital problems' is to recognise or endorse the centrality of a particular definition of marriage within society as a whole.

Such a perspective also implies that there exists a specialised knowledge in relation to such problems, as well as a body of experts (such as marriage guidance counsellors) to whom couples can turn for help with their marital difficulties.

However, for many social theorists, when it comes to definitions of the family, the social unit is assumed to be the conventional nuclear family household. This is complicated by two main issues: first, that for many (whether theorists or practitioners), there is a 'commitment to a three generation model of processes and structure which assumes links between households as well as processes within them', while others may extend this to the wider kinship network. Second, while the theoretical analyst may have in mind a particular definition, when some intervention is considered necessary, then the whole issue assumes a central focus. Morgan describes a model of four elements, all involved in exchanges with one another – the family, the state, class and gender – each of which are capable of six distinct exchanges with one another. In this sense he considers that the family might be considered as any one of the following:

1 The actual distribution of the population as households, within which the members share at least one meal.
2 'Relationships between persons which are understood' by them 'to be in terms of blood or marriage, or which are understood to have the same status as these relationships'.
3 'Ideals, images and understanding and evaluations of such terms as "family", "marriage", "parenthood", etc.' As he points out, a more complex model would demonstrate that each of these separate components are constantly interrelating and influencing one another. Morgan considers that there is an intimate interconnection between the various theoretical concerns and issues of public policy as well as practical applications.

The reader is referred to the original for Morgan's selective focus on the various attempts to build a mid-range theory. This includes a lucid appraisal of systems, family history and phenomenology, as well as of the work of the Rapaports which, while essentially eclectic and liberal humanist, nevertheless reflects their original academic backgrounds in psychodynamic psychiatry and social anthropology.

SYSTEMS THEORY

Morgan points out that Parsonian functionalism has many similarities with systems theory – as, for instance, that all systems (whether personality, family or social system) can be analysed in similar and parallel ways; as the idea of levels, and the concept of the whole, irreducible to its individual constituents. However, there are differences, as Parsons (1964) does not give so much emphasis to boundary maintenance, interchanges between systems, and the emphasis on dysfunctional systems (see page 42, 'Marital breakdown').

These essentially academic considerations will not be considered here, as this is an attempt to develop a theory for practice. It must suffice to state that it is probable that the systems framework does have some advantages when one is trying to comprehend the complexities which are integral in any attempt at defining that elusive collectivity known as 'the family'. It is perfectly possible to focus both on the individual and the family unit (see page 38, 'The marital system'), although there is as yet no sufficiently well-established *theoretical* framework for so doing. However, although it is entirely possible to use systems theory both in order to focus, as a framework in attempting to understand problematic behaviour, and also to facilitate change in all human systems (and indeed many human relations consultants are doing so), in this book the level of analysis will be on the social unit which is generally understood and referred to as 'the family'. Therefore a systems framework, as developed into a family systems perspective, will be used here in order to build up a model which encompasses families in transformation between marital breakdown, divorce and remarriage. This model, expressed as a *re-formed family systems model* (from *The Oxford English Dictionary*'s definition 'altered in form or content; especially put into a better form, corrected, amended'), will be described below. The choice of the word 're-form' is intended to convey both the alteration and the need for change, as well as taking a neutral stance in attempting to indicate that the transformed family which ultimately emerges can be regarded as neither better nor worse than the original nuclear family, *merely different*.

TOWARDS A RE-FORMED, EXTENDED FAMILY SYSTEMS MODEL

The definition of a family which will be the basis of this book is one which incorporates the following elements, developed from some of those described by Morgan (1985) and already discussed. Other elements, such as those of systems, constructs, life scripts, and the meanings within relationships, will be defined more fully and discussed in later sections. Some of the other components described by Morgan, most notably the idea of a family household who sometimes eat together, have been omitted from the model, so as to devise a more open, even diffuse, and extended family system. The elements of such a family definition are included in a *re-formed extended family systems model*, the levels of which are distinguished in terms of a hierarchy of contexts as follows:

1 *Constructs* about the way in which the re-formed extended family knows its world, family myths, traditions, legends and general conceptions of how society and family relationships work. These would include ideas, images, meanings and evaluations which are generally given to such terms as 'family', 'marriage', parenthood', 'stepfamily', 'remarriage', 'former spouse','stepparent' and 'step-parenthood' and so on. Such constructs are likely to be shared only by family members who have a common family history together; for other members who have not, these very constructs are the subject of intersubjective conflict as they have no shared way in which they can 'language' this situation (see page 34 and

Chapter 3, 'Guidelines for the practice of therapeutic conversations', page 59).

2 *Life scripts*, individual conceptions of themselves according to social actions and roles, which would include ideas about the self in the roles given above. These too are likely to be incompatible at first and to require mutual negotiation in order to accommodate to one another.

3 *Relationships* between persons which are understood by them to be in terms of blood, or marriage (or to have the same status as in adoption).

Such definitions would thus allow the inclusion, as an integral part of the family system, of previously married, now divorced former spouses, couples where one or both have been divorced, or lost a previous partner through death and have remarried or remained as single parents. These would also include intergenerational expectations of behaviour as between 'parents' and children; and also the newest and the most vulnerable developing 'collusive' partnership relationship between parent and stepparent (see page 38, 'The marital system').

Such a model would therefore include nuclear families, adoptive families (perhaps long-term foster families also) and stepfamilies created through the remarriage of one or both parents. It also includes stepfamilies created through cohabitation, where the intention of the partnership is commitment to each other and any children of previous partnerships as well as those of the present partnership. This extended family system would notionally include all the children of either partner, some of whom might be brothers and sisters to one another, some might be stepchildren, and some of whom will be half siblings in terms of blood or marriage (or to have the same status, as in adoption). It would of course also include grandparents, step-grandparents and others of a variety of relatedness, whether cognative or affinal kin. In the consideration of such a re-formed extended family systems model, it would be important to recognise that its boundary would be much more diffuse than that of a nuclear family consisting only of two married parents and their biologically related children.

During the process of becoming a re-formed extended family system, the family belief systems or world view of themselves would undergo what is known as a 'second order change' (see page 36, the sixth feature in a shift to circular thinking). The model would therefore allow the recognition of various degrees of relatedness and attachment, whether they might be close, more distant, overtly negative or even apparently unrecognised. For the observer, particularly when considering the problem systems which often result, at least temporarily, from divorce and remarriage, it would be helpful to keep in mind this re-formed extended family system in its complexities, even though the members of the family under focus might be only a part of such a family network. The role of practitioners in the interventionist professions often requires them to intervene with individuals (a child or one of the parents), pairs (the couple, or a former partner now remarried, or a parent and child), or groupings (a stepfamily) of such re-formed extended family systems. Yet it is likely that the 'family' who seek or are referred for help, will have a world view of themselves which may be at variance with that of others in the extended family system. Such a view is also likely to differ from that of the person who seeks to introduce new ideas or information into the system, now defined by at least some of its membership as a problem system.

ADVANTAGES AND DISADVANTAGES OF A FAMILY SYSTEMS MODEL

In addition to the above, some of the other advantages of such a family systems framework outlined by Compton and Galaway (1979) are as follows:

1 'that such a framework allows an appreciation of the entire range of elements that bear on social problems, including the social units involved, their interrelationships, and the implications of change in one as it affects all'.
2 It 'shifts attention from the characteristics possessed by individuals or their environments to the transactions between systems, changing the vantage point of the data collector and focusing on interfaces and the communication process that takes place there', though (as will be discussed below) more recent thinking would stress the shared beliefs which underlie these, as well as including the observer or data collector in the system. Such a shift also allows the avoidance of blaming as a way of dealing with a problem and points towards attempts at interactional understanding.
3 People are 'seen as active personality systems capable of self initiated behaviour and thus able to contribute and alter their behaviour or even to create new environments'.
4 'If change and tension are inherent in systems' and they are

purposive, then the view of causality can be shifted from invididual responsibility to which blame might be attributable (and often is), to a multiple responsibility for causality and capacity for change.
5 'Such a perspective also places the family and any other agency and its workers in the same transactional field.'

There are three main disadvantages of the systems model, although none of them is absolute. In the first place, the *indiscriminate* selection of such a focus can diminish the value and therefore the rights of the individual, and an awareness of the context of such practice is important. Because the systems model is an evolutionary one, which originally derives from the mathematical theory of cybernetics (that is, control, regulation and information exchange and processing from the sciences) which the anthropologist Gregory Bateson (1967) recognised also had relevance in the understanding of human relationships, the language may appear mechanistic and is sometimes criticised as dehumanising (see the following four sections of this chapter). The third disadvantage arises from the fact that until recently the theoretical formulations have tended to accept the predominating definition of the power dimension in families, thus implicitly adopting a patriarchal stance which accepts the imbalance of power between men and women. However, recent feminist writers have attempted to reformulate a framework which brings the idea of gender into family therapy theory (McGoldrick, Anderson and Walsh 1989).

THE FAMILY AS A SYSTEM

In his final consideration of issues related to the definition of the family, Morgan comments on family varieties and types of families; the personal and the structural (macro/micro, society/individual, institutional/personal, public issues/private troubles, and how these are related) concluding that the family may be located at various theoretical positions, occupying as it does an active space between the individual and society. He also raises the question of time: as, for instance, interactions over and also across time; peculiarities of the family; the question of ideology; and finally a further consideration of definitions. In the absence of one comprehensive *theory*, all these issues can be subsumed within a *systems framework*, by the inclusion of elements drawn from various theories, although it is necessary to be aware of the theoretical discrepancies which may result.

How can the essential elements of a family systems perspective be described? The basis of such a framework involves a circular rather than a linear explanation of the phenomena of human interaction. This most crucially important idea, which involves a complete shift in perception, is primarily attributed to Bateson (1979), and is distinguished from the long-established linear thinking which is the traditional way of perceiving phenomena. Hoffman (1980, 1981, 1988, 1990), one of the most elegant commentators on his work, writes that he considered 'we need a new grammar, a new descriptive language to depict what is going on in the living world'. This is a recursive language which allows for the reflexivity between living systems, which, it is argued, react back and change one another in an ongoing circular process. This *concept of circular epistomology, the recursive way through which we acquire and develop our knowledge*, is a central idea of the systems approach, and has far-reaching implications for the study of the family. The essential features of such a shift to circular thinking in relation to the family can be described as follows:

First, the family (or any other social system) can be understood as a whole, made up of interdependent elements, which through their communication and behaviour will influence and be influenced by one another. According to Bateson (1973), family members develop shared patterns of behaviours through systemisation of habit and from the 'sinking of knowledge down to less conscious and archaic levels' – what he called the 'ecology of ideas' – and that it is this which determines who does what with whom.

Thus families over time gradually build up shared meanings or constructs based on beliefs which become embodied in myths, premises (propositions which follow from one another) or belief systems about the world, and, although these are usually unconscious and therefore unavailable to families, they nevertheless operate according to them (Hoffman 1988). These shared constructs both reinforce the beliefs and through their interrelatedness and interconnectedness of behaviour continue to hold them together. These belief systems are the way in which the family knows and understands the world, and as a result *families interact in ways which are unique and different from the way in which they interact with other systems*. In so doing, families build up what are known as family rules which govern their behaviour, rules of which all the family members are apparently aware, yet often seem to be largely unconscious and thus apparently lie buried and therefore are rarely openly discussed.

Second, the ways in which they operate are often described as family rules, which through feedback govern their relationships,

communication and patterns of behaviour. It is through these feedback processes – often known as feedback loops (which are experienced in terms of a number of different levels simultaneously) – that
the family operates in positive or negative feedback loops, which
both serve to maintain the system and allow adaptation in response
to environmental conditions. It would appear that some kind of
balancing mechanisms or compensatory cohesiveness of key aspects
of family patterns increase when the family comes under stress (Lask
1982, Minuchin et al. 1978 and Reiss 1981). While the family system
operates within limits these are often unrecognised by the family, or
recognised only implicitly, so that, for example, certain family
behaviours may be experienced as being unacceptable within the
family because of precepts which have apparently been laid down by
previous generations. Because families interact within a relatedness
over time, they develop self-perpetuating behaviours, and participation in a *shared world view* provides in turn the ideology which
supports them (Sluzki 1983) although this is not necessarily an
accurate perception of the world outside, nor would it be necessarily
shared by others outside the family.

Third, therefore, it could be said that family patterns of behaviour
take place inside an implicitly specified boundary between the family
system and its *context*, and the boundary may be inflexibly rigid, or
relaxed, even amorphous. There are also intergenerational boundaries, as between grandparents, parents and children, and boundaries
between the sexes based on beliefs about gender roles and what is
appropriate behaviour.

Fourth, it is argued that within the family system there are different
levels of meaning through which, by employing communication as a
social process, the family manages structures and coordinates actions
(Cronen and Pearce 1985). These range from the deepest, though
'highest' level, to the surface, each of which is informational for the
family and arranged hierarchically according to the meanings attributed to them, each serving as context for the interpretation of
others. Cronen and Pearce describe five typical levels, from higher to
lower order in a hierarchy, each affecting and being influenced by the
others through feedback loops. The highest level, that of beliefs,
exercises an influence on the lower levels through each of the levels
embedded within them, which is described as 'contextual force'. The
lower levels may influence the higher levels through an 'implicative
force' which moves upward, both these processes implying a recursive relationship between levels:

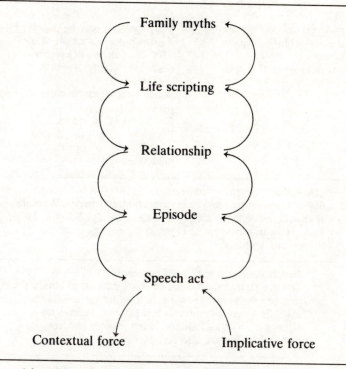

Source: Adapted from Cronen and Pearce (1985)

Figure 2.1 Embedded levels of context

5 *Family myths*, which are general concepts about society, personal roles and how family relationships function, as for instance, beliefs about marriage, parents and children.

4 *Life scripting*, the conception of the self in social action based on personal history and expectations, as for example, 'I am cautious and caring'.

3 *Relationship*, the relational concepts as to the terms on which and how two (or more) people interact with one another. An example might be, 'I am assertive, s/he is gentle'.

According to Bateson (1973) relationships may be *symmetrical*; that is, the behaviours of the two persons are similar and the given behaviour of one stimulates the same behaviour in the other. Or the behaviours can be *complementary*, in that although the behaviour is dissimilar, the behaviour of one fits with that of the other (Campbell and Draper 1985).

Cultural
Married couples do split up,
but someone/thing is usually
to blame.
Parents have right of access to
their child.

Legal
Marriages can only be dissolved
if broken down – on proof of
'fact' of adultery, behaviour,
desertion, specific length of
separation.
Ancillary matters: Welfare of child
paramount.
Child's 'right' of access.
Financial matters negotiated
according to appropriate
guidelines.

Agency and professional context
Conflict between parents' rights and children's needs. Who are
our clients, individuals, children, couple, family? What is the
primary task of our agency? How do we manage conflicts
between our agencies?

Family beliefs: scripts, myths, premises
Divorce should/should not be more difficult to obtain than
it is now.* Parents should stay together for children's
sake/ Personal fulfilment is first priority/ Parents may
divorce each other/Parents do not divorce children. Bad
husbands/wives are also bad parents.

Relationships
Husbands/wives. Co-parenting. Parent/children
Family

Behaviour
Following provocation s/he leaves home.
Evidence of grief and anger. Family unites
against departed parent. Children refuse to see
'out of house' parent. Parents in conflict when
they meet/ controlled distancing.

Key –
In the context of:

Contextual force ⌊   Implicative force ⌉

Sources: * *Social Trends*, 1989: 37% agree, 33% neither agree nor disagree, 27%
disagree. Developed from Burnham (1986); Adcock (1988), ch. 2, Fig. 1

Figure 2.2 Family reconstruction during divorce: levels of embedded
context

2 *Episodes* are conceptions as to patterns of reciprocal acts, such as 'We had one of our usual arguments about money'.
1 *Speech acts*, the relational meanings of both verbal and nonverbal messages; for instance, 'trustworthy' or 'negotiable'.

Fifth, it could therefore be considered that families, like any other system, are experienced as meaningful systems within the *context* of other systems, perceived as relevant and of which they see themselves as components or parts – as, for example, of society. These ideas of context and boundaries are also important to take into consideration when families are perceived as problematic by the agency systems which are acting on behalf of society – such as the legal context, as for instance, when considering the family reconstruction of reality during the divorce process (as Figure 2.2 shows).

Sixth, it is argued that there are two different types of change within systems: first-order change in which a particular system, such as a family, itself remains unchanged; and second-order change in which the system itself becomes changed, what Watzlawick et al. (1974) describe as 'change of change'. Second-order change occurs unexpectedly, as a kind of quantum leap, which sometimes occurs paradoxically in response to an apparently insoluble problem.

Seventh, according to what is known as 'second order cybernetics' we compute our vision of the world rather than perceive it as it actually exists. Second-order cyberneticians include von Foerster (1981), who originated the idea of the 'observing system', through which we map a territory which does not exist independently of ourselves. A later contributor, the cognitive psychologist von Glaserfield (1984), argued that one of the implications of this view is that because there is no one truth, then in our attempts to understand the world the best that can be achieved is through a 'fit' rather than a 'match'. In a recent article Epstein and Loos (1989) argue that 'the world is composed of a "multiverse" of realities and these are continuously invented and reinvented, rather than "discovered"'. There are therefore many views as to what constitutes a family, even within the same family, as the mother's view is different from that in the child's mind. The views of the family in the minds of those who intervene in families are also different, and to talk of the family as if it exists independently serves only to reify the concept of the family and thus limit options which may be therapeutic for any given family.

LANGUAGE AND THE CONVERSATIONAL DOMAIN

The biologists Maturana and Varela (1980) concluded as the result of their experiments that because nervous systems are 'information-ally closed systems' there can be no direct transfer of information between human systems. Such conclusions led to an emphasis on language because it is by engaging in conversation and dialogue in what are described as communication networks that human systems communicate with one another. This implies a shift to the domain of meaning which Anderson and Goolishian (1988) describe as a 'linguistic or conversational domain'. Rather than taking the psycho-linguistic definition of language in which meaning and understanding are thought to be derived from signs and symbols and from gram-matical structure, which have a logic separate from their use, they broaden the focus of language by defining the 'linguistically mediated and contextually relevant meaning that is interactively generated through the medium of words and other communicative action. This generated meaning (understanding) within a particular social context is evolved through the dynamic social process of dialogue and conversation'. It is thus through language that we share a reality in which we are able to maintain meaningful human contact. Epstein and Loos (1989) consider that

> language is ... a social creation, ... an active negotiation or attribution of meaning and ... a local phenomenon that is con-stantly evolving. [They consider] human systems as existing only in the domain of meaning or intersubjective linguistic reality ... humans, then, can be defined as language-generating, meaning-generating systems engaged in an activity that is intersubjective and recursive.

Meaning is thus a negotiated reality that does not occur outside the context of human interaction. It is therefore through language that social structure and role are derived. The interactional system that is relevant to any problem is therefore determined in language (see Figure 2.1).

THE DEVELOPMENT OF BEHAVIOUR WHICH IS PROBLEMATIC FOR THE FAMILY

The implications of second-order cybernetics on the development of family therapy have been considerable as, according to Hoffman (1988), the earlier family therapists (among whom she includes herself) had seen themselves as repairmen outside (meta to) the family system, whose task was, in effect, social engineering.

At about the same time as the early second-order cyberneticists were developing the ideas discussed above, the family therapists Keeney (1983) and Dell (1985) returned to a former argument that Bateson had with the early family therapists (notably Haley) and introduced the idea that reality, rather than being 'out there' and discoverable, is constructed intersubjectively by the family members. If this is so, then the implication would be that in attempting to understand family interaction, the best that observers can achieve is a 'fit', between their constructs and those of the family.

These arguments are at variance with those of the earlier 'first-order cybernetics' in which the family was considered to be a self-correcting system which, through oscillations of behaviour, endeavoured through various mechanisms to maintain a balanced functioning of the family known as homeostasis. As Anderson and Goolishian (1988), as well as Hoffman (1988) and others, have pointed out, this has resulted in a major perceptual or paradigmatic shift for many family therapists, in that the field of family therapy has moved in two different and 'opposing directions concerning the understanding of human systems, the problems they present and how therapists might usefully understand and work with them'. One paradigmatic shift, which has derived 'meaning and understanding from observing patterns of social organisation, such as structure and role', is essentially based on a Parsonian view of social systems, which they described as 'onion theories'. The other paradigmatic shift is that human systems generate meanings intersubjectively and recursively through linguistic systems, 'that these can be described as existing only in language and communicative action ... [and] the system to be treated includes those who are in a languaged context about a problem'.

THE FAMILY LIFE CYCLE

This idea of a family as a system with a shared world view and patterns of behaviour interacting through feedback over time can be given further clarity when considered within a developmental model. Several writers on the family have developed Erikson's (1950) psychoanalytic and essentially interactional concept of the individual life cycle into the idea of the stages of family interaction, in which they are confronted by psycho-social changes and expectations (see Dare 1979 and Gorell Barnes 1984). Carter and McGoldrick (1980) propose a six-stage model of the family life cycle, whereby families are perceived as going through a series of stages, each necessitating emotional processes of transition which arise from the normative events of procreation, child-rearing and development. Such emotional processes of transition entail a key principle of expansion, contraction or realignment of the family system:

1 The unattached young adult who is between families, in which it is necessary for there to be acceptance of parent/offspring separation.
2 The joining of families through marriage, which requires a commitment to the new system.
3 The family with very young children, the principle being that of accepting new members into the system.
4 The families with adolescents in which the flexibility of family boundaries is necessary so as to allow for the children's independence.
5 Launching the children and moving on, in which it is essential to accept a multitude of exits from and entries to the family system.
6 The family in later life, which entails that the family accept the shifting of generational roles.

At each stage, these key processes and their concomitant 'second-order changes' in the whole family system are necessary to allow the family to proceed developmentally. In the same volume, Terkelson (1980) writes of the elements of structure, first- and second-order change. These elements of structure are behaviours which characterise the day-to-day behaviour of a given family, and first-order changes are incremental adaptations and mastery achieved by the individuals within the developing family system. Second-order changes are those necessitated within the family in response to the normative development of individual members – as, for instance, the advent of puberty in one of the children, or to a paranormative event such as a marital separation, divorce, disabling disease or death within the family system. These second-order changes result in reverberations throughout the whole system, thus producing a re-arrangement of the elements at all levels. At that time Hoffman (1980) extended Terkelson's ideas by postulating that not all such changes are a continuous process but may be characterised by a sudden leap or transformation.

The natural history is usually as follows. First the patterns that have kept the system in a steady state relative to its environment begin to work badly. New conditions arise for which these patterns were not designed. Ad hoc solutions are tried and sometimes work, but usually have to be abandoned.... [T]he state of dissonance eventually forces the entire system over the edge, into a state of crisis.

Eventually the system either breaks down or creates a new way to monitor the same state, or spontaneously leaps to a new and more functional integration. It could be argued that family breakdown, which might ultimately lead to a divorce and eventually remarriage, is an example of such a discontinuous and unpredictable second-order change.

Combrick-Graham (1985) argues that the idea of the family life cycle does not consist of such linear events as beginning with a stage and ending with the deaths of members of a particular generation. She therefore extends this concept by superimposing the developmental tasks of each generation in the family upon one another, thus creating a family life spiral, the generations coming closer together or drawing further apart according to the developmental tasks with which they are preoccupied. A family systems approach which includes a developmental family life spiral does not preclude the consideration of other theories of the family. While this may not allow for a fully coherent theory of the family, and while some aspects may be discrepant, there are pragmatic arguments for the inclusion of any theoretical models which might prove of use when attempting to understand and also to intervene in family systems which are dysfunctional. One of these theoretical models is that of family history, both in the fairly long term of providing social benchmarks, but also in the shorter term, such as providing role models, or in terms of an individual family, as, for instance, a family tree (or genogram).

Another theoretical model which is not precluded by a family systems framework is a transactional psychoanalytic model. Indeed a number of recent writers – see Feldman (1979), Wynne (1984), Byng-Hall (1980, 1986), Willi (1984, 1987), Robinson (1986), and Solomon (1989) – have all attempted to develop an integrated model by a linking a family systems approach with a psychoanalytic perspective, either in relation to the marital system, or as regards the family as a system – Dare (1979), Will and Wrate (1985) – many of them building on Bowlby's original work (1969, 1973, 1980) on attachment theory.

THE MARITAL SYSTEM

It is appropriate at this point to introduce a brief discussion about marriage, both as a pattern of behaviour and as a stage in the family life cycle. Rice and Rice (1986) point out that, while marriage in the post-adolescent period serves society's need for procreation and the maintenance and survival of a culture, it also provides a socially sanctioned milestone that is part of a rite of passage into independence, responsibility and adulthood. Mansfield and Collard (1988) go even further when they conclude from their research on newly wed couples that 'marriage crystallises a sense of the future in [the] way it is bound up with its definition as a commitment for life'. They found that the young couples' commitment in planning their weddings reached far into the future; indeed, they seemed to be planning who they would become.

The element of Erikson's (1950) individual life cycle which characterises the young adult is the conflict between intimacy and isolation. Since that time a number of mainly psychoanalytically oriented marital therapists have taken up the theme of this conflict – see, for instance, Dicks (1967), Byng-Hall (1980), Morley (1982) and Birchtnall (1986). Willi (1984) criticises psychoanalytic theory as lacking relational perspectives and ignoring the phenomenon that relational structures allow for certain specific behaviours, but not others. He postulates the idea of an 'interaction personality' which is that part of a person's behavioural potential which can be expressed within a specific partnership. By pointing out some of the fundamental differences between marital and family systems, he also raises some of the debatable concepts in systemic family therapy:

1 In marital therapy a problem may consist in the *existence* of the marital system, while in family therapy the family as a system is unquestioned.
2 'In forming and maintaining a marital system there is a continuous process of making choices,' while 'in family systems there are no such choices, children cannot select their parents and parents cannot [yet, except in adoptive families] choose their children'.
3 In therapeutic work with couples, it is necessary to deal with the motives, fears, needs and the views of growth of the dyadic system. In working with separating couples this is even more important, because insight and understanding assist the partners in the process of uncoupling and in becoming free for a new relationship.

4 While marital systems can and do break up, family systems do not. Though parents and children may change their relationships with one another they cannot dissolve them, parents are forever the parents of their children. However, one of the main strands of argument in this book is that the re-formed extended family system becomes changed and different rather than lost altogether.

In our present society the expectation of many couples for a companionate marriage could be characterised as a search for intimacy in which each is touched, held, comforted and nourished. Building on Dicks's (1967) earlier concept of collusion, Willi develops the idea that both in their choice of one another and by developing a collusive relationship married couples, through complementarity, attempt to manage both their regressive and progressive needs. Marriage as a 'developing and ongoing process of partnership ... offers a framework ... in which the partners in stable marital relations require delay of personal needs, mutual responsibility and commitment to common goals, but also provide for satisfaction of a variety of regressive needs'. It is therefore apparent that the various normative stages of the life cycle such as childbirth, as well as paranormative events such as unemployment, will challenge such collusive regressive and progressive behaviour, in which one spouse compensates for the other as their marital roles are progressively redefined.

Another marital therapist, Feldman (1979), develops arguments which are not dissimilar as, according to him,

> intimacy is characterised by a close, familiar and usually affectionate or loving personal relationship; sexual relations; detailed and deep knowledge and understanding from close personal connection or familiar experience. The level of intimacy which is acceptable (tolerable) in a marital relationship is both determined and regulated by the complex process by which an interpersonal system is 'calibrated'.... As two people develop a relationship they communicate both overtly and covertly a set of expectations, desires, needs and fears regarding the kind of relationship they want. Over time this process leads to the creation of implicit and explicit relationship rules that define a range of acceptable deviation for a variety of interactional behaviours.

Family therapist Lyman Wynne (1984) has developed a richer and more comprehensive model of the epigenesis of relational systems, in which he describes four major processes, each fluctuating between positive and negative poles (see Figure 2.3) These are attachment care-giving, communicating, joint problem-solving and mutuality. Though these processes are essentially sequential, they necessarily all overlap, each recursively affecting the other, and each having the potential of a second-order or transformational change. According to Wynne, it is mutuality which is necessary for enduring relatedness; intimacy, though much valued, is only achieved fleetingly. If considered at the level of relationship (as described above), clearly the struggle for intimacy would be recursively influenced, through contextual force, by family myths and life scripting and also, through implicative force, by episodic behaviour and speech. Wynne's (1984) model of the epigenesis of enduring relational systems also demonstrates the types of relationships which result from degrees of failure in the development of these processes. But as indicated, although there are differences between writers regarding the ability of the couple to achieve intimacy, there is little doubt that it is the wish to do so, which is one of the main motives to seek a marriage partner and for remarriage should the first partnership prove unable to fulfil expectations.

Solomon (1989), writing about love and marriage in an age of confusion, also manages to integrate both psychodynamic and systemic concepts by describing marriage as the combination of two partners' individual subsystems whose task, both consciously and unconsciously, is to create a mutual and workable system. She uses Kohut's (1977) idea of the self-object, whereby each uses the other 'to maintain, restore and consolidate the internal experience of the self' as the basis, and draws on ideas from both the object relations psychoanalytic school (Dicks, Winnicott (1965) and others) as well as systemic thinkers (such as Bowen (1972)) to explore the evolution of reciprocal agreements which couples make with one another. Her concepts are in some ways similar to the models of Feldman and Wynne, as she developes a model of a narcissistic continuum which has three levels: archaic, transitional structures, and those which are more mature. However, while both the Feldman and Wynne models seem to imply that because individuals have become stuck at some level, then their interactional relationship too becomes more or less fixed, Solomon's model allows for more flexibility. She considers that in marital partnerships, while at each level the partners have an internal experience of the self, because they also have a capacity for object relations, they interact at each of these levels and that these prototypical interactions are based on their earlier building blocks. While many deep emotional experiences remain unconscious, events in adulthood may trigger affect, emotion and feelings, even

1 Attachment/ Caregiving	Emotional over-involvement	'Flat' detachment	Criticism/ withdrawal
2 Communicating	Amorphous communication deviance	Constricted guarded communication	Fragmented communication deviance
3 Joint problem-solving	Cyclic 'solutions' and ruptures	Evasion of problem-solving	Disruptive disagreement
4 Mutuality	Unstable pseudo-mutuality	Rigid syntonic pseudo-mutuality	Pseudo-mutuality
5 (Intimacy)	(Romanticised relatedness)	('Ho-hum' relatedness)	(Coercive/sub-missive relatedness)

Source: Wynne (1984)

Figure 2.3 Major processes and illustrative dysfunctions in the epigenesis of enduring relational systems

from the most archaic level, which in turn evokes similarly primitive defensive mechanisms from their partner.

In their work with divorcing couples Rice and Rice (1986) have devised a less complex developmental model of life-cycle development, and argue that two key tasks of human development occur and recur throughout life, though their meanings differ according to the stage of the life cycle. These concepts they describe as '*intimacy*, where the key task is *communion*, the ability to be close to another individual and *identity*, where the key task is successful separation or individuation'. As the Rices' model has been developed specifically in relation to couples and divorce, it is as yet insufficiently developed to integrate with the ideas of the family life spiral, though this would clearly be possible.

In earlier therapeutic work with couples in marital breakdown Robinson (1986) attempted to integrate the two models of Feldman and Wynne and to develop a clinical model of intervention with married couples who are trying to decide whether or not to make the commitment to work on improving their marriage, or to separate, perhaps with a view to divorce. This entails the marital therapist making a hypothesis as to the level at which the couple are 'stuck'; in engaging them in a therapeutic conversation which explores the hypothesis, it is either verified or the therapist develops another hypothesis. When the hypothesis is confirmed the therapist, through appropriate interventions, attempts to help the couple to move to the next level of relatedness. Solomon's model would seem to imply additional interventions requiring an interpretation of the partners' defensive reactions to each other as well as that of the level at which these take place.

MARITAL BREAKDOWN

Willi (1984) distinguishes four different types of couples whose relationship, while functional initially, breaks down and becomes dysfunctional under stress. These are based on the psychoanalytic terminology of oral, anal, phallic and narcissistic developmental concepts and are shown in Figure 2.3.

Partner A	*Circle of interaction*		*Partner B*
is intending to take over the regressive role:	by choosing of the partner		is intending to take over the regressive role:
helpless passive pliant dependent idealising the partner	I can behave as regressively because you ...	I can behave as progressively because you ...	caring for active concerned guiding autonomous, independent claiming admiration
denies and delegates to the partner:	in marital conflict		denies and delegates to the partner:
caring capacities activity being concerned active guiding autonomy, independence claiming admiration	I must ... become ever more regressive because you ...	I must ... become ever more progressive because you ...	helplessness passivity pliancy dependence idealisation of the partner
	The progressive–regressive dynamics in a dyadic collusion		

Source: Willi (1984)

Figure 2.4 Exaggeration of the progressive–regressive polarisation leads to dysfunctional behaviour

Willi points out that more and more couples with symmetrical narcissistic collusions have been seeking treatment. Each of the partners strives for maximum individual freedom and independence within the relationship, but they each deny their regressive need for closeness by projecting it on to the other partner. By avoiding the complementarity which increases cohesion and interdependency they have become involved in a mutually frustrating process of denying each other any true intimacy. Such couples often separate and either enter into new relationships also with the illusion of avoiding serious commitment, or end in lonely isolation.

Lawson, a social anthropologist (1988), carried out research into adulterous relationships (during which she and her colleagues heard the stories of approximately 2,550 such liaisons) and found that the patterns of adultery are changing. Increasing numbers of women are engaged in adulterous affairs, although they are less likely to tell their husbands about them than are men. Divorce is more likely for the adulterous, even in marriages where couples have an 'open marriage' arrangement; the more such liaisons, the less likely are the couple to remain married. Only serious affairs are likely to lead to a man's divorce, while if a woman had only one such liaison she is more likely to separate. Hart (1976), a social anthropologist who undertook her research among the members of a club for the divorced and separated, describes marital breakdown as an unstructured status passage. She points out poignantly that almost everyone in her sample 'thought of the end of marriage as the end of an era in their lives'. She discusses the main features which mark the termination of marriage by separation, and divorce, and these are as follows:

1 A significant part of the social identity is being changed, so that the transition is especially critical. As marriage is a 'multiplex role identity' the transition spills over into considerable aspects of social life.
2 'Because "divorce" is a deviant social category it is undesirable and the status passage transgresses life career norms prescribed by culture.'
3 For these and other (presumably psychological) reasons, according to Hart, individuals are generally unprepared for marital breakdown and because of lack of socialisation many are also unable to recognise the events that precipitate marital breakdown.
4 Marital breakdown is a 'non-scheduled' status passage and 'its temporal sequence lacks direction and inevitability', and in the general absence of 'institutional mechanisms for getting the occupant in and out of beginning, transitional and end statuses' the law

as the 'only legitimating agency of transition' only plays its part 'when most people have had to negotiate the crisis of status passage alone'.

At another level altogether, the societal level, it is interesting to note that Hart's fieldwork was conducted during the late sixties and therefore prior to the implementation of the 1969 Divorce Reform Act in 1971. While it could be argued that in view of the rising divorce rate many individuals are prepared for marital breakdown, there is little general recognition of the stages and behaviour which might be expected during a process which still lacks direction and through which people do not necessarily follow predictable patterns. As will also be apparent in the subsequent discussion, there are no generally available societal and institutional mechanisms which serve as signposts and support for persons who are embarked on the process of divorce. Nor is there any clear and easily communicable understanding as to what divorce actually means to those who experience it.

DIVORCE AND REMARRIAGE AS ADDITIONAL STAGES OF THE FAMILY LIFE CYCLE

Carter and McGoldrick (1980) describe divorce as a paranormative event, and in doing so seem to concur with the negative connotation of many other writers towards divorce. On the other hand Rice and Rice (1986) argue that, as nearly half first marriages end in divorce in the USA, it is time to review approaches to divorce that are considered to be normative, and they introduce a developmental model of divorce. They have been followed by Ahrons and Rodgers (1988) who take a similar approach to divorce and remarriage. In the United Kingdom, where the divorce rate is lower, and is projected as one in three of marriages currently taking place, it is more doubtful that divorce could be considered as 'just another phase of the life cycle'. It is hardly likely that taking a more neutral and developmental view of divorce would lead to more *laissez-faire* attitudes than there are generally perceived to be at present, as we seem to be in the midst of a transition of values towards both marriage and divorce. In their model of the family life cycle, Carter and McGoldrick (1980) also include additional stages – those associated with divorce, single parenthood and remarriage – which they consider are necessary in order to allow the family to restabilise and proceed developmentally.

However, it is important to recognise that whereas at least one of the partners of the divorcing couple seeks to end the marriage, this is not the case for their children. Recent research, for example, Wallerstein and Kelly (1980), Mitchell (1985) and others (see Chapter 8) – shows that while children may adapt to the divorce of their parents this is not what they wish. At least for a period the needs and wishes of the parental and children's systems are in conflict, a conflict which places the stability of the family unit in jeopardy, thus affecting the decision-making capacities of parents and putting them in conflict with their children, whether directly or implicitly. The additional stages related to divorce which Carter and McGoldrick (1980) distinguish could therefore be said to be more marital and parental than family-oriented, and are as follows:

1 The decision to divorce, which involves the parents in accepting the inability to resolve their marital tensions sufficiently to continue the relationship.
2 Planning the break-up of the system, which requires supporting, viable arrangements for all parts of the system.
3 Separation, which requires not only a willingness to continue a cooperative, co-parental relationship, but also to work on the resolution of attachment to the spouse.
4 The divorce, which requires more work on the emotional divorce.

Carter and McGoldrick's developmental outline for stepfamily (remarried family) formation includes the following steps:

(a) Entering into a new relationship, which implies recovery from the first marriage, including an emotional divorce.
(b) Conceptualising and planning a new marriage and family, which involves accepting the fears of both partners and children about forming a stepfamily. This includes accepting the need for time and patience to adjust to the complexity and ambiguity of multiple new roles, boundaries, space, time and authority; and also affective issues, such as guilty loyalty conflicts, desire for mutuality and unresolvable past hurts.
(c) Remarriage and the reconstitution of the family, which involves the final resolution of the attachment to the previous spouse and relinquishing the ideal of an intact family and acceptance of a different model of family whose boundaries are more permeable.

More comprehensive, extended and also more complex models of these additional stages of the family life cycle, which also include models for intervention during the divorce and remarriage process, will be discussed in Chapters 3, 4 (Figures 4.2 and 4.3), 5, 6 and 7.

3 The family as a system
Models of intervention

I am the family face
Flesh perishes, I live on.

Thomas Hardy (1840–1928), 'Heredity'

Language is called the garment of thought; however, it should rather be, language is the flesh garment, the body of thought.

Thomas Carlyle (1795–1881) *Sartor Resartus*, Book 1, chap. 11

FAMILY SYSTEMS THEORY AND MODELS OF INTERVENTION

Family systems theory, like psychoanalytic theory, has often been confused with various therapies which are based upon it. In fact the definition of the word 'therapy' is the medical treatment of disease. Systemic thinking is indeed the basis of most family therapy models of intervention, as psychoanalytic theory is the basis of psycho-analysis and many (though not all) of the psychotherapies. These models are not essentially therapeutic models, but adaptations which allow their application in the form of interventions which are specifically designed within a particular framework or context. Because psychoanalysis, for example, was developed within a medical model, assumptions are made about symptomatology or malfunctioning. Family therapy, on the other hand, has been developed from a systems model, and while avoiding some of the excesses of the medical model such as the search for a cure, as is implied in some models of psychotherapy, nevertheless became incorporated into the medical model with its basic premise of healing. Although it is not the intention of this book to provide a history of family therapy, it is necessary to point out that what are now known as 'first-order cybernetics' are relied upon as fundamentals by many family therapists, particularly those of the structural and strategic schools of family therapy; see, for instance, Minuchin (1974), Papp (1983), Haley (1987), Hoffman's (1981) earlier work and that of many others.

The implications of 'second-order cybernetics' (see Chapter 2, 'The family as a system', page 28) were expanded by a number of writers who argued that the presence of an observer, both by definition and perception, would necessarily intervene in the systemic interaction of the family – Keeney (1983), Watzlawick (1984) and Dell (1985) – indeed, that *both* the family and the 'observer' would be affected by such a process. For many family therapists, these ideas resulted in a redefinition of the focus of therapy from the behaviour of the family to the meanings, often unconscious, which underlie behaviours. It will be apparent that there are many different models or, as they are often called, 'schools' of therapy, and each of these therapeutic models enables the therapist to select an appropriate therapy through which to perceive the client couple or family as if through a lens. The therapist, in engaging with the client(s), creates a new system which can provide the leverage for change.

Recently some constructivist family therapists began to develop the idea of the configuration of relationships around a given problem – see Cecchin (1988), Anderson et al. (1986), Anderson and Goolishian (1988) and Hoffman (1988). Hoffman (1988), employing one of her vivid metaphors, describes it as being like the folk tale of the young man who stole a magic goose: 'anyone who touches the goose becomes stuck to it, and anyone who touches that person gets stuck too. Eventually there is a long line of people running through the countryside all stuck to each other and the goose.' As she points out, 'a problem system is a network of meanings rather than a collection of people'. Therefore, as Anderson et al. (1986) point out, 'the interactional system that is relevant to any problem under study is determined in language, not in social structure'. More recently, taking what might be called a chicken-and-egg perspective, they argue that it is not the system which makes the problem, but that the 'system to be treated includes those who are in a languaged context about a problem' (Anderson and Goolishian 1988). They argue that 'languaging about a problem makes systems' and consider 'such a defined system as a problem-organizing problem dis-solving system'. According to them 'we live with each other in a world of conversational narrative, and we understand ourselves and each other through changing stories and self descriptions. ... Meaning is derived from the intersubjective and communicative uses to which meaning is put.' Problems are not necessarily specifically in any socially defined unit, but are in 'the intersubjective minds of all who are in active communicative exchange and as such, are themselves always changing'.

Their colleagues, Epstein and Loos (1989) state unequivocally that they see the process of problem definition as one in which the therapist and client(s) engage in a collaborative venture rather than the therapist as being a diagnostic expert. This implies that any assessment or diagnosis must be developed together and can no longer be based on so-called objective notions of health or psychopathology. Wynne et al. (1986) have gone further and recently argued cogently for a total shift from the idea of family therapy, which they consider 'tend(s) to confuse and mislead both the public and professional colleagues about intentions and . . . actual functioning' to that of systems consultation. This apparently novel idea underlies the processes of intervention described in subsequent chapters (but particularly in Chapters 9 and 10), which will focus on ways and means of intervention during the divorce and remarriage process. Because so-called therapy is usually, though not always, voluntarily entered into, the traditional title of 'therapist' will be retained, though the inverted commas will be used to indicate that such a role is a consultative one.

THE CONSTRUCTIVIST APPROACH TO FAMILY INTERVENTION

The constructivist approach to family systems based on 'second-order cybernetics' has already been briefly described, and there are an increasing number of family 'therapists' – see, for instance, Penn (1982, 1985), Andersen (1987), Anderson and Goolishian (1988), Tomm (1987a, 1987b, 1988), Cecchin (1987), Hoffman (1988), White (1986,1988), Epstein and Loos (1989) and others, including the present author – who attempt to base their most recent therapeutic work on this model. Rather than doing something 'to' or 'for' their client(s) (or patients), their intention is to construct, through a conversational domain, a shared process of meaning, which co-evolves as between themselves and the others (clients or patients) involved.

As has already been discussed, this development is based on the work of Varela (1979), who distinguished the observing system (that is, the 'therapist' together with an observer community such as the team) who, through conversation with the client(s), constructs a meaningful process, which from then on develops a life of its own. The view of Anderson and Goolishian (1988) is similar to that of

Maturana and Varela, that 'communication and discourse define social organization and that reality is a product of changing dialogue. . . . Human social systems require the linguistic coupling of their components (i.e. individuals) such that they can operate with each other as observers in language'.

It is argued that as there is no belief in objective reality, therefore problems exist in terms of meanings. While of course there are actual situations and events which are problematic, in essence it is the beliefs of those involved in them which influence their perceptions and definitions of such situations or events. Such a stance indicates the need for a shift in focus from behaviours to the development of cognition. This implies an emphasis on change in inner as well as outer structures – in other words, on intersubjective and reciprocally maintained ideas, rather than on the Freudian tradition of the intrapsychic, or the earlier family therapy tradition of interactionally defined behaviour. The system to be treated thus includes those who are in a 'languaged' context about a problem, which may be a family, though it can be a smaller or larger system. It is these people who 'language' about what they call a problem. As Anderson and Goolishian indicate,

> no communicative account, no word, is complete, clear and univocal. All carry unspoken meanings and possible new inter- pretations that require expression and articulation . . . therapy is a process of expanding and saying the 'unsaid' – the development through dialogue, of new themes and narratives, and actually the creation of new histories.

Through such dialogical conversation new meanings are allowed to emerge, and change takes place. The process of change through therapy then becomes an exploration through which 'other descrip- tions and meanings will emerge that are no longer labelled in language as a "problem"' (Hoffman 1988). This kind of conversa- tional domain is one in which 'therapist' and family (namely, the clients) together create a context in which change can come about spontaneously. According to Hoffman it is at least possible that in creating such a shared consciousness together 'therapist' and client(s) may also develop a shared unconscious which can be approached through symbols, dreams, stories or trance, as linking elements which human beings collectively share, and which, as it is always unfolding, can be tapped like an underground spring. This idea seems to have some links with the idea of the collective unconscious of society as conceptualised by Jungian psychoanalytic theory – see, for instance, Storr 1972.

Meaningful conversation is thus 'based on mutual respect and understanding, a willingness both to listen and to test one's opinions and prejudices, together with a mutual seeking of the rightness of fit of what is said' (Anderson and Goolishian 1988). Some of the other aspects which Anderson and Goolishian (1988) distinguish evolve as follows:

1 the occasion for the conversation; the relationship of the participants to each other;
2 what each knows of the situation and intent of the others;
3 what the participants hope to accomplish;
4 the applicable social and cultural conventions and the ever-changing intended meanings of the participants.

Because of such a co-evolution, the understanding and meaning in dialogue is always changing and fluid; and therapeutic dialogue is basically no different from any other. The heart of therapeutic communication is still essentially a process of people trying to understand one another, and who comprise the social system which becomes the target of discourse. As they describe with deceptive simplicity, 'Change in therapy is no more than changing meaning derived through dialogue and conversation.' Epstein and Loos (1989), in setting out the ethical implications of such a 'dialogical constructivist position', consider that this

> implies that the reality of each person has a validity within his or her domain of existence. Normative views of what constitutes a family, what characterises healthy interaction or what defines appropriate communication represent an imposition of moral values with disrespect for the other's position.... The participants in a conversation codevelop a meaning system as they engage in a dialogue [and] these intersubjective realities are generated out of the understanding of each other's position ... new meanings arise out of the continuance of the conversation.

They consider that the task of the 'therapist' is 'to continue or manage the conversation out of which new meaning will emerge. Both client and "therapist" change as the result of the creation of new meaning, and it is through the conversation that options are created.'

GUIDELINES FOR THE PRACTICE OF THERAPEUTIC CONVERSATIONS

Each of the following writers has set out principles and guidelines for the practice of such therapeutic conversations (Hoffman 1988 and

1990, Anderson and Goolishian 1988, and Epstein and Loos 1989); and their ideas have been drawn together in an attempt to achieve a workable synthesis, on which, except when required to act as an agent of social control (see Chapter 10) practice may be based.

First, social systems do not create problems; problems themselves define and determine the relevant systems for involvement and intervention, and in this way the problem therefore creates a 'system'. This is a particularly important concept as it implies that there is no distinct 'unit' of treatment, there is just a group of people who are having a particular kind of conversation about a problem about which some of the people are complaining and others are not (Hoffman 1988). This could be described as the 'problem-organising problem-dis-solving system' (Anderson and Goolishian 1988).

Second, if we ourselves construct reality, we cannot therefore find an outside place from which to perceive and consider it; in other words, there cannot be a higher (or meta) position to the problem as proposed by many family 'therapists'. Thus there are no experts in the sense of authoritative omnipotence, and therefore the task of the 'therapist' (as consultant to the system) is to try to enable everyone's private reality to be understood and to keep the enquiries within the parameters as described by the clients.

Third, the 'therapist' is not constrained to think solely in terms of social units, such as the marital couple, or the nuclear family, as such problem-determined systems often overlap different social structures. However, every 'therapist' must include themselves, as well as the referring agent, in any conceptualisation of the problem system. While it may not be necessary for the 'therapist' actually to see together everyone engaged in active communication about the problem – it may even be inadvisable – it is important to acknowledge all these different perspectives.

Fourth, the 'therapist' is neither neutral nor impartial. She or he seeks to find the meaning behind even the most unpleasant actions or events, and sides with everybody involved, attempting to 'get behind' each person in the situation. This implies the simultaneous holding of several, often contradictory, ideas, and using the interview to move towards mutual enquiry about the prevailing ideas and thence to a broadening, a shifting and a shared creation of new meanings for all the participants, including the 'therapist'. Any diagnoses are mutual creations, emerging out of the dialogue, which then either limit or expand the possibility for generating new ideas (Epstein and Loos 1989).

Fifth, the 'therapist' tries to learn, understand and use the language of the client(s) because that is the metaphor for their experiences and what is happening in their lives.

Sixth, by using only cooperative language the 'therapist' may offer a view of aspects of the problem system, and which those present are free to accept or reject, or to come up with an alternative definition (to which the 'therapist' not only listens respectfully, but also does not understand too quickly, so as to promote dialogue and the emergence of new meaning for client(s) and 'therapist' alike).

Seventh, the 'therapist' asks both information-seeking and closed questions which are lineal (answered Yes or No), also those which are open and may be directed to any family member. Such purposeful questioning may be generic or specific and is designed both to check on a hypothesis developed by the 'therapist' and to promote self-questioning in the clients. For instance questions may be circular (inviting the expression of comments on the views of others), strategic (having a constraining effect), reflexive (facilitative of new links or views), contain embedded suggestions (see Tomm 1987a, 1987b and 1988, Cecchin 1987 and White 1988), or future oriented (Penn 1982, 1985). It is the 'therapist's' skill in asking questions which is the essential tool of the therapy.

Eighth, the 'therapist' takes responsibility for the creation of a conversational context that allows for a mutual collaboration in the process of problem definition. Although such a model de-emphasises hierarchy, it does not do so in such a way as to negate distinctions. Rather, it distinguishes the idea of positions, in which where one stands influences what one sees and thinks about the problem. This implies a need for clarity about boundaries in order to get a valid sense of the different perspectives.

Ninth, while change is still a goal in the (so-called) therapy, the aim is less one of intent than one in which the 'therapist' and family join together in setting up a context in which change can come about spontaneously. This would indicate that in certain situations, such as marital therapy with couples in conflict, the 'therapist' makes a clear contract as to what are the goals which the couple would hope to achieve.

Tenth, the 'therapist' maintains a dialogical conversation with himself or herself and is as prepared to change his or her views just as any other participant in the problem system. This includes the responsibility to consult with his or her own belief system.

In such a model there is much less focus on issues of the power and control associated with the 'therapist', but more a responsibility to share with the clients the possible implications for them, should their views be perceived differently by others. Recent work on the importance of gender in family therapy – see, for instance, Walters, Carter, Papp and Silverstein (1988) and also McGoldrick, Anderson and Walsh (1989) – indicates that the 'construction of gender emphasizes the difference, polarity and hierarchy, rather than similarity, equality and commonality of experience in human thought and action' (Hare Mustin 1989). This would also include taking into account the influence of the gender of the 'therapist'.

Hoffman (1988) differentiates between 'imposed' and 'reciprocal' power, the former being any unilateral attempt to control the circumstances without regard to the benefit of everyone present, and the latter attempting mutually to enhance the balance of interests of everyone involved. However, she also points out that in situations of risk, as for example when a child is at risk of violence, it is the responsibility of the 'therapists' not only to consult with their own belief system but also that of the agency for whom they may be working. This would also imply that it is the responsibility of the 'therapist' to share with the clients the implications of alternative views, such as those which might be held within the legal system.

In some therapeutic situations there is a 'reflective' team, (that is, one observing the 'therapist' and family from behind a one-way screen, as described by Andersen 1987) and there is a relative absence of hierarchy, as the team allows the family to become party to their thinking. Such a reflective team comment spontaneously when discussing the family, sharing their own beliefs which the family may choose to interpret in the light of their own subjectivity. This is different from the status which is built into the structure of most family therapy models, as the family is not only able to listen in, but also invited to comment on what the team have said, and are given the last word.

THE MEDIATION MODEL OF INTERVENTION DURING THE DIVORCE PROCESS

Like family therapy, conciliation or mediation in family disputes is a developing field of intervention (see Chapter 9, 'Conciliation/ mediation', page 195, and 'Combinations of conciliation and therapy with the same family', page 201, and Chapter 10, 'Conciliatory or investigative?', page 228), about which there is a burgeoning literature both in North America and in the United Kingdom – see, for instance, Haynes (1981), Haynes and Haynes (1989), Saposnek (1983), Folberg and Taylor (1984), Folberg and Milne (1988),

Robinson and Parkinson (1985), Parkinson (1988), Robinson (1988) and Walker (1988) and others. As there is considerable confusion attached to the use of the words 'conciliation' and 'mediation', the process of intervention will be described as mediation, the practitioners will be described as conciliators, and the independent services described as conciliation services.

There are two major distinguishing features of the conflict between marital partners during the divorce process and family conflict at other stages of the family life cycle. In the first place, the family and its whole future are in a state of total flux, and second, such a dispute takes place within the legal context or in the shadow of such a possibility. The task of the law is to settle disputes, at the same time protecting the rights of the individuals in so far as it is possible so to do. It therefore will be apparent that the balancing of needs and rights becomes a herculean task in the case of families going through divorce, and it is one for which in many ways the law is ill equipped, as such decisions require the wisdom of Solomon (Clulow and Vincent 1987). A major implication of such an interconnection with the legal system is that if the parents are not able to resolve their conflict on behalf of the family then the ultimate decision will need to be made by the court. If parents who are in dispute about custody and access for their children (and perhaps also financial matters and the family home) cannot resolve the conflict themselves, either with or without the help of their lawyers, then eventually the court will necessarily be required to make a judicial decision (see Chapter 4). While the tasks of the legal system and those of conciliation services are distinct, they are also overlapping. This can lead to some difficulties for the families who may be the clients of both lawyers and conciliators (see Chapter 9). The family transition during the divorce processs is a second-order change of some magnitude, in that the changes required of the family are so comprehensive and often also potentially cataclysmic (at least for some family members).

Whereas many couples are able to resolve their differences regarding future plans without intervention, for others the conflict becomes so entrenched that it is only possible to change within a holding structure, and for relatively few this ultimately leads to a court appearance and a judicial decision. It is this holding context which mediation attempts to provide in which the conciliator controls the process, but not the decision-making. It is perhaps unfortunate that the word 'conciliation' not only sounds very similar to 'reconciliation' but also can be used in a number of different ways, and, indeed, is so used (see Chapters 4, 9 and 10). Similarly, 'mediation' also is used with many different meanings. For our purposes here 'conciliation' (or 'mediation', which are used inter-changeably) is taken to mean a method of brief intervention as defined by Robinson and Parkinson (1985)

> which focuses on particular issues of family conflict, where there has been pressure from inside or outside the family systems for decisions to be made within a legal context; and where such decisions have long term legal and often financial implications for those involved. The context within which conciliation is practised influences the process, particularly if the practitioner has implicit or explicit power in the decision making process,

and, (the author would now add) 'also the long-term implications for the attachment and bonding of the family members'. While it is regarded as a brief intervention, with relatively few sessions, these may be spread over some months, the intention being to mesh with the psychological processes in which the couple are involved and if possible, in parallel with those of the legal system.

There is a steady growth of independent conciliation services, and those whose professional standards accord with those of the National Family Conciliation Council may become members. The Council, founded in 1983, has become a well-established association which now has a membership of approximately fifty affiliated services, provides a core training programme and is currently planning more advanced training modules, as well as accreditation. It is also active in lobbying for conciliation for divorcing families and in promoting links between the various services already provided.

Mediation is a developing field of intervention which is aptly described as 'bargaining in the shadow of the law' (Mnookin and Kornhauser 1979). While various models of child-focused mediation are adopted, in essence the differences are on a continuum as between the minimalist and legalistic approaches which primarily focus on the negotiation between the individual disputant partners, and a more 'therapeutic' approach which includes that based on a systemic perspective which takes into account the family system in transition. This may include such family therapy techniques and strategies as would be compatible with the principle of what is usually known as 'party control'; which essentially means that the parties involve themselves voluntarily and are in agreement with the issues which are being discussed. The family systems approach to media-tion, which is the focus here, has been criticised as 'subjecting families to covert forms of treatment' (Roberts 1990; see Chapter 9, 'Conciliation/mediation', page 195).

As Robinson (1988) indicates, there is an increasing interest in the United Kingdom in adopting a broader approach to mediation, so as to incorporate focusing on all aspects of the conflict, which include financial matters such as the payment of maintenance and the disposition of the matrimonial home, and this is usually referred to as 'comprehensive mediation'. A result of such developments has been to involve lawyers more directly in the process of conciliation. In the United States particularly, many lawyers have undertaken additional training and have become mediators themselves, while in this country a small but increasing number co-mediate with a conciliator in comprehensive mediation (Parkinson 1989). As the law requires that each partner should be separately represented in court, should this become necessary, the Law Society requires that lawyers acting as mediators cannot *also* represent their clients. Therefore, it is suggested that any mediation agreements are made 'without prejudice' and approved by the solicitors of each of the partners. Nevertheless, as Walker (1988) succinctly states, 'conciliation is task oriented, [and] the skills of both therapy and legal practice need to be blended'. Figure 2.2, which shows the reconstruction of the family's reality during the divorce process (see Chapter 2) demonstrates there is a choice as to which level to intervene, and the 'therapist' or conciliator needs to recognise the impact and effectiveness of the intervention upon the other levels. Kelly (1983) distinguished between conciliation and psychotherapy, and Robinson (1988) differentiated between the interventions of conciliation, psychotherapy and family therapy (see Figure 3.1).

Haynes, who originally began his career in labour relations, has recently outlined the assumptions on which he bases his practice in comprehensive mediation (Haynes and Haynes 1989). Many people are afraid of conflict, although it is a useful aspect of everyday life; it is only when it is unresolved that it becomes dangerous, and most people do want to settle the conflict between them. They distinguish between conflict resolution in mediation, which is over issues, from conflict over behaviour, which can be resolved in therapy; and point out that when people need to continue an ongoing relationship (as do parents following divorce), negotiations are more likely to be successful. Whereas the mediator is responsible for the process of the mediation, the outcome is the responsibility of the parties. The Hayneses believe that there is good in everyone, and that it is the mediator's task to reconnect the parties with their own wisdom.

	Conciliation/mediation	Psychotherapy	Family therapy
Knowledge base	Family systems approach, attachment theory, negotiation theory, family law	Psychoanalytic, behavioural, Rogerian, etc.	Family systems approach, structural, strategic, Milan, constructivist
Goals	To achieve attitudinal change and negotiated agreement	To improve mental health	To restore family functioning
Contract	Explicit	Generally implicit	Varies according to model
Tasks	Concrete, focused on external data and issues	Focused on internal psychic reactions	Focused on family transactions, communications and meanings
Length	Short term	Varies from brief therapy to long term	Varies from brief to medium length
Role of worker	Very active Manages process not outcome, educator, clarifier, organiser	Ranges from fairly passive to fairly active	Varies according to model – often fairly active
Relationship	Neutral, balanced	Partisan, dependency on therapist features	Varies according to model from neutral to partisan
	Empowers parties as individuals yet still co-parents	Assumes primary responsibility for mental health	Assumes primary responsibility for mental health of members
Power relationships in client	Balances power (a) financial (b) ability to think, organise and plan (c) raw power or ('muscle mediation')	Indirectly only (b) ability to think, organise and plan (c) assist in coping	Varies (b) Ability of members to think, organise and plan (c) redistribution

(Continued)

	Conciliation/mediation	*Psychotherapy*	*Family therapy*
Expression of feelings	Not main focus	Main focus	May or may not be main focus
Conflict management	Major skill Circumscribe area, partialise, identify and specify, encourage self-interest, proscribe behaviour	Minor skill Identify and interpret Encourage self-interest	Varies according to model Identify, partialise Encourage enactment, Proscribe behaviour
Orientation	Future	Present and and sometimes future	Varies, usually present and future
Reality testing	Provides a forum for financial as well	Provides a forum	Provides a forum
Negotiation strategies	Bargaining Continuing educational process to make sure each partner understands details Asks each to justify why other should accept proposal Stress win/win philosophy	Rarely	Sometimes encourage family members to negotiate and set tasks for each other

Source: Robinson (1988); developed from Kelly (1983)

Figure 3.1   Comparison between conciliation/mediation, psychotherapy and family therapy

Finally, they believe that because the ways in which the mediator behaves during the process is determined by the situation, therefore as each family is unique so is the conduct of mediation. Haynes himself sometimes explains what is he is doing and at other times is strategic. According to these assumptions the objective of conciliation is to assist the couple to reach their own agreements, and any therapeutic benefits which may occur are the result of spin-off rather than intent; whereas the focus of the various therapeutic interventions are to improve mental health or family functioning, and any decision-making which may result is, as it were, of secondary importance.

GUIDELINES FOR THE PRACTICE OF MEDIATION

Several writers, particularly in the US, have described the stages of conflict management in conciliation/mediation (Folberg and Taylor 1984, Haynes 1982, Haynes and Haynes 1989, Folberg and Milne 1988), and Robinson (1986) has adapted these in accordance with a family systems approach to conciliation practice in the UK. This process can most easily be described in stages, and it is important to note that the mediation process attempts to complement both the psychological processes of marital breakdown and divorce, and those of the legal processes in which the couple are likely to become involved.

Prior to first interview

The parties are often referred by their solicitors, who will usually explain the implications of the mediation process to them, also support the referral and suggest that any legal steps are deferred until the outcome is known. They may be referred by counsellors (and others) or may refer themselves to the conciliation service. The referral process is a particularly delicate one, as the first contact is usually made with one partner, who not infrequently indicates that the other is unwilling to attend. Some services initially conduct an individual interview, while others insist on both partners attending in the first instance.

Stage 1

In attempting to engage the parties in the process, the conciliator tries to join with each of them and, through the development of a trusting relationship, begins to build a framework within which they can all work together. This is particularly important, as especially at this stage there is usually little trust between the parties themselves. Indeed, many have not previously met since one partner left the matrimonial home.

This first interview includes the introduction of conciliator and agency to both parties, preferably at the same session, explaining the link with legal procedures, and the need for cooperation with their lawyers.

Addresses and telephone numbers are obtained for each of the parties, sometimes in confidence, as well as factual information, such as the names and ages of the children and where and with whom they are presently living.

It is also necessary for the conciliator and couple to develop procedural rules for the process of the conciliation. Where the conflict is particularly high, the conciliator may seek the parties' agreement to interrupt or even curtail the session, so as to allow the dissipation of a highly charged atmosphere.

The issues to be mediated begin to emerge and may include the possibility of the children becoming involved, though the arrangements and objectives of including them are to be clearly set out and sanctioned by both parents. The existence of pain and anger is acknowledged, but the conciliator focuses on the issues and the couple's expectations as to the outcome. The focus is in the present with an orientation towards the future rather than the past. Both parties are given equal opportunities to put their point of view, and the goals and suggestions for working procedures are agreed between the conciliator and the couple.

Stage 2

Through careful questioning and in dialogue with them the conciliator tries to isolate and help the parties to agree the issues over which they are in conflict and which need to be worked on – for example, custody, access, and, for comprehensive mediation, perhaps also including maintenance and the matrimonial home. In many instances the arrangements for the children are intricately linked with the decision as to which partner will retain the family home, as well as with the maintenance for the children. Many couples have already agreed on some issues, while other issues present apparently insuperable difficulty.

The structures for the working procedures are agreed; as, for instance, whether the sessions are to be dyadic or joint, or a combination of both, and as to the possible inclusion of children in the process. The existence of conflict is acknowledged and the issues for conciliation are agreed and prioritised. The ensuing processs is strictly task-focused, although, if necessary, the mediator attempts to equalise the power between the parties. The conciliator encourages them to begin brainstorming for possible solutions, perhaps adding or amending suggestions. This leads to the consideration of some concessions made by each to the other and opens the way to the possibility of some compromise between them. The aim is that any agreements which are subsequently reached as far as possible meet the needs of those involved, the parties and their children, and are reasonably equitable.

Stage 3

While the conciliator may employ therapeutic skills, such as reframing (redescribing more favourably so as to effect a more positive alteration in the parties' negative perceptions of the situation), these are focused on attempts to reduce the conflict and to help the parties to create options which are mutually acceptable. The conciliator focuses on the needs of those involved, especially those of the children of the family. The parties are helped towards the consideration of future needs and opportunities for all the family members, as well as ways in which the possible options might be affected – as, for instance, by job moves or financial constraints. If appropriate, the conciliator introduces a broad consideration of legal and financial norms as well as stressing the need for professional advice. The possibility of new attachments is also anticipated for the parents, as well as their implications for their children.

Stage 4

This is the stage of decision-making for the parties. The issues relating to the possible decisions are clarified, the priorities are finally defined and the negotiations towards parenting agreements and plans for the future begin. Possible plans are outlined and tried out while details are rehearsed and, if necessary, revised. It is at this stage that the children might be seen, though only with the agreement of *both* parents either together with them, or individually, with each of them; or, if the children are older, perhaps on their own, either singly or altogether.

Stage 5

The final stage is that of implementation, review and formal revision. In some services, the conciliator checks how the plan appears to be working, and if this is agency policy, together with the couple writes an agreement which is legally 'without prejudice', and which they take to their lawyers. In other agencies, and with the permission of the parties, letters are sent to their lawyers indicating in outline what issues have been agreed and which have not. All conciliation agencies recognise the importance of professional collaboration and have devised a recognised policy for communicating with the lawyers of the couple.

A COMPARISON OF CONCILIATION AND A CONSTRUCTIVIST FAMILY THERAPY APPROACH TO INTERVENTION

When comparing conciliation as a method of intervention during the divorce process with a constructivist approach to family intervention it will be apparent that while there are differences, particularly as to the goals and the focus of the work with the couple, many of these are really differences of emphasis. For conciliators who use a systemic approach to their work, the strategies and skills which they use are often those of family therapists, such as reframing, positive connotation (a positive re-evaluation of behaviour which is regarded by one or both parties as mad or bad) and diversion (changing the subject). It is significant that in the Hayneses' latest work (1989) they make specific reference to the questioning strategies described by Tomm (see page 52), including those which are aimed to create doubt in the parties' perception of the original position, which they regard as the first step towards change. The goal of both models of intervention is change, but that of mediation is more specific, short-term and task-focused, while in constructivist family therapy the pace and process of change can be lengthier and less specific.

There are however two main differences, the major one being the effect of working within or alongside the legal system, which imposes a time frame on the decisions which have to be taken. This also makes it necessary to recognise that, as the legal position of each of the partners is of great importance, it is also therefore necessary for them to respect and work collaboratively alongside their solicitors.

Ideally the work of mediation intervention should mesh with those of the legal processes, so that the parties have begun to make the necesssary emotional changes, particularly those of individual differentiation from their relationship as a couple, before they have to tackle the decision-making processes which the law requires. Second, whereas the aim of therapy is primarily therapeutic, that of mediation is primarily task-focused, while any therapeutic effect is a spin-off from the process. Unlike therapists, conciliators do not work with the losses which the family are experiencing, though these are acknowledged.

Both family therapist and conciliator are impartial, rather than neutral, though the family therapist would try to get behind the meaning of the changes for the couple and their children, and the conciliator would try to focus on the here-and-now of the decision-making process, unless the couple seem to have become so seriously stuck that they cannot proceed. Families going through the process of separation, divorce and remarriage are undergoing both a process of transition and a redefinition of family rules (see Chapters 4 and 5). Therapists and conciliators alike would both help couples to create a framework within which they could function as parents in future, although they might have no future together as a couple, while the family therapist would be likely to emphasise the meanings for the family, and the conciliator stress the need for decision-making.

CONCLUSION

The preceding discussion of theoretical frameworks and models of intervention shows that there is no one comprehensive and proven theory either for the study and understanding of families or for intervention for families who perceive themselves or are perceived by others as being in difficulties. Family life is not just one rich, interwoven and living tapestry, but a complex system moving through sequential individual and family life cycles or spirals, as well as those of the society in which they live. Each of these individual and familial cycles consists of a series of interacting levels and patterns of beliefs, relationships and episodes within which the family members, through communication, co-evolve and script their mutual life histories.

The interventionist practitioners to whom the family, whether as a group or individual members, turn for help need to recognise that their practice (and especially that of therapy and conciliation) is in the domain of ethics, and therefore they need to be aware of and to take responsibility for how their own belief systems influence their values and the ways in which they work (see Chapter 9, 'Whose choice of intervention?', page 185, and Holmes and Lindley 1989). Bearing their own value position in mind they only then can merely try to select an appropriate theoretical model of intervention as a lens for the family, so that together they can attempt to explore and highlight some of these patterns, while trying to make others more muted; and in this way enabling such changes as are necessary to be more mutually acceptable and beneficial for the family.

4 Families through the divorce process
Divorce as a private sorrow

All happy families resemble one another, but each unhappy family is unhappy in its own way.

Leo Tolstoy (1828–1910), *Anna Karenina*, chap. 1 (Tr. Maude)

All violent feelings ... produce in us a falseness in all our impressions of external things, which I would generally characterize as the 'Pathetic Fallacy'.

John Ruskin (1819–1900), *Modern Painters*, vol. IV, chap. 20

There is an increasing amount of academic and clinical research which seeks to describe the aspects and stages of the divorce process from various theoretical perspectives. On the one hand there are those who view the social processes of divorce, while on the other there are those who seek to describe the psychological process, either from the experience of the individual, the couple or the children, or from that of the whole family. When marital breakdown results in divorce, as is often the case, then the process also crosses the somewhat amorphous boundary which divides the private sorrows (Wright Mills 1959) which lie within the family and those of divorce as a public issue, and one which may come under the purview of the civil (or private) law as it relates to the family. One of the earliest researchers described a stage-theory approach to divorce, distinguishing the six stations of divorce – the emotional (two stages), the legal, economic, co-parental, community (networks of friends, neighbours, schools and so on) and ultimately, the psychic divorce (Bohannon 1970) – and this has formed the basis of much subsequent work.

Among those who consider divorce as a social process are two sociologists, Hart (1976) and Vaughan (1987) one of whom describes the process from the perspective of the individual and the other from that of the couple. Hart (whose work has already been referred to in

Chapter 2, 'Divorce and remarriage as additional stages of the family life cycle', page 44) considered marital breakdown and divorce as an unstructured and unscheduled status passage in which an important aspect of social identity is being changed, and that this is one for which the individual is ill prepared, lacks role support, and (at the time of her research) transgressed social norms, although society is now more tolerant of divorce. Vaughan researched the underlying patterns which lie beneath disintegrating partnerships and, while clearly introducing ideas drawn from stage theory, also describes the un-coupling process in interactional terms. Her work shows clearly how the private troubles of the partners eventually become a public issue.

The seminal work of Bowlby (1969, 1973, 1979, 1980), on attach-ment and loss, revolutionised the existing ideas and understanding about the making and breaking of affectional bonds. Bowlby developed his comprehensive theory from ideas drawn from ethology, develop-mental psychology and psychoanalytic theory, as well as clinical studies on the separation of children from their mothers.

Weiss (1975), a US sociologist, drew on Bowlby's work in his research on marital separation, and writes of the process of ending a marriage and becoming single again, in interactional terms of the individual with important attachment figures. He describes the erosion of love, the persistence of attachment, the decision to separate, as well as subsequent phases, including the effects of the separation on children, relatives and friends, some of which will be referred to later in this chapter. Weiss, sensitively compelling in his description of the pain of separation, prefers to focus on the dyadic interactions of the couple, or the parent and child, and therefore does not include a family systems perspective, thereby excluding the circularity of the interactions and processes.

In the United States Kitson (1982), also developing the work of Bowlby, Weiss and others, undertook a longitudinal study of 322 men and women at various stages of the divorce process, who were interviewed in an attempt to discover empirical indicators of their attachment during the divorce, which she concluded were less affected by resources and social supports than is subjective distress. She found that substantial numbers of the divorced remain attached to their spouse, although there was some association of this with the spouse's request for a divorce, and also with a recent decision to divorce. Like Bowlby, Kitson distinguished attachment from dependency, describing the psychological distress experienced by many divorced persons as related to difficulties in adjusting to the divorce, rather than their dependency.

A more recent study by Berman (1988) of sixty recently divorced women selected from court records, distinguished attachment and distress as separate constructs. He found that, although many factors had led them to divorce, one group of the divorced women still continued to 'experience a sense of being "drawn"' to their former spouse and felt a 'profound sense of sadness and confusion at the loss of the relationship regardless of what existed objectively'. These included

> recurrent thoughts and images of the ex-spouse; attempts to contact or learn about him . . . feelings of emptiness, as if one were missing a part of onself; loneliness and panic that occur suddenly when the ex-spouse is inaccessible; and expressed positive feelings towards the ex-spouse.

He concluded that following divorce, in those who had continuing positive feelings for their former partner these elicited a higher frequency of thoughts about them and are linked to increased distress. Vaughan too draws on the work of Bowlby, Weiss and others in presenting an interactional model; but, as has already been described, also indicates the length of the process, beginning with the minor disillusions and concluding with the final uncoupling.

In considering the boundary issues between divorce as a private sorrow and a public issue, Kressel (1985), a social psychologist in the United States, considers divorce from the point of view of the professional therapists and lawyers who try to help the couple with the necessary decision-making for the family's future. He focuses particularly on the strategies which assist the couple to negotiate agreements and also on the issues of therapy and mediation in divorce, which will be explored subsequently (in Chapter 9).

A number of family therapists, drawing on their therapeutic experience, have developed projects with particular sections of the divorcing population. For instance, in the United States, a number of psychologists and family therapists – Isaacs, Montalvo and Abelsohn (1986); Kaslow and Schwartz (1987); Johnston and Campbell (1988) – describe their work as therapists with families in divorce. Isaacs et al. and also Johnston and Campbell, although from a different context and perspective, describe their experience in projects with those divorcing families where the couple become entrenched in family warfare, and where the children may also be drawn into taking up battle positions alongside one or other of their parents (see also Chapters 7, 8 and 9).

Kaslow and Schwartz in their comprehensive study of the dynamics of divorce give an excellent and up-to-date review of the US literature on divorce. They conducted their own research as well as drawing on their considerable experience as practitioners in the divorce field and, in common with others, adopt a life-cycle perspective in which Kaslow's seven-stage dialectic model of the divorce process is a development of earlier work. However, in describing the context of divorce, she and Schwartz have developed a model which combines family systems with the stage theory of development. Each of these stages involves the couple confronting and attempting to cope with the intensity of feelings engendered in them as individuals. At the same time they are beginning to carry out certain tasks which eventually will allow them to achieve the necessary separateness and autonomy to build a new life style. The family system which emerges as the result of the structural changes which follow from the divorce have been described as a binuclear family (Ahrons 1980a, 1980b; Ahrons and Bowman 1982).

One of the major tasks of the divorce process is that in which the divorcing partners who are also parents redefine their parental roles, while relinquishing those of husband and wife. The model developed here by the author (a marital and family therapist and conciliator) which is shown in Figure 4.1 and described below is also based on a family systems perspective and takes a developmental model of family dislocation during the divorce process in which the family life cycle of the nuclear family is transformed and extended so as to include additional phases.

The phases are: recognising the marital breakdown, the decision to separate or divorce, preparing and planning the outcome, the actual physical separation, the legal process and the post-divorce family. Each phase of the divorce process over time involves changes at the various interacting levels of the family system, with each of the partners as an *individual* both within themselves and as between each of them, and between others; and also as between them as a *couple subsystem*, by working at certain emotional processes both individually within themselves and together with each other so as to make the necessary changes to enable them to shift from being husband/father and wife/mother, which allows them to let go of their marital partnership and yet retain and even improve their co-parenting relationship with their children. At another level – that of the *children's subsystem*, their children, with assistance from their parents, will need to work on the meaning of the impact and effects arising from the separation of their parents for themselves and their siblings, as well as their relationships with each of their parents

Phase	Emotional process of transition of couple	Second-order changes required in family status to proceed developmentally
1 Recognising marital breakdown	Working together to decide whether to make make recommitment to continue relationship	Mutual acceptance of both own and other's part in marital breakdown
2 The decision to separate or divorce	Recognition by one or both partners of inability to resolve tensions sufficiently to continue as married couple	Mutual acceptance of failure of marriage Agreement to end marriage by separation or divorce Consideration of children's needs
3 Preparing and planning outcome	Struggling towards ability to share responsibilities now and in future	Working cooperatively on problems of telling children, agreeing custody and arrange- ments for access and maintenance Dealing with extended family, colleagues and friends about difficulties
4 Separation	Working towards letting go attachment to spouse as marital partner and reinforcing co-parental relationship Begin mourning loss of intact family Supporting children's attachment to other parent	Restructuring marital and parent–child relationships Announcing decision to extended family and others in community
5 The legal process	Giving up phantasies of family reunion Resolving hurt, anger, bitterness, etc. through process of mourning Retrieval of emotional investment of self in marriage	Reviewing decision- making on legal, psychic, financial, co-parental and community divorce Staying connected with extended families and others

(Continued)

Phase	Emotional process of transition of couple	Second-order changes required in family status to proceed developmentally
6 Post-divorce family	Ability to maintain contact with ex-spouse and develop co-parental relationship	Forming more flexible relationships so as to manage access contact with minimum conflict
	Recognition that children do not divorce parents and therefore encourage children's relationship with the other parent	Realignment, organisation and management of two separate one-parent households
	Recognition that the former spouse may have new attachments which may lead to cohabitation or remarriage	Rebuilding own and acceptance of other parent's social networks

Source: Adapted and extended from Carter and McGoldrick (1979)

Figure 4.1   Dislocations of the family life cycle: family transformations during the divorce process

separately. The incremental changes in each of these subsystems may ultimately result in second-order changes not only in the *nuclear family* but also in the whole extended family system, though the point of no return is often only recognisable in retrospect. These second-order changes vary according to the stages of development which the original nuclear family had reached, and their resolution gradually allows a family transformation to take place, so that the family can proceed developmentally in the life cycle.

This chapter will primarily focus on the emotional changes of couple's relationship as a subsystem of the family and on an outcome for the family at each stage of the process. Although the tasks and changes for the children's subsystem are integral to the outcome for the family unit, as an attempt to clarify what is essentially a complicated and complex process, the changes for them will only be referred to briefly (see also Chapter 8). This model of the family life cycle in transition is further extended to include the life cycle and tasks involved in becoming a stepfamily (see Chapters 5 and 6).

One of the major psychological tasks for the divorcing family unit is to alter the way in which they construe themselves as a family; in other words, to change their beliefs about their family. Such changes might permit the reorganisation of the family's patterns of attachment, although with different structures and ways of achieving need attainment, so as to promote the survival of the individual members and thus allow the possibility to resume the family's functioning, and thence the survival of the family unit itself, albeit in a different form. The six phases of family transformation during the divorce process are distinguished and discussed as if they are each discrete and complete in themselves, although in practice they often overlap. Nor do they necessarily follow a predictable pattern, as there are frequent deviations and pauses during the process, sometimes with many separations and reunions. However, within the processes, which evolve day by day, the boundaries between the stages are more amorphous, and the gradual transformation is also cyclic in nature, becoming clearer only as they are worked and reworked at various levels, by the individual family members, the couple, their children and the whole nuclear and extended family (as Figure 4.1 shows).

Nevertheless, it is often possible to distinguish the stage in the divorce process which the family system and subsystems have reached. Each phase describes the emotional processes of transition for the couple, which shows the potential tasks necessary for them to complete together before they proceed to the next stage. In view of the size and complexity of the task it is hardly surprising that relatively few couples are able to negotiate these stages altogether smoothly.

RECOGNISING MARITAL BREAKDOWN

Many couples experience some difficulties with distance and closeness within their relationship, although most, by a process of often unconscious negotiation, manage through a process of progression and regression to come to some flexible accommodation of each other's need for psychological and physical space. Some only do so by drawing their children into their implicit (rather than explicit) marital struggles, so as to keep their own distance, thus 'triangulating' their children; while others may avoid closeness by breaching the generational boundaries and becoming closer to a child (or children) than to each other. These shifts in the search for intimacy, which were discussed earlier (see Chapter 2, 'The marital system', page 38), are often unconscious and in psychological terms may mean that one partner begins to invest more emotional life apart from the other, perhaps in their work or a hobby. The subsequent disillusion with the relationship may lead to one partner either opting out, or seeking more intimate mutuality within another relationship.

Vaughan (1987) vividly describes the process of uncoupling as one which often begins unwittingly as a serie of small and secret dissatisfactions for one partner, the initiator, and which are not intended to jeopardise the partnership. Nevertheless, the initiator begins to create a social location apart from that shared with their partner. These secrets, often unimportant in themselves, and created merely to relieve minor discomforts or aim at self-improvement, are not shared with the partner who could offer an alternative view. Although she does not stress the systemic and circular nature of these turning points, Vaughan makes the collaborative nature of the partnership breakdown clear, and indicates that it could be either of the two partners who becomes the initiator. This process of unshared secrets may heighten the ordinary disappointments and dissatisfactions which lie within any marriage, but are usually manageable. Such disillusionment may increase and the initiator may start a process of belittling, which may be begun by the husband to the wife as she begins to search for new interests when the children need her less (Gold 1988). Or the wife, who now has more space for her own needs, may needle her husband in an attempt to gain his attention. The dissatisfied initiator may then begin to explore and consider information which could lead to a transition to a different life style.

As the dissatisfied partner *privately* begins to focus more and more on flaws (which of course exist within any couple relationship), a bond may be created with a transitional person who acts as a bridge between their old life and a possible new one. While there is usually an affectional bond with the transitional person, this may not necessarily lead to a permanent and intimate new relationship. In this way the initiator begins to recreate an image of herself or himself which ultimately leads to the creation of a point of departure, thus anticipating a transition. There may be more than one transitional person rather than a potential alternative partner – as for instance, a therapist or lawyer who will help them through the maze of creating a new life, and may indeed actively encourage them to do so. The initiator's partner may consciously become aware that the relationship is deteriorating but collude in a collaborative cover-up, or this may be unconscious, with only feelings of vague and unshared dissatisfaction (see Willi 1984, Vaughan 1987 and Solomon 1989). It is only when this breaks down, initiator's 'cover' is blown and both partners can admit the seriousness of the situation that they can begin to do something about the point of breakdown which their relationship has reached. The following case shows the mutual nature of marital breakdown.

The Ashtead family

Alec, a middle-aged married business man who commuted to London daily, knew that he might face early retirement and this gave him considerable anxiety, which he kept to himself, becoming withdrawn and uncommunicative. He and his wife Marie had been married young and were the devoted parents of two late teenage children, the older of whom had recently left home and would shortly be followed by the younger. Since becoming parents, they had neglected their own relationship and most of their communications were focused on their children, friends or household matters. Marie, who had given up her own career on marriage, was now menopausal, generally resentful, irritable and at times depressed. The couple often argued about minor matters, which left Marie feeling unappreciated and Alec feeling guilty, but also resentful. On the train Alec met several regular travelling companions and began to confide his worries to a younger middle-aged woman who, though she herself had never married, listened with interest and sympathy. On one or two occasions, Alec broke his journey and had a drink with her at her home, conveniently near the station. She, misinterpreting his wish to explore his dissatisfactions as interest in herself as a possible alternative partner, telephoned Marie to tell her of their meetings and her own interpretation of them. Alec was horrified as was Marie, and for the first time, the couple were shocked into the realisation of each other's concerns. Marie suggested that, together with a counsellor, they confront their problems, to which Alec, with relief, agreed.

The Ashteads realised that they each had played a part in what had happened, and by exploring their relationship openly and together, began to make a recommitment to their marriage, which they both wanted to continue. Wynne's (1984) model (Chapter 2, Figure 2.3) might explain this failure in mutuality in terms of the couple's constricted communication patterns, which in turn led to failures in problem-solving, something which in fact they were eventually able to resolve in therapy. Indeed, many couples do decide to make a recommitment to work at their marriage, or reconcile even after apparently embarking on the path to divorce, or even subsequent to it. Research undertaken by Davis (1982) shows that about 13 per cent of couples reconcile after they have become involved in the legal stage of the process.

However, such turning points (as Vaughan 1987, Kaslow and

Schwartz 1987 and others show) so often result in the initiator attempting to persuade the unwilling partner to accept what is for them an unwanted transition – uncoupling. While many regard divorce as a legal event, as this chapter will explore, it is a process which commences with the marital breakdown, a private sorrow and, only following reverberations throughout the family system, culminates in the legal divorce, a public issue, one in which some cherished value of the public is considered to be threatened. As was shown (in Chapters 1 and 5), it is not always the initiator in the process of uncoupling who is also the initiator in the divorce process. In most marriages which end in divorce, it is the initiating partner who experiences the greater stress *before* the actual separation, while the other, the rejected partner, experiences more *after* the confrontation or separation (Kelly 1986).

Hart's earlier research (1976) had also demonstrated that it is the unwilling partner who only reluctantly recognises the end of the marriage, is less likely to comprehend what is happening and consequently is often unable to organise the process. For them the transition is all the more distressing because of its lack of structure. The fact that the two partners are experiencing their greatest stress at different times of the divorce process makes it even more difficult for them to communicate effectively so that they are able to act in unison about the decisions which have to be taken. As is shown (in Figure 4.1) the emotional process of transition for the couple pre-divorce relates to their ability to decide whether or not they wish to make a recommitment to their marriage and together work towards improving it. Often this means improving communication as a prelude to more constructive problem-solving which is made necessary by the vicissitudes of life which happen to most couples. This is a preliminary to the second-order change which would be necessary for a couple, such as the Ashteads, who were able to accept that each had some responsibility for the parlous state which their marriage had reached.

THE DECISION TO SEPARATE OR DIVORCE

The reasons which underlie the initiator's ultimate decision to separate or divorce become crystallised and are conceptualised in different ways and at different levels, according to the context. It has already been indicated that for most, if not all, divorcing couples there is one partner who wants to end the marriage more than the other; but it is also important to reiterate that this partner is not necessarily the one who initiates the legal proceedings. Almost inevitably such imbalance leads to conflict between the couple, whether or not it actually becomes overt. In order for the couple to realise that their marital difficulties are such that they cannot sufficiently be resolved in order to continue as marital partners, it eventually becomes necessary for the more reluctant partner to fall in with the wishes of the initiator.

There are many strategies which the initiator may choose in order to shift the responsibility for ending the marriage and initiating a divorce on to the spouse. One such strategy is provocation through a series of escalating actions aimed at disrupting the marriage in anticipation that the other will seek a divorce out of exasperation. Another is sabotage, in which the initiator provokes the spouse, who is however resilient, and the actions are accelerated until the spouse begins to retaliate by hurtful behaviour, whereupon the initiator indicates that he or she 'wants out' (Haynes 1981). Davis and Murch (1988) in their conciliation in divorce study also found that husbands and wives perceived the reason for the failure of their marriage somewhat differently. Some wives considered failure of communication as a long-standing problem. Others seemed to have regarded their husbands almost as an additional child, for whom they had responsibility, while another theme was that husbands had other sources of satisfaction, whether in their work or leisure activities. However, a significant proportion of wives perceived their husbands' alcoholism and violence as the major difficulty and they gave horrifying accounts of long-standing battering, which had often begun quite early in the marriage. On the other hand, while many of the husbands regarded the marital breakdown as inexplicable and sudden, others put it down to sudden desire for independence on the part of their wives at a time of mid-life crisis (see also Chapter 5, 'The post-divorce family', stage 2, page 101).

Kressel et al. (1980), taking an interactional perspective, identified a typology of divorcing couples as the result of their research with American couples in divorce. The patterns of the couples' divorce decision-making are based on three intercorrelated dimensions: the degree of ambivalence towards the fate of the relationship; the frequency and openness of communication about the possibility of divorce; and the level and overtness of the conflict with which the decision was reached. The categories distinguished were enmeshed, autistic, direct and disengaged patterns of decision-making. If these are explained in terms of Wynne's (1984) different levels of relational systems, then it would be possible to speculate that the enmeshed couples are 'stuck' at the over-involved level of the attachment/care-giving stage; the autistic couples, perhaps at the level of constricted or guarded communication stage; the direct conflict couples, at the disruptive disagreement of the joint problem-solving level. The couples whose conflict seemed almost non-existent and are described as disengaged appear to have already divorced in all but deed.

It is common during this stage of uncertainty, as to whether to continue or to end the marriage, that the intensity of feelings engendered between the partners interferes with their ability to come to terms with what is happening as well as jeopardising their capacities for decision-making, whether as individuals, or as a couple. The rejected partner may feel shocked, despairing, bitter, inadequate and fearful of the future. The initiator may be angry, anguished and equally desperate, while both may experience a sense of disappointment and shame about the failure of their marriage. As with marriage (Bernard 1975), for any divorcing couple there are always two (if not three or more) versions, the husband's divorce and the wife's divorce (and also those of the children), each of them trying to make their own sense of what is happening and also attempting to justify their own explanation of events, and thereby to salvage some self-esteem. Indeed, one US longitudinal study of seventy-two divorced husbands and wives found that the women had been dissatisfied longer and considered separating earlier than had their husbands (Hetherington et al. 1981).

At this stage in the divorce process it is not unusual for one of the partners to seek information or attempt to gain the help of a supportive outsider, perhaps by a visit to the Citizens' Advice Bureau. Either the unwilling or the initiating partner may consult a solicitor, perhaps as an SOS, with a view to induce a reconciliation; as a strategy to force the other partner to accept their point of view; or as a last-ditch attempt to maintain the status quo, or even to force a divorce. As already indicated (in Chapter 1), it is clear that it is wives who most often petition for divorce, but it is not known how many of these have ultimately done so in order to safeguard their own position and that of their children, or succumbed to the pressures and even threats of their husbands; nor how many husbands have 'allowed' their wives to become the petitioner.

If the couple find it so intolerable to be together that one of the partners leaves, only to return later, either of their own volition or at the behest of the other, as quite often happens, this is likely to have some effect on their children and also the extended family. Unless one partner's occupation frequently takes them away from home it is difficult to manage to keep the distress and anger discrete and between the couple. For many couples for whom the situation becomes intolerable, who eventually agree to live apart for a time, in order to reflect on the possibility of seeking divorce later, or to separate as a prelude to a divorce, then such a decision has implications for the whole family as individuals, for the parent–child relationships and for the family as a unit. Such an agreement entails at least some mutual acceptance that the marriage is in severe difficulties or has failed, and also implies some recognition that certainly the relationships within the family and perhaps ultimately also the future organisation of the family system may be in jeopardy. Whether or not the couple are able at this stage to consider their children's needs is often in doubt, as they are inevitably preoccupied with their partnership rather than their parental relationship and responsibilities. For instance, the Californian study of Wallerstein and Kelly (1980) found that the parenting capacities of both partners become both unreliable and diminished for about two years during the early stages of the divorce process, and are especially limited around the actual physical separation, when so many major changes are occurring.

There is now a significant body of research both in the United Kingdom (see, for instance, especially that of Mitchell 1983, 1985, Richards 1982, Walczak and Burns 1984 and others), as well as in the United States (see, for instance, Isaacs, Montalvo and Abelsohn 1986, Johnston and Campbell 1988) which indicates that all too frequently parents are virtually unable to consider the implications of their separation for their children (see Chapters 5, 6, 7, 8, and 11). In many families, it is only immediately prior to the separation, or even following it, that many parents are able to comprehend that their children need to be informed about what is happening; and this despite the impending radical changes for their children's future (see 'Separation, Telling the children' (page 83) and 'Sharing the parenting after separation and divorce' (page 86)). For their children this failure may result in serious implications (see especially Chapter 8). The children, according to their age, stage of development and understanding of the situation, will be trying to make their own sense of what is happening both to them and to the whole nuclear family, and this will in turn have repercussions on their parents, as the following example shows.

The Bexley family

Tom, a young business man who was highly successful financially, had rebelled against his own family's conventional values by becoming involved in an untraditional and socially down market-business. In the early thirties, he had married a young woman in her early twenties, Kate, who had also rebelled against her own family.

Each of them had felt undervalued and misunderstood in their families of origin: Tom, who had hated public school and had not done well, and Kate, who had had to act as surrogate mother to siblings because of her own mother's long illness and hospitalisation. Kate had 'run away' to Europe during her adolescence, becoming part of a rock group. For a time she lived in Italy, where she had become pregnant and given birth to a child who had subsequently been adopted. Kate's own perceptions of this experience were that she was not only given little care and support, but considers that she was also condemned by the nuns for her immorality.

Soon after her return she had met Tom at a pop festival, and they had married. Kate, still grieving for her lost child, became pregnant very quickly, which initially angered Tom, who, though he wanted children, had also wanted some time for the couple to be on their own. Nevertheless Harry, who proved to be a highly intelligent and attractive little boy, was much loved by both of them.

Two years later they had another child, who died soon after birth. Each of them was very distressed but unable to grieve either together or separately. For a while Tom found solace in joining and becoming actively involved in a spiritual community, which eventually disbanded, and persuaded Kate to join him in some of the activities. Kate went along with these, but found little consolation in them and was in any event exceedingly busy with Harry; she also wanted to resume her career plans.

Each of them had sexual relationships with other people, although their partners had little emotional importance to them. While they remained good friends and devoted parents to Harry, they quarrelled a great deal, mainly about Tom's dictatorial behaviour towards Kate and her inconsistency towards him, sometimes wanting to be very close and at other times insisting that she needed space for herself and going off and leaving him with Harry.

The Bexleys had a house abroad, and during the summer in

which Harry was rising 4, Kate took him to live there in order to 'sort herself out'. There were frequent telephone calls between Tom and Kate and he visited often. During these visits they would be very close for a few days and then the rows would start again and he would return to England. That autumn Kate decided that she would return to England but that she and Tom would not live together. He reluctantly agreed with this but insisted on having Harry while she found a flat. Harry was looked after by a daily nanny, of whom he became very fond. When Kate found a flat, he spent the weekdays with his mother, though his father often fetched him from school and he spent most weekends with him. Kate and Tom continued to see each other, to have a sexual relationship and Kate often stayed at the father's home at weekends. They explained carefully to Harry that they were living separately and telephoned and wrote to him when away from him. At first, Harry seemed to cope with this quite well, though under the circumstances, it is doubtful whether he realised that his parents were trying to live apart. However, he did seem to need the reassurance that if he needed either his mother or his father urgently, they would come.

This arrangement, however, broke down when it became apparent not only that Kate was having an affair with someone else who was important to her, and that Harry, by now aged 6, was finding it difficult to settle in school. Used to undivided adult attention of one or other parent, he expected this from his teacher. Used also to being part of a rather adult world, he found it difficult to make friends with other children, nor could he amuse himself.

His parents could not make up their minds whether to try to live together again or have a period of separation, and they sought help from a therapist who agreed to see them for a limited period to try to decide what to do. At first they actively enjoyed the sessions, laughingly teasing each other about the behaviour which neither of them liked about the other and referring to the good times past. They left each session planning to meet over meals or outings with Harry. Gradually, the therapist began to confront them with their underlying pain and uncertainty about their future together. Kate revealed that she had been seeing a bereavement counsellor to help her grieve for the child who had died, and though this was revealed only later, Tom started therapy for himself. On two or three weekends, Kate went abroad, and it later emerged that she was still seeing her boyfriend, though she had avoided revealing this. Tom also had a girlfriend whom he denied had any importance, yet who appeared to be waiting in the wings for him to decide whether or not to continue his marriage. Harry became more insistent on the attention of both his parents at the same time, and they became worried about his school situation.

The therapy sessions became more and more painful as Tom and Kate began to explore the past hurts and disappointments between them and their doubts as to whether these could sufficiently be overcome. They wondered if they should not see each other for a time in order to see whether they could manage apart, and agreed not to meet for a while, except in the sessions. This agreement was broken the next day by Kate going to Tom's work to say she still loved him. Tom responded, but this was followed by his discovery of where she had been at the weekends and her countering this by accusing him of having his girlfriend at the house when he had Harry there. Harry himself became more and more insistent that he wanted his Mummy and his Daddy, and played up his nanny incessantly.

Tom and Kate found Harry's anxious demands very difficult to resist, especially as they were both so uncertain themselves of what each wanted from the other. On one occasion, when Kate had been away for nearly a week, allegedly attending a friend's wedding abroad, she (arriving at the session on time, while Tom, held up in the traffic, was late) confessed to the therapist that she could not bear to be apart from Harry as she felt so guilty about what she had done. In this session – which proved to be the final one (for the present) – not only were they able to reveal the full extent of their other relationships, but also their fear of losing Harry and determination to find ways of sharing his parenting with the other partner.

The Bexleys showed how difficult it was for each of them, neither of whom had received sufficient attachment care-giving in their earliest years; each was in need of demanding this exclusive care from the other, obscuring this by a variety of diversionary tactics and attempting to manage their own emptiness by giving Harry excessive and exclusive attention.

PREPARING AND PLANNING THE OUTCOME

The ability of couples who are intending to separate both to communicate about possible plans for the future and to attempt to solve the possible problems together, is, as with the previous phases, dependent on the stage of relational development they have reached, as well as the amount of conflict which has been generated between them. Not only do they share the responsibilities of their children and their home, but it also becomes necessary to work out the financial arrangements, at least for the immediate future.

Some couples manage this phase of the planning reasonably well, though others, particularly where one partner is reluctantly going along with the separation, may drag their feet, or suddenly introduce new difficulties, predominantly as a diversion or to delay the actual separation because they cannot face what is about to happen, or both. It is often at this phase, prior to the departure of one spouse, when one or both partners become aware of the finality of what is happening and they actually begin to confront each other with this state of affairs, that violence erupts. This may precipitate a hurried and abrupt departure of one partner, usually the husband, who is most frequently the perpetrator of the violence. When this happens, the couple often avoid meeting – the woman because she is afraid that the violence will erupt again, and the man because he may be ashamed and guilty about the violence as well as about his departure.

Yet it is precisely at this phase that parents need to be able to work cooperatively on what to tell the children. It is important for both the divorcing parents to recognise and to inform their children what is happening and also to prepare for the responses of their children. These are issues to be faced by them both, a difficult and upsetting task, as this will confront them with the distress of their children about what is to happen to the family and to the children in particular. There is the question of whether the parents are able to tell the children together; and if not, which of them will tell which child? What they actually will say? And how will the other parent respond if the children come to him or her with their questions and distress? While the age and level of understanding of the children are relevant, there are arguments for being them told all together, so that they can support one another, thus allowing the sibling relationships to strengthen in the times immediately ahead. It is particularly difficult for only children, who often remain unsupported and isolated.

Further questions which need to be addressed are the arrangements regarding custody and access for the children, as well those for their maintenance. For the father this may well be the first full realisation of what is more than likely to happen, as many men not only lose their wife and their home, but also their day-to-day relationship with their children, and perhaps face a final separation from them. For the mother, this is the phase when she ultimately realises that it is likely to be she who will be left alone and with the major responsibility for the children. The financial position will be of deep concern to them both, the woman because of the loss of much of her husband's financial support and the man because of his fears for where he will be able to afford to live and for the future maintenance that he will be expected to pay for his children, if not also for their mother.

It is often when the couple begin confront these kinds of issues that hitherto simmering conflicts ultimately emerge, and may start to become bitter and eventually entrenched. The whole nuclear family by this stage is graphically confronted with the impending changes which are about to take place and which will either split the family into separate and semi-closed systems or allow a new and more open, binuclear family to develop (Ahrons 1980) which, although involving the same members, becomes a different system (see Chapters 5, 6, 7, 8, 11 and 12) and one which ultimately includes new members.

Finally, at this stage there is the need to deal with the extended family, who begin to make their own sense of what is happening and wittingly or unwittingly may take sides with one of the parents. Grandparents are particularly important at this stage, for it is often they who remain the only people to whom the children can turn in their distress. Friends, neighbours and particularly the children's schools also need to be informed, as these are the additional or surrogate care-givers who can support the children at times when their parents are not able to do so. The role of the friendship network and extended family will be discussed in more detail in Chapter 11.

The following example shows both the circularity and the complexities of preparing and planning the family system for separation.

The Chigwell family

Charles and Patricia Chigwell, a professional couple in their early forties, had three children: Debbie (6), Annabel (4) and Colin (2). Tricia worked three mornings each week, and the two younger children were looked after by her parents who lived nearby and with whom all the family were close. Charles, the only child of a widowed mother, became very preoccupied with building up his professional practice and Tricia was very lonely. Their intimate life, which had never been very satisfying, dwindled to almost nothing, and, when Tricia complained, Charles either criticised her performance or said he was too tired. During the course of her own work, Tricia met a married man with whom she had a brief affair.

As a 'liberated' couple they had previously talked of having an open marriage, so Tricia told Charles, who to her surprise, became very angry. He utterly refused to talk about her affair, and after several months told Tricia that he had remet an old girlfriend, started an affair with her and wanted a divorce so that he could marry her. Tricia in her turn was very angry and hurt, and particularly that Charles was preparing to desert three young children, as she saw it. She felt very guilty about her affair and sadly withdrew into looking after her children. Charles, who was confused and distressed himself, suggested that they seek help from a child psychiatrist so that they could assess the effect of their impending separation on the children. Tricia at first saw this as a reflection on her ability as a mother, but, as she became more and more depressed, eventually agreed. The psychiatrist gave them active help in what to tell the children and how to manage the actual separation. They were able to agree that Charles would see the children one evening a week at the family home, and on Saturdays, and have them every other weekend to stay when he found somewhere to live.

Tricia also explained the matrimonial situation to her own parents, who, while at first they were upset with their daughter for jeopardising her marriage, withdrew for a time. Tricia, guilty and very hurt with her parents, as well as with Charles, went to a therapist, who supported her through the next stages of the divorce process. However, Charles, who had been particularly close to his father-in-law, also had a talk with him explaining that things had been wrong for a long while; and the grandparents, fearful of losing touch with their daughter and grandchildren struggled to manage their own concern and began to give Tricia their much-needed support.

It is difficult to assess at what level of relatedness Tricia's and Charles's relationship stopped progressing, though it seemed that until they were faced with a possible separation they had not been able to engage in joint problem-solving. Although providing for his family, Charles had more or less left the children to Tricia other than as a playful and loving father, and she had turned to her parents, rather than to him for support. In Kressel's typology, Charles and Tricia were a direct conflict couple who, with the help of the child psychiatrist, became able during the process to reach agreements related to their children.

SEPARATION

This is the phase which includes the relocation of one of the parents – for some, either to live alone or with another partner, or even return to their family of origin, while the other partner, together with the children, may remain in the matrimonial home. It is at this time that there is an overt implication that some action is to be taken, and it is one of the most difficult stages of the divorce process. While in many families this physical separation is carefully planned and painfully carried out, as has already been discussed, in others it is sudden and abrupt, apparently done as a last straw and on the spur of the moment. In some families, both parents doggedly remain in the matrimonial home, each pressuring and manipulating the other to move out. This struggle, often with barely veiled threats and sometimes spilling over into violence, is waged either directly or through champions, perhaps extended family members or their solicitors (see the next section). Some couples attempt to live separately in the same house, sometimes for years, while in other families one partner moves out, only to return and leave several times more before the physical separation is finally achieved.

As men are more likely to remarry fairly soon after divorce, and as most custodial parents are mothers, the single-parent household typically consists of a custodial mother and children. For many younger women the single-parent household phase of the process is a relatively temporary, though exceedingly stressful phase, as they are more likely to remarry or find a new partner. However, for perhaps the majority of older mothers, single parenthood becomes a way of life, and the loneliness, privation and parental overload they experience, with little support either from the former husband or the state, is considerable.

Research shows (see Chapter 8) that the crucial time in the parent–child relationship are those first weeks after one parent leaves the matrimonial home. It is at this time that it is important to reinforce the attachment between parent and child, and also to lay the foundations of a different relationship, one which in the future will be separate and distinct from the relationships which have previously been based within the family unit and home. There is increasing evidence that noncustodial fathers find it particularly difficult to both maintain and restructure their relationships with their children (Kelly 1988).

Divorce as bereavement

The divorce process is inevitably a bereavement, although it differs from bereavement as the result of the death of one partner, which can usually be ascribed to fate rather than fault, while divorce usually means failure and is perceived as rejection of one partner by the other. There are few men, women or children from families of divorce who believe in a no-fault divorce and there is always some blame and/or guilt. A divorce almost always a leaves a legacy of considerable guilt, anger and shame, particularly for those who remain behind. After all, it is possible to idealise the deceased without any possibility of an unexpected meeting. Each spouse when confronted with the loss of their partner, tries to find a new meaning through the reworking of the history of their relationship at all levels, while attempting to come to terms with what has happened. The bereaved husband or wife, through reliving the memories of happy times, can often find comfort to assuage their present loss. But many of those bereaved through divorce are trying also to cope with the actual rejection, feelings of abandonment and shame which often result in a considerable loss of self-esteem. Only those bereaved by divorce have to manage an unexpected challenge to their perception of the situation through some kind of confrontation with each other, whether this be an unwished-for meeting with their former spouse, an interview with a conciliator or their lawyer, or even an appearance in court. Living through divorce is therefore both a slow and turbulent process for the couple, their children and indeed the whole family, during which they and their previous lives are painfully turned upside down and inside out.

Although it seems that relatively few couples seek therapeutic assistance either for themselves or their children, and many are able to cope with this rite of passage without formalised outside assistance, there is nevertheless a considerable fall-out of casualties, both children and adults, as the result of incompletely resolved processes of divorce, which are not always recognised as divorce-related.

It is useful for those in the interventionist professions (see Chapters 9 and 10) working with family members from divorcing or divorced families to assess which stage each of the parties, both individually and jointly as well as parentally with their children, seem to have reached. When a family member dies, while the psychological processes of grief and mourning which face the family may be unknown and therefore fearful, there are nevertheless generally recognised practical tasks to be carried out, as for example, the rituals of the burial and grieving, and the necessary reorganistion of family life, which can assist the process of mourning. A death in the family is still generally considered as sad but respectable, whereas a divorce, though now less stigmatising, is still often regarded as a shameful event in which one partner may be perceived as seeking a new life at the expense of the other.

When a couple divorce, the process is a transition for which there are as yet no clearly recognisable maps; and so for the parties involved there are few landmarks other than the legal process, for which the family are often ill prepared. Indeed, many divorcing partners try to deny the significance of what is happening to them and to their family, and this is a significant factor which often leaves each of them and their children isolated as well as bewildered and distressed.

The children of the divorcing partners also need to make their own sense of what is happening to them as the result of their parents' divorce and ultimately to come to terms with what they are experiencing. The ways in which they can best be helped will largely depend on the abilities of their parents not only to continue to support them emotionally, but also to maintain their parent–child bond and the child–parent attachment to each parent. Nevertheless, the effects of divorce on children are particularly related to their age and stage of individual development at the time of the marital breakdown (see Chapter 8).

Telling the children

At the early stages of marital breakdown, the couple's children may at some level be aware that their parents' marriage is in difficulties; they may have heard their parents quarrelling, noticed their father's frequent absences, or found their mother in tears. The level of recognition and awareness is both related to their age and stage of development, their own personality structure, and also the abilities of their parents to manage the generation boundaries sufficiently to keep their difficulties to themselves. However, Kelly (1986) discovered that for some children, particularly those whose parents had managed to achieve a good enough co-parenting relationship, the knowledge that their parents are thinking of seeking a divorce comes as a bolt from the blue, and this adds considerably to the distress which most children experience during their parents' separation and divorce. From their position in the family, everything seems to be going well enough, and they are often unable to comprehend why it is that their parents cannot continue to remain in their family as it is, nor, of course, do most children want their parents to separate anyway.

According to Wallerstein and Blakeslee (1989) it is important that children should be told where the parent leaving (usually the father) is going to live, and for young children it is helpful to be taken there and shown the accommodation so that they have a mental picture of their parent and how their mother or father will be looked after. If parents tell children that things will be difficult for a time, but they will all try to help one another, this is not only truthful but also helps to maintain the children's trust in both parents. It is not usually immediately necessary for children to be told about third parties or other details, but they should be informed in a general way so that they understand that their parents are sad about what is happening and that a divorce is intended to make things better ultimately.

It is hardly surprising that many parents avoid such painful issues, either directly or by trying to convince themselves by such rationalisations as the children must know already, or are too young to understand. While most children (other than the very young) need to be consulted about the arrangements for their future, it is generally considered that they should never be asked which parent they would like to live with as this will involve them in feeling that they have chosen one parent at the expense of the other. However, adolescents may well have strong views about where they will live and may need to be consulted more directly, though in the clear understanding that it is their parents who will ultimate decide. There are likely to be long-standing problems for children whose parents have involved them in taking sides in their conflicts, as children are usually loyal to both parents and, being enjoined to take sides with one or other parent, whether or not this is explicit, may well be to their ultimate detriment.

Sharing the parenting after separation and divorce

As well as the detachment of uncoupling and the grief which accompanies the divorce-as-bereavement process for the husband and wife as a married couple, there is the major issue as to how they are going to continue as parents to their children. Changing their customary patterns of interaction is yet another aspect of the multiple changes which confront the couple. Although Wallerstein and Kelly (1980) found that the quality of parenting often deteriorates during the divorce process for a priod of approximately two years, they did not distinguish specific types of co-parenting. They did, however, describe the specific types of parent–child relationships following separation and divorce, and also the response of the individual parents; as for example, the depressed parent and the embittered chaotic. Lund's (1984) small UK research study on thirty families two years after separation showed that the parents' relationships fell into three groups: harmonious co-parent families, conflicted co-parent families and families where the father is absent. The results of this and other research studies (which will be discussed more fully in Chapter 8) indicate that in families where the parents can continue to share the parenting of their children then the benefits to the children are considerable.

Ahrons (1980), who has carried out many of the US studies into post-divorce relationships, stressed that the relationship of the parents is a crucial factor in the redefinition of relationships in the post-divorce family. She distinguished three main groupings according to the frequency of parental interactions: low, medium and high. Those who have a mutually supportive and cooperative co-parenting relationship, as well as interacting frequently, often establish a binuclear family structure with two interrelated households, maternal and paternal. Her more recent work (with Wallisch 1987) distinguished parental and nonparental interaction between divorced parents, and found that, whereas one year post-divorce about 40 per cent of the eighty couples in their research sample indicated that even if they had no children they would want to continue a relationship, by three years post-divorce this had dropped to 32 per cent. They conclude that about half of divorced parents have post-divorce relationships which are so angry and conflict-ridden that they are not conducive to the continued involvement of the noncustodial parent.

The quality of post-divorce relationships between the parents is one of the most crucial factors which influences their children's future development. A study carried out by Rosenthal and Keshet (1981) with fathers during the first two years post-divorce (see Chapter 5, page 100) found three patterns of relationships: cooperative but distant; the unsorted husband father, who presented a picture of confusion as regards his ex-wife; and those for whom co-parenting had failed, who removed themselves sooner or later from contact with their ex-wives and children.

In her most recent work, Ahrons (with Rodgers 1988) has developed a four-fold typology of former spouse relationships which is based on the quality of their relationship, as follows:

1 Perfect pals: those whose non-parental interaction was highest between the formerly married who had not remarried and who enjoyed spending time together, including shared activities with their children.
2 Cooperative colleagues, who are able to get along well, but interact mostly only about their children.
3 Angry associates: those who are quick to get into conflict and only communicate about their children.
4 Fiery foes: those who went out of their way to avoid each other and who often forced their children to take sides.

This last grouping has been the subject of two important US clinical research studies, one of which was the Families of Divorce project of Isaacs, Montalvo and Abelsohn (1986) at the Philadelphia Child Guidance Clinic, which followed the structural shifts and emotional fluctuations in 103 separating families during the first three years of separation. This study of chronically warring parental couples distinguished two specific groups: first, the sporadic and scared fighters who engage in a cycle of avoidance and noncommunication, during which they fight through the children; a process during which the couple become heated up over unresolved issues followed by periodical collisions, yet are held together by a tense and angrily based status quo. The second group consists of the frequent and direct fighters, who seem to thrive on a process of chronic confrontation which is often accompanied by physical violence.

Since 1981 Californian law has required divorcing parents who are in dispute regarding the custody and care of their children to attempt to mediate their differences, which is based on the premise that divorcing parents should be empowered to make their own decisions. As in the United Kingdom this court-based mediation (see Chapter 10) is usually brief, focused and problem-centred, and those who are 'unable to reach agreement or are disputing the mediated settlement or court order' may be referred to the Child and Family Divorce Counselling Service at the San Francisco Children's Hospital, which takes only referrals from the courts.

Johnston and Campbell (1988) carried out a research study interviewing eighty families whom they followed up two years later. The 100 children were aged from 6 months to 12 years, fifty boys and fifty girls. Significantly, two-thirds of these children were only children, and this seemed to indicate that they were a precious resource. They distinguished the divorce transition impasse which is multilayered and at three different levels: external, interactional and intrapsychic.

At the external level the conflict can be exacerbated by significant others such as extended kin and new partners, including interventionist professionals (that is, lawyers, mental health professionals, therapists who typically only saw one of the partners and encouraged uncompromising stands). At the interactional level 'disputes were broadly of two different kinds: those that were the legacy of a destructive marital relationship and those that were the product of traumatic and ambivalent separations'. At the intrapsychic level, unconscious conflicts both motivated the disputes and impeded the parent's capacity for making decisions. These were usually related to the feelings of loss, anger, helplessness, humiliation and guilt which divorce typically provokes.

Wallerstein (with Blakeslee, 1989) as the result of her latest (and controversial) research (see Chapter 8, 'Long-term outcome and conclusions', page 169) on the 'visiting relationship' also distinguishes such conflict-ridden families but points out that the fight over the children may have little to do with the child, but much for the wish for revenge. She describes the 'Medea syndrome', where, because one or both parents have lost control over their anger, one partner wishes to murder the relationship with the child of the other. They become preoccupied with the rage and experience of betrayal which serves to keep away a profound sense of depression. They have a real need for and a psychic dependence on the child. The function of the child is to hold the parent together psychologically, and the child may well therefore develop the phantasy that it is he or she who is keeping the parent alive. There are also parents who develop an obsession with a particular child who is usually young, sensitive and/or attractive. Such parents may function extremely well, but the child seems to be chosen as a mirror of their self-esteem, and the interparental battles for such a child are often accompanied by a Greek chorus of extended families, psychotherapists, lawyers and the threat of litigation.

In summary, therefore, it could be argued that there is a continuum of five roughly distinguishable types of parental relationships among divorcing couples, which range from various forms of co-parenting, to hostile, negative and exclusive parenting by the custodial parent. First, there are those who are able to manage the collaborative parenting, in which the couple try to change their relationship to one of tentative friendship through which they can more or less manage to support each other and help to maintain the children's attachment to the other parent. The second relationship is one of collateral parenting, where their own interactions are minimal and generally cautious, yet they support each other to the children and maintain some degree of attachment through regular contact and access visiting. The third type, rigidly uncooperative parenting, is similar to those described by Ahrons and Rodgers as angry associates and by Isaacs et al. as sporadic and scared fighters, their interactions being often characterised by a kind of implacability in which the children are also caught between their loyalty to both parents (triangled), unable to change and develop their own relationship with their out-of-home parent. The fourth type, aggressive parenting, is similar to Ahrons and Rodgers' fiery foes, the frequent and direct fighters of Isaacs et al. in which the couple seem to survive only by constant, noisy and sometimes violent disagreement, in which the children often become involved. This group perhaps also includes those described by Johnston and Campbell as proponents in a divorce transition impasse; after all, fighting is one way of maintaining contact. The fifth type, paranoid parenting, of which a small sub-group form the Medea syndrome, occurs most often in so-called single-parent families in which the custodial parent maintains a steadily hostile and embittered relationship towards the other parent, sometimes accompanied by a steady barrage of threatened or actual litigation. This absent parent, while missing in actuality, nevertheless is often ever-present in phantasies of the remaining parent and the children, who may themselves have a very different phantasy from their custodial parent – indeed, may idealise this absent parent. There also seems to be a process in which the parental attempts to co-parent their children follow a process which runs parallel to the psychological processes of the divorcing couple. The co-parenting relationship of the couple may therefore gradually change from one of extreme hostility to a collateral or collaborative one during a period of about three years following the decision to separate.

The Epsom family

Tony and Marilyn Epsom had been married for five years and had two children, Joe (5) and Ben (3). Marilyn was pregnant with 'little Tony' when his father suddenly and apparently inexplicably gave up his job and walked out to live with Sharon, who was pregnant with another man's child. Marilyn was angrily desolate, and sought out a counsellor who had previously helped her family through her brother's drug addiction. Tony, who had been brought up in care himself, was determined to keep contact with his children, with which Sharon reluctantly concurred. Their relationship was uncertain, and often after a row with Sharon, Tony would return to

Marilyn. Eventually, after a fight between Marilyn and Sharon over the children, Marilyn refused to allow Tony to see them. Tony was desolate and Marilyn, who really believed that children should be in touch with their father, and who was having some difficulties with Joe (by now 7), who idealised his father and was very aggressive at school, sought further help, to which Tony agreed. After a few meetings between Tony and Marilyn with a conciliator access was restarted, and within a few months the boys were having staying access with their father and Sharon, and the two women were struggling to find ways to manage their own relationship. Tony's and Marilyn's relationship had changed from one of rigidly uncooperative parenting, to one which they referred to as friendship, but could be described as collaborative.

The visiting parental relationship

The relationship between noncustodial parent and child is a difficult one to maintain, partly because it is so ambiguous, partly because there are no guidelines which help parents to develop what is in effect a new relationship with their children. Not only are there no guidelines, but there are also no role models for such relationships. As the majority of children actually live with their mothers, even in families where there is joint custody, it is usually the father–child relationship which needs the greater redefinition.

Recent research seems to indicate that it is especially difficult for fathers to redefine their relationships with their children post-divorce, and these often take on an unreal quality, particularly with young children (Hetherington, Cox and Cox (1976), Wallerstein and Kelly (1982) Kelly (1988) and others) and little help is available to them. There is also little information available about how to divide their time with their child or children – as, for instance, when they should see all the children together and when it would be best for them to have individualised contacts with each child. Initially at least, each contact involves further painful goodbyes at the end of each visit, which reopen distress at the separation of the family. There are few places to go to where the visiting parent can interact in what is a customary way with their children. Wallerstein (with Blakeslee 1989) describes the visiting relationship as 'ghost ridden', and (as they indicate) some men opt out because of the painful nature of rebuilding a relationship with their children. Because the visiting parent is now on the outside of what was after all their family unit, each visit is a distressing reminder of their role as an outsider.

Yet recent research by Kressel (1988) seems to indicate that many noncustodial fathers are their own worst enemies! In a recent study of mediation he and his colleagues unexpectedly identified and distinguished the interpersonally dysfunctional parent (of whom seven out of eight were fathers) and whom they described as preoccupied with their own needs at the expense of those of their children, disparaging or irresponsible towards their former partner, and particularly regarding child care and regarding access visits, engaging in overt or covert incitement of the children to be disrespectful to the custodial parent and with 'a studied incapacity to acknowledge their own role in the continued conflict'. Many such visiting relationships seem to 'freeze' at the developmental phase which parent and child had reached when the parent left, and this results in behaviour which is perhaps too protective or restrictive, and which is also inappropriate to the present age of the child. For instance, the father of a 9-year-old daughter was still bathing and dressing her as he had done when his daughter was 3 and he was living with the family.

Initially it is almost always hard for separated (and later divorced) parents to work out and accept guidelines for a workable and acceptable visiting relationship. Family rituals such as weddings, even funerals, are often particularly difficult for separated and divorced families, and there are few guidelines available other than a sensible pragmatism, which is often difficult to achieve. Christmas, that idealised family festival (though often far from the everyday reality), is nevertheless an opportunity for the reinforcement of family solidarity, but for separated families can be a painful reminder of the losses which the separation has brought about. Many of the practical pitfalls which commonly arise in post-divorce families, such as attendance as school functions, can often be overcome with foresight and prior negotiation (Goldstein 1987).

5 Families through the divorce process
When divorce becomes a public issue

It is so far from being natural for a man and woman to live in a state of marriage that we find all the motives which they have for remaining in that connection, and prevent separation are hardly sufficient to keep them together.

Samuel Johnson (1709–1784), 1772

Marriages would in general be as happy, and often more so, if they were all made by the Lord Chancellor.

Samuel Johnson, 1776

THE LEGAL PROCESS

When looked at in systemic terms, the legal system, like any other, operates with shared constructs based on beliefs which are enshrined within the law, and this operates according to premises traditionally laid down within the legal framework. In family law there are practice directions, issued from the President of the Family Division of the High Court, which lay down requirements or guidelines for the implementation of any particular law. The legal context of divorce and remarriage has already been discussed in outline (in Chapter 1, 'The legal process of divorce', page 7), and this section will describe the impact of the legal processes on the family and its subsystems, as, for example, the divorcing couple or their children.

As has been suggested (Robinson 1986, Davis 1987, Parkinson 1988), it is only when the legal framework begins to impinge on what are essentially the private sorrows of a particular family that their troubles become a public issue, as, for instance, when one partner petitions for a divorce. Of course, there are other legal processes related to the matrimonial breakdown, such as judicial separation (where the partners have a legal agreement to live separately) or injunctions (which require one of the partners, usually the husband, perhaps to refrain from certain behaviour, or to move out of the matrimonial home), each of which has the same impact of making what is happening to the family a matter for public scrutiny and comment. When the family's troubles also result in a child protection issue, as they do when there is a matrimonial supervision order on a child, then the impact on the family of the involvement of the child protection agencies becomes an important factor as will be discussed later (in Chapter 9), as will the probable effects of the 1989 Children Act (in Chapter 12).

When a couple become involved in the legal process and especially when they instruct solicitors to petition for a divorce, they effectively lose control of a process which not only affects the future lives of each of them and their future partners, but also those of their children and indeed their whole nuclear and extended family. Although the laws are laid down by Acts of parliament, their implementation is essentially in the hands of the legal system, which has strong traditions largely based on the professional values of those who work within it, particularly the judiciary and the legal profession. This will be discussed in more detail later (in Chapter 10, Figure 10.1), but the impact of the legal system on that of the family can exacerbate what is as painful a situation for them as it is difficult for them to understand. Davis (1987), who conducted large-scale surveys of consumer opinion as part of his research into the Special Procedure in Divorce and Conciliation in Divorce, concluded that the parties involved in the legal process of divorce have mixed feelings about it. On the one hand, many, if not most, couples were relieved to have their own advocate, who would translate their situation into legal constructs and language, become their champion in speaking for them in court, as well as guide them through the labyrinthine legal processes. On the other hand they also felt helpless and often shamed by the indignities of the process and by their inability to engage directly with the court.

The choice of facts on which to base the divorce petition alleging matrimonial breakdown is also not without effect on both the parties involved, and as was earlier indicated (in Chapter 1), a significant proportion of divorce petitioners are wives, over 70 per cent. Such a petition involves the process of writing and signing a detailed affidavit in which the allegations are described. It is not unusual, particularly in families where there are economic and other stresses, that marital breakdown leads to violent behaviour between the partners. While there are different explanations as to the cause of such behaviour, there can be little doubt that the husband is usually the dominant partner, both economically and physically, and that many lawyers suggest to the wife that grounds do exist for a divorce petition based on the behaviour of her husband. However, there are also indications that such petitions and the adversarial nature of the present matrimonial laws sometimes also inflame and further polarise what is already a volatile situation.

As legal proceedings are differentiated into the diverse aspects of the case, what are known as 'ancillary matters' are dealt with separately from the actual petition, as previously described (in Chapter 1). The economic issues such as maintenance and the disposition of the matrimonial home are, as far as possible distinguished from matters regarding the children, though in the minds of many, if not most, of the divorcing partners, these are inextricably intertwined. Descriptions of the experience of being in court seem often equivalent to that of depersonalisation. As Eekelaar (1986) writes, 'there is something odd in the notion of an individual applying to a court for a finding that he has committed adultery and that his partner finds it intolerable to live with him, or that he has behaved in such a way that his partner cannot reasonably be expected to live with him'. Perhaps especially in the circumstances when the respondent of the petition defends the grounds on which it is based, both partners may hear themselves and each other described by their advocates in terms which seem to be a dramatisation of the experience of their marriage as they knew it.

It is now generally acknowledged, if not generally agreed, that under certain circumstances the state has the responsibility to safeguard the welfare of children (and indeed other vulnerable groups such as the elderly and mentally ill) though there is little agreement as to how this should be carried out. Within the legal framework and the practice directions, each judge and court have their own procedures for the way hearings are conducted. During the course of the brief Section 41 Conciliation or Mediation Appointments – sometimes as little as five minutes – the judge is required to scrutinise and, if she or he considers them appropriate, also to sanction the arrangements proposed by the parents as regards their children. In cases where the divorcing couple are in conflict over their children, they may be referred to the court welfare officer to see if they can come to an agreement prior to the mediation appointment. Couples who are in conflict over the arrangements for their children may be 'invited' to see the Divorce Court welfare officer beforehand to see if they can come to some agreement (though see Chapter 10, 'The client's search for a settlement', page 225). If this proves impossible, then they may be asked to withdraw with (usually) a different Divorce Court welfare officer during the mediation appointment, which may be adjourned to see if they can agree. At some Divorce Registries (for example, the Principal Divorce Registry) when parents are in conflict about the arrangements for their children they are required to bring those aged 9 and over to the court, and the judge or registrar and/or Divorce Court welfare officer may interview them in chambers. Despite the good intentions and often (though not always) sensitive interviewing by the judge in chambers, children often find this experience both daunting and confusing, and for many, whose disputing parents cannot help them beforehand or afterwards, these visits are experienced as quite terrifying. The Booth Committee Report (1985) recommended that children should not attend the initial hearing (which may also be concerned with the granting of the decree and financial matters), partly because they wished to emphasise the responsibility of the parents to make arrangements for their children, but also because they were generally concerned about requiring children to attend in order to assist in resolving disputes which concern their parents and where they might experience their parents engaged in active dispute across a crowded corridor.

After the decree nisi has been granted, and all the court appearances are concluded, then the partner who has been awarded the decree can, after a minimum of six weeks, apply for a decree absolute. This is usually granted automatically, and the judge will read out in open court a list of the decrees made absolute on a particular day.

Custody matters

The pronouncement of the decree absolute is usually the final public ritual through which the family system is changed forever. The parents are no longer husband and wife – they may be divorced from each other but they remain the parents of their children. Their children will live primarily with the parent who has their 'care and control' either by agreement, or by the decision of the court. It is rare for courts to change the status quo with regard to the children, who usually remain with the parent with whom they have been living since the parents separated. There is also a guiding presumption that young children should normally live with their mother (Eekelaar 1984 and Cretney 1984) as well as the legally recognised expectation that the noncustodial parent should have access to the child.

The decisions about custody and access are often inextricably interconnected with financial matters and indeed, whereas most parents cannot live at the same level as they did prior to the divorce, for many lower- and some middle-income families this necessitates either the sale of the family home or the transfer of a tenancy to the custodial parent (see Chapter 1, 'Financial consequences of divorce', page 17). Such a situation not only exacerbates the conflict between the parents, but also adds to the burdens and distress of the children, who may additionally have to cope with changes of home and school and the loss of their friendship networks.

Joint custody

In families where parents have joint custody of their children, they usually live day to day with one parent, seeing the other parent regularly and both parents having joint responsibility for the major decisions regarding their lives. As Parkinson (1988) points out, there are confusions of nomenclature as well as the powers as between the magistrates' domestic courts where many custody decisions are made at the time the couple separate and the county courts where the divorce petitions are heard. Magistrates' courts cannot award joint custody, and the term 'actual custody' effectively means care and control, although there is no mention of care and control in the Matrimonial Causes Act (1973). There are also wide variations as to the award of joint custody as between different courts, as recent research by Whybrow and Priest (1986) shows, with a small but increasing tendency for joint custody to be awarded to middle-class parents in the South, although even then there are apparently inexplicable differences between individual courts. The Review of Child Care Law by the Law Commission (1986) proposed that parental responsibility should 'run with the child' on a time-sharing basis, much as happens at present in a number of states in the USA. The Booth Committee (1985) deplored a situation in which an order vesting the custody of the children in one parent, carries with it a condemnation of the other parent, and even the termination of his or her role in the children's lives. This is not only unjust to the noncustodial parent, who may be deprived of parity in terms of parental status, but may also exacerbate conflict by implying that the parent awarded custody is the better parent, sometimes leading to further loss for the children as well as damage to the post-divorce family. Indeed, the US research in Denver of Pearson and Thoennes (1982) found that many custody disputes were based on a belief that one parent is disposable after the divorce. Some children, whose parents live near to each other, regularly spend part of the week with one parent and part with the other, under a freely negotiated and even flexible arrangement. The issues relating to sole or joint custody and the implications of care and control on the children will be considered in later chapters (Chapter 8 and Chapter 11, 'Custody', page 258), as will the radical changes which will result from the Children Act (1989) (see Chapter 12).

Case example – the process

The Chigwells (first described in the previous chapter, page 81) finally decided that they could not continue with their marriage, after Charles had left and returned for a few weeks, during which time they agreed that Tricia would tell the children they were getting a divorce and what that would mean to them. They also agreed that Charles would talk to them on the next weekend when they were staying with him at his new flat. The children, particularly Annabel (now 5) were all upset, and for several weeks begged their mother to ask their father to come back. Debbie (now 7) refused to talk to her father for several visits, and Colin became very clingy and became enuretic, although he had been completely toilet trained. Both Charles and Tricia separately, painstakingly and carefully explained what was happening to the family and why, in words that the children could understand. They reassured the children that they both loved them although Charles and Tricia did not want to live with each other any more. Tricia also explained the situation to Debbie's teacher at school.

Their solicitors too did not hurry them into the legal process despite the eighteen months to two years of arguments as to who would divorce whom and on what grounds. Eventually, Tricia and Charles both cross-petitioned on the grounds of adultery, withdrew their petitions and agreed to divorce on grounds of two years' separation.

It was also agreed they should have joint custody of the children, though the care and control would remain with Tricia. By this time they were able to agree to have 'flexible access', though there had been a time when the children refused to stay overnight with their father and his new partner. At this Charles had threatened to demand 'defined access' once a week.

Tricia's parents, despite their strong religious objections to divorce, supported both parts of the binuclear family, allowing Charles to collect the children from their home (though not with his girlfriend) and giving as much to their daughter and grandchildren as they had ever done. Charles's mother, however, who had been very fond of her first daughter-in-law, could not cope with the new situation, and on the rare occasions that the children met her, made things very difficult by being very effusive about Charles's girlfriend, and expecting the children to agree with her.

Soon after the decree absolute had been agreed Tricia visited her therapist and announced that she was now divorced. Her therapist asked her what that meant to her and she replied that she was now resigned to it, and even relieved, but she wished that it had not been her birthday on the day on which the decree absolute finally came through.

Mother custody

Where one parent is awarded sole custody of the child or children it is usually the mother. Research shows (see, for instance, Hetherington, Cox and Cox 1982, and Weitzman 1985 in the US, and Finer 1974 and Eekelaar and Maclean 1986 in the UK) that mothers with custody experience particular stresses, both economic and emotional, as well as the additional tasks which becoming a single parent involve. It is the first time in their lives, for many divorcing women, that they are expected to define themselves as individual persons separate from a relationship. Custodial mothers are less likely to have the education, job skills or experience which permit them to obtain a sufficiently well-paid position or to pay for child care. As well as the downward mobility, constraints in employment possibilities and task overload, the family may also have to move home, which results in further losses, dislocation and social isolation. Research also shows – Wallerstein and Kelly (1980), Hetherington, Cox and Cox (1981), Kelly (1989) – that boys in mother-custody families show higher rates of hostile behaviour and interpersonal difficulties both at home and at school. The evidence too suggests that mothers are not only less perceptive of the needs of their sons, but also more likely to identify them in a similarly negative way with their fathers. Hetherington, Cox and Cox (1982) found that 'fathers are usually much more concerned than mothers about the maintenance of stereotype sex-role behaviour in their children and more likely to vary their role as they relate to male and female offspring'. The influence of gender in families will be discussed in more detail on page 104 (see 'Gender differences and the divorce process') and after remarriage in Chapter 11, 'Single-parent house-holds', page 226.

Father custody

Although there are fewer fathers seeking custody of their children, the numbers are increasing. Studies in the US (Gersick 1979, Santrock, Warshak and Elliott 1982) found that the reason why the fathers sought custody was also an indicator of its success. Santrock, Warshak and Elliott found that some men seek custody either because their former wives do not want custody; others actively want it, some because they believe they are the better parent, others because they feel vindictive enough to use a custody battle to intimidate their former wives, while still others seek it for economic gain. O'Brien's (1982) UK study of fifty-nine custodial fathers indicates that the success of the transition to sole custody depends not only upon the father's choice, but also upon the extent of the discussion, the amount of hostility involved, the abruptness of the transition, and whether the child's needs were put first. She distinguished three more or less equal groupings: the conciliatory negotiators (where the decisions were made jointly with the children's needs uppermost), the hostile seekers (where the decisions were made by either by default or where the children became pawns in the matrimonial battle in which the fathers were outraged by the conduct of their wives) and the passive acceptors (who became custodial fathers as the result of their wives' desertion).

Unlike many custodial mothers, particularly those who are older, most custodial fathers subsequently remarry, which leads to the formation of stepmother households (see Chapter 11, 'Single-parent households', page 246).

This section has primarily discussed the legal processes of decision-making in relation to the matters of custody and access. As the law stands at present a parent may be awarded sole custody – that is, legal custody and care and control; both the parents may be awarded joint legal custody, and more rarely this might also include shared care and control; or the children would be split, some being in the custody of one parent and some in the custody of the other (although the courts are generally reluctant to split siblings).

Psychological implications of types of custody decisions as between sole custody, joint custody or split custody will be discussed later (see Chapter 11, 'Custody', page 258).

THE POST-DIVORCE FAMILY

Herz Brown (1989) considers that the process of becoming a single-parent family can be distinguished by three separate stages, each of which requires major changes within the family unit, but places particular burdens on the parent who takes the major responsibility for the children.

The aftermath of the break-up of the marriage and the divorce

This involves becoming a single parent, managing money in circumstances when there is almost certainly less than when the parties were married, and, as has already been indicated, becoming a single parent. In most families the parents do not often consciously distinguish between their marital relationship (the exception being those aspects related to their sexual relationship) and their co-parental one, yet it is the separation of these two familial aspects of interaction which become a necessity during the divorce process. Nor do the children usually think of their relationship with their mother and father as separate and distinct, unless the marital relationship is one of acrimony or violence, though generally they may have special aspects of relationship with each parent, and at different times in the family life cycle.

The task of the family during the divorce process becomes that of forming more flexible relationships, so that the parents can maintain and even strengthen their co-parental relationship and both grieve for and relinquish their relationship as husband and wife (though as Ahrons and Wallisch 1987 found, a significant proportion retain a non-parental relationship). At the same time they will be attempting to differentiate and individualise their parenting of the children, both one to one and as a sibling system and also reinforcing their children's individual and collective relationship with the other parent. These attempts at change inevitably continue throughout the whole of the divorce process and often also for a number of years after the legal divorce and even remarriage (see Chapters 7 and 8). It is well known that many parents find this an impossible task – indeed, Wallerstein's (1989) most recent research in which she has followed some of the families of her earlier study (conducted with Kelly 1980) shows this to be the case.

Realignment

The second stage is that of realignment. Each parent and former partner will have the task of establishing, organising and managing a separate household. In many families post-divorce, the parent with whom the children are living remains in the former matrimonial home with the children. Such an arrangement at least minimises the additional stress necessitated by a move to a new home, a different neighbourhood and perhaps changes of school also. For most, if not all, families post-divorce, there is inevitably a reduction in living standards, particularly for women, and for some there is the necessity to move 'down market' because of the terms of the financial settlement, which may result in neither of the two single-parent households being able to remain in the former matrimonial home.

Weiss (1975), as well as Weitzman (1985) and others, distinguishes three common sources of strain which single parents experience – responsibility overload, task overload, and emotional overload. When the custodial parent has to move home, this requires coping with reorganising a household, finding and arranging new schools for the children, perhaps finding a job for the first time for many years, and all this single-handed. The phase of realignment also necessitates changes in social relationships, as it is likely that some of the relationships, whether with friends or colleagues, will not survive equally with both divorced partners, if at all. If there has been a relocation of household, then some friends will be lost as a result, so there will be the tasks of finding and exploring new friendships and support systems. As the parents often have a nurturant and supportive role regarding the social relationships of their children, these will also need monitoring as part of the realignment phase.

As already indicated, the terms 'custodial' and 'noncustodial parent', which are in common usage, neither indicate that both divorced parents are equally important for their children, nor do they imply that both parents have equal responsibility for them, whether or not they are living with them day-to-day; yet there is no other terminology in common usage, although this will be changed following the implementation of the 1989 Children Act. For the noncustodial parent their new life style post-divorce involves a change of home as well as the loss of living as a family with their former spouse and children. There are a considerable number of noncustodial parents, particularly fathers, who have nowhere to take their children for their access visits. Although there are now some access centres, which are comfortable, homely and open at weekends, these are few and far between, and many more are needed.

Restabilisation

The final phase is that of restabilisation. During the divorce process, each partner attempts to retrieve their emotional investment from the marriage, to salvage their self-esteem and develop a new world view of themselves which allows them to begin a relatively autonomous life style. Indeed this is seen as one of the objectives of seeking a divorce, at least initially. As will become apparent when stepfamilies are discussed (in Chapters 6 and 7), many couples or partners have far from completed the emotional divorce processes by the time they remarry; and may frequently carry unresolved problems and emotional 'baggage' from the breakup of their first marriage into their second. Adjustment to the post-divorce re-formed or binuclear family implies an acceptance by each formerly married partner that each of them needs to develop a new social network in which their children may also become involved. The case example given below shows the process of becoming a post-divorce family for one older couple and their children.

The Farnborough family

Frances Farnborough (the only member of the family with whom there was contact) came to this country from overseas, having had an emotionally deprived childhood. Perhaps this had led to her becoming pregnant and, following the birth and subsequent adoption of her baby, experiencing a deep distress which she had never resolved. She fairly quickly married Neil, a Regular Army officer, and they had three children, the first of whom was mildly brain-damaged. The marriage was not at all happy, Neil drank heavily and bullied her, while she devoted herself to being a loving and protective mother to her children (perhaps neglecting him in the process).

Neil soon left the Forces and their family life swung between impoverishment and his somewhat grandiose schemes (some of which were successful), according to his phases of sobriety. Both parents were intensely competitive over the children, who, though fond of their father, tended to side with their mother. All of them were frightened of him when he was drunk.

Eventually, following a particularly violent incident during which one of the boys, then aged 9, tried to stand up to his father who had made insinuations about her past, Frances decided to get a divorce. This decision took her a number of years to implement, and by the time she was eventually legally divorced the eldest son had left home and the two other children were in their final years at school. Because she believed in the children having access to their father, and because he at first had nowhere he could see them, she allowed him to come to her new home.

After a number of hospitalisations and failed attempts to stop drinking Neil joined AA, but remained depressed and emotionally dependent upon Frances, and the children. Now both over 60, neither of them had been able to detach themselves sufficiently to begin to build autonomous lives of their own. Frances continued to be a dependable if somewhat over-protective parent to her children, and Neil, when he could get his foot in the door, would try to intrude on her frail new social life with her few friends and some neighbours, many of whom she also allowed to lean on her, as he had done.

Eventually, after a trip to her country of origin where, to her surprise, she was greeted with pleasure by members of her family and old friends, Frances decided to seek help from a counsellor to begin a new and autonomous life for herself.

GENDER DIFFERENCES AND THE DIVORCE PROCESS

It is not known how many couples have agreed to separate for a time in order to take and/or give each other a 'breathing space' in order to come to a final and possibly cataclysmic decision about their marriage, though the numbers are probably considerable. Certainly, a number of couples who file a petition do not seek a decree nisi (12–15 per cent), some, perhaps, because the grounds for the petition are amended; and a few (2 per cent) do not apply for a decree absolute. At least some of these are likely to have become reconciled.

What is known is that a surprisingly high number of women who escape from violent marriages and enter women's refuges often return to their husbands. There are two general explanations for this apparently inexplicable behaviour. The feminist argument relates to the economic and physical powers of the husband. The other is a psychological argument, which indicates that some women in violent marriages have grown up in violent families and know no other ways of relationship. There is probably some validity in each of these arguments, but what is generally accepted is that the power balance between the couple is a crucial variable in their attempts to sort out their marital difficulties (see Chapter 3, 'The mediation model of intervention during the divorce process', page 53, and Chapters 9 and 10).

Recent research also shows that differences in attitude to certain issues which arise during the divorce process are affected by gender and societal expectations about the roles of men and women (see Davis and Murch 1988). For some men who have been the initiators, this may be the first time when they fully realise what they stand to lose – all too frequently, not only their wife, but their children and home as well. For other men whose wives have been the initiators, it may be at this time that their despair or jealousy at their impending loss leads them to erupt into violence, either against their wives and children, or themselves. On the whole men in our society are not socialised into talking about their emotions, and indeed for many they have only been able to discuss their feelings with the wives who are now about to desert them (see also Chapter 4, 'The decision to separate . . .', page 73).

Kaslow and Schwartz (1987) comment on the gender influence on the differential impact on the divorcing partners; referring to the research of Hetherington et al. (1979) in which the divorcing fathers of preschool children, in an effort to regain their self-esteem and perhaps their youth also, reverted to styles of dress and behaviour which they described as the 'Hip, Honda and hirsute syndrome'! Other men – such as the professional man whose common-law wife left with their 3-year-old daughter without telling him – are shocked and initially utterly unable to assimilate what has happened and become dangerously distraught, even suicidal or murderous (see also Chapter 7, 'Physical and sexual abuse in stepfamilies', page 149, and 'Factors prognostic of problem development in stepfamilies', page 157).

For women, on the other hand, a crucial issue appears to be whether or not they are the initiators of the suggestion to divorce. They too often change their appearance by hairstyle or dress and show weight changes either of loss or gain, which may be related to their post-separation depression. For many women it may only be at this stage of planning that they begin to realise the size of the responsibilities they will be carrying in the future and just how desperate their financial situation may become.

Weitzman's (1985) research shows very clearly how widespread is the feminisation of poverty, particularly for young mothers, older housewives and women in transition, since the changes in US legislation. Although purporting to treat men and women equally at divorce, the legislation not only ignores the economic inequalities between men and women in marriage, but also the differences in society in general. As Wallerstein (1989) indicates,

> many young women are driven into a Herculean struggle in order to survive emotionally and physically ... while many older women are emerging from marriages alone and unhappy facing old age with rising anxiety ... they lean on their children, with mixed feelings for support and companionship, ten, even fifteen years after the divorce.

One of the few UK research studies relating to men following divorce (Ambrose, Harper and Pemberton (1983), see Chapter 1, 'The increase in households headed by a lone parent', page 16) found that the majority of the ninety-two men in their study gave, on average, two of the following reasons for the divorce:

1 Reasons internal to the marriage, either concerning the couple alone (seventy-one) or internal to the marriage but concerning both the couple and their children (fifteen).
2 Pressure from outside the marriage – relationships by one or both parties with another or others (forty-five), tensions related to career of either party, or other money matters (twenty-one), pressures from mother-in-law (eight).
3 Reasons related to an original inappropriate choice of partner (fifteen).
4 Illness of either party (nine).

Kelly's (1986, 1988) ongoing and comprehensive longitudinal study, in which she is monitoring 437 men and women in the process of separating (two-thirds of whom are already separated), either when they file a petition or go for mediation, reveals nine major clusters of factors which they regard as having led to the separation:

1 Two-thirds, both men and women, reported a loss of closeness, sexual and intimacy difficulties and revealed a major sense of growing apart.
2 More than half, both men and women, reported high levels of conflict.
3 More women reported divergent life styles.
4 More women reported an angry, demeaning and violent spouse. Both partners were extremely angry and there were also high levels of child conflict. For men this was associated with their lower levels

of education, and for 22 per cent this was a second marriage ending.

5 Both men and women reported employment or money problems, though the women had a high level of stress and the men a high level of guilt.
6 More women reported substance abuse or emotional difficulties or instability of their spouse. Both the men and the women were depressed and felt exploited by their spouse and had low levels of guilt.
7 More men self-reported extra-marital affairs or drug abuse; and this was the only factor associated with women who stay at home.
8 More younger women reported role and career conflicts, particularly related to a level of education.
9 More men reported their spouses' jealousy of their own activities, particularly their sporting activities.

Some also reported severe or chronic illness, including the death of a family member, where the feelings related to this loss were displaced on to the marriage.

A recent joint UK–US survey carried out by the universities of Brunel, Alaska and Michigan, Institute of Personnel Management (Jones 1990) of 500 managers and professional people separated or divorced since 1980 produced results which seem to indicate a changing trend, particularly amongst women, who are more likely to do better than men at work. Women seem to adjust by investing in a career in order to gain self-esteem and self-worth. Men, on the other hand,

> have already made that investment, so it is not an option for them and they experience a downward spiral affecting many aspects of their work. ... Divorced men spend more time in hospital than married men; they have a shorter life expectancy and are twice as likely to die of cirrhosis of the liver.

Half of the women and one-third of the men reported that their relationships with colleagues had changed after divorce from just-work relationships to more personal friendships.

Rosenthal and Keshet's (1981; Keshet and Rosenthal 1978) US research study, conducted through depth interviews carried out by a male interviewer, explored the relationships during the first two years following the break-up of their marriage between 129 middle-class fathers, and their children aged 7 or under. They distinguished four types of father:

1 *The occasional father*, who is likely to be living alone, though he has close women friends who are usually childless. His two children are likely to be an older girl and a younger boy, and he regards his primary role as that of a regular provider. Such men have strong beliefs in family life and wish to maintain the ties with their children, but are unwilling to make major changes in their life style to achieve this. They disagree with their ex-wives about child-rearing, especially discipline; and their fatherly relationship with their children is as a helpful visitor, calling fortnightly to take them out, and spending traditional father's free time entertaining them at weekends and in the holidays.

2 *The quarter-time father* is more likely to see his children more than once a week, but does not have strict access arrangements for their two children, the older usually being a boy. Many of these fathers consider they have a special post-divorce relationship with their children, and find it difficult to enforce discipline. Their women friends are more likely to be divorced women with children of their own and, as they frequently have their children for all or part of the weekend, they are more likely to be present when they visit, so that the family has a characteristic sociability. These fathers are likely to have a high degree of ambivalence towards their ex-wives, and seem to have a conventional image of the male fatherly role.

3 *The half-time father* has a low level of conflict with his (usually) separated wife, with whom he also has less contact although he keeps in touch with her over matters related to the children. There are rigid arrangements with regard to his children, only one of whom is likely to be of school age, usually a boy, whom he takes to and from school, thus avoiding contacts at the mother's house. His house is set up to include living arrangements for the children and, where possible, he orients his usually low-level work and social life around the access arrangements. He has women friends, usually single, but they are as likely to stay at home as to go out. These men, by defining themselves as half-time fathers, have oriented their home life around their children.

4 *The full-time father* is usually one in whose situation the arrangement is likely to be involuntary, in that the mother has willingly or out of necessity given up her rights to the custody of her children. He is likely to have arranged his life so as to take care of his children by arranging child care or having a live-in lover. He feels very different, particularly from his male colleagues, whom he regards as unsympathetic to his situation. He is keen to remarry and goes out with women who are single and childless.

Huntington (1986) concludes from her US research that men are frequently unsure what caused the break-up of their marriage; for instance, men who are workaholics and often away from home perceive this as dedication to the welfare of the family. She points out that it is of supreme importance to many men that they have control not only of their feelings, but also of their marriage; thus men whose divorce is not of their own choice experience this as having lost control, and their anger becomes a real issue. She categorises five groups of men following divorce. One group seem to feel very little, who came from marriage where there was not only little commitment, but also little intimacy. A second group are those who experience a severe narcissistic injury with an intense sense of betrayal. And a third group are often the parents of young children who are devastated by the loss of contact with their children. A fourth group, also crushed by the divorce, are those who know themselves to have been the warmer and more selfless of the two parents for their children; while a fifth group includes those who experienced relief as they had realised that the marriage was not psychologically good for them. The influence of gender in 'good enough' re-formed families will be discussed in Chapter 11, 'Step-mother households', page 252.

CONCLUSION

Although for each couple the marital relationship is unique and many-faceted, there are variations of degrees of attachment as well as of distance and closeness, particularly at different stages of the life cycle. As will be apparent in the divorce process the partners go through a dissonant and lengthy process of disillusionment, erosion and detachment, which results in a voluntary or involuntary physical separation, each stage usually being accompanied by grief and mourning, although for some this is never finally resolved.

There are clear gender differences between the men and the women as the partners struggle to understand and make sense of what is happening to themselves and each other, try to comprehend the implications, and begin to change their own interaction. The fact that women frequently complain of lack of responsiveness and communication and men about criticism, arguing and nagging, indicate common patterns of dissatisfaction. There are also different patterns of psychological distress, the women experiencing the time before the decision to end the marriage and the decision to divorce as more difficult and the men the realisation of how much they valued their relationship with their wives and children after they have divorced (Hetherington and Tryon 1989). Gradually each begins to make a new sense of their shared history and present position, which allows them to develop new meanings, and these in turn change their communication and behaviour.

Many researchers and clinicians argue that a continued bond with the former spouse is significantly related to post-divorce emotional adjustment. Those (such as Kitson 1982 and Berman 1988, and others basing their work on that of Bowlby 1969, 1973, 1980, and of Ainsworth 1973) who have clearly conceptualised attachment as a transactional concept affected by and influencing both of the partners in a dyad, stress that though residual attachment appears to be fairly common, such feelings are distinct from general distress. Distress and attachment can both influence and interact with each other in a complex feedback system involving emotional, familial, social and economic systems.

In the meantime the children, perhaps at first relatively unaffected by what is happening to their parents, eventually begin to discern the changes in their parents' relationship to each other and to themselves. This in turn affects the way they communicate and interact with their parents, who in response change their own interactions with them, perhaps beginning to exclude or even disqualify the other parent.

At another level the whole nuclear family is also changing. Patterns of behaviour and the largely unconscious rules by which they operate become dysfunctional and are suspended, or abruptly changed, often without understanding or explanation because no one is really aware of what is happening. The family becomes at first puzzled, then confused, and often only later becomes distressed, affected by the emerging changes and by the circularity of their interactions and behaviour.

The processes of divorce are ambiguous and overlapping, and may include other attachment figures of minor or increasing importance, for one or both parental partners. The diagram (Figure 4.1) attempts to show this spiralling circularity of the internal life of the nuclear family, together with the second-order changes as, during the divorce process, the family moves through the process of redefinition and transformation necessary to become a re-formed family.

The now re-formed family will ultimately separate into two separate households, although the decisions relating to the matrimonial home may not always have been concluded by the time the divorce decree is made absolute. Wherever possible the children remain in the family home with their custodial parent, although in situations where the noncustodial parent's livelihood is tied to the matrimonial home, this may not be possible.

However, for many middle- and lower-income families, the sale of the matrimonial home will be necessary in order to complete the financial settlement. For the custodial parent and children, this often entails a move to a cheaper area, with subsequent loss of support networks for the vulnerable single-parent household, changes of school for the children and frequently greater distance from their noncustodial parent. For the noncustodial parent (usually the father) this may not only entail the loss of spouse and family but also the loss of the home and the financial inability to purchase another, at least initially.

The specific effects of divorce on the children will be considered in Chapter 8, but it is important to point out that the amount of parental conflict, the subsequent adjustment of the custodial parent, and the post-divorce relationship between the custodial and noncustodial parent are the crucial factors in relation to the children's adjustment.

Wallerstein's latest research (see Wallerstein and Blakeslee 1989) which follows up some of the families originally seen with Kelly ten years earlier, has led her to come to some controversial conclusions, which have been criticised (see Chapter 8, 'Long term outcome and conclusions', page 169), yet also seem to indicate that for children the long-term sequelae of divorce are more serious than have yet been recognised. These seem to indicate:

1 That the child's long-term relationships with both parents, who also are able to cooperate with each other, remain vital to proper development.
2 Following marital breakdown, both men and women experience a diminished capacity to parent their children.
3 Because following divorce, most children live with their mothers, her mental health and the quality of her parenting is the most important factor.
4 That the children continue to need their fathers, and this need increases at adolescence, particularly when it is time for them to leave home.
5 Many fathers seem to lose their sense that their children are part of their own generational continuity and act as a protection for their own fears of mortality.
6 In some families, the new relationships which develop leave the child overburdened by the responsibility for the psychological well-being of their parent.

6 Becoming a stepfamily

Starting out

O let not Time deceive you
You cannot conquer Time
In the burrows of the Nightmare
Where Justice Naked is,
Time watches from the shadow
And coughs when you would kiss.

W. H. Auden (1907–73), 'Birthday Poem'

According to Rimmer (1981), one in three of all marriages are now remarriages for at least one of the partners, and recent figures indicate that about half of these are likely to end in a further divorce. The stepfamily is not a new family phenomenon, though until this century stepfamilies were more likely to be created following the remarriage of widows or widowers. Since the increase of longevity as well as the rise in the divorce rates, most stepfamilies are now likely to be those which result from divorce and remarriage.

Although nuclear families are frequently idealised, mythology and folklore indicate that stepfamilies are regarded with intense ambivalence if not outright negativity, on one hand featuring wicked stepmothers who dominate a passive father and terrorise their children; and on the other, sexually predatory stepfathers with an innocent young girl who may or may not ultimately triumph (see 'New beginnings', page 127). Another view is that of the classic Oedipal triangle of sexual rivalry either between the girl and her stepmother or between the boy and his natural father for a usually much younger stepmother (Maddox 1975). Such cultural negative stereotyping of the stepfamily is evident, even in the euphemisms for stepfamily – such as 'blended', 'reconstituted', 'remarried', 'second', 'merged', 'combined' or 'reorganised'. This negative stereotyping distorts perceptions, 'so that what is perceived is believed about the group', which leads to a less favourable evaluation regardless of what behaviour is observed (Coleman and Ganong 1987). A further example of this can be seen by the stereotyped media mythology, following enquiries into child abuse cases which have resulted from the death of a child at the hands of their stepparent – as for instance, Maria Colwell (1974), Wayne Brewer (1976), Jasmine Beckford (1986) and Kimberley Carlile (1987); and the 'discovery' of child sexual abuse (see Chapter 7, 'Physical and sexual child abuse in stepfamilies', page 149).

It may be at least partly because of these negative attitudes that there are few normative expectations of roles and relationships in stepfamilies. In nuclear families there are clear expectations and opportunities to learn through perception and modelling, as well as indications of the consequence of failure to meet such expectations. Because nuclear families are regarded as the norm (and perhaps because of their idealisation) stepfamilies are often compared unfavourably with them, being considered as a 'deficit model' (Coleman and Ganong 1987). Until relatively recently societal pressures assumed that stepfamilies were expected – and indeed, expected themselves – to behave as if they were just another nuclear family, and yet because the stepfamily is regarded as an incomplete institution, no guidelines or supports were provided to help them to conform to society's expectations (Cherlin 1978). Such research as there has been into the definition of parental and stepparental roles has clearly shown the lack of institutional norms and the stress which results from such ambiguity (see, for instance, Duberman 1975, Visher and Visher 1979 and 1988, Robinson 1980, Robinson and Smith, forthcoming, and Smith 1990). Each stepfamily, therefore, has to negotiate their roles in an *ad hoc* way, often during periods of considerable stress and in isolation. Many stepparents have likened the experience of admitting that they were stepparents to that of 'coming out' as homosexuals.

Burgoyne and Clark (1984), in their study of stepfamilies in Sheffield, point out that many of the troubles of the remarried arise from earlier stages of their biographies and that the remarriage is often seen as a fresh start with high hopes. The previous chapters have shown how family transformation during the divorce process requires the couple, their children, and indeed the whole nuclear family, to negotiate a series of processes of transition as the result of the death of a parent, or the divorce of the parents. If these transitional tasks are not more or less complete when one or both partners remarry, then those that remain unresolved are likely to impede the initial stages in the process of becoming a stepfamily. Parental remarriage which includes becoming a stepfamily is yet another transformation and one which results in further disequilibrium and disorganisation. It is this double transition, often occurring within a relatively short period of time, that, if unrecognised, can compound an already vulnerable situation, particularly for the children. (For instance, according to Ihinger-Tallman and Pasley 1987, in the US the median period between divorce and remarriage is three years.) This double transition, when coupled with the lack of received wisdom about roles and relationships in step-families, very often creates additional stress for the newly established stepfamily, despite the parents' positive hopes for the future. The failure to provide emotional and social maps has added to the confusion and isolation of many stepfamilies, particularly at the outset.

CHARACTERISTICS OF STEPFAMILIES

Visher and Visher (1988) have distinguished some of the common characteristics of stepfamilies, which they consider are important as they contribute to some of the confusions, uncertainties and ambiguities of stepfamilies. These characteristics have been adapted and extended in an attempt to provide a normative map and some understanding as to the expectations for stepfamily development. While many of these characteristics will be discussed in more detail subsequently, they have been outlined as a way of demonstrating the elements which are common to most stepfamilies. Some remain fairly constant over time, while others change as the stepfamily develops.

Complexity of stepfamily structures

There are a large number of people in the stepfamily network with whom connections need to be forged. Stepfamilies are not usually confined to one household; there are two or more house-holds, which result in ambiguous boundaries as both need to be involved in any decision-making as well as managed by the binuclear family members. The structures which stepfamilies need to develop are not the same as those of nuclear families and initially are related to the tasks that they must undertake in order to create a stepfamily system with its own rules. More and more couples are living together, especially post-divorce, some as a prelude to remarriage, though for many this recoupling results in a firm cohabiting commitment. Their experiences of previous marriage(s) frequently leave those who have divorced with a disinclination to remarry; and their hard-won independence, often forged as the result of some emotional and financial cost, also leaves them unwilling to relinquish it.

Stress

It will already be apparent that stepfamilies have to cope with and manage more stress than their nuclear counterparts. This is at least partly because of the ambiguity of their situation, though also because of unresolved problems following the divorce or death of a biological parent (see later and Chapter 7).

The integration of a stepfamily into a functional family system

The integration of a stepfamily takes years, rather than months, and depends on many factors. Among the most significant are the age and sex of the children at the time the stepfamily is formed and the type of stepfamily. The minimum is generally considered to be two years, a rough guide being that of the age of the eldest child at the time of the remarriage as s/he has already lived in another family system for that number of years. For some stepfamilies functional integration is not achieved before the stepchildren leave home.

Cut-off relationships

There are frequently cut-off relationships in stepfamilies. These are most common in stepfather households, as within two years of the divorce half of biological fathers lose contact with their children (see Chapter 1, 'Marriage matters', page 11, and Chapter 8). Clinical impressions seem to confirm that the overall adjustment of children who are cut off from a parent is poorer and that they also have more difficulty in forming relationships with a stepparent. These cut-offs may be partial, as when siblings live in different households, or temporary, as in the case of very young children, or when adult children seek out their absent parent.

Continual transitions

A common feature of stepfamily life is the movement of children between households. These may be for access visits to the other parent whether for a day, overnight, for holidays, or because the children live more or less equally with both parents. In order to enable these transitions to take place stepfamilies need to develop permeable boundaries.

Less cohesiveness

In stepfamilies where the parents and stepparents try to maintain the children's attachments to biological parents and therefore because of the necessity for permeable boundaries in stepfamilies, it is likely that stepchildren, other than the very young, are likely to become less attached to their stepparents. Research also shows that stepchildren generally feel less close to their stepparents than they do to their biological parents (Ganong and Coleman 1987).

Variety of patterns in stepfamily households

In addition to the unique patterns which are idiosyncratic to all households, there are diverse custody and access arrangements in stepfamilies which necessitate different ways of managing day-to-day living. Each stepfamily household needs also to develop their own way of living together, and the children can learn to live within life styles which are very different.

Unrealistic expectations, lack of norms and information

These are affected by the mythology related to stepfamilies and the hope that the stepfamily can become just another nuclear family. There are few normative guidelines for stepfamilies, perhaps because they been evaluated on a deficiency comparison with nuclear families (see particularly 'New beginnings', page 127 and Chapter 7). The lack of research on stepfamilies, until very recently, is a striking example of societal attitudes towards them.

No common past history as a family

New stepfamilies as yet have no established interactional patterns which enable them to function on a day-to-day relational basis. Nor do they have a familiarity with the family environment and their own behaviour within it. Initially at least, this usually leads to a self-consciousness as regards their own behaviour and an acute awareness of that of others in the household. This is often experienced as a kind of 'culture shock' and the feeling of being in an alien environment.

Even the most trivial things can seem important and sensitive respect becomes necessary. There is no shared history or intimacy as a family, and expectations of creating family togetherness easily lead to discomfort.

No common solid foundation of understanding of relationships

Relationships within stepfamilies have no foundation of caring or understanding as they do in biological nuclear families, based on shared beliefs, which is largely unconscious. Because there is no such shared experience, stepkin have to learn to understand and build up over time the implications of communication, both verbal and nonverbal.

Loyalty conflicts

Because of the structure of stepfamilies, loyalty conflicts are likely to be more prominent. The subsystems in stepfamilies, whether parental, parent–child, or between siblings will have psychological bonds to other family members who are not physically present in the stepfamily household. Such loyalty conflicts are initially strong, but diminish as the stepfamily gradually becomes integrated as a unit.

Ambiguity of roles

This has already been mentioned and will be discussed in more detail later. Recently, clinical experience and research has demonstrated that such ambiguity allows freedom of choice and provides the freedom for a range of roles with different children.

The premise of Visher and Visher (1988) is that 'these normative characteristics have often been labelled as dysfunctional . . . that they can be expected, even anticipated. Indeed in that acceptance lie the seeds of change, where change is possible.' Such a premise not only begins to provide some kind of map for stepfamilies themselves, but also normative expectations for them and those in the interventionist professions who try to help them.

THE SUPRA FAMILY SYSTEM

The importance of the binuclear households and the extended families of parents and stepparents cannot be underestimated. A US research study carried out by Sager (a family psychiatrist, together with a group of family therapists) at the Jewish Family Welfare Service in New York (1983) combined a research study with their treatment of remarried families who came to their consultation service. Sager et al. described this complex network as a supra system (indeed, this has many similarities to the re-formed extended family system). The supra system includes all the individuals who, through kinship, or as the result of the remarriage and additional subsystems, impinge on the stepfamily. This may be a positive or negative force, or a mixture, but one which needs to be considered. The differences between such a remarried family system (which Sager et al. describe as REM families) and the systems of nuclear families lie along seven parameters: structure, purposes, tasks, the nature of bonding, factors that influence both the adults and the children in the system as well as the forces which impinge upon the system. These elements will be summarised below, and some of them have been found to be especially prognostic of future difficulties (see Chapter 8, 'Children living in stepfamilies', page 175).

Structural factors

Structural factors include the following. Because the stepchildren have been previously parented by only one of the adults, the parental tasks are not exclusive to the parent–stepparent dyad as they usually are in nuclear families. The parent–child relationship pre-dates the marital relationship, and at least two members of the stepfamily have been (and in some sense remain, at least historically and relationally) a part of another system. This results in the need for a relatively open boundary between the systems, whose membership cannot therefore be clearly defined. Thus there are other 'family' members who have an influence on the system and who may be perceived ambivalently or even negatively, as indeed they often are. Attempts to 'close off' part of the system, such as the custodial parent, children and one set of grandparents, result in cut-offs which are now recognised as among the most damaging factors for children (see Visher and Visher 1988, Skynner 1989, and others). Finally, unlike the structures in nuclear families, the legal ties (which include some of the major decision-making matters, including inheritance) are asymmetrical.

Purposes

The purposes are similar to those of nuclear families – to establish a marital partnership and care for the children, and to see that a variety of needs are met, and yet the previous experience of loss and failure adds pressure to the expectations. The existence of such an 'instant family' may make the possibility of procreation more doubtful, especially where there is a discrepancy in the life-cycle stages of the remarried partners.

Similarities with nuclear family system

There are many similarities between the tasks of the nuclear family system and that of the remarried family. These include the consolidation of the marital system, the resolution of individual life-cycle and marital life-cycle tasks, the preparation for the parental role, and the shift from dyadic to triadic family structure. However, the attempt to fulfil the intimacy needs of the partners is complicated by the existence of the previous marriage and the presence of the children. The lapse of time between the first marriage and the remarriage means that at least one partner already has some experience of day-to-day family life, while the pressure to establish a functional household adds urgency to the situation. The age, stage of development and characteristics of the children also lead to loyalty conflicts for children and parent(s).

Bonding

The nature of bonding may be less strong because of the experience of failure and loss, which may lead to cautiousness about commitment. The family rituals which in nuclear families customarily reinforce attachment may be experienced on such occasions as reminders of loss, rather than enhancing bonding. There may be less sense of security and spontaneity, and therefore ambivalence may be more difficult to tolerate. Initially at least, there may be not be acceptance and support from an extended family, who are likely to have their own ambivalences regarding the failure of the first marriage and the introduction of a new partner.

Other influences

The adults are influenced by a number of factors – one or both have been in a previous marriage, which may be subtly compared and evaluated with that with the present partner. There is often continuing contact with the previous partner, which, whether experienced and perceived as positive or negative, will have some impact on the remarried couple. At least one of the partners has previous experience of the married life style, which will affect their attitude to remarried living, though again this may be positive or negative. The life cycle of the stepfamily is therefore lived on two different marital and family life-cycle 'tracks', which are likely to lead to confusion about responsibilities and may well result in conflict Finally, one or both partners are likely to be experiencing guilt about the failure of the previous marriage, the present situation of the previous spouse and, perhaps particularly, the effects on the children

Factors influencing the children

The factors which influence the children include the need to mourn the loss of the former nuclear family system, a loss which they did not want and about which they were not consulted. They are likely to experience the disruption of their roots, perhaps followed by the advent of stepsiblings, which may even alter their ordinal position in the new stepfamily. The arrival of a half sibling born to the parent and stepparent is often experienced as positive by the stepchildren and may help with the development of bonds within the stepfamily. (On the other hand the children may be jealous of this newcomer, who is now the baby of the stepfamily.) One particular child, who may be adolescent or even adult, can become scapegoated or extruded from the family. They may also experience the loss of a recently established primary role in the single-parent household.

As the role and function of each child is not yet fully established, becoming a stepfamily may lead to changes which provoke anxiety and confusion. Either one or both of the natural parents may demand the exclusive loyalty of the children and there is often special anger towards the natural parent and/or stepparent who either is perceived as having deserted the child, to have been the cause of the breakup of the nuclear family, or both.

Forces impinging on the stepfamily system

The forces which impinge on the stepfamily system, particularly where there are young children or those of school age, may include one or both natural parents using the children as go-betweens or spies. In such families the presence of a former spouse often means that the emotional divorce is not fully complete and there is residual guilt. There may also be financial pressures which in turn affect the children.

The continuing co-parental relationship can be experienced as threatening by the new spouse, especially in the early stages of development of the stepfamily. Grandparents, particularly those who may have taken an important role between marriages, can be experienced either as supportive or an intrusive influence in the new stepfamily. The presence of siblings and intimate friends of both remarried adults similarly can promote or detract from the developing stepfamily. Forms of communication – for instance, letters and telephone calls between members of the re-formed family – can intrude on the privacy and life space of the stepfamily.

The shadow of the law and possibility of legal processes because they regulate maintenance, custody and access, but also because of their adversarial nature, may accentuate conflicts, rather than provide a constraining balance. The legal position regarding stepparents' rights and responsibilities is at present confused and even contradictory.

Money is a crucial and complex factor for the stepfamily. A remarried man who is maintaining his former wife cannot provide his family with the same standard of living as was possible in his first marriage. The remarried woman may perceive maintenance to a previous spouse as being taken away from the stepfamily, although she may have her own maintenance reduced as the result of remarriage. The issue of finance has links with the expected role performance which in turn is related to gender (see Chapter 11, 'Stepmother households', page 252).

TYPOLOGIES OF STEPFAMILIES

Stepfamilies have also been variously described as reconstituted (Duberman 1975, Robinson 1980, Shulman 1981), blended (Wald 1981), or remarried (Wald 1981, Sager et al. 1983, Ihinger-Tallman and Pasley 1987), and different criteria have also been used as factors in constructing a typology of stepfamilies.

Burgoyne and Clark (1984) classified the stepfamilies in their study according to the goals they set for their family life, distinguishing five different types, as follows:

1 *Not really a stepfamily* – those who have young children at the time of the divorce and remarriage, and as a result are quickly able to think of themselves as an ordinary family.
2 *Looking forward to the departure of the children* – those older couples who consider themselves too old for children of the new

marriage, and whose children are teenage and who are awaiting their departure so that they can focus on their own relationship.

3 *The progressive stepfamily* – the prototype of a modern stepfamily in which conflicts with former spouses have been resolved and who stress the advantages of their situation. They perceive few barriers to additional children of the new marriage.

4 *The successful, conscious pursuit of an ordinary family life together* – in which the stepparent becomes a full 'social parent', transferring allegiance to children, and in which the initial problems have been resolved or ignored successfully. Children in the new marriage symbolise the 'normality' of family life.

5 *The conscious pursuit of ordinary family life frustrated* – in which the legacy of their past frustrates the couple's attempts to build an ordinary family life together. Continuing problems make the possibility of children of the new marriage unlikely.

Some writers (see, for instance, Ahrons and Rodgers (1988, chapter 5)) base their classification on co-parenting relationships, or the lack of them, which exist between two households of the now binuclear family and the complexities, which range from those in which the custodial parent has not remarried to those in which parents share joint custody and the children are split between two households.

The classification of Robinson (1980) is on the legalistic basis of the marital relationship between the biological parent and stepparent, thus minimising the re-formed nature of the extended family system:

1 *Legitimating*, where the biological parent had not previously been married and the children were illegitimate.

2 *Revitalised*, where the biological parent had remarried following the death of the other natural parent.

3 *Reassembled*, where one or both partners have previously been divorced, and the biological parent brings into the family a stepparent who had not previously had children.

4 *A combination* (first described by Shulman 1972 and 1981), where both parents have previously been married and have children from their first marriages, who may or may not live with the stepfamily full-time. A common example is that the children of the remarried woman live with the family and the husband's children are regular visitors.

Pasley and Ihinger-Tallman (see Ihinger-Tallman and Pasley 1987; Pasley 1987) have devised a nine-fold structure which is based on the levels of complexity in the remarried family, which includes childless remarried spouses, those with their own child in common, those where at least one of them has an adult child who does not live with them, those who have a child in common and at least one of them also has a child from a previous marriage, those remarried partners where at least one of them has a child from a previous marriage who does not live with them, those where such a child does live with them, those where both have a child from a previous marriage who lives with them, those who are similar but also have a child of their own, and those who both have a child from a previous marriage, a child of their own who lives with them and another child or children who do not. This is similar to Wald's (1981) classification of parent–child subsystems where there are fifteen different combinations of arrangements regarding parents and their children as the result of prior unions of either husband and wife or both.

STEPPARENT HOUSEHOLDS AND PATTERNS OF PARENTING IN STEPFAMILIES

Stepfather households

Because the majority of mothers retain the custody of their children following divorce, the majority of stepparent *households* are those with a stepfather. Remarried parents whose children are primarily living with them have two usually distinct sets of co-parenting to manage, one with the children's biological parent and one with the stepparent who is living in the household. In stepfather family households, where stepfathers have been divorced, it is more likely that they will be sharing the parenting of their stepchildren who primarily live in the household, while their own children, who may or not visit the household, are living with their mother, the previous partner of the stepfather.

Research in US (Clingempeel, Brand and Segal 1987) found that the quality of their marital relationship influenced the quality of the stepfather's relationship with both their stepsons and stepdaughters. Another study suggests that the relationship of stepfathers with their stepchildren was not adversely affected by the children's contact with their father (Furstenberg and Spanier 1984).

Hetherington's (1987) comprehensive longitudinal study of parenting found that for children living in mother custody households after the divorce the stepfathers' relationship with stepsons improved over time, but that the relationship with their stepdaughters continued to be characterised by negative behaviour despite positive attempts by stepfathers. Because of the heightened sexual activity within new stepfamilies there are also increased sexual phantasies, including the fears and the possibilities of stepfathers becoming perpetrators (see Chapter 7, 'Physical and sexual child abuse in stepfamilies', page 149).

Stepmother households

In stepmother households, the quality of the marital relationship was not found to be linked to the quality of the stepmothers' relationship with their stepdaughters, though it was to their relationship with their stepsons (Clingempeel et al. 1987). Another study (Santrock, Warshak and Elliott (1982) compared boys and girls from intact families with those in stepmother households where fathers had remarried following divorce, and found that the boys were less affectionate with their fathers, and that the girls showed less self-esteem than those in intact families. Despite the fact that many of the stepmothers had undertaken a good deal of the caretaking and had made consistent attempts to build relationships with their stepchildren, stepmothers felt less involved with their stepchildren in a number of important areas. In general the negative view of their relationship by both stepchildren and stepmothers may well be linked to their attachment to their biological fathers, which would inevitably be closer than that to their stepmothers (Santrock and Sitterle 1987).

Parenting in stepfamilies

Hetherington (1987) was able to distinguish four types of parenting styles, *permissive, disengaged, authoritarian and authoritative.* The most frequent style of parenting for all mothers (except those who are divorced and have sons) is authoritative parenting, which is characterised by warm involvement, low conflict and maturity demands. In contrast, while stepfathers' authoritative parenting increases over time, this decreases with girls and is increasingly likely to become disengaged. The stepchildren's perspective will be considered in Chapter 8, as will the research which is based on data collected from more than one stepfamily member, which therefore gives a more systemic view of stepfamily life (see Chapter 11, 'Single-parent households', page 246, and 'Remarriage/cohabitation', page 247).

THE STEPFAMILY LIFE CYCLE

Many writers on the stepfamily take a developmental life-cycle approach (see Robinson 1980, Carter and McGoldrick 1980, Wald 1981, Sager et al. 1983, Mills 1984, Papernow 1984 and Visher and Visher 1988), either comparing and contrasting the stages of the nuclear family life cycle with those of the stepfamily (Wald and Sager et al.), or focusing on the dislocation of the family life cycle and the formation of the stepfamily as requiring additional developmental tasks and an extension of the life cycle of the nuclear family, before the transformed family can resume functioning as a 'good enough family' (Carter and McGoldrick, Robinson and Papernow). Terkelson (1980) (see Chapter 2, 'The development of behaviour which is problematic for the family', page 34, and Chapter 1, 'The hierarchy of needs', page 243) distinguishes between normative life crises and paranormative crises, such as divorce (and presumably also remarriage), which require second-order changes in the family structure and functioning in order to restore family functioning. (Second-order changes in systems are those which result in 'changes in the body of rules governing their structure or internal order' (Watzlawick, Weakland and Fisch 1974).

As with the family during divorce, the developing stepfamily life cycle can be distinguished by various phases, each with their own emotional tasks related to the process of transition, and the second-order changes which it is necessary to achieve before the stepfamily can move to the next phase. Like the stages of the divorce process these transitions are not discrete, and the interactions which bring them about are circular rather than linear and need to be worked and reworked at several levels simultaneously. There are thirteen phases in all which encompass the whole process of family transformation during divorce and subsequent remarriage. There are seven which relate to the stepfamily life cycle: new beginnings; efforts at assimilation; awareness; restructuring; action; integrating; and resolution.

The major task throughout the development of the stepfamily system is the recognition and acceptance that the stepfamily is not a nuclear family and that attempts to try to function as a relatively closed system, as most nuclear families do, are likely to be doomed to failure.

Phase	Emotional process of transition of couple	Second-order changes required in family status to proceed developmentally
7 New beginnings	Recognition of myths and phantasies about step-families	Recognition of need for co-parenting while resolving emotional divorce Recognition that parent–child bond precedes that of remarriage
8 Efforts at assimilation	Allowing time and space for stepparent and stepchildren to develop their own relationships	Recognition of grief, jealousy and loyalty conflicts from loss of original intact family system
9 Awareness	Reaffirming generational and household boundaries	Recognition of key and position and authority of biological parent Recognition of remarriage and place of stepparent
10 Restructuring	Mobilisation and airing of difficulties	Acceptance by re-formed extended family that changes are necessary for stepfamily to become functional
11 Action	Beginning to work together	The creation of new rules, rituals and boundaries which are achieved through renegotiations throughout re-formed extended family network
12 Integrating	Achieving contact and intimacy in stepfamily	The stepparent achieves a unique role which does not compete or usurp roles of biological parents, is accepted throughout the re-formed extended

(Continued)

Phase	Emotional process of transition of couple	Second-order changes required in family status to proceed developmentally
		family network and sanctioned by rest of stepfamily, especially the spouse Roles include generational boundaries between stepparent and children
13 Resolution Becoming a binuclear family	Holding on and letting go	Relinquishing the last hopes of living like a nuclear family Accepting interrupted parenting and family life Ability to negotiate family rituals and changes of access and custody

Note: This figure only shows the transformation of a two-generation nuclear family during the divorce process and does not focus on the complexities of the family life spiral, which would reveal the fluctuations of closeness and distance with the extended families, which are typical of families at the key points of transition of the family life cycle and at times of crisis such as divorce and remarriage.

Source: Developed from Papernow (1984)

Figure 6.1 The stepfamily life cycle: family transformation during remarriage

NEW BEGINNINGS

One of the earliest tasks of the couple contemplating remarriage is to recognise the myths and phantasies about stepfamilies. It has already been indicated, as Robinson (1980), Maddox (1975), Smith (1990) and others have described, that there are many myths and folk tales which depict the stepfamily as cruel and unhappy and which Freud and others considered as rationalised versions of deeply held unconscious phantasies. Stepmothers in folklore (as, for example, in the stories of Snow White and Cinderella) are believed to be envious and wickedly cruel, and stepfathers are often seen as sexually rapacious and/or cruel (as, for example, Humbert Humbert in Nabokov's novel *Lolita*).

However, there is also a more up-to-date modern mythology and some current phantasies which are prevalently associated with step-families, and which need to be recognised and even dispelled by the remarried couple of biological parent and stepparent. One such common phantasy is that of *instant love*. Parents who remarry often believe that because they have chosen and love each other, the children of one or both parents will automatically feel the same, although this is usually far from the case. Another aspect of this frequently held phantasy is the fear of the separated or divorced single parent, that the stepparent will steal the love of their children who will in turn reject them. According to Papernow (1984), there is a further and complementary phantasy to this belief which is that the *children must be rescued* from the inadequacies or excesses of the previous spouse, who is also one of their biological parents.

Much, if not most, family law is based on the premise that the welfare of children is paramount; but perhaps at least partly because of the adversarial nature of the legal system, when there is a conflict over custody this allows the articulation of such rationalisations in the form of affidavits presented to the court. Whether or not they are found to be substantiated, the affidavits can serve to reinforce the phantasies which often underlie the accusations. The presence of these powerful phantasies of instant love and of rescuing the children have been expressed by many authors: Shulman (1972, 1981), Visher and Visher (1979, 1988), Robinson (1980), Goldstein (1987). On the other hand, as research shows (Wallerstein and Kelly 1980, Walczak with Burns 1984, Mitchell 1983, 1985 and Smith 1990), the hopes of the children are often quite different. Younger children, particularly, believe that if they are good or bad enough their parents will get back together again, while older children may attempt in a variety of ways to dislodge the new and unwanted stepparent.

As has already been indicated, a third phantasy, which is almost universally held (see, for instance, the first section of this chapter and Sager et al. (1983) in 'The supra family system', page 117) is that the purpose of the stepfamily is to *become the same as that of the nuclear family*, and it is this phantasy that encourages unrealisable expectations, as well as adding to the conflicts between biological parents whose children may be members of stepfamilies. The characteristics of stepfamilies already outlined above clearly indicate that such a phantasy, which is often reinforced by the interventionist professions, is not only unrealisable, but if unrecognised can also be destructive to the stepfamily (see 'Unrealistic expectations', page 154).

At the beginning stage of stepfamily life the adults in the re-formed extended family may fail to recognise that, while they may have completed the psychological aspects of the ending of the marriage, the remarriage has plunged the family into a further transition and there is a need for further work on the co-parenting aspects of their relationship, as well as that of the parent and stepparent. It will be apparent that many formerly married couples have not completed their emotional divorce prior to remarriage, so that developing a co-parental relationship becomes even more problematic. For the step-parent in remarried families it is not always easy to recognise, let alone accept, that the bond of the children with their custodial parent pre-dates their own marital relationship with their remarried spouse. This is often the cause of jealousy and misunderstanding, as the stepparent's own uncertainties can be exacerbated by the stepfamily in a situation where relationships are still tenuous and as yet undefined. Re-formed stepfamilies are also un-formed during the early stages, and indeed may never fully complete the stages of becoming a stepfamily.

The Chigwell family (continued)

As soon as his divorce was made absolute, Charles married Corinne, who, though she had previously been married, had never had children. Charles did not tell Tricia he had remarried and Debbie, Annabel and Colin (now 7, 5 and 3) at their next access visit to their father discovered that they had a stepmother. Although they had met Corinne once or twice, she had usually been away when they spent the weekend with their father. It was therefore a shock when they discovered that Corinne not only shared their father's bed, but was now also his wife.

Debbie, who was very close to her mother, was very angry and would have nothing to do with either her father or Corinne, despite their attempts to reach her. Corinne and Charles sat on the sofa together with Charles's arm around her shoulder, and Corinne tried to entice Annabel with the offer to read her a story. Annabel, who was learning to read, was initially fascinated and then, remembering Snow White (as she told her mother later), suddenly looked from Corinne to her father with wide eyes, pulling abruptly away. Their father remonstrated with the girl and Corinne, hurt and puzzled, turned her attention to Colin, who accepted her offer to sit on her lap. That evening, when their father put the girls to bed he tried to explain to them that Corinne loved them and they must love her as he did. Corinne put Colin to bed, but did not know he wore a diaper at night, and he woke in the night screaming as he had wet his bed.

When the children returned to their mother next day, confused and upset about Corinne's sudden change of role, Tricia, who had done her best to maintain the children's attachments to their father, was shocked, hurt, angry and fearful that Corinne, who was many years younger than herself, would steal the children's affection from her. When Annabel asked whether her mother liked Corinne and was she now going to be their stepmother, Tricia angrily said that Corinne had stolen their father from them, and would never be their mother. Annabel repeated this to Debbie, who was able to ask her mother why she was so angry with Daddy and Corinne. Tricia was by now in control of herself and able to explain to Debbie, that though she did not like Corinne herself, she was indeed their stepmother and that not all of them were necessarily wicked and cruel. Debbie said sadly, 'But if you are the Mummie Duck and if you don't like her, because we are your baby ducks we have to follow you, or we won't find our way across the pond (i.e. we must like you).'

Corinne's lack of experience in relating to children irritated Charles, and during the subsequent access weekends he was often exasperated with her ineptness, which frequently resulted in her retiring to bed with migraine. It was many years before she and the children were able to have a mutually rewarding relationship.

The part-time stepfamily of Charles and Corinne Chigwell reveal some of the clinical findings of Carter and McGoldrick (1980), Sager et al. (1983) and others. Corinne's youth and the fact that she had not been a parent led to difficulties for Charles and herself. The fact that there was a short interval between divorce and remarriage as well as the expectation that the children would automatically take to Corinne led to an exacerbation of the difficulties. Charles's failure to inform his former wife not only deprived Corinne and himself of her possible support, but also made it difficult for her to help their children with their confusion and distress.

EFFORTS AT ASSIMILATION

Stepfamilies need time for the biological parent to reinforce and also to adapt their relationships with their children, at the same time allowing space for the stepparent and stepchildren to begin to form their own attachment. Jealousies are the predominant problem at this stage of the stepfamily life cycle. The stepparent, especially if he or she has not previously been married, becomes jealous of the biological parents' relationship with their children. Even if they have children of their own, husbands may be jealous that their wife has her children living with them, and guilt-ridden and grief-stricken that their own are still living with their mother. The parent with whom the children do not live is both jealous of the custodial parent and the stepparent. The children also are jealous of their biological parent's new relationship and fearful that they may be excluded. Thus the differing jealousies of all the stepfamily members not infrequently cover the deep uncertainties around the changes that these new and developing relationships might bring.

Amongst the findings of Duberman's study (1975) of eighty-eight remarried couples, were the following: that family integration was better if the new spouse had been divorced, rather than had been a bachelor; and that men who had left their own children behind on remarriage related less well to their stepchildren than bachelors. She also found that all the parent–child relationships were better when the wife's children of her first marriage remained with her, and that they were best when the extended family approved of the remarriage and worst when the extended family cut off or were indifferent.

As already indicated (see page 123) Hetherington's (1987) longitudinal and comparative study found that in the first two years of marriage both authoritative and authoritarian parenting by the stepfather led to high rates of behaviour problems in both stepsons and stepdaughters in the first two years of remarriage. After two years, authoritative parenting by stepfathers related to fewer problems in stepsons, though not in stepdaughters.

This early stage of stepfamily life can be compared with a rules roundabout relating to family patterns of behaviour. The biological parent – perhaps particularly the custodial parent – and children already have a belief system about 'this family' which has its own established patterns of behaviour and communication which they are attempting as far as possible to maintain. A stepparent, who has not shared the previous family history and is at a different stage of their own life cycle, may try to join the roundabout, but finds himself or herself out of phase. This may lead to what Sager et al. (1983) describe as the *conflict of multiple tracks*. The custodial parent and children are attempting to continue on their shared track, the stepparent is doing likewise, but it is a different track, while the newly remarried couple are only beginning to build their own new, shared track. Many conflicts which arise can quite simply be explained by this useful concept, though resolving them takes longer and involves honest and open communication and tolerant understanding.

The developing stepfamily will also be carrying unresolved emotional baggage; Carter and McGoldrick (1980) distinguish three sets of such carry-overs: from the family of origin, from the first marriage and from the process of divorce and the period between the two marriages. Another factor, the sheer complexity resulting from the numbers of relationships within stepfamilies, is considerable. Indeed, Visher and Visher (1979) gave a striking demonstration of this by pointing out that in a nuclear family of two parents and two children and four grandparents, there are twenty-eight pairs and 247 different combinations; in a remarriage of one of these parents with a new partner who has three children, there will be 136 pairs and 131,054 combinations!

The lack of guidelines about the role of stepparent adds to the tension and confusion. What kind of role should the stepparent try to play, and where should he or she look for guidelines? Draughon (1975) discusses the possible roles for stepmothers – as, perhaps, primary mother (where the first marriage has ended in the death of the parent, or the child joined the stepfamily very young and is not in contact with the biological mother) or 'other mother', or 'friend'. Guidelines and suggestions for stepfathers are (perhaps significantly) absent (though see Chapter 11 for gender issues). There may be some similarities between stepfamilies and foster families with a view to adoption, at least as regards the role which the stepparent might attempt to adopt. While both adoptive parents choose the child whom they adopt with the intention of becoming legal and psychological parents, stepparents have chosen only one parent of their stepchildren, not the children themselves who come 'as a job lot' with their biological parent. Nevertheless, some stepparents can hope to become a sort of aunt or uncle who is special to their stepchildren if the stepfamily life cycle allows for functional development. Mills (1984) points out that the future goals in the stepfamily need careful discussion and clarification, perhaps realism should also be added. Papernow (1984) indicates (as the above example shows) that moves made by the stepparent towards the children of their spouse will often induce a loyalty conflict for them. The children and their biological parents have a mutual loyalty to one another consisting of consanguinity and family lineage, as well as 'earned merit' (Boszormenyi Nagy and Spark 1973); but probably this also serves to remind them of their as yet unresolved grief over the loss of their original nuclear family.

The Greenwich family

Nick and his wife Sarah had a stormy marriage and broke up soon after their daughter Nicola was born. Sarah, a teacher, took a job in a residential community and formed a relationship with Stephen, a colleague who was also somewhat vulnerable. She had three further children, eventually marrying him. Nicola hardly saw her biological father after she was 3 years old, and though he paid maintenance and eventually also school fees, he did not maintain a steady contact with her. Nick formed a long-standing relationship with a colleague Bridget, whom he eventually married, though not until much later.

At the age of 11, when secondary education was being considered for Nicola, Nick became more involved with the planning for her future as he was deeply concerned about her progress. Nicola was very angry with her father, but as a developing adolescent intrigued to know him better. Bridget, herself the child of divorced parents, understood something of the tensions and conflicts of stepfamilies, and encouraged Nick to meet Nicola and negotiate with Sarah, while keeping well in the background herself. Nicola began to trust her common-law stepmother, and was 14 by the time of their marriage. Apparently coincidentally, at the time of their wedding there was a big family row between Nicola, her mother and stepfather, and also between her mother and father. This was partly over her adolescent struggles, but also partly because her mother and stepfather had decided to move to another community which was far away from Nicola's school, from her friends and from where she had spent most of her life. At another level this row, which rippled throughout the re-formed extended family system, was another stage of the long-standing battle between Nicola's parents. This family conflict eventually resulted in Sarah agreeing that Nicola could spend her holidays with Nick and Bridget, who would try to find a more suitable school for her. Bridget and Nicola explored a number of schools, for which Nick agreed to pay, and eventually Nicola went to a school within reach of her father and stepmother.

The Greenwich family shows a binuclear reassembled stepfamily in which Nicola became a casualty of the re-formed family system when she became adolescent, although both her biological parents had long since re-established themselves, her mother in a nuclear family with her second husband and their children, and her father with his new wife as a childless couple.

AWARENESS

At this stage, biological parents have two major tasks: the need to reaffirm the generational boundaries, and to recognise the boundaries between the households. For some children in step-families, particularly eldest children and those who are adolescent, they have occupied a semi-adult or even parental role in the period between the breakdown of the first marriage and the remarriage. It may become necessary for their biological parent to find ways of helping them to accept that they are still children without the responsibilities and privileges of adulthood. As the majority of families post-divorce are mother-custody families, it is often the advent of a stepfather potentially disturbing the privileged position of the oldest son, who may have become established as a kind of surrogate father or even husband to his mother and who now experiences the arrival of a stepfather as displacing him. Daughters, on the other hand, may have had more responsibility and power in the single-parent household and find this even more difficult to give up (Hetherington 1987). Something similar, but with the roles reversed, can also happen in a father-custody household, although for the daughter this has often included some aspects as a replacement wife.

In stepfamilies where the children are regular or occasional visitors to the remarried parent, there is less likelihood of the generational boundaries being breached in such a semi-permanent manner, as the parent and stepparent can revert to developing their relatively new spousal roles *vis-à-vis* one another between visits of the stepchildren. Nevertheless, as research and clinical practice shows, the parent–stepparent relationship is the newest and most vulnerable relationship in the transformed extended family system. Unless the remarried couple allow themselves time and support to enhance their mutuality, attempts by the children of the natural parent(s) may make inroads into their compatibility with each other. It is often only at this stage that the stepfamily members begin to recognise that a stepfamily is not a nuclear family, and perhaps may never be able to become one. This may be particularly difficult for the stepparent who has not yet become a parent, as she or he may begin to realise that even if they do have children with their new spouse, the chances are that they will not be able to (or feel they should not) have several children, as they might well have done had their spouse not previously been married. Indeed, it is often the stepparent who has tried and failed to join in the implicit family rules of the ongoing and now partial segment of the previous nuclear family, who first recognises either that the family is stuck, or that changes are beginning to happen which are denied or unrecognised.

The boundaries also need redefinition and recognition by adults and children alike, as the stepfamily household is usually only part of the re-formed extended family. According to Pasley (1987), remarried families are characterised by subjectively determined rather than socially determined boundaries. In most nuclear families there is a congruence between physical and psychological presence in the family, while in stepfamilies this is not usually the case, the nonresident parent often being psychologically, though not physically, present in the stepfamily household. As Mills (1984) points out, outstanding problems between the ex-partners can lead the stepfamily to locate their dissatisfactions outside their own household, focusing on what may be unresolvable issues, rather than concentrating on those between themselves for which solutions might be found. Research findings (Wallerstein and Kelly 1980, and Hetherington, Cox and Cox 1978, Pasley and Ihinger-Tallman 1987) found that after a period of destabilisation, usually about two years (though often longer and for some embittered chaotic families apparently this never occurred) and according to their age and stage of development, children can begin to manage to divide their time between two separate households. However, this will be impeded or enhanced according to the ability of the adults to recognise and support the rules of the other household, while they are beginning to develop their own different rules.

Failure to resolve the conflicts related to relationship issues which belong to the first marriage are likely to lead to difficulties for the whole extended family system in transition. Some families deal with these difficulties by trying both to draw and close the boundaries around one household system and to attempt to command loyalty to developing the cohesiveness in the new family (Carter and McGoldrick 1980). While some attempt to exclude, or even disqualify, the place of the natural parent and/or combat the influence of the grand-parents, others try to infiltrate the new stepfamily, either directly or by using the children as go-betweens or spies, which leads to even greater loyalty conflicts and bitterness.

The Hartlepool family

Douglas Hartlepool, a farmer, and his wife Doris lived on the family farm, and their three children grew up used to having plenty of space and their own animals, which to some extent helped to shield them from their parents' long-standing unhappiness. When Sheila, Naomi and Jonathan were in their early adolescence (14, 12 and 11), Douglas met a widow about his own age who also had two adolescent children, Derek and Diana, and eventually moved in with her, returning daily to his work on the farm.

After a good deal of conflict prior to the divorce, Doris and the children moved to a new house nearby, and Douglas, now re-married to Diana, moved into the farm with her children. The legal proceedings were protracted – particularly the financial arrange-ments for maintenance – and the children, who were very angry with their father, were very aware of their mother's distress and anxiety about money matters. Douglas, who was very guilty but also concerned about his former wife and children having to leave their family home, kept the children's animals, encouraging them to visit whenever they could.

The children themselves found it very painful to visit their old home, now occupied by their father and stepmother, stepbrother and stepsister, and with Doris's collusion, blamed Diana for the break-up. Doris, while overtly encouraging her children to visit the farm, subtly undermined the arrangements in Douglas's stepfamily – as, for instance, by asking about changes of room use and also confusing arrangements so that the children would arrive when they were not expected and their father was extremely busy about the farm. Diana herself, a forthright woman, became very angry with her stepchildren when her new husband became upset and on one occasion, when they 'forgot' his birthday, gave them a piece of her mind. This led to Naomi, by then 14, refusing to visit, and her brother and sister scapegoating her. Douglas, who was by now also very angry with Doris whose sabotage he recognised, reacted by becoming more rigid in his expectations of what he considered were the poor standards of his children's behaviour and, to his great distress, became in danger of losing touch with them altogether.

The Hartlepool family, three years after the divorce and Douglas's immediate remarriage, were still having considerable difficulty in reaffirming the household boundaries, and neither of the parents were sufficiently able to reconcile their own feelings about ending their marriage to give recognition to the importance of the other parent for their children.

These three early stages of the stepfamily cycle of development

(Papernow 1984) may need reworking, especially if the stepfamily have tried to rush the process. In describing such process in relation to stepmothers, Smith (1990) stresses that gentleness and understanding is needed, especially in letting go of the myths and phantasies which subsequently may be looked back on with embarrassment.

7 Becoming a stepfamily

Getting it together

Round and round the circle
Completing the charm
So the knot be unknotted
The cross be uncrossed
The crooked be made straight
And the curse be ended.
                    T. S. Eliot (1888–1965), 'The Family Reunion'

If we offend, it is with our good will.
That you should think we come not to offend
But with good will. To show our simple skill,
That is the true beginning of our end.
    William Shakespeare (1564–1616), *A Midsummer Night's Dream*

RESTRUCTURING

The stage of restructuring is heralded by the recognition, often first by the stepparent, that it is necessary for some changes to occur in the stepfamily. The stepparent begins to try to initiate such changes, sometimes through a series of confrontations with their spouse. Stepfathers tend to try to establish rules about discipline, those who have not previously been fathers seeing this as a way to find a role in the stepfamily, while those who have left their own children often feel guilty about not being a full-time father to them and try to compensate by being a firm father figure to their stepchildren. Stepmothers, on the other hand, tend to try too hard and too soon to develop affectionate relationships with their stepchildren and, when they fail to do so, blame themselves, become depressed and may ultimately seek help (usually) for themselves.

While stepchildren may well be beginning to develop affectional bonds with their stepparent, the conflict of loyalties which may result for them is often unrecognised by parent and stepparent alike. These confrontations may lead to problems arising between the parent and stepparent, who will need to explore their differences together. The struggles among themselves may result in their attempting together both to distinguish and express the difficulties that are occurring, and they may well confront the rest of the family with their view that things have to change, if they are to get along with one another in ways which sufficiently accommodate to each of their individual needs. Frequently this also involves open communication with the former spouse about the impact of possible or even proposed changes on their life.

Restructuring entails confronting where the power lies in the re-formed extended family. Who is really responsible for decision-making, and how can they set up structures which can promote the possibility of negotiation between them, and which also allow other family members to be consulted? It means making stepfamily rules about discipline, disagreements, expression of hostility and affection as well as household rules about division of labour, manners and other behaviour. Because of the ambiguous boundaries of the system it is necessary to clarify who are the members of which family and how they might try to relate to others in the re-formed extended family system.

There are also issues with regard to space and time. In many stepfamilies living space is at a premium and the advent of step-children, or half siblings from the now remarried parents impinge on what are often regarded as the territorial rights of the children of the first partnership. This may be exacerbated by a change in a child's ordinal position; for instance, by the acquisition of an older or younger stepbrother or stepsister, thus changing their place in the family from oldest or youngest child. Another factor is the management of time. By now, the remarried parent and stepparent's relationship may be sufficiently established and secure enough for them to recognise and allow the biological parent to give some individualised time to their children from the previous marriage, and this can allow the stepparent time for their own pursuits. It becomes clear that the stepfamily needs to be much more flexible over the issues of such boundaries, as these can rarely become fully stabilised, and must contract and expand according to the custodial and access arrangements.

Attitudes towards sexuality can be a problem, and what is known as the 'incest boundary' needs recognition, careful discussion and negotiation (see also 'Physical and sexual child abuse in stepfamilies', page 149). For many families, particularly those with young children, parents and children bathe together, or the children join their parents in bed. Indeed, during periods of stress, including that of the divorce process, children often may sleep in the parental bed. In families where there are adolescent children, particularly in stepfather families, or where there are adolescent stepsiblings, the heightened sexual ambience of the new partnership, or the arrival of a nubile teenager, may cause sexual tensions for the young people. In many families who become stepfamilies at the time of the adolescence of the children, this can lead to some difficulties, as sexual attraction between stepfather and stepdaughters or between stepsons and stepdaughters are confronted. In other stepfamilies where the natural children and stepchildren have grown up together, this is likely to be less of a problem.

The Ilford family

Henry and Louise Ilford had recently married. Louise's first marriage had ended in divorce some years previously and she had brought up her two sons and two daughters primarily on her own. Her first husband, Leonard, had had a schizophrenic breakdown early in their marriage and had spent many years in and out of psychiatric hospital. After taking him back many times, she eventually decided to divorce him in order to give her attention to her children who, she felt, were being neglected.

Henry's first marriage had ended abruptly when his wife committed suicide, leaving him with three young children whom he brought up single-handed, but with a good deal of support from his elderly parents. By the time Louise and Henry met, her children Jonathan, James, Nancy and Angela, were aged 24, 20, 18 and 16. The boys were away from home in higher education, Jonathan studying medicine, though James was not doing well in his first year at technical college and was threatening to leave and travel to the Far East. Nancy was supposed to be taking her A levels, but had become involved with a crowd of youngsters on the edge of the world of drugs, and Angela was taking her O levels.

Henry's children were also young adults. His eldest son, Mark, was 20 and at Oxbridge with an academic career before him; Alison, 19, was an art student in London; and Georgina was 17 and in her first year at the local sixth-form college.

Neither Henry nor Louise had been happy in their first marriages and their new relationship was particularly precious to them both.

As they each had a house, they decided to move into Louise's house together and allow the 'children' in various permutations to be organised by the stepsiblings themselves, to live in Henry's former home, which was in London. The 'children' showed their resentment of their parents' remarriage, first by exploiting them in what was, in effect, typically adolescent behaviour, either by not managing their finances properly or in skirmishes with the law, which Henry and Louise found particularly shameful as they were trying to re-establish their social position in their town. Second, the 'children' began to engage in what was effectively a game of 'whispers', in which the objective seemed to be the sabotage of the remarriage of their parent.

In desperation Henry and Louise sought help from a family therapist who stressed their right to have a happy remarriage, and offered to see whichever of the children cared to come. Two of the children did so, and one sent a message to which the therapist responded with a message. Effectively, these sessions redefined the boundaries between the parents and their own children, encouraged the 'children' to leave home and get on with their own lives, free to choose with which of their stepbrothers and sisters they would engage in relationship, and demonstrated as well that their parents also had the right to theirs!

Both Henry and Louise had spent a number of years as single parents, as neither of their previous partners had taken an active spousal or parental role during the last years of their first marriages. For them remarriage had allowed them marital fulfilment for the first time, yet it seemed to them that this was apparently at the cost of their relationships with their children, which grieved them considerably. While there can be little doubt that some of their parent–child relationships were distorted as the result of the unhappiness of their first family relationships, some of the behaviour of the 'children' was clearly a mixture of difficulties about leaving home, coupled with their very natural resentment at losing the almost total commitment of their parent and the experience of sharing them, not only with their stepparent, but also with stepbrothers and sisters. As will be discussed below, the remarriage of parents when the children are in late adolescence or young adults presents them both with the dilemma and a choice as to how much they want to be part of the new stepfamily, and how much they want to be free and independent.

ACTION

This stage might also be described as taking steps through which the remarried couple together begin to explore workable solutions. As Papernow (1984) points out, some of the old ways of interacting are likely to be preserved, but new ones are added so that new rules and boundaries are negotiated with firmness and clarity.

At this stage of stepfamily development the most frequent continuing conflict between the former partners is usually over custody and access for their children. Burgoyne and Clark (1984) found that it was frequently the stepparent who seemed most resentful of the intrusion of the noncustodial parent into their family life. They describe three separate 'solutions' which the families found in order to resolve these conflicts. In families where the first marriage has ended acrimoniously and the couple have not had the opportunity to make some shared sense of what has happened to them, they are increasingly unlikely to be able to resolve their difficulties sufficiently to be able to begin to develop a cooperative relationship, the result being that the noncustodial parent finally withdraws. In other families, particularly where there are practical difficulties, usually because of distance, then the boundaries which become drawn around the developing stepfamily are accompanied by the gradual withdrawal of the noncustodial parent. The third solution is the development of flexible access arrangements which allow the noncustodial parents to remain in active contact with their children.

The changes which are necessary in the developing re-formed extended family system require the recognition of the key position of both biological parents as well as the recognition, if not the actual acceptance, of the remarriage, and that a place must be found for the stepparent. The implication of the relatively open boundaries between the binuclear family households is that the children have to learn to move between two sets of family belief systems and patterns of communication and behaviour. At this stage the differences between the two sets of rules can be openly recognised and stated. Providing that this overt recognition of the differences is stated with clarity and without covert or actual criticism of the other parent, it has been found that most children can tolerate and eventually move comfortably enough between the two households. As will be discussed (in Chapter 8), it is particularly painful to children to hear their biological parent criticised by their parent and stepparent, as this not only places them in a conflict of loyalties but also leads them to deny what is (in effect) a part of themselves. Young children, particularly, are quick to recognise that behaviour tolerated in one household – as, for instance, rules about bedtimes – will not be tolerated in the other. If these are clearly and neutrally made explicit, after a period of testing out, they will learn to accept (and even enjoy!) the differences. Ephron (1988) gives an amusing and delightful account of her developing relationship with her stepchildren, which starts with her battling to get them out of an empty fountain in an attempt to establish her right to discipline them.

This issue of discipline is often the one which provokes the necessity to review the conflicts which are developing between the two different sets of family rules. In addition to indicating the need for negotiation between the remarried couple, it may also lead to a renegotiation between the formerly married spouses, and even members of the extended family, such as grandparents. It has been found that until the stepparent and stepchildren have been able to begin to build their own unique relationship, disciplinary matters are if possible best left to the biological parent. As will be discussed (in Chapter 11), recent work by Carter (1987) and others has shown that stepfamilies are in fact leading the way in the renegotiation of gender roles within families.

At the present time most stepfamilies are either those living in households in which the children primarily spend their time, or those in which they are visiting children. Although most young children can adapt to having two homes, it is more difficult, both psychologically and often economically also, for the parents to do so. It is therefore easy to slip into describing some stepfamilies as custodial stepfamilies and others as part-time or visiting stepfamilies. There are multiple subsystem combinations of children from prior unions in the stepfamily, ranging from all his or her children living full-time in the family, some of his or her children living and some visiting, through to all the children of both parents living elsewhere (Wald 1981).

It is often as difficult for those who try to help stepfamilies consistently to recognise the necessity to think in terms of open and extended re-formed family systems as it is for stepfamilies themselves. It is therefore useful for those in the interventionist professions who are trying to help stepfamilies to try to ascertain from the stepfamily members who are their clients those whom they perceive as being inside the family unit, and those whom they regard as outside. Perhaps the single major developmental task in becoming a stepfamily is to accept that such a family can never become a nuclear family and therefore cannot operate like one. The challenge therefore is for each family to work out its own goals, which are relevant to the stage of the family life cycle of parents and children and are likely to be a compromise between those of the parent and stepparent and the biological parents and children.

The Jarrow/Kingston family

Linda Jarrow had married very young and against the wishes of her parents, who did not like Dave, the brash Londoner who had already been in trouble. The young couple had nowhere to live for the first two years of their marriage, but when Alan was born, moved into a council flat. Alan was the first grandchild and Linda was very involved with her family.

The marriage deteriorated and Dave eventually left. Though he wanted to return, Linda, encouraged by her mother and sisters, refused. Dave became increasingly desperate and reacted in the only way he knew how, by getting into trouble, so as to bring in the authorities who had helped in the past. Alas, this was not to be, and the result was a legal injunction to prevent him from molesting his separated wife. Furthermore, there was also defined access to Alan, whom Dave could only see at his maternal grandparents, and they soon froze Dave out of their home. The couple were divorced, and some five years later both remarried.

Linda never talked with Alan about his father, and when he was 8, she met and and married Brian Kingston, who had not previously been married, and she told Alan that Brian was his father. As the child of a serving soldier Brian had spent much of his childhood on various overseas postings and he set out to make a friend of Alan, which Linda encouraged. During all this time, Dave Jarrow, who had also remarried, continued to send maintenance for Alan, and though Dave heard news of him through various mutual acquaintances he never saw him.

When Alan was 11, Brian and Linda, who by now also had a daughter of their own, applied to adopt him. They had already (illegally) changed his name to Kingston. Among the many implications of the adoption application was a social worker's visit to Dave and his wife Diane. It became apparent that Dave and his new family had always considered that Alan was a part of their family (albeit only in phantasy) and that Dave particularly had hoped that one day his son would be returned to him. Linda, on the other hand, was quite clear that Alan was the son of Brian and herself and that the adoption order would merely legalise this. The social worker found that Alan had only the vaguest memories of his father (he thought he had a beard) and found it most difficult to challenge his mother's wishes.

Linda was very angry with the social worker, but Brian intervened and began to talk to Alan about his 'born father', gently distinguishing the two roles for him. Alan's asthma suddenly worsened and he had several disturbed nights, in which his stepfather comforted him. Dave himself began to accept that Alan would be most upset by being transplanted from one family to another, but reassured by Diane, hoped when Alan was old enough he might one day choose to visit them. The adoption order was granted.

The Jarrow/Kingston story demonstrates how unresolved difficulties arising from the failure of a marriage were exacerbated by the failure to resolve the outstanding difficulties over parenting. The family situation was further complicated because of the denial by mother and her family that another parent existed at all, which led to considerable distress for the whole re-formed extended family when the invocation of the law attempted to resolve the past.

INTEGRATING

The stages of stepfamily development are of course not discrete, but are attempts to distinguish the necessary preoccupations of the family as the stepfamily develops. At first contacts are re-established between biological parent and children within a family system, which now also includes a stepparent who is attempting to make contact with the stepchildren; by the stage of integration as a stepfamily, the whole family is working as a system in order to face the challenges and solve the problems of day-to-day family life. By now at various levels the belief systems within the family will have been changing, as will the rules which accompany such second order change. The premises on which stepfamily life is based will have altered, and a new family scenario of day-to-day living will have developed, which in turn will have led to new family rules, patterns and behaviour.

As Hetherington (1987) concludes from her research with remarried mother/stepfather households,

the best strategy of the stepfather in gaining acceptance of the stepchildren seems to be one where there is no initial active attempt to take over and try to actively shape and control the child's behaviour either through authoritarian or the more desirable authoritative techniques. Instead, the new father should first work at establishing a relationship with the children and support the mother in her parenting.

Some of the examples described above show how the stepparent (see Mrs Greenwich, page 133, and Mr Kingston, page 144) delicately and carefully began to engage their stepchild in a relationship which was unique to the two of them, rather than attempting to impose one as a given right, merely because they had married the child's biological parent. When at a later stage a crisis threatened to overwhelm the family, it was the stepparent who was able to support the biological parent and child and thus maintain the delicate balance which had been achieved. This is the stage of integration in the stepfamily, one in which, contact having been achieved, the relationship can develop into family intimacy, albeit of a different kind from that of a family who have grown up together. In chronological and historical terms the stepfamily is always younger than the stepchildren but can provide an alternative which allows the biological parents some freedom from parenting, and the children a different model of family life.

According to Papernow (1984), the time needed for the stepfamily to manage the early stages and move through the two middle stages of restructuring and action towards the final stage of integration is from two to five years, if the children are young at the time of the remarriage. A useful rough guide for a custodial stepparent is that of the chronological age of the child plus the length of the remarriage (Mills 1984). It is not easy to postulate the length of time it will take for latency age children, as so much will depend on the children's attachment to their biological parents, the quality and consistency of parenting prior to the divorce, and the parents' ability to resolve their conflicts relating to their children. For adolescent children, because this is a period of differentiation and sexual development it is not unlikely that the 'ordinary' difficulties of leaving home may be exacerbated in the stepfamily. Yet stepfamilies need to remind themselves that many nuclear families go through a period of difficulty at the time the children are preparing to leave home. It is no accident that most of the previous examples of stepfamilies are those with adolescent children who came for help because unresolved difficulties from divorce or remarriage related to the age of the children at the time the stepfamily formed. Indeed, it is these families which Burgoyne and Clark (1984) describe as 'not really stepfamilies'. Nevertheless, because stepfamilies are such complex systems it is not easy to predict which stepfamilies will develop difficulties during the adolescence of the stepchildren.

The stepparent role is a unique one, which should neither compete with, nor usurp, the role of the biological parents. If this is accepted throughout the re-formed and extended family system and sanctioned within the stepfamily, then the stepparent may also take a mediating role when tensions threaten to break into conflict either between biological parent and children, or between biological parents. While stepparents can develop true and intimate friendships with their stepchildren, it can become confusing if in so doing the boundaries between parent and children are breached. In some ways stepparents are damned if they try to behave as if they are biological parents, thus competing with the natural parents, and damned if they become such an intimate friend that the generational boundary is breached and the stepmother or stepfather becomes enmeshed with the children against the parental coalition. These are the Scylla and Charybdis roles which have to be carefully negotiated and maintained by and within the stepfamily.

There are, however, rewards associated with stepparenting (Ihinger-Tallman and Pasley 1987). One major benefit is that, providing the parents have a sufficiently cooperative relationship, then the burdens of parenting can be shared with the 'other' subsystem of the re-formed extended family system. This not only gives both parents and each household some respite, but it also brings greater objectivity into the whole system than is usually possible for the biological parents to achieve. A stepparent who is able to take a more detached perspective and remain impartial at times of crisis can often provide an alternative view which is impossible for other family members because of their own (often stormy) family history, which often results in a partiality towards a particular perspective. A stepparent who is able to develop a deep friendship with a stepchild is given the opportunity to become a source of support or even a mediator between that child and his or her natural parent, though, as earlier indicated, the generation boundaries need to be maintained. In addition, a stepparent can often bring into the family new knowledge skills and ideas from their own experience and background, as for instance in education or in the arts. Finally, when a child, after divorce, has the choice of living in two households, she or he not only has an alternative residence as a back-up, but also alternative models of adulthood, of relations and behaviour between partners and of models of parenting.

RESOLUTION: BECOMING A RE-FORMED FAMILY

The stage of resolution is one which is rarely reached during the childhood of the stepchildren. If the stepfamily's stages of development are consonant with those of the stepchildren, and the other stages have been completed sufficiently for the family to have been 'good enough', there are a number of possibilities. As has already been indicated, in a number of families the 'other' biological parent may have dropped out of the family picture, but this has been accepted and resolved, so that there are no secrets which cannot be discussed. Other stepfamilies will be only loosely in touch, through occasional regular or irregular meetings, perhaps for family rituals, which are compatible with other interactions of the extended family. For families which have come together during later stages of the family life cycle of the children and the original nuclear family, they may have achieved sufficient intimacy and closeness so as to allow changes of access and even custody and where the whole binuclear family system functions with mutual acceptance and respect. This final stage of stepfamily life, in which the children are reaching the stage of young adults, is best described as holding on and letting go (Papernow 1984).

Most extended families have regular rituals, when there are family meetings to reinforce bonding and renew the sense of family solidarity, whether for formal family festivals such as Christmas, or for those which recognise and mark the stages of the family life cycle – christenings, bar mitzvahs, weddings and funerals and so on. During the years, the stepfamilies will have been struggling to find their own place in these rituals, perhaps at first being excluded altogether, perhaps facing the fact that only some part of the binuclear family is recognised by other segments of the extended family. While stepfamilies who reach resolution have by now gained sufficient solidarity to stand together and attend such festivals as a system in their own right (whomever they consider that might include), they also face regrets which are unique to them. Stepfamilies at this stage invariably have the feeling that they are still seeking to find some 'nuclear intimacy', which as yet seems elusive, or they are facing the real regret that it will now never be realised. While all families experience regrets and sadness when negotiating the departure of the children, for stepfamilies this implies poignant reminders of the early times and family history which were not shared and now can never be. For many stepfamilies this is the final realisation that they are not, never have been, and cannot now be a nuclear family, and this means relinquishing a dream, which most of us nurture however secretly, and which is implicitly (if not explicitly) encouraged by societal attitudes towards families.

PHYSICAL AND SEXUAL CHILD ABUSE IN STEPFAMILIES

It is only within the last decade or so that Western society has begun to accept and begin to confront the realisation that there are many people who use their power as adults to involve children in sexual activities which they neither understand nor to which they are capable of giving informed consent; and which through force, threat or deceit they are required to keep secret. The area of child sexual abuse is relevant to the study of divorce and remarriage, and the sexual abuse of children by stepfathers or mother's cohabitees seems to give expression to one of the deepest anxieties of society.

Whereas on the one hand it is likely that as the result of their mother's divorce many children will have been removed from long-term paternal abuse, others, as the result of the increase in the divorce rate and the further couplings, will have been exposed to the possibility of abuse from their mother's lovers and from stepfathers. It is difficult accurately to gauge the exact incidence of child sexual abuse which occurs within stepfamilies, as the findings seem contradictory; though many of the incidence studies single out sexual abuse by stepparents as a distinguishable group, the prevalence studies often refer to intrafamilial abuse, which includes male members of the households, thus including fathers, stepfathers and male cohabitees as one group. However, one of the leading US researchers in this field points to the risks (Finkelhor 1984, 1986), particularly for girls in families with a stepfather; his latest figures indicate that having a stepfather increases the risk factor by 6 or 7 times.

Although the findings of the Cleveland Inquiry (1988) as well as research into child sexual abuse have shown a significant proportion of such abuse, particularly in relation to girls, as having been committed by a stepfather (or cohabitee), a recent review of the research (La Fontaine 1988) on child sexual abuse indicates that girls and boys are abused (by fathers and stepfathers or cohabitees) more or less equally. The Leeds study of Hobbs (1989) of children referred to the hospital's paediatric department shows that, of the 237 children who were found to have been abused, 31 per cent were abused by their natural fathers but only 4.5 per cent by their stepfathers or mother's cohabitee, while 19 per cent were abused by perpetrators who were unrelated and 10 per cent by brothers. The

1987 figures from the NSPCC's research register of child abuse found that only 40 per cent of the registered children were living with their natural parents, while 26 per cent were living with their natural mother and a father substitute. The person suspected of abusing the child was recorded for over 90 per cent of the injured and sexually and emotionally abused children. Stepfathers and male cohabitees were implicated in 19 per cent of the injury cases, 3 per cent of the emotional abuse and 24 per cent of the sexual abuse cases. Nevertheless, these figures are considerably lower than those for natural fathers (35 per cent for physical abuse, 61 per cent for emotional abuse and 33 per cent for sexual abuse cases), or for brothers and other relatives (5 per cent of the injury and 31 per cent of the sexual abuse cases).

It is becoming clear from all the research of incidence of child sexual abuse that there is likely to be an underestimate of its true extent, and it is also therefore not unlikely that occurrence in stepfamilies is also an underestimate, and it is a possibility that should be considered, especially in medical settings where a young child presents with sexualised behaviour, and in adolescence with apparently poor self-esteem, running away, anorexia, self-injury and/or genital symptoms such as soreness, bleeding, discharge or pains. As the result of this deeply distressing discovery and the resulting questions and moral issues which have been raised there has been a rapid development of research which it is not possible to cover here, and readers are referred to authors such as Finkelhor (1984, 1986), Bentovim et al. (1988), Glaser and Frosh (1988) and many others.

At a recent conference on child sexual abuse, Finkelhor (1988) speculated on the importance of the factor of gender socialisation for men, who are more likely to abuse children sexually than women. In the first place, he commented that in Western society we tend to deprive young boys of the emotional and physical expression of affection; and it is only later in adolescence and early adulthood that they can express this in sexual relationships, through which they also try to get their other emotional needs met. Men carry this emotional baggage into adulthood and therefore find it more difficult to relate with children, who are open in their needs for affection and evoke the desire to be close and intimate. For men, therefore, expression of affection and closeness can be accompanied by a sexual connotation and discomfort. Many men realise this and can manage to put it aside; and while some men deal with this discomfort by distancing themselves, for others these feelings and phantasies tend to become overwhelming and they become involved in sexualising relationships with children.

Second, Finkelhor distinguished what he described as the 'sexualisation of subordination', in which children are part of what he called the 'attraction gradient'. Whereas women are socialised into regarding those older, larger and stronger as attractive, men are socialised into regarding the young, small and weaker than themselves as attractive. Finkelhor considers this is more than just having the power; it is also eroticised and, as well as other unequal power relationships, such as those between boss and employee, it can also relate to the eroticisation of children, thus leading to sexualisation of the relationship.

Third, men tend to be exempted from intimate care and responsibilities for children and therefore have some difficulty in empathising with children. Some recent research (Parker and Parker 1986) has shown that incestuous fathers are more likely to have been out of households during the children's early years and therefore much less likely to have spent time in the actual care-giving to their children. There is some biosocial theory that intimate care, such as the tactile contact with the skin of a young child or the need to take care of the child's genitalia, inoculates and thus prevents parents from finding their children sexually attractive. Among those men, including stepfathers, who generally have not been involved in the child's early years, and thus have not been 'inoculated', some may be eager to get rid of the emotional baggage of their childhood through eroticisation of their relationships with children, which then can lead to attempts at sexual gratification.

FACTORS PROGNOSTIC OF PROBLEM DEVELOPMENT IN STEPFAMILIES

Research and clinical experience indicate that some aspects of stepfamily life are particularly problematic (Carter and McGoldrick 1980, Robinson 1980, Sager et al. 1983, Finkelhor 1984, 1986, and others). Some of these are unresolved mourning from the original nuclear family, structural aspects, boundary issues (including those of sexuality), wide discrepancies between the binuclear family life cycles and unrealistic expectations.

Unresolved mourning issues from the original family

In many stepfamilies the parent and stepparent remarry or cohabit, and set up home together very quickly after divorce. Such a short interval allows little time for the family members of the re-formed family even to begin the necessary processes of mourning, let alone complete them. There are several strands which tend to stem from failure to grieve for the loss of the original nuclear family.

The first strand of mourning relates to the children. For instance, it is known that many children do not give up their hopeful phantasies that their parents will get together again until one of them remarries, and it is only then that they begin to grieve for the loss of the original nuclear family. Many parents and stepparents, perhaps because of their own attitudes and hopes for the future, expect that the children will accept the remarriage. Their failure to recognise that the remarriage may cause some emotional difficulties for the children is likely to lead to difficulties within the parent–child relationship as well as delay in bonding to the stepparent. In some stepfamilies the parent and stepparent may even deny that such a loss has occurred, and this prevents the open acknowledgement of grief within the stepfamily.

The second strand of mourning, relating to the natural parent, is the failure to resolve intense relationship issues from the first family. Most divorcing spouses attempt to manage their disillusionment, pain about rejection and damaged self-esteem by blaming their previous partner, at least in the initial stages of divorce. If relationship issues such as intense anger which appropriately belong within the first family are not resolved, then they will be taken into the stepfamily where they may become reinforced by the new partner and thus become entrenched and less likely to be accessible to resolution.

A third strand is the attitude of the stepparent towards the need for the rest of the stepfamily to grieve for the loss of the original nuclear family, for although it will continue to exist, the family of the future will be in a new form; it will never again be the nuclear family it once was.

Structure

Many remarried partners, in order to protect the vulnerability of their own relationship as well as the development of the new stepfamily, attempt to draw boundaries around the stepfamily household. Their aim in doing so is usually an attempt to promote the cohesiveness of the new family, as well as trying to ensure that the primary loyalty is to the stepfamily. This may well result in the exclusion of the other natural (nonresidential) parent, which not only arouses their distress and anger, but also results in increasing the loyalty conflicts for the children.

Another aspect of structural difficulties which may occur is when there is a change in the custody of the children near the time of the remarriage. In this case, at the same time as the couple are beginning to create their own partnership together and work out their rules for managing their separateness and togetherness, a child who, at the very least, is likely to be distressed, joins their household. The stepfamily will then be struggling to create a couple relationship, develop some household rules which are comfortable for them, and simultaneously cope with all the implications of becoming a stepfamily which have already been discussed.

In some stepfamilies the parent and stepparent also attempt to exclude the grandparents in an attempt to combat their influence, which arouses their distress and also their ire, with resultant repercussions throughout the extended family system. This may be so particularly in families where the grandparents have been considerably involved in care-giving for the children between the break-up of the first marriage and the remarriage.

Wide discrepancies between life-cycle stages of the binuclear family

In many stepfamilies, but particularly in those in which it is the father who remarries, the father is likely to choose a partner who is some years younger than himself. While some stepmothers may already be mothers (as they are in combination stepfamilies), others are not, and may indeed have not previously been married or cohabited within a committed partnership, as in reassembled stepfamilies. This may mean that not only are they living in the close proximity of a spousal relationship for the first time, but they are simultaneously moving into a family system where they are also for the first time expected to become part of the parental generation. Even in combination stepfamilies, where both partners have children from previous marriages, the children of one partner may be adolescent, while those of the other may still be prepubescent. Similarly with stepfather families, while custodial mothers may marry younger men (and there is some evidence that this is increasing), it is very likely that the stepfathers, even if they have already been married, will not have yet been fathers, or if they have, they may not have been part of a nuclear family household for some time as the remarried mothers have been; so that, they too may be required to move into a role in the stepfamily unit which will be novel to them.

Thus the essential features of the conflicting family life cycles are that the stepparent may not only move into a new and different role, but simultaneously move into a stage of the life cycle of which they have not yet had any experience. Such a double move is often confusing enough for the spousal couple, who may or may not recognise this, but in families with adolescent children it can also be particularly difficult for them to have a stepparent who may be more or less their own age (as was shown in the case illustrations of the Bexley family, the second Mrs Chigwell and the Greenwich family, although Mrs Greenwich, who was older, was able to use her own experience as a child in a stepfamily).

Permeability of generational and sexual boundaries

Many of the difficulties which seem all too frequently to result when the life cycles of stepfamilies conflict are the result of the general uncertainty regarding the role of the stepparent together with the additional lack of experience of a particular stage of the life cycle. The fact that this is often unrecognised adds further confusion. Some stepparents eventually resolve this difficulty by developing a real friendship with their stepchildren; however, if this fails to include the recognition (as with Mrs Greenwich) that the parents are of a different generation and will at times need to stand together with their spouse and act in a disciplinary role, then at such times their stepchild is likely to feel a betrayal of friendship. Some of the researchers on child sexual abuse (see Finkelhor 1984, 1986, 1988 and others, and 'Physical and sexual child abuse in stepfamilies', page 000) postulate that it may be at least partly the stepfather's lack of paternal experience, particularly the intimate care which fathers give to their very young children, which leads to the breaching of the incest boundary which results from child sexual abuse. Finkelhor also speculated that some of the extra-familial child sexual abuse in stepfamilies results from the friendship network which such stepfathers introduce to the family, who, because of the loosening of the incest boundary, also may not regard the stepchildren of their friend as 'out of bounds'.

Unrealistic expectations

It has already been made clear that stepfamilies cannot expect to become the same as nuclear families, and yet many of the functions of stepfamilies are the same, perhaps particularly those of need fulfilment. The urge to creativity through becoming parents is both biological and psychological, as is the desire to perpetuate our own lineage. From our earliest years, both within our families of origin, in school, through the media and indeed, politically, this expectation is impressed upon us, so it is therefore not surprising that it is the hope to recreate a nuclear family which includes stepchildren which is often the hardest to give up. Indeed, it is what might be described as the parental wishful thinking (albeit unconscious), which allows stepparents not only to take on such an onerous task in the first place, and take their place as partners alongside their spouses who are already parents, but which also sustains them through many of the disillusioning early days as a stepparent. Parents in nuclear families too are gradually confronted with the loss of a similar phantasy of the idealised nuclear family as they grapple with the hard work which parenthood entails for most of us.

However, for most stepfamilies much of the disillusionment is accompanied by the realisation that such gratifications of parenthood which can be realised cannot be limited to the stepfamily alone. It is not surprising that many stepfamilies, when consistently disappointed, deny that families are different and, at the same time are struggling against all the odds to maintain their illusion that they are or can become a nuclear family, and one which makes stepfamily life even harder than it might otherwise be. Although the ambivalent attitudes of society towards stepfamilies are gradually diminishing, not infrequently they also serve to reinforce and compound such denials. However, Chapter 11 summarises some of the current empirical and clinical research which is based on the perspectives of more than just one stepfamily member, and offers some guidelines which attempt to provide some support as well as offering some realistic goals for 'good enough' stepfamilies.

8 Children during divorce and remarriage

O body swayed to music, O brightening glance,
How can we know the dancer from the dance?
> W. B. Yeats (1865–1939), 'Among School Children', VIII

Be near me when my light is low,
When the blood creeps, and the nerves prick
And tingle; and the heart is sick,
And all the wheels of Being slow.
> Alfred Lord Tennyson (1809–92), 'In Memoriam A.H.H.'

A systemic approach to families during divorce and remarriage essentially allows a focus on the whole family interactional system during the processes of transition and change, rather than emphasising the effects on the individual members as elements of the system in transition, although these are not necessarily precluded. Beals (1979) considers that the concept of emotional attachment is a cornerstone of family systems perspective, and points out that compensatory mechanisms maintain the balance of emotional forces in the family; and he instances physical and emotional distance, or emotional conflict between individuals, and child focus. He argues that children in child-focused families, whose parents are considerably emotionally invested in them, are highly relationship-oriented and less task-oriented, and are therefore likely to have more difficulty in coping with parental divorce or separation.

This chapter, therefore, while considering divorce and remarriage as they generally affect children in greater detail, will also pay particular attention to how these relate to age and stage of development of the child. The likely effects of divorce on the children need to be taken into account in any decision-making, whether it is by parents themselves, the interventive professionals whose task it is to advise or help them, or by the courts, which may ultimately called upon to be the final arbiters. It will be therefore be apparent that because of the societal responsibilities to protect children, however these might be embodied in the legislation, it is necessary to consider the process of transition during divorce and remarriage from the perspective of the individual child. In Chapter 11, on the 'good enough re-formed extended family', the focus will return to the family systems approach in which the child is perceived as part of the interacting stepfamily.

CHILD-CENTRED PERCEPTIONS OF SEPARATION AND DIVORCE

There is now a good deal of child-centred research in relation to divorce, particularly from the United States, and, while I am not undertaking a comprehensive review of the research literature, I shall make a selective attempt to summarise and present some of the findings of academic and clinical research projects so as to highlight some of the issues. (For a full review of the US studies, see Hodges 1986 and Emery 1988, who includes some of the UK studies in his review.)

One of the earlier US studies was conducted by Jacobson (1978), who studied thirty families of fifty-one children ranging from ages 3 to 17, all of whose parents had separated during the twelve-month period prior to the first research interview. This study found that an important aspect of child adjustment is the amount of interparent hostility to which the child has been exposed. In Wallerstein and Kelly's (1980) well-documented research, the data – which were obtained from sixty families, including 161 children who attended a mental health centre in California, by clinical interviews at one year, four years and ten years after the separation (Wallerstein 1984) and (with Blakeslee, 1989) – revealed that the most distressed children were those who became the focus of their parents' conflict. At the one-year follow-up, nearly half the preschool group and over one-third of the latency children either were still showing dysfunctional behaviour or had deteriorated, while none had had any previous psychological or psychiatric difficulties.

Richards and Dyson (1982), in their earlier review of the research on the effects of divorce on the development of preschool children (2.5 – 6 years) conclude that young children are frightened and confused and often blame themselves for what is happening. With the irrefutable logic of the very young, they reason that if one parent can leave them, so can the other! They have a great need for physical contact and often express fears of being sent away or replaced. Only the older children are able to express their feelings and have some conceptual ability to comprehend the divorce-related changes which occur. The small but significant UK study of Lund and Riley (1984) of thirty custodial parents and children, which found that those who do best are those whose parents have a harmonious co-parental relationship and who have regular access to their noncustodial parent, seems to confirm this view.

However, in a recent and important US study, the authors, Isaacs, Leon and Donohue (1987), point out that much of the research on the effects of divorce on the adjustment of children has been based on data collection from families who have requested counselling for their children (thus a skewed sample), and then the findings have been generalised to *all* separating families. They studied approximately 100 families, of whom half had requested counselling and the other half had agreed only to take part in the research project. The cohort of children were drawn from a wide age range (4–16), and consisted of twenty-two boys and twenty-seven girls, of whom 27 per cent were white and 27 per cent black. The children were given standardised tests of adjustment and the results were compared. The parents of the group of requestors (that is, those who requested counselling) had been separated on an average of 5.8 months, while that of the nonrequestors was 8.3 months. Although the findings were similar to those of other similar research projects which indicated the likelihood of post-separation emotional or behavioural problems for the children, there was no indication that clinical levels of disturbance predominated; indeed, these were only slightly more than would be expected in any randomly chosen normal group. Comparing the findings between the two groups led the authors to question the assumption that those children whose parents sought counselling for them are representative of all children of divorcing parents, although they were more likely to be rated towards the clinical extremes of maladjustment than the children of those parents who had not. As the authors themselves point out, while they did not find the levels of adjustment to be related either to the child's age or sex, other studies are needed which examine a different age range, or which rely upon more qualitative measures.

Recent research has also begun to explore children's perceptions of their parents' divorce. In the US Kurdek and Siesky (1980), in open-ended interviews with 132 white children (aged 5–19) found that the nature of their responses consistently related to the age and level of both locus of control and interpersonal knowledge, which therefore significantly influenced their perceptions of their parents' divorce. They found that the older children were more likely to react less negatively to the news of divorce; to be given a two-sided explanation of the divorce; to define the divorce in terms of emotional separation; to view the parents' separation as final; and to share this news with friends. They were also more likely to possess perceptions of both parents which were realistically based combinations of negative and positive attributes; to report the absence of parental conflict as a beneficial outcome of divorce as well as qualitative improvement in their interactions with noncustodial parents; and to acquire strengths and responsibilities as the result of the divorce.

Isaacs, Leon and Kline (1987), also in the US, investigated 200 children from joint custody, mother custody or father custody families through the use of the Draw-a-Family test, and found that joint custody, frequent visitation (access visits) and the child's perception that the parents get along well make it less likely that the child will omit the nonresident parent from the family drawing. As they point out, the findings of Wallerstein and Kelly (1980) indicate that noncustodial parents are more likely to withdraw from their children if they have no legal responsibilities for their care; and that the children themselves often take this as a sign of rejection. Isaacs et al. also quote Leupnitz (1982), who argues that children in joint custody arrangements maintain *filial* relationships with both parents, while children in sole custody arrangements are more likely to develop *avuncular* relationships with the noncustodial parent. They conclude that their findings indicate that the child's definition as to who is in the family is a realistic assessment of who is responsible for major aspects of the child's life, and also a reflection of the divorcing relationship between the parents.

Similarly, in the UK McGurk and Glashan (1987) studied (through doll play) the perceptions of continuity of parenting of 314 children (aged 4–14) following divorce. They identified three levels of understanding: unquestioned assertion of the inviolate nature of parenting; belief that the continuity of parenthood following divorce was conditional upon the place of residence, positive affection towards the children involved, or subsequent marital status; and recognition of the permanence of parental relationships, accompanied by differentiation of relationship and role. Children whose parents were known to be divorced tended to show more mature levels of understanding than children from intact nuclear families. They concluded that the experience of divorce gives the realisation even among the youngest children that a parent may need to live outside the family home and that affectional bonds can be maintained.

A retrospective study by Walczak and Burns (1984) describes their conversations with 100 adults whose parents had separated before they reached the age of 18. These revealed the poor communication between them and their parents about the whole process of divorce, including custody and access decisions, financial hardships, and even their parents' remarriages, as well as their lack of contact with professional helpers.

Saposnek (1983), a psychologist, therapist and mediator of child custody disputes in the United States, poignantly describes in an empirical study the strategies which children may innocently adopt, but which make a functional contribution to the custody dispute. He distinguishes a number of these, those of younger children which are often aimed at reuniting the parents; such as becoming ill, or regressing to earlier levels of behaviour, or attempting to reduce parental distress, by becoming distressed themselves at the beginning or end of access visits. Some children will offer themselves as a scapegoat in order to absorb the hostility between parents, while others (at least temporarily) will withdraw from the relationship with one parent out of loyalty to the other, with whom the child may ally in order to prove it. Some children, in an attempt to attract the attention of parents who are emotionally unavailable, will try to test their parents' love for them. Such emotional withdrawal and/or physical absence frightens some children sufficiently to sacrifice their loyalty to one parent, by taking part in the marital conflict. Other children, who are aware of the fragility of their parents' self-esteem will, out of empathy or for their own self-survival, hide their own feelings, and their parents assume they are not upset, or are sufficiently resilient to recover fairly quickly.

Kelly (1987) and others describe the role reversal of children of 9 upwards who themselves become a nurturing parent in an attempt to protect their own parent. She considers that unless this goes on for too long, it is not necessarily damaging for the child. It is the disorganisation of the two-parent structure which is the major crisis for children, who are often both unprepared and anyway have no experience of divorce. This will also apply to those who have witnessed violence, though those in conflictual families may well be relieved. Those children who come from well-knit and functioning families, perhaps because their parents have protected them from their own difficulties, are uncomprehending as well as deeply shocked. Indeed, on the whole children are not told about their parents' reason for divorce.

Chethik, Dolin, Davies, Lohr and Darrow (1987) in the US

explored the effect on the normal developmental processes of identification of children when a parent leaves, and describe what they call 'negative identification'. They distinguish internalisation by the child as a defence against the sadness of the loss, against the anxiety of helplessness, as warding off threatening aspects of the self, and as a defence against abandonment. They also describe the child as 'splitting' (not necessarily the primitive splitting described by psychoanalytic theory), whereby in order to keep the absent parent alive the child idealises them, partly to serve a defensive function, but partly because there is no opportunity for the reality testing which results from the normal frustrations of day-to-day living. Parents going through divorce often polarise and exaggerate their differences, and this derogation of the other parent may come to symbolise them negatively and therefore become gender-linked. Parents may also give similar negative descriptions both to their child and about them, perhaps out of empathic concern for them, but also sometimes out of displaced rage at the other parent.

In their recent US study of eighty families referred by the courts because of a divorce transition impasse, Johnston and Campbell (1988) interviewed 100 children (fifty boys and fifty girls) whose parents had been separated on average for two years, and they followed them up over two years. As well as individual counselling sessions followed by mediation, they undertook direct play sessions with the children over a brief period with the aim of maintaining attachments to both parents, despite the conflict between them. They estimated that one-fifth of the families resolved their impasse, forming 'beneficial, rather than vicious cycles of interaction' through which the layers of impasse were able to be unravelled; while for two-fifths, although the resolution was less than optimal, there was a marked improvement. However, for the remaining two-fifths, there was almost no improvement and there remained severe conflict; indeed, for 15 per cent of the total sample this had deteriorated into ever-increasing new or renewed accusations of abuse, neglect or sexual molestation.

These results as well as empirical experience show the need to try to discover not only the children's perceptions of divorce, but also those relating to post-divorce parenting. More research needs to be undertaken in order to reveal how far these perceptions are age- and stage- or gender-related and when changes in perception are likely to occur over time. Such discoveries might point the way to the most appropriate time for preventive interventions, or family life educational projects in schools, both of which are sadly lacking at present (see Wallerstein and Kelly 1980, Mitchell 1985, Isaacs et al. 1986, Johnston and Campbell (1988) and many others).

YOUNG CHILDREN

Some of the research discussed above covers a wide age range of children, including the very young (Wallerstein and Kelly 1980, Kurdek and Siesky 1980, McGurk and Glashan 1987, Isaacs et al. 1987, Johnston and Campbell 1988, and Wallerstein 1989), although it is not specifically related to them. Young children have little awareness of family relationships and tend to seek secure relationships in the immediate family situation. In their US study, Hetherington et al. (1979) compared forty-eight white, middle-class preschool children from divorced families with a group of forty-eight children from nondivorced families who were studied at two months, one year and two years following the divorce. Shortly after the divorce their patterns of play were less socially and cognitively mature, and by one year, while both boys and girls showed high rates of dependent help-seeking behaviour and acting-out behaviour which was noncompliant, this lasted longer in the boys. At the first year post-divorce, they found disruptions in play and social relationships for both boys and girls. However, by two years post-divorce, most of these had disappeared for girls, though not for boys, and especially if their parents could sufficiently manage their own anxieties.

The research sample of Wallerstein and Kelly (1980) included thirty-four pre-school children and confirmed the findings of Hetherington et al. in which the children showed regression in toilet training, a possessiveness of toys, and an increase in sleep problems and aggressive and acute separation anxieties. The children's play was constricted and characterised by aimlessness and desperate searching in which they attempted to fit objects together. Their research confirmed the findings of the longitudinal study of Hetherington et al. Kelly (1986) concludes that the major symptom which appears in young children is separation anxiety, but considers that the compartmentalisation of their lives can be managed. However, Wallerstein's ten-year follow-up found that almost half the children 'entered adulthood as worried, underachieving, self-deprecating and sometimes angry young men and women' (with Blakeslee, 1989; see also 'Long-term outcome and conclusions', page 169).

Guidubaldi et al. (1983) studied the predictive significance of divorced and intact family status of all the 115 kindergarten children entering one school system (Ohio, USA) who were given an extensive battery of tests. The families of the children were generally representative of the lower middle class, and the 23 per cent of the sample came from single-parent households which were the result of divorce. The results of the study provided evidence that children from homes where the parents had divorced enter school with significantly less academic and social competence than those of intact families, and that single-parent status and socio-economic status variables were demonstrated to be more powerful and consistent predictors of competence than other family background and health development. The young children in Johnston and Campbell's (1988) study experienced considerable separation anxiety and were found to be multi-symptomatic during the periods of transition from the house of one parent to the other. Many of them witnessed the verbal and physical aggression between their parents and often became passive weapons in the dispute; for example, being withheld from access if maintenance was not paid.

In the UK Hildebrand (1986), drawing on her clinical experience of working with the families of young children who were seen at a children's hospital, identifies the common stress symptoms of increased illness and aggression, management problems, anxiety and regression, as well as the failure to thrive which had led to the referral. She points out the emotional effects of marital breakdown which lead to changes in the emotional climate, loss, experience of overprotection and the tendency for the children to become pawns in the battles of their parents.

The importance of the family home for young children is indicated by Stirtzinger's (1987) small, comparative US study of preschool children (aged 3.6–6). From the results she formed the hypotheses that the family home may provide for the retention of a transitional representation of family structure which allows the child both to store memories of past love and at the same time to develop and organise new ways in which they will now experience to both parents.

Wallerstein's most recent work (1989) reveals a disturbing feature for the subsequent relationships for children whose parents had a violent relationship, but who experienced no violence from the age of 6. While 26 per cent of them had observed violence between their parents during marriage, 57 per cent had not done so subsequent to their separation. Although many of these mothers (as the usual custodial parent) had subsequently remarried, had other partnerships or remained on their own, they seemed to have transformed themselves and their lives, yet many of their children had not. These children, now adult themselves, had apparently retained the image of violence, as half were involved in violent relationships themselves, the boys as perpetrators and the girls as victims (though see 'Long-term outcome and conclusions', page 169).

CHILDREN OF SCHOOL AGE TO ADOLESCENCE

The seminal study of Wallerstein and Kelly (1980) again provides important knowledge in understanding children of school age, who they found fell into two groups – the younger latency children (aged 7–8) and the pre-adolescent children (aged 9–12). The younger children predominantly expressed feelings of sadness and abandonment. The children found it difficult to express their anger to their departed father, and they entertained phantasies, often in secret, that their parents would reconcile. They were fearful of expressing anger towards their custodial mother and showed divided loyalties, even when their parents were not pressing them to take sides.

The older children demonstrated surprising poise and courage when they were seen, and their soberness and apparent clarity of thought was in stark contrast to the younger children, who frequently appeared immobilised by their grief. In attempting to overcome their humiliating powerlessness these children seemed galvanised into activity, through which they tried to manage their feelings. Perhaps the most striking feeling from this group was their capacity to express and direct their anger. The researchers point out that children of this stage need parental figures, not only for protection and nurture but also in order to consolidate their age-appropriate identification. Another important feature was the children's vulnerability to being swept up into the anger of one parent against the other, and they were often battle allies with one parent (usually the mother) against the other, even though they might have been very close with that parent prior to the separation. A finding which they found surprising was that a significant number of the boys of this age, at the five-year follow up, had remained as angry as they had been just after the separation.

A comparative US study by Hess and Camera (1979) of two groups of children (aged 9–11) from sixteen intact families and sixteen divorced families whose parents had been separated for two to three years, measured the relationship between the family processes and child outcomes. Their results led them to conclude tentatively that the study of family processes indicate the results of the effects of divorce more clearly than the establishment of differences. They also concluded that the family relationships which emerge affect the children as much or more than the divorce itself, that the relationship of the children to their parents is more significant than the level of parental discord; and that their relationship to the noncustodial father is of equal importance to their well-being and distinct from that with the custodial mother. A nationwide US longitudinal study was carried out by Guidubaldi and Perry (1984, 1985) on 699 children, six being selected at random in each grade, from first to fifth (that is, aged 7–12), one child from an intact family, one from a divorced, single-parent household. The study included a multi-method and multi-factorial approach to evaluating the cohort's intellectual, academic socio-behaviour and adaptive characteristics as well as those of their family and school environments. They found that on slightly more than one-third of the mental health measures, the children of divorce perform more poorly. These include more dependency, irrelevant talk, withdrawal, blaming and inattention and decreased work effort; and higher frequencies of inappropriate behaviour, unhappiness and maladjustment.

In her review of the research on children's adjustment to divorce Kelly (1988) mentions Zill's (1983) study of more than 2,000 children of 7–11, which, as well as finding that children of divorce experienced more loneliness and boredom, indicated that those in unhappily married families reported the most neglect and humiliation as compared with the children in happily married families and those in separated or divorced groups.

Much of the research on this pre-adolescent age group of children (Hess and Camera 1979, Wallerstein and Kelly 1980, and Guidubaldi and Perry 1985, as well as the self-reporting questionnaire study of Kaslow and Schwartz 1987) reveals gender differences as between boys and girls, maladjustment and aggressive behaviour, which seem to suggest that boys are more developmentally vulnerable than girls, particularly in the older age group. Warshak and Santrok (1983) attribute this to mother custody being more customary, though others (for instance, Hetherington 1987; Wallerstein and Kelly 1980; Kelly 1987) comment that there are gender differences in parenting, which provide less emotional support for boys.

Hetherington's (1987) comparative study of relations between parents and 10-year-old children in nuclear families, divorced families where the mother is the custodial parent, and remarried mother/stepfather families in which the children were also interviewed, shows some interesting findings. The boys in divorced families both recognised their own aggressive behaviour, which often led to antisocial behaviour that their mothers knew nothing about, and recognised that their mothers had little control over them, yet also demonstrated high levels of warmth towards them. The girls in divorced families, on the other hand, were assigned more responsibility and had more power; and for some, this, coupled with the tendency to mature earlier, led to more conflict with their mothers during adolescence.

In Johnston and Campbell's (1988) study of Californian families where custody and access had been the subject of litigation, and the children had been given continuing and fairly frequent access with both parents as the result of a court order, there were forty-four children of elementary school age. More than half of them also witnessed verbally and physically abusive incidents between their parents, although being more mature, they were often drawn into the disputes, either as support, or for comfort or reassurance for the emotional distress of one or both parents. But they were also often used to collect evidence or as spies or messengers carrying threats and insults to the other parent. The loyalty conflicts they suffered were considerable, making it difficult or even impossible to maintain a neutral or balanced position. Indeed Johnston and Campbell describe their experience of

> witnessing the birth of tricksters, reminiscent of those cultural folk heroes from myths who survive by dint of their astute social awareness, imagination, foresight, distance from, and manipulation of the system, [their] clinical judgement ... [being] that at higher levels of moral development ... these children looked like clever mediators or diplomats, [while] at lower levels ... we feared the early onset of antisocial tendencies in that some children aimed to get what they wanted without consideration or respect for others.

Richards and Dyson's (1982) summary, written before the latest research, showed the gender differences, indicated that the older schoolchildren had a more realistic understanding of separation, were more able to express feelings of intense anger and were often morally outraged by the behaviour of their parents. They frequently felt both rejected and lonely, and their loyalties were divided between their parents. The mechanisms used to manage these processes were age-appropriate.

ADOLESCENT CHILDREN

There are major difficulties in evaluating the effects of parental divorce on adolescents. First, it is necessary to make some assessment of their development prior to the separation and divorce; and second, it is hard to disentangle the divorce-specific reactions from those of normal adolescent differentiation and what are commonly described as 'leaving-home problems' (Haley 1980, and others). The US study of Kurdek and Siesky (1980), who conducted open-ended interviews with 132 children ranging in age from 10 to 19, resulted in three major findings. In the first place, the children's reactions were primarily negative and varied according to their developmental level. Second, the child's level of adjustment was affected in a large part by the functioning of the custodial parent, particularly during the first year post-divorce. Third, the adjustment of older children was related to the parent's ability to refrain from perceiving them as sources for meeting their own emotional needs.

Wallerstein and Kelly (1980) found that adolescent children often experienced pressure towards independence, though this was frequently accompanied by greater maturity and moral growth. Many were concerned about their sexuality and the possibility of their own marriage. Their relationships with their parents, which characteristically change during adolescence, often fluctuated wildly, exacerbated by perceptions of their parents as sexual persons, which they found embarrassing, and they sometimes felt deeply betrayed by their parents' own regression to somewhat adolescent behaviour, which resulted in heightened competition between them. Their loyalty conflicts were also frequently characterised by deep anger. Some adopted the policy of strategic withdrawal from the family, while for others relationships within the family sometimes swung between responsible overprotectiveness to frantic social overactivity.

In Scotland, Mitchell's (1983) retrospective research with seventy-one divorced parents and fifty of their adolescent children (twenty-eight boys and twenty-two girls) who, six years after the divorce, were aged from 16 to 18. Of the thirty-nine children who were able to describe their feelings, nineteen said they had been upset, six were relieved, three angry and three surprised, and the rest had mixed feelings. Ten children admitted they had wept, usually in secret, and five said that their school friends had seemed more upset than they were. The young people reported that while fifteen mothers were still single parents, twenty-nine had one new partner and four had had two or more, while two were now living with their divorced husbands. One in six had always liked the new partner, but one in four had never liked him, and this disliked partner was more likely to be living with the noncustodial parent. Mitchell, like many other researchers, comments on the the fact that the child was often left in limbo as regards the reasons for the separation, and while absent parents often failed to keep in touch, the custodial parents did little either to encourage access or to help the child maintain links with the past.

Wallerstein's ten-year (1984; Wallerstein and Blakeslee 1989) follow-up of the earlier study was stimulated by the findings of the five-year follow-up which focused attention on the anxiety of the young people as to their capacity to make and sustain a love relationship. She and Kelly had originally been struck by the intensity of feelings which had persisted, both as regards anger at the parent who had initiated the divorce and the longing for the parent who had departed or was only minimally in contact. Wallerstein herself had hypothesised that adolescence might offer the young people a positive opportunity for reworking and resolving the divorce experience. She was able to trace fifty-four of the sixty families from the original study (conducted with Kelly) and interviews carried out. Of the children 74 per cent were still in school (52 per cent in elementary and 22 per cent in junior school or university), while 22 per cent were working. Almost half of those who were 19 at the time of the follow-up were still in school or university and, apart from three young women (one of whom was married, and two others who were dependent on parents or boyfriends to support them), all the others were fully employed. Twelve had been arrested for serious delinquency, while twenty-two (the majority females) had engaged in minor delinquency. Several had married, five of them very young, one had been divorced and remarried. Ten young women had become pregnant, although only one, who married at 17, had children of her own, and eight elected to have abortions.

During the open-ended interviews it was apparent how often the young people had soberly reflected on their parents' divorce; and their memories were still vivid and fresh, particularly the sharp memory of their pain. Their predominant mood on looking backwards was one of regret and yearning, and restrained sadness; they seemed to have lost the experience of growing up within the nurturant protection which an intact family can provide and their predominant feelings about this were sorrow, resentment and a sense of deprivation. A significant group had continued to be angry with their parents for what they regarded as their irresponsibility or immorality. A small but significant number of young women who were either late adolescent or young adult seemed to be drifting from job to job and man to man. However, the sibling relationships proved to be a supportive network which had provided some of the nurturance of family relationships as well as actualising some lasting experiences of fidelity and intimacy.

The exploratory study of Kaslow and Schwartz (1987) of thirty-two respondents to a survey (by then aged 11–40), while echoing the findings of Wallerstein and Kelly, showed no clear patterns, though this might be related to the wide age range and personality differences. However, they did stress the importance of peer networks and demonstrated that not all older children of divorce were affected negatively.

LONG-TERM OUTCOME AND CONCLUSIONS

Wallerstein (1984) considers that it is the preschool children who are the most vulnerable group, while those who are adolescent are the second most vulnerable group. She found that whereas 34 per cent of the children whom she followed up had 'recovered' and resumed their developmental tasks five years subsequent to the divorce, 37 per cent had not. She concludes that although 50 per cent of the children were doing very well, 50 per cent were not doing well at all. In the latest follow-up (1989) she also discovered in young women entering adulthood a previously unrecognised phenomenon, which she describes as the 'sleeper effect'. Such girls apparently manage the divorce of their parents well and their development appears to be unimpaired; but at the time when they begin to make adult relationships with young men, fears of commitment, and other anxieties about making relationships, suddenly emerge and with crippling results.

Hetherington (1987), in common with other researchers (see Santrock and Warshak 1979; Santrock and Sitterle 1987) and following her comparative longitudinal study (1987) of mother custody families concludes that there is some evidence that following divorce the children may adjust better in the custody of the parent of the same sex. In her review of the research on the adjustment of children of divorce, Kelly (1988) points out that much of the literature has 'emphasised the pathology rather than adaptive coping; and that this has led many mental health practitioners to generalize these findings to the larger, normative divorcing population' which is heterogeneous. She stresses that high-conflict parents in families prior to a divorce may behave very differently towards their children; indeed, her own findings demonstrate that 'overall divorcing parents reported significantly less child-specific conflict than marital conflict, and significantly better cooperation at separation regarding their children than overall levels of cooperation'. There is converging evidence from long-term studies that, as compared with children in intact families, children of divorce experience more psychological, social and academic problems (see also Guidubaldi et al. 1983 and Hetherington et al. 1985). The research also indicates a stabilisation of behaviour over time, the boys externalising difficulties and the girls internalising them. She points out that almost all the research has been based on assessment of children in mother custody families where their access to their fathers is constrained by traditional arrangements.

For the children whose parents separate and later divorce, the central architectural structure of their family has collapsed, and with it a generally held belief that marriage is forever. But even this disaster is not all: their life script has been irrevocably changed, though not at their behest; and their relationships will never be the same again. As has been discussed above, the emotional development of children following the divorce of their parents will not only be affected by the age and stage of development which they had reached at the time of the *de facto* divorce, but also by the post-divorce relationship between their parents. There seems to be increasing evidence that boys and girls are differentially affected, the long-term effects on boys apparently being greater. Societal pressures and parenting of boys are influential factors, and while this is controversial, there is some evidence that lack of contact with the parent of the opposite sex does influence the sex role development.

Recent US research (Guidubaldi and Perry (1985)) has demonstrated that decreased conflict between former partners resulted in the better conduct, classroom behaviour and cognitive development of children, with several of the studies pointing to the effects on learning. The post-divorce adjustment of the custodial parent is clearly linked with the eventual outcome for the child; but the primary negative aspect is that of the loss of contact with the noncustodial parent. The influence of divorce on the social development of children, while also related to the age and stage of development and the influence of post-divorce parenting, seems to indicate that some children regain their social faculties, while others withdraw into semi-isolation.

Wallerstein's most recent retrospective study (1989), in which she interviewed at least one member of the fifty-two families from the earlier study (Wallerstein and Kelly 1980), including 110 children in families who had been divorced some ten years previously, has resulted in a storm of harshly critical reviews from many of those in family research (see Hetherington and Furstenburg 1989, and Kelly and Emery 1989). It is not difficult to see why this is the case, for in contrast with much of the previous research she concludes 'that divorce takes a far heavier toll on children's self image and their capacity to form satisfying male/female relationships than has previously been believed' (Nord 1989).

Her book, written with medical journalist Blakeslee (1989), makes vivid and moving reading, striking the chords of the painful experiences of many; yet as a research project it has been criticised in a number of ways. Among her main findings are that even years later, half the women and a third of the men are still immensely angry with their former spouses. Two-thirds of the girls, many of whom apparently initially adjusted well, are frightened of betrayal and unable to make lasting commitments, which she attributes to the 'sleeper effect' (although this is an attribution not uncommonly made of many young people today). Both spouses report satisfactory lives following the divorce in only 10 per cent of the families; and it is usually the spouse who initiated it who seems able to live a happier life. Some of the most serious criticisms are that in the first place, by building on the previous small, exploratory study, Wallerstein has built in some methodological problems, such as the self-selected sample and the lack of a baseline comparison group of children in intact families. Second, she is criticised for going beyond the evidence provided by the research data and 'delivering a sweeping and dire message' to the public at large, which is not always backed up by direct evidence (Hetherington and Furstenberg 1989). Nevertheless, some of Wallerstein's conclusions are certainly supported by Johnston and Campbell's families in the divorce impasse transition study who were referred by the courts, as the result of their inability to comply with the Californian law which requires that divorced parents who are in a custody dispute should attempt to mediate their differences.

However, the earlier conclusions of Wallerstein and Kelly (1980) distinguish seven criteria in which the divorce process seems to influence the long-term effects and outcome for their children. They are: the extent to which the parents are able to put aside and contain their own conflicts; the changes in parent–child relationships; the extent to which the child is able to continue a nonrejecting relationship with the noncustodial parent on a regular basis; the characteristics and personality of the child; their ability to turn to parents and others, and the availability of supportive people; and the sex and age of the child and the absence of continuing anger and depression.

Recent UK studies using the data from the Medical Research Council's National Study of Health and Development of 5,362

children born between 3 and 9 March 1946 (the most recent contact
of the depleted sample of 3,996 being when they were 36 years old)
examined the educational achievements of the men and women, now
in mid-life, whose parents had divorced twenty-one or more years
earlier (Maclean and Wadsworth 1988). Studies showed that among
those children whose parents had divorced before the age of 5,
an incidence of delinquency of both boys and girls, was twice as high
as normal (Wadsworth 1979). Further, by the age of 26, there was
also a higher rate of hospital admissions for emotional disturbance
and stomach ulcers. Wadsworth and Maclean found that among the
population of unemployed who were seeking work, parental divorce
may demonstrate an initial point in a future chain of vulnerability.
Poor educational attainment, chronic illness in adult life (in 17 per
cent), appeared to have a cumulative effect, rendering them insecure
and irregular workers at the lowest end of the employment range.

Leach's most recent research (forthcoming) seems to confirm the
long-term findings of Wallerstein (1989); her longitudinal study
followed up children born in the same week in 1970, and found that
none of the children wanted their parents to separate, even those
whose parents abused them. These children were less likely to do well
at school and more likely to become juvenile offenders, to be
asthmatic, suffer from eczema and other stress-related diseases; and
that these effects lasted through until adulthood.

In summary, therefore, it is useful to mention the tasks which
Wallerstein and Blakeslee, in an earlier study (1989), considered that
children of divorce need to master. As Kaslow and Schwartz (1987)
also stress, during the first year it is important for the children to
master the first and second tasks both of *acknowledging the reality of
the marital separation,* and *disengaging from their parental conflict so
that they they may resume their customary pursuits.* The third task of
resolution of loss may need reworking several times. This includes
that of losing one parent on a day-to-day basis, and feelings of being
unloved and rejected, and indeed the loss of meaning about the
family because previously held family traditions no longer prevail.
The fourth task which involves the child in *resolving anger and self-
blame* is for some children (especially for older children) particularly
difficult to resolve, as divorce characteristically leads to anger with
either one or both parents, either for seeking divorce, or for their
lack of consideration of their children's needs. By and large the fifth
task, which is to *accept the permanence of the divorce,* is easier for
older than younger children, as they are more likely to be able to
make their own sense of what has happened. Wallerstein's final task

is for the child to *achieve a realistic hope about their own future relationships*. As with any major experience of loss, the children of divorce need to return to and rework their experience in the light of their increased understanding.

In his excellent review of the research on children's adjustment to divorce, Emery (1988) indicates that there are many methodological and conceptual issues in divorce, not least of which are 'unrepresentative sampling, insufficiently reliable measurement problems in inferring causation from correlation and complexities in longitudinal designs', which are hardly unique to this field. He concludes that 'divorce is evidently associated with some undesirable outcomes among children, increased utilization of mental health services, more conduct problems, less success in school and an increased likelihood of eventually getting divorced'. Nevertheless, some of the common assumptions made as regards the short- and long-term effects have not been substantiated. In the first place, there is little support for the hypothesis that there are 'strong associations between family status and children's adjustment problems', especially those of 'father absence' and 'parental loss'. Second, while economic and racial factors seem to explain some of the differences as between single-parent and two-parent families, they do not explain them all. Third, those children in divorced, single-parent households seem to have more difficulties than those of children from other single-parent families. Fourth, there are some outcomes which seem to be related to sex differences, with regard to the increased externalisation of problems among boys, and possible increased internalisation of problems and early heterosexual involvement among girls. Thus the results for children following parental divorce do seem to indicate that some of the effects are long-term.

THE CHILD IN THE SINGLE-PARENT HOUSEHOLD

Previous chapters (3,4,5 and 6) have discussed the idea that divorce and remarriage are processes which commonly lead to additional stages of the family life cycle; and that these result in tasks which need to be mastered at all levels in the family system. For many, though not all, children living in a single-parent household this is an interim stage between living in a nuclear, two-parent family and becoming a stepfamily. Although there has been some child-protection research focused on single-parent households, where for various reasons it has been necessary to receive the children into care, there has been very little on what might be described as 'good enough' functioning single-parent households.

Weiss (1979), for instance, as the result of his US research – which is based on conversations with single parents, whether mothers or fathers, who were on their own with their children, many of whom have to go out to work as a necessity – describes their children as 'growing up a little faster'. He points out that in most two-parent households which function well enough, there is little opportunity for the children to take part in the decision-making related to the household. For these single parents a shift has taken place in their relationships with their children; and some children, at least for a time, take on the role of parenting their parent; others may compete with them for the leadership role, and many make a greater contribution to the functioning of the family and the running of the household than is usually the case in the two-parent family. On the other hand, younger children who spend the greater part of their childhood in single-parent households may grow up to be more self-reliant, but also may have had to suppress their need for parental nurturance, which may result in their having special vulnerabilities. Children who continue to parent their single parent may come to take on a pseudo-spousal role to the lonely parent and, if this situation is allowed to continue for any length of time, it is clearly fraught with danger for both child and parent.

Some children, particularly those who are adolescent, may take on a surrogate parental role in relation to their younger siblings and, although this premature independence may be source of some pride to them, it may also lead to their missing out on the development of peer relationships which provide a 'holding network' while they differentiate from their parent and become their own person.

Schlesinger (1982), in the US, interviewed forty children (average age 14.9 years) who had spent an average of 4.7 years in a single-parent household, in order to ascertain their perceptions. He found that some of their views about outcome were diametrically opposed – as, for example, regarding being closer to or more distant from one parent, helping in the household, getting along or not getting along with their siblings, having more or less responsibility and moving to a new area.

Ferri's (1984) study of children growing up in a one-parent family, who formed part of the National Child Development (longitudinal) Study of children born 3–9 March 1958, in which either father (418) or mother (33) were absent, found that problems of financial hardship and poor accommodation were more frequently found in one-parent households headed by mothers than in father-headed households. The major aim of the study was to explore the effects on the development of the children, and the results demonstrated that, overall, children in these families were less well adjusted than their peers from two-parent nuclear families. The results of this study also supported the findings of Rutter's (1972) research, which demonstrated that losing a father through divorce or separation seemed to produce more lasting effects, although there was some evidence that it might be the 'distortion' rather than the 'disruption' of family relationships which is detrimental to the children's development.

Morawetz and Walker (1987), both family therapists, who undertook a clinical study of brief therapy with single-parent families in the US, describe families where problems had developed in the children, in which the negative aspects of the unfinished emotions pertaining to the marriage continued via the children, or because of a family failure to accept that a divorce had happened, or because an adolescent boy sought to find his missing father through delinquent behaviour.

Hodges (1986), in his recommendations for professional and clinical interventions for the children of divorce, points out that single-parent families are likely to have significant problems, such as lower incomes, which have a major influence. There are frequently disciplinary problems, and especially in families where there is a relationship between parent and child which is too close there are also likely to be problems over individuation for the children. There is some indication that sex-role behaviour is affected, but this is inconclusive, partly because of the influence of economic factors and partly because there is such a limited number of studies.

CHILDREN LIVING IN STEPFAMILIES

While many of the effects of divorce on children will still be with them when they move into stepfamilies, it must be reiterated that this is a double transition, which brings new changes and difficulties for the children. It has already been indicated that for many children they are faced with the final implications of the divorce or death of a parent only when one or both parents remarry. Particularly for many young children this is the time when they begin to realise that their parents are not likely to have a reconciliation, struggle to accept this and begin to complete their mourning for the loss of the nuclear family. Indeed, it may be that for some children it is only at this time that their repressed anger emerges, and they may even work towards breaking up the new marriage. For some children whose trust in adults has been diminished as the result of their pre- or post-divorce behaviour towards them, they will be cautious about investing in new relationships with adults.

The initial problems for stepfamilies have been considered in Chapters 5 and 6, but there are particular issues for children, many of which are age- and stage-related. On the whole, young and early school-age children take to stepparents fairly easily, though much depends on the attitudes of their biological parents and the cautious approaches of the stepparent. However, later latency-age children are generally more cautious and loyalty-conscious than younger children.

An important US study by Perkins and Kahan (1979) compared the differences between twenty biological families with twenty step-families where there was a stepfather, with one child aged 12–15 (selected randomly where there was more than one) who had access to their natural fathers twice a month on average. These were upper-middle-class families, and most of the mothers in the stepfamilies had initiated the divorce, which had usually been three years previously which indicates a fairly biased sample. This is one of the few studies in which *all* were interviewed and the findings demonstrated agreement that the adjustment and satisfaction scores were higher for the biological father than for stepfathers, from all family members. The authors concluded that these results ran counter to the commonly held belief that mothers turn their children against noncustodial fathers.

Adolescents too frequently have intense loyalty conflicts, particularly if one parent has not remarried. The parent's sexual intensity, which is likely to be reawakened with the new marriage, is also likely to be anxiety-provoking to the adolescent's own emerging sexuality. For some young people, their own psychological and physical leave-taking preoccupations also lead them to such intense ambivalence that their resistance to bonding with new stepparents is considerable. For adolescents who have spent some years in a single-parent household it is likely that they will not only lose status as the result of the remarriage, but they may also lose freedoms and responsibilities which enhanced their self-esteem. Disciplinary problems may become exacerbated in stepfamilies, especially when the single-parent mother remarries. Adolescents in stepfamilies both have a handle for their rebellion in threatening to leave and go to live with the other parent, and sometimes do so with unhappy results. On the other hand, if such a move is carefully planned and agreed to by both parents, it can provide fresh opportunities and perhaps more freedom for the young person.

The long-term US study of Hetherington et al. (1985) found that the children who had been living in a stepfamily for less than two years demonstrated increased behaviour difficulties. Subsequently the boys who had stepfathers did not differ from boys in families where there had not been a divorce, while the boys in divorced families continued to have problems. The girls, on the other hand, continued to demonstrate both behavioural and internalised problems even after two years in a stepfamily. Hetherington's (1987) longitudinal comparative study of mother custody families following a divorce when the children were aged 4, demonstrates that the age and sex of the child is of relevance to their ability both to recover from the effects of the divorce and to assimilate the changes of remarriage. In the six-year follow-up of those children whose mothers had remarried for more than two years and were living in stepfather households, she found that the boys no longer demonstrated such aggressive, non-compliant behaviours; but that mothers, sons and their teachers report the boys' behaviour more positively than their stepfathers do. The girls however, continue to 'view their stepfathers as hostile, punitive and unreasonable on matters of discipline'. An important finding was that in stepfamilies where there is a close marital relationship, this is associated with high levels of conflict by the children, especially the daughters, with both their mothers and their stepfathers. As has already been indicated, it is postulated that this is the result of the girls having to give up both their powerful position in the household and their close relationship with their mothers.

In stepmother families, Santrock and Sitterle (1987) found that the stepmothers were sharing many of the parenting activities with their husbands, yet, despite their persistent attempts to involve themselves with their stepchildren, their stepchildren continued to 'view them as detached, unsupportive and uninvolved in their lives'. They give several reasons for this mutually negative view of the relationship between them. In the first place, because of their biological relationship and early history between the child or children and their father, the children are likely to be closer to their mothers. Nevertheless this does not explain their negative attitudes towards their stepmothers; though secondly, because there is already physical separation between them and their biological mothers, the stepmother's presence in the household may threaten the children's attachment to them. Third, the presence of the stepmother may be a constant reminder to the children that the loss of their mother is final. This may be the reason for the children's displacement of the disappointment, pain and anger with both parents, on to their stepmothers.

The previous marital and parental status of the stepparent is likely to influence the development of bonding between the children and the stepparent, many of whom who have little or no experience of parenthood, and whose lack of parental experience may be revealed in insensitivities or undue caution towards their stepchildren. As the focus of this book is on divorce and remarriage, the death of one parent and subsequent remarriage of the widow or widower has been given insufficient attention. Losing a parent through death is not the same as losing a parent through divorce; there are many differences, not least the likelihood that a deceased parent is idealised, while the feelings of attachment towards a divorced parent are likely to be ambivalent, if not overtly negative, at least for a year or two.

CHILDREN OF DIVORCE AND THE SCHOOL

Despite the increase in divorce and stepfamily-related research, until recently there has been little specifically written for the teachers of the approximately one in five children from divorced families who spend two-thirds of their waking life at school. The succinct discussion of divorce and remarriage from a school perspective by Cox and Desforges (1987) goes some way to remedy this gap. Lund and Riley (1984) point out that the school is often caught in the middle between parents in conflict, and Rodgers (1982), an educational journalist, considers that schools are in the front line when it comes to dealing with the practical and emotional difficulties when a family breaks up. It is not unlikely that many of the problems which children may take to teachers and school counsellors are linked with their parents' divorce and/or living in stepfamilies. However, the teacher may be in a dilemma as, at times of extreme stress, the school may be the *only* place in which a child can experience life continuing as normal.

In a film made for television – Thames Television's (1985) *Voices in the Dark* – when a teacher, noticing a teenage girl weeping in class, enquires what is the matter, the girl denies that anything is wrong, but nevertheless is able to share her unhappiness with her best friend. However, another teenage girl whose parents were about to separate was very distressed at having to leave them both to return to boarding school, where she felt unable to tell her friends what was happening to her. Those of her friends whose parents were together she felt would not be able to understand her unhappiness, while those whose parents were divorced she felt would understand, but her worries would be an added burden to them.

Morawetz and Walker (1987) comment that where single-parent families are involved, the school, with the best of intentions, tries to compensate for the missing parent; but they point out that, on the other hand, the parents' strained relationships may also strain relations between the family and the school. If, however subtly the school is perceived as blaming the parents for the child's failure to conform to the school's requirements, then the parents in turn can blame the school, thus setting in motion a vicious circle of resentment and lack of cooperation in which the child becomes the victim. As the research demonstrates, children who are preoccupied with grieving or torn by their loyalties to parents in conflict are hardly likely to be able to make the most of their educational opportunities.

CHILD ABDUCTION

There has been a steadily rising incidence of child abduction by noncustodial parents (or by a third party with their connivance), who have either not returned them from access visits, or who have seized their children from the care of the custodial parent, often taking them overseas or bringing them into this country. So far the numbers have been relatively small – thought to be between 200 and 500 each year in the UK, though many more in the US – and these numbers appear to be increasing. Many of these children are born to parents of differing nationalities and cultures, while others may have one parent who has been working overseas, and, following a matrimonial rift or legal loss of custody, the parent who feels they have lost out, often in considerable distress, kidnaps their own child.

There is no legal definition of child abduction, though the Children's Legal Centre, which has produced an information sheet, has defined it as 'the removal of a child from the care of a settled caregiver [for example, parent or fosterparent] without the consent of that caregiver and without legal authority'. This definition extends the concept of (and as a result probably also increases the numbers involved in) child abduction so as to include children who are subject to care orders and therefore in the care of local authority social service departments, although they may have been placed with foster parents. The arrangements for the care of these children when they are traced are likely to be reviewed, and it is open to their parents to make an application to the court for discharge of the care order. Since the coming into force in 1986 of the Child Abduction and Custody Act (1985), as well as the clarification of the criminal law, and also some practice directions, the law has been considerably tightened up, but distressing cases of children who have either been brought into this country or taken abroad still come to light.

Two recent television programmes illustrate the delicate balance as between the deeply contrasting parental perceptions and those of the needs of their children. In the first (Independent Television's *Stolen*, written by Moggach), a Pakistani father, distressed by his English wife's behaviour (which includes an adulterous affair, largely as the result of his neglect), kidnaps their two children and takes them back to Pakistan to be brought up by his own Muslim parents and extended family. The series shows the resulting attempts by the mother to 'rescue' her children, and includes a realistic and moving court scene which demonstrates how ill equipped is the law and the courts to handle such situations, let alone to resolve them.

The second, a BBC '40 Minutes' programme, attempts to give a balanced picture of a real family situation in which a mother, pregnant and divorced after a marriage of only a few months, after allowing the father access to his daughter for two years, refused to allow any further contact because she had (what seems to be clear) evidence that he was sexually abusing her, though he denies this. While sexual abuse was considered by the judge to be neither proven nor unproven ('in equipoise' is the legal term in the US), he still ordered that access should continue. The mother sent the little girl 'into hiding' and served a two-year prison sentence for refusing to comply with a court order to allow her daughter to spend two weeks with her father. After serving two years, her sentence was revoked through a special Act of Congress, as the result of the uproar which followed. Meanwhile, the child has since seen neither of her parents; and one can only conclude that the resultant loss of her attachments has compounded the original trauma, whatever it might have been.

Many countries throughout the world now have extradition treaties with the United Kingdom through which the abductor (rather than the child) is brought back to this country. For countries which subscribe to The Hague Convention on the civil aspects of child abduction, the authorities of that country are obliged to trace the child who has been wrongfully removed, where possible to secure their voluntary return, to exchange information regarding the child's social background and to initiate judicial proceedings or administrative arrangements for their return. In every case of children being brought into the UK, the course to be followed, as far as possible, is determined by the best interests of the child. It has to be said, however, that for children who have been removed from this country, especially those whose parents come from differing cultures and religious beliefs, then such a situation is likely to be much more difficult. Because of the complexities of, the secrecy involved in, and often the international nature of the offence, very little is known about the effects of abduction on the children, and for many it may take years for them to be returned to their custodial parent. Although children who are abducted may initially welcome being reunited with a loved parent, it is possible to conclude that the child who is abducted in such a manner will also experience confusion and distress at their abrupt removal from familiar surroundings and will also grieve for the parent from whom they have been removed. Other children may not even have a consistent attachment to their abducting parent, and their removal to a strange place, even a different country, may compound their unhappiness.

9 Ways and means of intervening during divorce and remarriage
Outside the courts

Go with me like good angels, to my end;
And as the long divorce of steel falls on me,
Make of your prayers one sweet sacrifice,
And lift my soul to heaven.

William Shakespeare (1564–1616), *Henry VIII*, III. i. 75

Words move, music moves
Only in time; but that which is only living
Can only die. Words after speech, reach
Into the silence.

T.S. Eliot (1888–1965), *Burnt Norton*

As Murch (1980) writes, 'marriage breakdown involves all family members in a task of reorganising their family relationships, adapting to separation and loss, redefining old relationships, discovering a framework for new ones'. Many families complete the transformation through divorce, single-parent households, remarriage and re-formed extended families without formal help, though not without pain. For some their contact with the legal system is minimal, although it is, of course, only through the final recourse to the law that a marriage is formally ended. The focus of this chapter will primarily be on the many ways in which members of families who are going through the divorce and remarriage process may be given emotional support while retaining their customary autonomy. The next chapter will focus on ways in which the legal context, in addition to legal advice, can also provide emotional support, although, given the present legal system, this may ultimately be at the cost of what is known as 'party control' (Davis 1988).

It is rare that both partners simultaneously and equally want to end their marriage; usually there is an initiator, with whom the other partner eventually goes along either willingly or unwillingly (see

Chapter 5, 'The legal process', page 93). It is also unusual for both former spouses to make a firm commitment to new partners at more or less the same time, as it is for their children to become assimilated into binuclear stepfamilies, which usually takes between two and five years – sometimes longer, even if all goes well enough. Children almost never want their parents to divorce (see Chapter 8), but in any event they may not even be informed, nor included in some of the discussions about custody or their access to the out-of-house parent. This delays their recovery, as they have first to confront the actuality of the end of their parents' marriage before they can begin to realise, let alone accept, their own losses. Although some couples who agree to end their marriage (we do not know how many) do not go through the legal processes of judicial separation or divorce, most do pass through the boundaries that redefine private sorrows into a public issue. However, there can be little doubt that *all* the members of the families which are in transition during divorce and/or remarriage need support from their customary extended family and friendship networks, as well as from those whose function it is to provide them with assistance both individually and also in various subgroupings.

SUPPORT

Most families going through such painful transitions need support, both practical and emotional, as well as some legal advice. Some family members turn to family and friends; indeed, because divorce is now so common few of us remain untouched by it, whether directly or indirectly, so advice based on personal experience is readily available. Yet, the endeavour to give such support involves a real test of integrity for those who attempt it, as it is also likely that only a few of us are able to be objective and supportive at one and the same time. In attempting to give assistance to members of families during the divorce and remarriage processes we are likely therefore to perceive the situation through the lens of our own experience and to react accordingly, albeit often unknowingly. Indeed, for some there may be a danger that the embers remaining from the fires of our own divorce may result in our fanning the flames of those of our friends and relations who are currently going through theirs.

In the light of the findings of current research (see Chapter 8) as regards the plight of children of divorce, it is hardly surprising that many identify with the needs of the children and bias their support towards pleading concern for them, perhaps alienating their equally needy parents, thus not assisting them to resume or change their patterns of parenting. Others will identify with one partner or the other, perhaps colluding with a one-sided perspective and offering sympathy, exhortations or criticisms of the other partner according to their own perspective. Taking a systemic view of the family which is undergoing traumatic changes can act as a constraining influence on what is a natural tendency to identify with one or other of the family members, and thus perhaps unwittingly to take sides which may exacerbate the conflict and prove unhelpful in the long run. Relatives and friends, as well as interventionist practitioners, can provide support by encouraging the parents as parties in conflict to seek appropriate help through which to attempt to settle their own disputes. Couples going through the process of divorce, and also often those involved in becoming a stepfamily, are attempting to reevaluate their previous lives, justify the actions they have taken and elicit support for their present decisions (see Chapter 3).

Partners who are separating or divorcing have needs from family, friends and community networks which can be summarised as follows. First, they need empathic listening which is consistent and reasonably objective; information as to available resources, where to obtain specialist advice, whether legal or psychological (for themselves or their children), or specialist services such as counselling or mediation (see below, 'Conciliation/mediation', page 195). Also needed is information regarding reading material, of which there is now much available. The distress involved in the processes of separation, divorce and even remarriage, often prevents people who are normally quite able to seek out information which they need and which, in other circumstances, they would be quite capable of finding for themselves.

For children, the place of the school has been stressed as the one place where they can perhaps pursue their normal lives (see Chapter 8, 'Children of divorce and the the school', page 178); and it was also emphasised that there is a serious lack of resources to which children can turn for support in distress about their parents' separation, divorce or remarriage. In the United States most secondary schools have school counsellors, quite separate from the teaching staff, with whom, within the safety of a confidential relationship, children can work out their own grief, within a counselling relationship which will not make them feel disloyal to either parent. Although in Britain there are now many sympathetic teachers, there are too few school counsellors who are recognised and accepted by the school teaching staff, and who, because they are *outside* the teaching system, can provide supportive counselling which is confidential (see Robinson

1976). The implication of this situation is that children either go without the help which they need, or they have to externalise their pain sufficiently noticeably so that they are referred to child and family clinics.

The second need is non-judgemental recognition of their distress, a continuing relationship in their life which remains constant at a time of turmoil. At such a time family members need practical support. One example might be to provide a neutral 'staging post' from which the noncustodial parent could fetch and return children, thus avoiding the unpleasant doorstep scenes which frequently occur, particularly in the early stages of separation. Friends and relatives might provide transport and a supportive presence for important appointments, particularly in connection with the legal proceedings. The children of parents going through the divorce process could be included in treats provided for their individual friends, thus allowing them to escape, albeit briefly, from the painful situation at home.

It is easy to underestimate the importance of an empathy which is impartial and yet also demonstrates a concern for each individual member of the family and for the changes they are all undergoing. Again, the needs of children are especially important, and members of the extended family, perhaps particularly grandparents, who are already known and trusted by them, can be supportive merely by giving children the time and care which in other circumstances they would be likely to receive from their parents. Indeed, it might be useful for the children and their parents alike if grandparents were able to put their grandchildren's needs before those of their own children. Children need someone they can talk to safely, who will realise that they are attached to *both* their parents and who may be able to reassure them that, although their parents might be quarrelling with each other, they do care for them.

WHOSE CHOICE OF INTERVENTION?

Davis (1988) points out that during divorce the law and legal procedures define the family conflict. As the next chapter will show, in the last resort the law will also make decisions for the couple who are unable to agree between themselves. This is also the case during remarriage, when the law does not intervene, unless there are disputed matters relating back to decisions made at the time of the divorce. It is not within the province of this book (nor the competence of the author) to recommend changes in the law, though there can be little doubt that such are necessary, and indeed are at present under consideration (see Chapter 12). The discussion which follows therefore primarily focuses on ways in which the members of a family in transition can seek help for themselves. The kinds of assistance which will be discussed are those which clients can seek of their own volition, and so retain their own autonomy while being given often much-needed support during the inevitable and very important decision-making at this time.

It often goes without saying, yet it is always evident, that our own beliefs will influence the choice of help we offer (as indeed these have affected the choice of models presented in this book – see Chapter 2) as well as our interactions with our clients, and will also underlie the discussion as to whether individual, marital or family therapy or mediation would be the intervention of choice. A recent book on values in psychotherapy (Holmes and Lindley 1989) discusses the ethics of therapeutic relationships and points out that the 'intimacy of therapy exposes the therapist's weakness ... and that therapists are often severely tested morally by their patients'. As they go on to argue, there is tension between intimacy and professionalism in all professions, and especially in psychotherapy. Nowhere is this more apparent than for any of the professions intervening in the divorce process. Therefore, their precept that there is a special responsibility to conduct oneself with the utmost moral delicacy based on considerable self-knowledge and maturity is particularly applicable to all those who become professionally involved with families during divorce and also becoming a stepfamily.

Those practitioners who intervene in the processes of divorce and remarriage need to consider in each of the families with whom they become involved (whether as individuals, couples, children or the whole family) where they stand as regards the primary rights of parents and children. Should the right of the child to have a continuing consistently supportive environment take precedence, or should the rights of the parents to the child take priority? What position should the counsellor or therapist take in relation to the legal process? These and other questions need to be reflected on if the practitioner is not to become caught up in the whirlpool of destructive processes which are often aspects of those involved in divorce.

It might, perhaps, be useful briefly to outline some possible principles regarding the general advice from professional practitioners to one or both partners (or others) who invite suggestions about the form of nonlegal help, which a couple might seek as they consider what to do about their future and that of their children. Although it will sometimes be impossible to adhere to the principles suggested below, they may serve as useful guidelines and, for the practitioner attempting to understand the reasons why they cannot be achieved, might also serve as areas for reflection or exploration. These guidelines are also applicable when a couple is already embarked on a process which may result in a separation and/or eventual divorce and the probable restructuring of family life. They are outlined below.

First, the couple should retain control of their own decision-making processes; and, subject to their children not being at risk of harm, as far as possible *they* should decide when to give up their autonomy. Second, if intervention should be necessary, then whenever possible both parties should be equally involved. Third, while it may be useful for their children to become involved as part of the process of intervention, this should only be with the permission of *both* their parents, and the objectives of such involvement should be clarified before the children are seen. Fourth, whatever form of intervention is eventually selected, whether individual, marital, family or conciliation, the repercussions on the whole family system and its possible transition into a re-formed extended family system should at the very least be considered by the practitioner, and whenever possible also reviewed with the client(s) as part of the process. Fifth, only in the event of couple's ultimate failure to make their own decisions should the statutory services become involved, except if it is clear that the children are at risk, when the child protection services should be notified. Inevitably, as at present, this will ultimately need to happen because there are many couples who are unable to manage their own decision-making. However, there are also many cases where the decision-making processes are virtually (or actually) and sometimes unnecessarily taken over by those whose task it is to help the couple to come to their own decisions (see Davis 1988).

It will be evident that in many situations it will not be possible to adhere to these principles. Nevertheless, even when it seems not to be possible to act according to these guidelines, such a situation could lead to an exploration as to why this might be so. For instance, it is now well known that men tend not to seek help for themselves, partly because of their differences in 'internal attentiveness' as compared with women, and partly because of their expressive inhibition (O'Brien 1987, Finkelhor 1988) that it is not manly do so. Indeed, women are generally regarded as being responsible for the nurturing of emotional relationships within the family.

Empirical research also suggests that during marital breakdown it is often initially difficult to engage both partners in any intervention which either one of them might select, in order to try to help him or her to make such important decisions regarding the future of their relationship, though gentle persistence can sometimes make this possible. In every divorce there are always two perspectives (often diametrically opposed), just as in every marital relationship there are always two marriages, that of the husband and that of the wife (Barnard 1972). Johnston and Campbell (1988), in their research with families where the couples were embedded in bitter conflict, found that 'coalitions with mental health counsellors were germane to some particularly entrenched disputes' and that for some these conflicts involved 'extensive participation of mental health professions, attorneys, police and court personnel [t]he impasse spread[ing] to involve ever widening circles of others'. Except for court-based interventions (see Chapter 1), it is always ultimately the choice and responsibility of the clients, but it is at least possible, and counsellors and therapists should bear in mind, that in attempting to help only one partner, they may be unwittingly assisting in the demise of a marriage, which in the last resort neither partner wanted to end.

COMPARISON BETWEEN MEDIATION PSYCHOTHERAPY AND FAMILY THERAPY

Fig 3.1 shows a broadly based comparison between psychotherapy, family therapy and mediation, which demonstrates the differences and similarities between them. Although the knowledge base of each of the methods of intervention may have some similarities (though mediation requires knowledge of the law and family therapy is based on systemic theory), the focus is different because the goals are not the same.

The goals of individual counselling or psychotherapy, marital therapy or family therapy are generally reconciliatory and restorative, either to improve the mental health of the individual, the couple's relationship, or the functioning of the family. Mediation, on the other hand, accepts the couple's intention to part, but aims to help them achieve settlement on various issues to be agreed between them. While there are implicit or explicit contracts for each form of intervention, that of mediation is spelt out in some detail, while in psychotherapy and family therapy this is not always the case. The role of the worker is also different, in family therapy sometimes being very active indeed (though this depends on the model selected, usually by the therapist), while in psychotherapy it is more likely, though not inevitable, that the therapist will be passive. In mediation the practitioner is often more active, managing the process though not the outcome of it.

There are differences too in the relationship of the practitioner with the clients. In mediation the practitioner struggles to be impartial and to empower the couple, while in the other forms of intervention the therapist generally takes some responsibility for improving the mental health of the clients, on whom they are likely to become somewhat dependent in psychotherapy, although in family therapy this is not usually the case. Two of the other differences between the practice of mediation and forms of therapy are in the areas of power and expression of feelings. In mediation the practitioner works to help the couple both retain and redistribute more equitably the power between them, usually as regards the children and the money, the woman often having power over the former and the man over the latter; while in the other two forms of intervention the practitioner assists the individual to take more power and the family to find ways of using it more effectively and mutually. The expression of feelings is the main focus of counselling or psychotherapy, as often in family therapy, but in mediation, while feelings are acknowledged, they are not worked with nor is their expression encouraged. In counselling and psychotherapy the orientation is often towards understanding the past as a way of managing the present, while in family therapy the focus is usually on the present as a way of managing the future differently. In mediation the orientation is distinctly future-oriented, and reflections which are backward-looking are actively discouraged. The ways of managing conflict and the negotiation strategies of each form of intervention vary according to the model used, though they form a major part of mediation and a minor part of psychotherapy and counselling.

Figure 3.1 neither includes nor takes account of interventions which are made within a statutory context, although many practitioners nevertheless adhere to one or other of the models to which the figure alludes. Where the practitioner intervenes from a statutory base this will inevitably impinge on the family system by providing an orchestral background of coercion to the decision-making, or will be perceived as doing so.

THERAPEUTIC INTERVENTION

Since depression and other symptoms of psychological distress are frequently aspects of the divorce process, some form of therapeutic intervention is often considered to be necessary. One of the partners, most often the wife, who is experiencing acute distress related to marital breakdown, separation, divorce or remarriage may seek therapeutic help for herself, either in an attempt to achieve a reconciliation with her spouse, or in order to manage her own pain. The partners may also be defined by others (such as general practitioners, or in the case of children, by their parents or through their school system) as in need of psychological assessment or therapy, which does not usually have any formal links with the legal system with which the family may also be involved. The exception may be in the case of children receiving psychotherapeutic help, in that a psychological or psychiatric report may be requested by the court in order to assist them with the decision-making with regard to custody or access.

Many people, and especially men (see, for instance, Keshet and Rosenthal 1978, Ambrose, Harper and Pemberton 1983), struggle through without any formalised psychological help. Since (as is shown in Chapter 2, Figure 2.3) there is almost always some dissonance, if not conflict, between the needs of the individual parents as well as between at least one of them and those of their children, it is hardly surprising that the therapeutic agencies with which the family members become involved have different perspectives of the situation. As indicated earlier, the family's conflict is often mirrored between those agencies, including those within the legal context, whose task is to assist the family to resolve these conflicts (see 'Whose choice of intervention?', page 185, Figure 2.2, page 32, and Chapter 10).

The arguments so far have stressed that any intervention with families in distress should be based on a family systems approach, whether related to divorce or remarriage, centred on an individual (adult or child), a couple, or the whole family, and it is perfectly possible to take such a stance even when working with one family member. The focus in this section will therefore be on the similarities with and differences between individual psychotherapy (in general), marital/divorce therapy, family therapy (particularly as related to the constructivist approach) and mediation, rather than the arguments for or against any particular therapeutic model of intervention. Because it will be apparent (and it is the author's belief) that the practitioner's construction of reality influences any work undertaken, it therefore must be stated that this underlies the discussion, as does the belief that families in distress should have access to various kinds of skilled assistance and, as far as possible, retain control of their own decision-making. It might also serve as a useful reminder that the model which has been previously been outlined is a re-formed and extended family systems one which redefines the family as a more open system than the nuclear family so as to consider stepfamilies as binuclear rather than confined to a single household. Such a belief is likely to change the normative expectations of post-divorce and family relationships, though it is as yet unkown whether they are also likely to change the perceptions of all relationships (Ahrons and Wallisch 1987).

Individual counselling/therapy

As has already been stated, many adults (and especially women) who are going through the process off marital breakdown and/or divorce seek therapy for themselves, often in order to help them come to terms with what they have lost and to regain a sense of self-esteem. It may take a number of months or even years before the husband or wife who feel they have been abandoned by their spouse begin to make their own sense of what has happened to them. Indeed, many seek what is usually known as 'divorce counselling' to help them come to terms with starting again. For some it is the impact of another loss, such as the children eventually leaving home, which triggers them into being able to confront what has happened to them and perhaps begin to be able to see their own part in the marital breakdown. For others, the failure of their own marriage allows them to understand for the first time how traumatic events of their own childhood (as, for instance, if their parents' marriage either suddenly broke down, or slowly disintegrated) has affected their own capacity for intimate relationships.

Gillian Lancaster

Gillian Lancaster, the elder of two daughters, was a young woman whose parents had had an unhappy marriage and had separated and later divorced just as she was about to leave school and go to college. While her younger sister was close to their mother, Gill had always been closer to her father and so felt particularly bereft when he left to work in New Zealand, during the first year of her degree. Gill, always a shy and diffident girl, found herself very alone and went for counselling, which helped her to get through her degree. During her second year at college she met another equally uncertain student, Christopher, whose parents had also divorced as he left home, and the two of them clung together.

After they qualified, both found jobs far from where each of them grew up. Within a year or so they married, because it seemed inevitable, and set about buying themselves a house. Gill did quite well in her post in the local authority, but Christopher changed his jobs several times and seemed unable to find what he wanted. Their sexual relationship, never very satisfactory, dwindled, and their marriage seemed to become a retreat from the world rather than mutually satisfying.

Some three or four years later, Gill met a much older man already divorced and remarried, and she began an affair with him. If anything, she was more upset by her behaviour than Christopher seemed to be, and she sought therapy in order to 'sort herself out'. Christopher was said to regard it as Gill's problem and refused to become involved.

During the therapy, she began to get in touch with the loneliness of her childhood, her awareness of her parents' unhappiness and how this had led her to choose an equally lonely young man. She realised that her choice of lover in some ways replicated her relationship with her father and this was not what she wanted. Christopher himself withdrew and within a few months they decided to separate, yet remain friends, which they did, helping each another to move to separate flats and meeting weekly for a time.

Some two years later, Gillian met another man, this time a confident and well-established Air Force officer, and, after her eventual divorce from Christopher, they married. She is now planning to give up her job to travel abroad with him and they are hoping to start a family quite soon.

In working with Gill over a period of two years, the therapist used her knowledge of Gill's wish for, yet fear of, closeness and intimacy, the roots of which lay in her too close relationship with her father, and her inability to identify with her mother whom she experienced as remote, even disapproving. At the initial stage of her contact with Gill the therapist made strenuous efforts to engage Christopher, and later offered to put him in touch with another therapist, but he could not accept this. As this couple had no children, the repercussions of their eventual divorce were minimised, but there are many couples like Gill and Christopher, where the repercussions are considerable and a referral elsewhere, such as to a child and family clinic, would be helpful to the whole family.

Marital/divorce therapy

At the present time many couples seek counselling or therapy as their relationship seems to have broken down and they do not know whether or not there remains enough between them to try to rebuild it. Many, if not most, of them have children to whom they are often both devoted, and it is often such parental affection and concern which leads them to seek help. Sometimes their relationship has foundered because they have concentrated their energies elsewhere, both physically and psychologically, frequently the husband on his professional career and the wife on their children, although with so many dual-career families this is not necessarily the case. Other couples have never achieved the intimacy which they hoped marriage would bring, and their disappointment leads them to seek help. Such a couple were the Nottinghams described below.

The Nottingham family

Ben and Judy Nottingham met while she was a staff nurse and he was at university in the Midlands. Ben had won a scholarship to go to Sandhurst, as had his father before him, but though be became secretly sure that he did not want an Army career, he kept finding ways to put off the decision. Judy was one of two children, the only girl, who had dealt with her own uncertainties by becoming extremely capable and felt quite ready to settle down and have a family. Ben admired her apparent strength and competence, and she found his boyish reticence most attractive after the aggressiveness of her own father.

Ben was the only son of his father's second marriage and was born a year after his older half-sister (then aged 12) had been killed in an accident which had also involved his parents and older sister. Ben's father had never seemed to have been able to discuss his grief with Ben's mother, who was a highly competent GP. He mourned his daughter in secret discussions with his son. Ben's father died while Ben was in his final year at university, at about the time he met Judy.

After Judy and Ben married, they moved to another town, where Ben became a lecturer in a technical college, though he always felt somewhat dissatisfied with his career. They had a daughter, and several years later, after several miscarriages, a son. Judy, who had made a personal and professional study of miscarriages as she worked part-time on a gynaecological ward, half wondered whether there was a psychological element about the miscarriages, but kept this to herself. Both Ben and Judy were especially devoted parents, with a wide circle of friends; and they convinced themselves and each other that they were very happy, although Ben secretly knew that he was not. Indeed, he had phantasy arguments with Judy while travelling in his car though actually they rarely quarrelled.

Ben's post involved him in some travel and on one of these occasions he found himself very attracted by a young woman, Anna, whom he met overseas. He could not understand what was happening to him, and yet he became more and more preoccupied with her. Later that year he had to pay another visit abroad where he met Anna again and found that the attraction was mutual. Eventually Judy, who sensed something was very wrong as he was so withdrawn, asked him what was the matter, and he told her what was happening and that he must spend some time with Anna to sort it out.

Meanwhile they agreed to try to rebuild their marriage and sought marital therapy, Ben to help him decide what to do, and Judy to save her marriage. As it seemed clear to the therapist who saw them that each had brought to their marriage unresolved issues from their somewhat deprived childhoods, it was agreed that they would each have an individual therapist and that some therapy would take place in foursome sessions to enable them explore what could be done to improve their marriage. The therapy continued for some months, with both Ben and Judy working hard in the individual and the joint sessions to understand what had gone wrong with their marriage and what might be done. Judy found herself surprised to learn of Ben's assertiveness and confidence with Anna, and he somewhat desperately sought Judy's approval of his relationship with Anna. Eventually Judy got so angry that she told Ben to leave, and only then did he begin to realise how much the loss of his children meant to him.

One of the children became ill, and Ben returned home at Judy's request and they continued in therapy trying to share some of the dissatisfactions which had built up between them over the years. Ben was adamant that he must meet Anna as arranged, and spent much time writing to her, talking with her on the phone and thinking of her. Judy, who sensed this, became quite depressed, and after a visit to the GP was put on medication. While Ben was away visiting Anna, Judy poured out her anger to her therapist. After Ben's 'holiday' with Anna he still could not make up his mind, and unusually for him, became angry when pressed by Judy, who continued to cling to the hope that they could save their marriage. From time to time they would have what for them were terrifying quarrels, ending with Judy in tears and Ben in retreat. Ben recognised that he was behaving in the same way as he had about making decisions about his career, and simply could not think about making the necessary practical plans either for his own future or for those of his wife and children. Anna, meanwhile, announced that she was planning to come to this country, whether or not Ben would leave his family to join her.

In working with the Nottinghams the two therapists tried to 'hold' them while they decided what to do about the future of their marriage. Through the construction of a 'shared process of meaning' (see Chapter 2) between each of the therapists and their individual client and between both of them and the couple in joint sessions they began to create a conversational domain through which they could begin to explore the meaning behind the unhappy situation in which Ben and Judy found themselves. The two therapists, by using their knowledge of the family life cycle, and the ideas of Feldman (1979) about the rules created by a couple in order to regulate their intimacy and those of Wynne (see Figure 2.2, page 32), were able to begin to hypothesise about the interactional level which they had reached, and the rules on which they were operating. Over some months of regular meetings with them, the therapists tried to help the Nottinghams to explore whether or not they could rebuild their marriage basing it upon different rules of interaction.

CONCILIATION/MEDIATION

There is considerable confusion over the use of the word 'conciliation' (see Chapter 3, 'Guidelines for the practice of mediation', page 59), which has here been used interchangeably with 'mediation', as it often is (see also Chapter 10, 'Professional guidelines', page 217), and this confusion is particularly apparent when it is practised within the legal context. In the United States conciliation is a form of intervention usually practised within a Court Service, as the Family Conciliation Courts (see, for instance, Haynes 1981, Haynes and Haynes 1989, and Milne 1983), while in Britain this is not necessarily the case and such intervention may also described as mediation (Jackson 1986, though see Chapter 10). In the US there are many mediators who are in private practice (see, for instance, Saposnek (1983), Haynes and Haynes (1989), either full-time or as part of their work, while in the United Kingdom, with the strong tradition of state provision of health and welfare care, there are very few private practitioners, although there are increasing numbers of independent conciliation services in the voluntary sector.

According to Hipgrave (1989) the word 'conciliation' is used 'in a confusing array of meanings'. It is used to describe a particular service offered to families, and sometimes in relation to anything practised by almost anyone in the context of family separation which aims to divert the family away from formal adjudication. The word 'conciliation' is also sometimes used to describe the legal processes involved in the Children's Appointments (see Chapter 5, 'The legal process', page 93) as Conciliation or Mediation Appointments; as well as the spirit inspiring practice whether by counsellors or lawyers as is described by the Solicitors' Family Law Association.

The overall goal of conciliation is generally agreed as being to assist couples in conflict to reduce the area and intensity of their conflict and work towards reaching agreements (National Family Conciliation Council (NFCC) guidelines for practice, Robinson 1988, though see Chapter 3, 'The mediation model of intervention during the divorce process', page 53, and Howard and Shepherd's 1987 fuller definition in Chapter 10). Although in the United States conciliators and mediators help the couple negotiate all matters (including financial matters such as maintenance and the matrimonial home), in Britain, at present negotiation is generally limited to matters concerned with their children (although financial matters and those related to the matrimonial home can be discussed in outline). However, this seems likely to change in the future. One such model has been developed by the members of the recently established Family Mediators' Association (which is accepted by the Law Society) and includes lawyers and conciliators who in co-mediating undertake comprehensive mediation on all disputed ancillary matters whether in relation to custody and access or as regards financial matters, including the matrimonial home (Parker 1989). At present neither in the United Kingdom nor in the United States can lawyers acting as mediators also act as the lawyer either to one or both parties.

As is indeed the case with conciliation, any agreements reached in comprehensive co-mediation are therefore made 'without prejudice' and are then passed to the parties' lawyers for the legal formalisation of the settlements reached. Many of the independent conciliation services affiliated to the NFCC practise mediation based on a family systems approach, including that at the Institute of Family Therapy (London) (see Chapter 2, 'Divorce and remarriage as additional stages of the family life cycle', page 44). Conciliators based in these independent services prefer their clients to be referred to them earlier rather than later, not only because this may avoid the conflict becoming too entrenched so that the parties take up polarised positions, but also because there is a greater chance that the couple may decide to work on reconciliation (as do approximately 10 per cent of couples).

In the earlier discussion about therapeutic interventions (see page 189), some attempt was made to differentiate between the models of intervention involved, although, because the bias throughout this book has been that of a constructivist family systems approach these were not explored further (see Chapter 2). However, because mediation is a relatively new form of intervention and one about which there is some confusion, it is thought that a fuller discussion of this model might prove useful. The models of mediation (that is, as a method of intervention) could be ranged on a continuum from the minimalist to the therapeutic; and the mediation conducted by the Civil Court welfare officers will be discussed in Chapter 10, 'Conciliatory or investigative?', page 228. Nevertheless, it is especially important to recognise that *all* family mediation usually takes place either alongside the legal context, within the shadow of the law (Mnookin and Kornhauser 1979), or actually within the legal system (see Chapter 5, 'The legal process', page 93; and Chapter 10, 'Professional guidelines', page 217).

The arguments for and against a family systems approach to conciliation have been expanded and discussed more fully in the recent literature on mediation (see, for instance, Robinson and Parkinson 1985, Howard and Shepherd 1987, Parkinson 1988, Marian Roberts 1988, Simon Roberts 1988, Davis and Marian Roberts 1988, Walker 1988, Marian Roberts 1990). Some of the differences seem to rest on the difficulty of understanding the central concept of the systemic approach, that of circular rather than linear thinking, which allows for reflexivity between systems. Others appear to result from a confusion between the theory and its application in models of practice. This debate, which seems to have aroused some intensity, is likely to continue (see Walker and Robinson 1990, and Robinson forthcoming).

The principles on which the practice of mediation is based have already been briefly described (in Chapter 2, 'Divorce and remarriage as additional stages of the family life cycle', page 44), but can be re-stated as follows:

1 Separating, divorcing or divorced couples voluntarily involve themselves in the conciliation process. Even when they may be referred from the court for such 'bargaining within the shadow of the law' (Mnookin and Kornhauser 1979) their voluntary participation is essential.

2 As indicated above, the primary goal of conciliation or mediation is to assist the couple to reduce the area or intensity of their conflict and to work towards reaching agreements, especially in disputes which are related to their children – as, for instance, their custody and access. Although this may not prove immediately possible, a change in attitudes can result in parents in conflict beginning to separate issues related to their relationship as husband and wife from those concerned with their children, thus paving the way for sharing their parenting in the reorganised re-formed extended family.

3 The conciliator works for the empowerment of the couple so that they are able to consider the best interests of the whole family. Where the balance of power is inequitable, the conciliator may endeavour to equalise it during the sessions, so as to promote the focus on the management of the conflict (see, for instance, Robinson and Parkinson 1985, Kaslow and Schwartz 1987, Haynes 1988, and Parkinson 1988).

4 The conciliator works with an explicit contract, using only overt techniques which empower the couple (though see Howard and Shepherd 1987).

5 The tasks are concrete, and focused on external data and issues, rather than on family communications or meaning. Although the expression of feelings is acknowledged, it is kept to the minimum necessary to achieve the tasks agreed upon.

6 The role of the conciliator, who is expected to maintain a high degree of impartiality, is that of managing the process, not the outcome, and acting as educator, clarifier and organiser, not as a therapist. The changes which result may well prove therapeutic for the couple, but these are by-products rather than the focus and objective of the process.

7 The methods used by the conciliator are commensurate with the goals and tasks agreed upon and also with the context within which the conciliator is operating.

8 The process of mediation is confidential (that is, it is legally privileged) to those involved and may not be reportable without the consent of the parties. (As will be discussed later, there are different implications for Divorce Court welfare officers based in the courts and within the legal system.)

9 The conciliator recognises and respects the legal context alongside or within which she or he and the couple are working.

The Oldham family

Jan and Michael Oldham had been married for some seven years. Michael had been previously married and had grown-up children. The couple set up an import/export business together and went through some hard times financially. They had a daughter, Stephanie, to whom Michael was particularly close and who was looked after by a daily nanny. Jan was also close to Stephanie, but as their marriage deteriorated, it was Michael who bathed Stephanie, now 4, and it was he who put her to bed most evenings. Then Jan met another man and they became lovers. He was already divorced and had custody of his children. Jan petitioned Michael for a divorce on the grounds of his behaviour and he cross-petitioned.

The family had always been very open in their behaviour about the home, walking about the flat in the nude, bathing together, and so on. Jan then became very concerned about Stephanie, who appeared to intimate that her father had behaved in a way with her which was sexually inappropriate (though it never emerged what he was actually supposed to have done), and in the situation of their acute conflict, she accused him of sexually abusing Stephanie. There was then a storm of accusations and counter-accusations in which a number of professionals became involved, although not the police. Stephanie and both parents were seen by a consultant specialising in child sexual abuse, who, while considering that some of the behaviour in the family was inappropriate for a 4-year-old, could find no evidence of sexual abuse. He therefore referred the couple for conciliation. They were seen for three very acrimonious sessions in order to try to explore whether and how Michael might see his daughter.

During these sessions further family material emerged which indicated that although the parental relationships with Stephanie had been close, the life style of the couple had always been unconventional. Nor was there evidence of sexual abuse. Indeed it seemed as if this was not only an exaggeration, but possibly also a ploy on Jan's behalf as she wanted Stephanie to join the family of her lover as she herself intended to do.

The couple broke off mediation as Jan had applied to the court, and the conciliator offered them an opportunity to return after the court hearing if they wished. Rather to her surprise they did so, as the hearing had been adjourned for them to return for conciliation. (In other circumstances they might well have been referred to the Divorce Court welfare officer (see Chapter 10, 'Divorce Court welfare officers', page 221) but it later appeared the Oldhams had asked to return to the Independent Service, and this was allowed by the judge. The conciliator then negotiated that Jan would bring Stephanie to the service, where her father would see her in the presence of the conciliator, and that in meantime the parents would approach a friend whom they both trusted who might in future agree to take part in supervised access.

The meeting duly took place as arranged and Stephanie greeted her father with considerable delight. He was close to tears, but recovered sufficiently to enjoy the access visit, during which it became clear that his parenting role included playtimes, putting her to bed, reading to her and a great deal of escorting her to and from playschool and to dancing classes, and so on. Jan collected Stephanie at the end of the hour, and when both parents met with the conciliator subsequently the supervised access was agreed. Michael wrote a letter which indicated that he was 'over the moon' with the arrangements which enabled him to see his daughter; and some months later, Jan telephoned to say that the court had confirmed what they had agreed to and to ask how she could refer a friend.

The work with the Oldhams covered only four or five sessions in all and did not entail any work at depth. The conciliator inevitably discovered something of the family history, but did not work with this in any way. The task of the conciliation was to explore whether or not an agreement could be reached in what were most difficult circumstances and in a situation of some anxiety for the conciliator. She had to point out to the parents that should there be any evidence of sexual abuse of Stephanie, then she would need to inform their local Social Services Department. These are the only circumstances in which the confidentiality of conciliation may be breached. The conciliator followed the process of the stages of conciliation as previously set out (in Chapter 2), though in these circumstances she did not write a memorandum of agreement as the couple were already engaged in the litigation process. She did, however, with the Oldhams' agreement, write a brief note to each of their solicitors.

Some would question whether to assist Michael to rebuild his relationship with his young daughter was in her best interests, especially as Jan had a ready-made stepfamily which she would join.

Others, however, would argue that Michael had not been either tried or convicted of any wrongdoing, and both he and his daughter had a right to continue a father–daughter relationship with each other.

COMBINATIONS OF CONCILIATION AND THERAPY WITH THE SAME FAMILY

Conciliation to therapy

Parkinson (1986) shows that of the couples who become involved in conciliation about 10 per cent are likely to change their minds about divorcing and decide to explore the possibility of reconciliation. The policy of most conciliation services is to refer such couples who want to work on reconciliation with a view to rebuilding their marriage to other agencies, such as Relate (Marriage Guidance) with whom the NFCC have worked out some guidelines for referral.

The reasons for such referral are predominantly because conciliation is task-centred and contract-based so as to attempt to help the couple reach agreement. But it is also at least partly aimed at conserving such scarce resources as are at present available, in order to retain the focus of helping the couples in conflict working together, and thus avoid the ultimate recourse to the courts which not only takes the decision-making out of their hands but is also likely to prove expensive (see Chapter 10).

The Preston family

Oliver and Naomi Preston married not long after she gave birth to Jamie, whose father had no contact with him and whom they treated as their own child. Both were professional people and ambitious in their careers, and Jamie was looked after by a daily nanny. Some two years after their marriage they had a daughter, Emma. When Jamie was 6 and Emma 4 they had a third child. Naomi was often unwell during the pregnancy and the child, a boy, whom they called Thomas, only lived a few weeks. His parents realised that it was unlikely that he would live.

Naomi was preoccupied with her own grief and the children, and buried herself in her career, shutting herself off from Oliver. He in turn, while continuing to be as close to the other two children as before, felt lonely and neglected by his wife. Always a sociable person, he met a woman through his work and began to go out with her, at least partly as a way of avoiding his own grief. The affair deepened and Oliver became attached to Marion. Naomi eventually discovered that Oliver was having an affair, and this was a cruel and shocking blow to her and to Oliver, who for the first time really faced his recent behaviour. He became confused and equally distressed, and there were terrible rows between them, Oliver eventually leaving to stay with a friend.

Neither of them was in any state to make such important decisions, yet Marion, in her angry despair, wanted to punish Oliver and insisted she wanted a divorce. They both consulted solicitors and a psychiatrist, who referred them to a conciliation service. The conciliator saw the couple together, which Naomi was very reluctant to do as she could hardly bear to see Oliver, she was so angry with him. It was a most painful interview for all of them, and both of them wept profusely between bouts of Naomi's understandable anger and distress. The conciliator saw them three times, during which they agreed that the most important priority was to try to find a way in which Oliver could see the children. As is customary, this was worked out in detail, so that the children could experience the least disruption to their normal programme. An important feature of this was that it was usually their father who put them to bed and read them stories. Naomi said she could not bear to see Oliver, so it was agreed that she would work late on the evening that he went to the home, and that on Saturdays she would go out so that Oliver and the children could be at home together. They agreed to put decisions related to their marriage 'on ice' for the time being, while Oliver sought therapy for himself, in order to try to sort out how he had got himself into such a situation.

At the third visit, the arrangements seemed to be working well, and the conciliator was about to suggest that the couple might return should this be necessary when they had made a final decision about the divorce, when they revealed that when Oliver visited the home they had resumed their sexual relationship with each other. Indeed, they were as confused as ever about the future of their marriage. Oliver did not think that he wanted to live with Marion, and the conciliator suggested that they might be referred back to the counsellor who had referred them to the service, but Oliver, particularly, did not want that. They asked the conciliator why they could not work with her, as they had all been through so much together. As the particular service was a separate department in a service which also included a marital and family therapy service, she agreed to take them on, but explained the manner of working would be quite different, as indeed it was.

The therapist thereafter began working with the couple on trying to explore what had happened to their marriage and how it was that it had not been possible for them to share their grief at the loss of their child with each other. They began to discover that for each of them marriage had been simultaneous with becoming a parent, rather than first being part of a husband and wife couple; also that both of them had been brought up in families with indulgent, live-in nannies and somewhat distant parents, and neither of them had an internal model of how husbands and wives managed the balance of their roles as marital partners and parent-hood. They agreed to work together on rebuilding their marriage.

The conciliator and the Prestons worked in very different and distinctive ways during the two types of work. During the first brief, task-centred work in mediation with regard to Oliver having access to his children, the focus was entirely on negotiating how this might be agreed. The conciliator worked in the here-and-now, and knew only enough of the couple's history to be able to work with them on the agreed task. The despair of the couple relating to their marriage was acknowledged, but not worked with; indeed, if anything their decision-making with regard to the future was frozen, while Oliver decided what he wanted to do. During the therapeutic work the contract was changed, and, unusually for this therapist, she focused almost entirely on the couple's marriage, rather than the family. This, by agreement, was because they had never really had the initial stage of marriage as they had become parent and stepparent as soon as they married. In fact, Oliver regarded himself and was regarded as Jamie's father, but it became clear that it would become necessary to explore how it was that Naomi had become pregnant when she had apparently not wanted to do so, and why it was that Oliver chose to marry a young woman who had only so recently had a baby. Indeed it seemed that this young couple had been stuck at the phase of attachment-caregiving as described by Wynne (1984), and that this was directed to their children rather than each other, though each secretly resented the lack of care given to them by the other.

Therapy to conciliation

As will already have become apparent, and with one in three marriages being a remarriage following divorce, many remarried partners take unresolved problems from their first marriage into their second marriage and stepfamily. The complexities of stepfamily life are such that the stresses on the new and most vulnerable relationship in the family, the remarriage, are considerable (see Chapters 6 and 7). It is hardly surprising, therefore, that the divorce rate is much higher for second marriages, and it is estimated that approximately one in four divorces is the second divorce for one or both partners. Many couples who survive the divorce and remarry without seeking help from outside find themselves in a similar position in their second marriage and seek help either as individuals or as a couple.

The Quinton family

When they sought therapy for their marital difficulties, Bill and Wendy Quinton had been married eight years and had a daughter, Sarah, aged 7. Both had previously been married. Bill and his first wife, Anne, had two daughters, Miranda, aged 10, and Carol, 8. Bill and Anne had married young (both aged 22), and their marriage had been a stormy one including violent scenes. Anne herself was the child of divorced parents and had lost touch with her father during her childhood. She was very close to her mother and since the divorce, the maternal grandmother had become very involved in the girls' upbringing. Bill was the only son of his parents; his father, a retired Naval officer, had not been around for much of his childhood, and he and Bill had never really got on well. Their relationship worsened when Bill, unhappy at his father's old college, managed to get himself thrown out. Bill and Anne married soon after in defiance of their parents and to their surprise, he did very well.

Wendy was the oldest of three siblings, two daughters and a son. Her father had been a prisoner of war and the effects of this on him had led to some difficulties in their family life when he returned. Wendy ran away from home and had a somewhat chequered late adolescence with various boyfriends, which led to an estrangement from her family, especially from her father whose favourite she had been, though this later became healed.

Wendy also married young, an Italian whom she had met on holiday, and they lived in Italy for several years, during which time she had two sons: Paul, now 15, and Charles, 13. The marriage was unhappy, and she came home to England with the boys and obtained a divorce, both the boys visiting their father, Luigi, every summer.

Wendy was divorced when she and Bill met; he and Anne were already separated. Nevertheless, his divorce was an acrimonious one, and for a number of years Anne, whose daughters had become her whole life, seemed to make it as difficult as she could for them to see their father.

Soon after they married, Bill, Wendy and the two boys went to the United States where, following his promotion, he had been transferred by his company. Sarah was born there. This was not a happy time for them. Bill, an assertive and ambitious man (with two families to keep) was preoccupied with his job which did not work out well, and Wendy was lonely and unhappy. There were rows in which Bill, desperate that this marriage too was going wrong, hectored and even bullied Wendy, who withdrew more and more into herself. When they returned, things were even worse as they tried to find somewhere to live. One day Bill returned home to find that Wendy, the boys and Sarah had left, and gone to Wendy's parents. He persuaded her to return and they sought marriage guidance, but Wendy found it difficult to talk to the counsellor. After tensions at Christmas, particularly between the boys and Bill, she left again also without telling him, this time going to his parents, which made Bill very angry as they had been very disapproving of his divorce and remarriage.

Bill by this time was involved in legal proceedings with Anne in order to get defined access to his older daughters. Bill and Wendy sought marital therapy for their own marriage and were seen weekly for a year. During this time they explored with the therapist Bill's aggressiveness and the link with his fear of rejection and Wendy's inability to cope with this, which led her to withdraw; and when it reached a certain pitch in which she could not express her anger back, to leave. They also did a good deal of work on where they had reached in the stepfamily life cycle. Bill still had some difficulties with Paul, but he and Charles began to do things together which they both enjoyed, like sailing.

The application for defined access to Miranda and Carol was successful, and every fortnight Bill drove to the West Country to collect them for the weekend. They formed a close relationship with Sarah and began to relax. Wendy managed to contain her irritation with Anne, who made all kinds of dietary requirements for the girls, and criticised the state of their clothes when they returned from access visits. On one visit she found sewn into their pockets a note saying, 'Miranda is on an access visit. In the event of an accident, please contact Mrs Anne Quinton' and her address.

Bill tried hard to repair his relationship with his parents, who refused to visit them, yet invited his daughters to stay with them, though Anne declined. On one occasion they offered to have Sarah to stay while he and Wendy went away for a week, but when their holiday fell through they cancelled it, to Sarah's disappointment, and invited Bill's sister's daughter instead.

Gradually this stepfamily began to move into another stage as their marriage improved and they decided to leave therapy. However, by now it had become very clear that Anne was finding it very difficult to share her daughters, and indeed refused to talk to Bill when he took them back from their access visits. Bill, now much happier in himself and his remarriage, became increasingly troubled about Anne's isolation and indeed her mental health, especially for the effect on the girls in the future when they became adolescent. After a discussion on conciliation during one of the therapy sessions, he decided to put this idea to Anne, so that they might try to find ways in which the access visits could be less of a stress to everyone in the re-formed extended family. The therapist therefore put Bill in touch with the local conciliation service which would try to see Anne and Bill.

With Bill and Wendy the therapist worked with their marital difficulties, but with a family systems approach which included all the children, and also their previous partners. They became aware of the circular pattern in which Bill's need for certainty that Wendy cared for him made him so anxiously demanding, which in turn led to Wendy's angry resentment, which she bottled up, withdrawing from him, in turn making him angry, until eventually after no discussion Wendy would leave. They began to be able to recognise and manage this for themselves.

Bill's troubled relationship with his parents also became a focus, as his anger and deprivation had affected both his marriages. Both Bill and Wendy wanted him to keep in touch with the daughters of his first marriage and were concerned about what seemed to be happening to Anne. It therefore seemed more appropriate for Bill and Anne to go for conciliation in her home town to see if they could work out a better co-parenting arrangement, rather than that the girls should return to heightened tensions at their mother's home after every access visit. They realised that it might be difficult to engage Anne but thought it likely that as the girls became adolescent this might become possible.

UNMARRIED PARTNERS

In view of the increasing numbers of couples who are cohabiting and have never been married, about whose relationships relatively little is known, it is probably useful to point out that these relationships too break down and one or both partners seek help of one kind or another. It may not be universally realised that much of the work of Relate (Marriage Guidance) is with either one or both partners of such a common-law relationship. Indeed, one metropolitan group of counsellors made the empirical discovery that a small but significant group of their clients were couples who were involved in an affair in which one partner (usually the man) could not come a decision as to whether or not he could or would leave his wife and children or give up the partner in his affair, who was usually a colleague at work. The same services for individual or couple therapy are of course usually also available for unmarried couples who are in relationship difficulties.

Mediation, too, is available for unmarried partners who have children and whose relationship is breaking down. It is useful for both to obtain advice as to their legal position both in relation to their children and any property jointly owned between them. A small number of such couples have not set up a home together, indeed have hardly shared their lives together, and yet many of the (usually young) fathers want to take a responsible paternal role as regards their child.

The Rochdale/Stockport family

Anita Stockport was in her early thirties when she decided to leave her job as a librarian and travel to Australia for a few months' holiday. At first she stayed with a friend, but on a trip to Melbourne she met John Rochdale, also in his thirties. While both had had previous relationships none of them had been important or long-lasting and each was ready to settle down. Anita, looking back, now considers that she was living in a dream during the first few months she was in Australia. She moved into John's flat and they tentatively talked of having children. Almost at once she discovered she was pregnant, which threw her into a panic. John wanted to marry her, but things were not going well with the relationship, particularly as regards his drinking, and at seven months pregnant, she decided to return home to see her parents and to sort out her flat.

She returned to Australia, and when their son David was born her parents flew out to see their daughter and grandson. John was 'over the moon' with his son, but resented Anita's complaints about his drinking and wishing to spend time with his own band of brothers whom she considered a bad influence on him. He had a row with her parents, which ended in some kind of fight between them, the details of which were never possible to ascertain as the accounts differed.

Anita's parents returned to London and she soon left with David to go into a women's refuge. By this time, David was six months old, Anita had no money and was also an illegal immigrant. John wanted Anita to return, but also to see his son, and was frantic that Anita wanted to return to the United Kingdom. A series of court cases followed in the Family Court of Australia, culminating in Anita and David being allowed to return to London. For the next year, telephone calls and letters were exchanged, but John sent no maintenance.

Anita returned to live with her parents and went into counselling to begin to replan her life. She was not working and so only had Supplementary Benefit for herself and David. John kept saying he would be coming to London, but she did not believe that he would until he suddenly telephoned to say that he would be arriving the following weekend and would be staying for three weeks and wanted to see David. Anita was in a panic, fearing that he would kidnap David and take him back to Australia.

With the help of her counsellor and after various telephone calls she and John went to a conciliation service, where they agreed the detailed arrangements for John to visit David, now 18 months old, at her parents' house, with Anita being present. Apart from one tense situation, these visits went well, John and David beginning to enjoy their times together; but John wanted to take David out on his own. This aroused all Anita's fears of kidnapping, which were not helped by John's somewhat heavy drinking. At the second conciliation session, the conciliator suggested that John handed his passport over to Anita, and it was eventually agreed that he could take David out on three occasions on his own.

The first two sessions went well enough, but by the third session John was getting desperate about his need to return to Australia and wanted Anita to promise to take David out the following Christmas. Anita who now regarded Australia as the place where her dream had turned into a nightmare, could not agree, and a stalemate ensued. Eventually, at the eleventh hour, the conciliator suggested that Anita find a solicitor in this country who would advise her with regard to her own and David's legal position should they go to Australia to see John; and that John would also ascertain his legal position regarding David, and Anita staying in his house. Anita would then return to see the conciliator who would discuss possible arrangements and write to John. John meanwhile, would also find whether it would be possible for a counsellor from the Family Court to support Anita during her stay and would write both to her and the conciliator.

These three sessions in three weeks at least allowed John to see his son, and Anita promised to continue to talk to David about his father. They also seem to have resulted in the beginning of a more cooperative relationship between Anita and John. In view of the relative youthfulness of Anita and John, and the likelihood of their forming future more permanent relationships, as well as the fact that David was barely a toddler, some might question whether a clean break with John might not be the best for Anita and David; while others would consider that David had the right both to know and have the opportunity to develop a relationship with his biological father.

CONCLUSIONS

The previous paragraphs have described the various ways in which partners going through separation and the divorce process not only can be helped to make their own decisions, but also can be given practical and therapeutic support. In their clinical research with the families referred to them for mediation by the Californian courts because they were at a divorce transition impasse, Johnston and Campbell (1988) developed a model which seemed to incorporate aspects of counselling and mediation which proved effective with some of these high-conflict families. There were three distinct phases. In the first place, there is a pre-negotiation counselling phase in which each of the parents is prepared to mediate by strategic interventions in the impasse, and the child's needs are explored and an understanding is built up. The second phase involves negotiation and conflict resolution, addressing specific issues as regards child care and co-parenting. And the final phase is that of implementation, when the same counsellor-mediator is on hand to help with monitoring, interpreting and modifying agreements for emergency consultations should the need arise. This model seems to contradict many of the carefully distinguished differences between mediation and family therapy, and yet is clearly differentiated into distinct phases and evidently effective for some of these high-conflict families. It will be clear that the context in which the practitioners work and the contract which they make with their clients will affect the work which they can undertake.

In this chapter a number of ethical issues have been raised in which the values of the members of the interventionist professions who try to help the families will influence their way of working and the mediation itself. There are no easy answers, but professional practitioners have a responsibility to be aware of how their own beliefs about families, children's rights, divorce and remarriage are likely to affect the way in which interventionist practitioners execute their task. Although the law is inevitably a somewhat blunt instrument which cannot be particularly sensitive to individual needs, its enshrinement of the rights of the individual as well as the settlement-seeking nature of family law can and does act as a check on the professional self-indulgence of some of the members of the interventionist professions. In the next chapter I will discuss how the legal system engages with those families which are unable to reach agreement, and some of the ways in which the attitudes of those who work within the legal profession can be changed by the acquisition of knowledge and even some of the skills of their colleagues in the counselling profession.

10 Ways and means of intervening during the divorce process

'Within the shadow of the law' – complementary roles or adversarial partisans?

There is only the fight to recover what has been lost
And found and lost again and again: and now, under conditions
That seem unpropitious. But perhaps neither gain nor loss.
For us there is only the trying.

                                        T. S. Eliot (1888-1965), 'East Coker'

The last chapter focused on the ways and means of intervening during the divorce and remarriage processes outside the legal context, though often in its shadow. The differences between the various types of intervention were discussed and some comparisons were drawn, particularly between psychotherapy, family therapy and mediation. The primary emphasis in this chapter will be on the ways in which the couple are *empowered to retain autonomous decision-making*, whether (as indicated by Mnookin and Kornhauser 1979) in the shadow of or within the legal system, by the two main disciplines which work within it – the divorce court welfare service and family solicitors – and to which each of the partners turn in their conflict. Although there has in many ways been a move towards participant justice (Murch 1980), there is still much to be said for finding ways in which the right to the private domain of family life could be better protected even when a family complaint becomes a public issue – as it does, for example, when the matter of custody and access for the children is considered during the divorce process. The concluding section will also briefly raise the question of how the family conflict can become mirrored by the professionals whose differing tasks are all connected with divorce as a public issue and yet, through lack of understanding, failures of cooperation, miscommunication and even competitiveness among themselves, often exacerbate the conflicts and pain of their clientele.

FAMILY SOLICITORS

A significant proportion of the individual clients of family solicitors are drawn from couples where one partner is either petitioner or the respondent (that is, they have received divorce petitions) and who consult solicitors for legal advice with a view to legal representation in court. There is an increasing trend towards specialisation in many solicitors' practices, particularly the larger firms which distinguish between (for instance) conveyancing and other work. Some solicitors do now specialise in matrimonial and family matters, which many consider to be low status work, while others combine such work with other litigation or criminal matters.

Clients' perceptions of the solicitor

Murch (1980), who surveyed a significant and representative sample (102) of petitioners in undefended divorce cases and interviewed a sample of 41 divorcing couples whose children had been the subject of a court welfare report, found that many clients, particularly women, found some difficulty in locating a solicitor. The majority asked the advice of a family solicitor, family or friends; others saw the office and walked in or had employed the solicitor before (usually for a house purchase); and once they had located her or him, most preferred to stay with one solicitor. Although many described 'feelings of not being accepted or properly recognised as a person worthy of the solicitor's professional concern and respect', slightly more than half found their solicitors approachable, helpful and friendly; and nearly all found their services satisfactory. Divorcing couples often did not understand the length of time the divorce process would take, yet most found that their solicitors were very good at letting them know about the reasons for the delay. They tended to evaluate their own solicitor according to whether or not they perceived him as partisan, yet saw their spouses' solicitor 'as inflaming the conflict by encouraging the former spouse to be more obdurate'.

In Scotland at the time of Mitchell's research (1981), all pursuers (petitioners) in divorce actions (though not the defenders unless they wished to defend the divorce or dispute the ancillary matters) had to use the services of a solicitor and an advocate; and a slightly smaller number than Murch's petitioners encountered difficulties in finding a solicitor. Nearly all of Mitchell's pursuers then found their services satisfactory, as did also a high percentage of defenders.

Davis has conducted several recent research studies (1988) connected with divorce, the Special Procedure in Divorce and, together with Murch, has examined 3,000 court files, observed 1,500 Children's Appointments and made two studies of the Bristol Family Courts (Out of Court – that is, independent) Conciliation Service. Davis also carried out a study of negotiation and settlement of legal issues, which as well as exploring '"mediation" on court premises, ... in practice involved studying the work of partisans (principally solicitors) just as much as that of mediators (welfare officers and registrars)'. Additionally, he has been monitoring the work of the South East London Conciliation Bureau (Davis and Roberts 1988), which, although 'out of court', is partially staffed by Divorce Court welfare officers. Three of these studies involved interviewing consumers in their own homes. In the Special Procedure study they found that about half the couples, although experiencing tensions and disagreements, struggled to maintain civilised behaviour towards one another, while slightly less than a quarter reported little or no tension and slightly more than a quarter either had no contact or what there was was 'far from amicable'.

Kressel's (1985) research, conducted in the US, found strong differences among attorneys relating to their professional role in divorce. After interviewing a small number of practitioners exclusively involved with divorce, and following a subsequent survey (of the Family Law Section of the New Jersey State Bar Association, and subsequent interviews) he distinguished six distinct stances according to which the lawyers perceived their work, which could be ranged on a continuum from the advocates, who take an essentially narrow legalistic and combatant view, to the counsellors, whose orientation is more primarily psychological. These, in ascending order, he described as follows:

1 *'The undertaker'*, who considers that the task is essentially thankless and that the clients are in a state of emotional turmoil.
2 *'The mechanic'*, who perceives the task as essentially a pragmatic and technically oriented one, and assumes that clients are capable of knowing what they want.
3 *'The mediator'*, whose 'stance is towards negotiated compromise and rational problem solving', the emphasis being particularly on cooperation and compromise with the other partner and in particular their lawyer.
4 *'The social worker'*, whose major concern is for the client's social welfare and post-divorce adjustment.

5 *'The therapist'*, who accepts the fact that the client is in a state of emotional stress and turmoil, and considers that the unless the lawyer engages with the emotional aspects and tries to understand the clients' motivation, the legal aspects cannot adequately be managed.

6 *'The moral agent'*, in which any attempt at neutrality is abandoned and the lawyer relies on his or her own perceptions of what is right or wrong, particularly in relation to a sense of fair play and parental duties.

In a subsequent discussion Kressel points out the stresses for lawyers in their efforts to solve dilemmas in professional practice for which they are ill prepared by their legal training, which virtually excludes areas such as child development, family dynamics and counselling skills. For the sizeable group who subscribe to the counsellor stance, their primary characteristics are a concern for the psychological and interpersonal issues in the lawyer–client relationships and a cooperative orientation to divorce settlement negotiations. The other equally large group are those who hold the advocate philosophy, and who eschew the psychological and interpersonal issues, defining their role in a more exclusively 'technical–legal approach', and choose to follow the adversarial approach. Kressel emphasises the lack of clear guidelines for helping lawyers decide which path to take: 'a zealous pursuit of the client's interests', or one in which 'the informal norms and the realities of professional life prompt compromise and cooperation'. He considers that

> the role of the divorce lawyer is unenviable ... the unhappy emotional and financial circumstances of their clients introduce significant tensions in the lawyer–client relationship; the adversarial nature of the legal system pushes lawyers towards tactics of competitive conflict, while the informal norms and ties to their colleagues, introduce strong counter-pressures to adopt a more cooperative stance.

It is important to stress that it is the clients who engage their lawyers, and it is entirely within their prerogative to choose to instruct another solicitor. Although there are conventions and organisational pressures which make it difficult for clients to change their doctors or social workers, it is a recognised possibility to change lawyers, though it is not easy to gauge how easy this is in practice. However, unlike social workers and some doctors, it is only in the past few years that lawyers have received training in the skills of the lawyer–client relationship in relation to divorce. Their clients too are often financially pressed and their conflict and distress are particularly acute.

Kressel points to the need for more direct observation of the lawyer–client interview to help lawyers manage interviews with such clients. He draws attention to a small study in the United Kingdom, where lawyer–client interaction was observed in seventy-seven cases (Cain 1979). In three of the six which involved divorce, only one lawyer rejected the clients' objectives in favour of his own: He was not willing to fight matters if there was a risk of being viewed as 'unreasonable' by court officers or fellow lawyers.' Kressel argues that lawyers also need knowledge of areas such as child development and family dynamics, as few of the issues that arise in divorce settlement negotiation could be described as strictly legal issues; indeed, many are likely to involve psychological expertise, such as the access arrangements which would best suit the emotional needs of children and parents.

In the United Kingdom until recently, when Murch (1980) and Davis (1988) carried out their studies, there has been almost no research into the performance of legal practitioners in civil matters. In describing the solicitor as 'more than just a partisan' Davis points out that it is not uncommon for them to be faced with clients who are as yet undecided as to whether or not they wish their marriage to continue. According to him, 'when parties are at their most vulnerable – in conflict with one another and confronted with legal machinery which they do not understand – the only "support" worth having may be that which is unashamedly partisan'; and that because in many people's minds partisanship coupled with sensitivity and understanding go together, solicitors who understand this 'provide a haven of support' throughout the divorce period. He considers that the nervousness of many solicitors in taking on a more definitively counselling role has resulted in the artificial dichotomy between issues relating to children and those related to money and property. While many of the clients interviewed valued their solicitor as a counsellor and valued his or her advice, whether neutral or partisan, others, notably those who remained on friendly terms as a couple, would have welcomed the opportunity of receiving joint advice from a solicitor, which at present is frowned on by the Law Society.

Davis discovered that the one area where solicitors do not appear to provide their clients with sufficient information is in relation to costs. He argues that there may be several reasons for this: first, the difficulty in predicting the costs; second, that it might be a deliberate tactic to enable solicitors to overcharge at the end of the day; or third, and as many solicitors themselves suggested, because at the outset of matrimonial proceedings many clients are so distressed that it would be clumsy and also unavailing for the subject of payment to be raised.

In a full discussion of the lawyer as negotiator and champion, Davis confronts the commonly held view that solicitors may be responsible for exacerbating the acrimony and misunderstandings which so frequently feature in divorce proceedings. He describes the approach of many solicitors 'as conciliatory within a framework of clear partisanship', and indeed this was how more than half the clients in the Bristol study perceived them. He gives one example of this by the way in which solicitors reduce the acrimony, which is the practice when on receipt of a 'behaviour' petition, by employing the 'face saving device of writing to the petitioner's solicitor setting out the views of the respondent and obtaining an assurance that the allegations will not be raised in the course of ancillary proceedings' (for example, when matters of custody and access are considered).

As he later points out, 'to lawyers the "adversarial system" does not imply anger, aggression, or ill-feeling; it merely acknowledges the fact of separate and competing interests'. Because of their familiarity with the patterns of settlement in other cases, lawyers are usually able to predict the eventual outcome, something which their clients, because of their emotional vulnerability at the time, are often unable to do. While he did find evidence that there were litigiously gladiatorial solicitors, according to their colleagues these were only a small group, as the figures were much less than folklore suggests. Only 19 per cent of the clients in contested applications considered their solicitors needlessly aggressive.

The legal expenses in obtaining a divorce are an additional burden for families already under financial stress, and may even be excessive. In a recent application for ancillary relief to make appropriate provision for the parties and their children following divorce in the Family Division (*Evans* v. *Evans*, 1990) the court was unable to make financial provision because the legal costs were out of all proportion to the assets available. In making her judgement, Mrs Justice Booth set out some general guidelines to be followed by the practitioner in the preparation of a substantial ancillary relief case.

Professional guidelines

In the Solicitors' Family Law Association (SFLA), founded in 1982, every member is recommended to adopt the code of practice (1984), which is as follows:

1 The solicitor should endeavour to advise, negotiate and conduct proceedings in a manner calculated to achieve a constructive settlement of [the parties'] differences as quickly as may be reasonable whilst recognising that the parties may need time to come to terms with their new situations, and should inform the client of the approach he intends to adopt.

2 The solicitor should treat his work in relation to the children as the most important of his duties. The solicitor should encourage the client to see the advantages to the family of a non-litigious approach as a way of resolving their disputes. The solicitor should explain to the client that in cases where there are children the attitude of the client to the other parent in any negotiations will affect the family as a whole and may affect the relationship of the children with the parents.

3 The solicitor should encourage the attitude that a family dispute is not a contest in which there is one winner and one loser, but rather a search for fair solutions. He should avoid using words or phrases that imply a dispute when no serious dispute necessarily exists; for example, 'opponent', 'win' or '*Smith* v. *Smith*'.

4 Because of the involvement of personal emotions in family disputes, the solicitor should, where possible, avoid heightening such emotions by the advice given; and by avoiding expressing opinions as to the behaviour of the other party.

5 The solicitor should also have regard to the impact of correspondence on the other party, when writing a letter of which a copy may be sent to that party, and should also consider carefully the impact of correspondence on his own client before sending copies of letters to the client.

6 The solicitor should aim to avoid or dispel suspicion or mistrust between parties by encouraging at an early stage where possible, full, frank and clear disclosure of information and openness in dealings.

The code of practice continues by making recommendations about the solicitor's relationship with the client, taking care that the client is immediately aware of his retainer; the impact of costs and his right to apply for legal aid; the preservation of his independent judgement;

and the need to ensure that while advising the client of their consequences regarding effects on children and financial matters, any decisions are properly taken by him. Further guidelines make recommendations regarding the relationships with other solicitors, dealings with the other party in person, and as regards petitions and proceedings. The final section sets out guidelines in relation to importance of the solicitor's duties in relation to the children – concerning the assistance of both his client and the other party in regard to the welfare of the child as the first and paramount consideration; the promotion of cooperation between parents in decisions concerning the child; the knowledge that the interests of the child do not necessarily coincide with those of either parent; the separation of issues of custody and access from those of financial matters; and the need strongly to discourage the 'kidnapping' of a child.

It will be apparent from the previous discussion that while it is beneficial for both parties in divorce to consult solicitors for legal advice and representation, legal training needs to include more knowledge and skills than it does at present. Indeed, the SFLA has initiated a series of seminars to deal with such issues as 'Acting in Child Cases' and 'The Importance of the First Interview' as well as one on the issues raised by becoming a stepfamily. Although further training is voluntary rather than compulsory, such courses are recognised by the Law Society as giving points towards recognition for recently qualified solicitors. These and many such issues continue to emerge which put pressure on family solicitors to adapt their expertise and change their current practice.

Solicitors and children

Many solicitors now work closely with other professionals, perhaps particularly with social workers acting as guardians *ad litem* in child-care cases. This has led them to begin to acquire an understanding and respect both for their different perspective and their skills. There are similarly good reasons for developing respect and understanding in order to promote cooperation between solicitors and other professionals, who may also working with the same clients during divorce.

Many, if not most, solicitors do not consider it appropriate to interview the children of their clients in divorce cases and avoid doing so. Yet, where the wishes of children considered to be competent differ from those of the guardian *ad litem*, solicitors are obliged to take instructions directly from the child. The collaborative relationship between solicitor and guardians *ad litem* has been shown not only to be fruitful for the child, but also for the court (Murch and Hooper 1989).

Should solicitors therefore become directly involved in interviewing the children of their divorce clients? They may certainly need to do so, if the proposed changes are adopted which relate to extending the powers of the court to order separate representation of children in some divorce cases, as, for instance, where custody and access are contested. If so, how can they acquire sufficient knowledge, skills and understanding to be more helpful regarding the children of their clients who are also parents in families undergoing transformation during the divorce process?

Is this another area suitable for conciliators and solicitors to work collaboratively and with more understanding than is often possible at present? Both the implications of the Children Act (1989) and Murch and Hooper's research (1989) on Support Services for Family Jurisdiction propose more cross-disciplinary training (see Chapter 12, 'The Children Act 1989', page 282, and 'Cross-disciplinary training', page 292). How might it be possible to explore ways in which the psychological processes which the family are experiencing as the result of the separation and divorce of the parents can be sufficiently understood? How might such understanding become incorporated and integrated within the legal processes so that families can experience legal proceedings as being less confusing and even more supportive than they are at present?

It is already the practice for some family solicitors to refer clients who initially consult them to one of the various agencies (often Relate (Marriage Guidance) or, though usually at a later stage, to a conciliation service, if one is available) rather than encourage preparation for litigation – although, as the research on children of divorcing parents shows, it is at the time of parental separation that children's relationship with the parent who leaves home is most at risk, and an early referral to conciliation could make a considerable difference in maintaining that relationship. Perhaps somewhat provocatively, Davis and Murch (1988) point out that

> since the state has virtually abandoned any attempt to sustain marriage through the law, this perception of separate and competing interests can be the only basis upon which divorce retains its identity as legal process, rather than an administrative matter. Once lawyers find it necessary to take account of the long term interests of the children, or the parties' future relationship, then

divorce as a legal process is called into question, because this is not legal knowledge.

They go on to ask why, once the partisanship of lawyers becomes tempered by a need for knowledge of child psychology or family therapy, they should continue to hold such a dominant position.

Lawyers as mediators

In the US matrimonial lawyers have increasingly shown interest in becoming involved as mediators, and there is now a body of literature written by lawyers, the earliest and perhaps the best-known being the Coogler (1979) Structured Mediation model, which is based on law. As Folberg and Taylor (1984) point out, lawyers acting as mediators tend to draw more skills and knowledge from their professional training and orientation, while therapists do likewise from theirs. Obviously a lawyer acting as a mediator is familiar with what the courts are likely to accept or can advise about financial matters, but as indicated above, would be cautious about advice relating to child development. Mediation offers an additional aspect to the lawyer's traditional practices, an alternative in which their legal expertise can be applied. As Melamed (1989) points out, lawyers

> are trained to give advice and to make [their] best judgements as to what is right and wrong, truth and justice. . . . [I]n mediation there are few things that will get the mediator into trouble quicker than giving advice or judgement. The mediative role must be understood as facilitative, with no decision-making role.

Fisher and Fisher (1982) a lawyer–therapist married couple, when ethically possible, have cooperated professionally to help divorcing clients. In writing of their own experience they emphasise the importance of boundaries. They point out that the lawyer is a counsellor at law, not a marriage counsellor. The lawyer presents the client with a range of alternatives, but the performance is by the lawyer, whereas the counsellor helps the client to help himself or herself. Their focus is on divorce counselling or therapy as insight-giving, where the focus is on the 'diminution and final dissolution of the marital relationship with correlative concern for the the intrapsychic needs of the individual spouse(s)'. They point out that the lawyer and therapist must be able to establish goals that are not in conflict and arrive at their objectives to their mutual understanding. Nevertheless they point to the importance of developing mutual respect and understanding of each other's discipline.

Another American married couple, a lawyer and mental health worker who now have a joint practice as private practitioners, have written a clear and straightforward account of the model of mediation which each of them practises individually and which is primarily based on a negotiations model. This entails promoting open and honest communication, attitudes which create trust, and negotiating methods which bargain about interests rather than positions, and outcome goals in which both will be winners rather than losers (Erickson and Erickson 1988).

There is a small group of solicitors based mainly in London who, as members of the Family Mediators Association (Parkinson 1989) have been practising together with a conciliator as co-mediators in *comprehensive co-mediation*, working with couples in dispute over financial matters and the matrimonial home and perhaps also over the arrangements for their children. It is as yet too early to assess such practice, which in any event is at the time of writing only available for divorcing couples who can afford to pay the equivalent of moderate legal fees. Alternative models which make selective use of family solicitors may well develop; and it is possible that this may lead to future developments on the boundaries between law and mediation.

DIVORCE COURT WELFARE OFFICERS

The Probation Service, whose practitioners are primarily trained as social workers to work with delinquent clients and related criminal matters, has a long-established and well-respected relationship with the courts. It also has a long-standing commitment to matrimonial work, particularly that arising from the Magistrates' Courts and, as the result of the rising divorce rate, gradually became involved in welfare of children of parents who were seeking divorce in the High Courts (see Parkinson 1986, 1988; James and Wilson 1986; Clulow and Vincent 1987; Howard and Shepherd 1987; James 1988; Robinson 1988). Following recommendations of the Royal Commission on Marriage and Divorce (1956) probation officers acting as welfare officers have been regularly posted to the Divorce Registry and, since 1986, to the County Courts, where they are now more often known as Divorce Court welfare officers, and are usually expected to provide both voluntary assistance to couples in conflict and also the investigative welfare reports which may be required by the court in order to assist the decision-making.

The primary duty of the civil work of the Probation Service is to provide information to the courts relating to the welfare of children and probation officers may also become involved in proceedings for separation, affiliation, wardship adoption, guardianship and cus-todianship, either to provide reports or even as a supervisor of arrangements for children (including, for instance, the execution of Matrimonial Supervision orders). However, the position of the Probation Service has been and remains somewhat uncertain in relation to civil matters, which are only a small part of its work (James 1988). Despite this, there has been a surprising increase in the establishment of specialist civil units for this purpose, and indeed, according to James, 80 per cent of the report work and 90 per cent of the supervision orders stem from matrimonial proceedings. James indicates that

> divorce courts have substantial powers to request reports: in advance of a hearing; to enable a judge to declare his satisfaction with consensual arrangements for custody; to provide information where custody and access are disputed; or in cases where an interim custody order is being sought.

Indeed, in 1988 the Civil Units prepared 27,000 welfare reports and undertook 10,000 conciliation cases.

A recent article by James and Dingwall (1989), which discusses the social work ideologies in the Probation Service with particular reference to its civil work, points out that

> there appears to be disagreement about the main unit of need in civil work. On the one hand, there is the individual child, whose needs must be protected, whilst on the other, there is the family, which must be helped through the difficult process of breakdown and reorganisation, thereby reducing the disruption to the indivi-dual child.

They go on to discuss the social organisation of civil work and point out that, 'while judges can define the purpose and focus of the enquiries to be made by a welfare officer, they only have limited influence over the officer's choice of methods' (see page 94).

Foden and Wells (1989), both experienced managers of civil work in the Probation Service, stress similar issues, pointing out that 'there has been a lack of management of the civil work of the Probation Service' and that this has resulted in most of the knowledge, experimentation and developmental thinking being held at practi-tioner level, because 'there has been a failure to identify the primary task of the service'. The result of this has been 'a failure to identify the primary client in divorce cases – the child, the parents, the family unit or the court'. They refer to the organisational dysfunction, which at least partly stems from the fact that the Home Office is the central government department for the Probation Service and the one which controls the resources available to it, and which 'spends its energies promoting more effective work with offenders'. Yet it is the Lord Chancellor's Department which is responsible for the courts; and it is the president and judiciary of the Family Division with whom the civil units have close links. The result seems to be a service which reflects the present uncomfortable split in the Probation Service and one which is virtually practitioner-led (see page 95).

During the divorce process the judge scrutinises the petitioner's proposed arrangements for the children, and, if these are accepted by the respondent, usually makes an order 'by consent' (see Chapter 3, 'Guidelines for the practice of mediation', page 59). However, if by the time the petition comes before the court the parents have failed to agree about arrangements for their children, then the couple and their legal representatives are invited to a Children's Hearing, often known as a Conciliation or Mediation Appointment – Section 41 of the Matrimonial Causes Act (1969) – see Chapter 5, 'The legal process', page 93. At this hearing, the judge (or in some cases the registrar) will listen to the arguments put forward by the couple's lawyers and may invite them to withdraw with the court welfare officer, to see if they can come to some agreement. If they fail to do so, then an investigative welfare report may be called for, and ultimately the court will make a judicial decision based on the welfare of the child as the first and paramount consideration. In fact this happens in only a small minority of cases – only 6 per cent of the parents who divorced in 1984 – but nevertheless involves 9,000 children (Priest and Whybrow 1986). At the present time there are two general presumptions: first, that young children should be with their mothers; and second, that there should be access to the noncustodial parent. The courts are also reluctant to remove children from whichever parent is currently holding their day-to-day care at the time of the hearing (see Chapter 3, 'Guidelines for the practice of mediation', page 59).

In many courts, before the Children's Hearing a court welfare officer through the intervention of voluntary conciliation may try to help the couple in conflict about custody and access for their children to come to their own decision. If this (semi)-voluntary bargaining fails, then another officer is required to undertake the investigative report which includes recommendations about custody and access so as to assist the judge to come to a decision.

In some cases, the courts (whether Magistrates' or Divorce Courts) will make a Matrimonial Supervision order, under the Matrimonial Causes Acts (1973) or the Domestic Proceedings and Magistrates' Court Act (1978). Such orders are usually made only in exceptional circumstances and often in order to facilitate access arrangements (see, for example, James and Wilson 1988). These orders may be supervised by probation officers or social workers from the Social Services Department and are statutory orders, and, if these are accepted by the respondent, usually (though not always) the Court makes an order 'by consent'.

The Oldham family (see page 199)

As it happened, in the Oldhams' case the judge was able to make an order for her father to have access to Stephanie, supervised by a mutual friend acceptable to both parents, with consent, as the result of conciliation intervention from an independent service (at the Institute of Family Therapy), but intervention from the court welfare officer through voluntary conciliation might well have given the same result.

The Quinton family (see page 204)

In the case of the Quintons, when Bill was unable to see Miranda and Carol for access visits, he applied to the court for defined access, and a court welfare officer did a full investigation of both binuclear family units and recommended that Bill should see the girls for staying access once a month. During their later difficulties, when the Quintons' therapist suggested that they might return to the court welfare officer and seek voluntary conciliation, Bill said that as she had made some comments in her report about Anne's over-involvement and restrictive behaviour with the girls, he thought Anne would be unlikely to agree to see her voluntarily.

Vignette

Mr Richmond has a long history of psychiatric illness. He and his wife had a particularly traumatic divorce in which his behaviour also distressed his children greatly. When he recovered he wanted access to his children, but they refused to see him. They were referred to an independent conciliation service, but his wife refused to attend. When the conciliator tried to encourage him to ask to see the Divorce Court welfare officer, his response was 'I've tried them – it was no good because they're ignorant, they only know about criminals'.

There must be at least some clients who think the same way as Mr Richmond. In his case it is particularly distressing as he clearly felt that the psychiatric label of mental illness was bad enough without (as he saw it) also being possibly becoming labelled a criminal.

The clients' search for a settlement

It is generally recognised that, in their search for a resolution to divorce-related conflicts, those couples who ultimately appear before the courts are further along the processes of divorce (and remarriage) and yet are also those most entrenched in acrimony because of their inability to reach decisions. In his consumer studies, Davis (1988) found that very few of the parents had resented a welfare report being ordered, though their views concerning the Divorce Court welfare officers were mixed. He considers that 'the Welfare Officer's role, as parents very quickly come to appreciate, is largely that of investigator on behalf of the court'. He found there were three major criticisms of the officers: 'lack of personal experience, insufficient knowledge of the family and an undue standardization of approach'. While Davis eschews taking a psychological approach to his findings, preferring instead to maintain a socio-legal perspective, he recognises the stigma of divorce and considers that this when linked with the client's experience of some welfare officer's authoritarian attitudes (as well as the perception of the main job of the Probation Service as being to 'regulate the poor and criminal classes') may lead to the client's initial acceptance and subsequent protest.

Another recent study of Divorce Court welfare practice was conducted by Clulow and Vincent (1987) who, perhaps because of their experience as psychodynamically oriented marital therapists, 'were critical of the courts when they operated in ways which failed to take account of the emotional purposes behind reasoned submissions, and when they encouraged and aggravated conflicts between partners'. Their view is that their training as probation officers and 'their professional identity as social workers, make it likely that they will regard themselves not only as reporters but as helpers, counsellors, therapists and conciliators'. Clulow and Vincent, together with colleagues from the Tavistock Institute of Marital Studies, joined the staff of a Divorce Court welfare unit as co-workers and participant observers in a core sample of thirty cases, welfare reports being required in seventeen custody applications (in which the majority of applicants were men), and twenty-eight divorce petitions (in which the majority of petitioners were women).

In the great majority of cases they found that a significant part of the context in which these disputes took place were unresolved attachments to the past marriage. They estimated that in more than three-quarters of their sample,

> although some partners were explicit about their wish for recon-
> ciliation, the shock of rejection and displacement more commonly
> resulted in vociferous and sometimes violent protest. A war of
> attrition could follow. Separation prompted the cut-off reactions of
> denial, the rapid substitution of another partner for the rejecting
> spouse and even seizing the initiative to divorce so that the one
> who felt spurned was seen to leave rather than to be left.

They distinguished three groupings which they described as 'nominal divorces, shotgun divorces, and long lease divorces', which indicated different positions on a continuum representing the stage in the divorce process which the couple had reached. The *nominal divorces* seemed similar to those described (see Kressel 1985) as enmeshed couples. Many of them continued to live together although divorced, although when seen separately would complain that their partner (and also the courts and court welfare officers) were failing to take the necessary action to break the deadlock. The *shotgun divorces* formed nearly three-quarters of the core sample, perhaps an indica-tion that these are the kind of divorces which ultimately reach the Divorce Court welfare units. Half of the partners in these cases perceived the divorce as a unilateral decision taken against their wishes by their partner. The shock of this experience resulted in different reactions by the men, who responded with angry abuse and sometimes physical violence; while the women, who would for some time have felt neglected by their husbands and withdraw from the marriage, became increasingly involved with the children, then when an opportunity to depart presented itself, would seize it (according to Clulow and Vincent 'like a turned worm'), leaving their husbands embittered and defeated by the legal process which they perceived as biased in favour of women. The *long lease divorces* – a small group in which, although there was a distant but persistent attachment between the partners, the men retained a 'proprietorial regard' which the women recognised and tacitly accepted. In such families one and often both the partners were in new partnerships, which were tacitly accepted, yet any shift in the distant but chronic affection seemed to trigger some kind of application to the courts in order to restore the previous delicate balance.

In each of these three kinds of families the attitudes and behaviour of their children was clearly related to the parental conflicts as well as their developmental stages. Like the parents in Davis' study, those in Clulow and Vincent's 'were aware that they were under observation and therefore vulnerable to the conclusions drawn by "strangers" about matters which were often felt to be of life and death importance to them'. It is interesting to compare this model with that already described (see Johnston and Campbell, Chapter 9, 'Combinations of conciliation and therapy with the same family', page 201), in which couples, engaged in such wars of divorce attrition, are referred out by the court-based services to a mediation service located in a children's hospital, with some resultant success in their reaching settlements.

Davis (1988) distinguishes three models of welfare enquiry, a combination of *'child protective* and the *quasi judicial'*, in which the welfare officer 'both seeks to identify those children who are being inadequately cared for by their parents' (perhaps because of the emotional and financial strains of the divorce) and 'to help determine the most appropriate child care arrangements in cases where the parents themselves cannot agree'. In the second model, *'settlement-seeking'*, the welfare officer primarily seeks to secure a legal settlement of contested applications using both the authority and expertise in child welfare matters as well as the position of trusted adviser to the court. The clients perceived the Divorce Court welfare officer as a reporting officer whose function was to advise the court. The third model is the *'therapeutic'*, of which Davis is particularly critical – partly because of the absence of any research, though he mentions the Clulow and Vincent study (as well as that of Howard and Shepherd 1987, to be discussed below). He points out that in the follow-up they encountered twice as many negative responses as they did positive ones, with men being especially critical. He nevertheless acknowledges that, like the settlement-seeking model, the therapeutic one can be seen

as an entirely laudable attempt to help parents escape the delusion that there can be a satisfactory legal conclusion to their problem; or

it may be construed as a bid for power of a subtler, 'therapeuti
kind' – and once again as a denial of legal rights.

Conciliatory or investigative?

The general confusion over the meaning of 'conciliation', couple
with the possible conflict between the role of the Divorce Cour
welfare officers' voluntary interventions with clients and investigativ
responsibilities to the court, together with the perceptions of th
service by a usually involuntary clientele, seem to have led t
particular difficulties for the Probation Service. Murch (1980) con
siders that it is essential to distinguish conciliation from the kind o
social investigation required in order to provide a welfare report t
the court. Jackson (1986) has also argued that, because there i
inevitably the coercive shadow of the court in the background, sucl
intervention should be known as 'mediation'. James and Wilso
(1986) point out that the term 'conciliation' is frequently use
indiscriminately, 'to refer to the objective of bringing peace to
dispute, to the process of trying to achieve settlement and to
method of achieving agreement between the disputing parties'.

However, Divorce Court welfare officers can and do use the terr
in relation to the objective of attempting to resolve the acrimony an
bitterness between divorcing partners; as a method to help disputin
parents gain greater control over the processes of agreement relatin
to their children; and also as the process of preparing an investigativ
welfare report requested by the court. It is this aspect of their rol
which seems to cause the greatest difficulty. James (1988) consider
that there is an argument that the Probation Service should reject thi
role as 'assessor of families and seek to return control over decisio
making to the families themselves'. Drawing on documents from th
Conference of Chief Probation Officers (1982) and the Nationa
Association of Probation Officers (1984), he points out that there ar
five elements to this argument. In the first place he states that report
are not requested in the majority of cases and that 'families ar
primarily investigated because they are in dispute'; if there ar
questions as to parenting abilities, these should be referred to th
child protection services (namely, the Social Services Departments)
Second, he states that the investigative model undermines th
authority and responsibilities of the parents. It is also questionabl
that when there is no child protection issue, it is appropriate t
make judgements about styles of parenting; in the majority of case
the courts merely endorse the existing arrangements. Finally, '

decisions have to be made as to the outcome of assessments they are legally the responsibility of the judge or the magistrate and ought not to fall on the welfare officer by default'.

Howard and Shepherd (1987), both senior probation officers with considerable experience of Divorce Court work (who take a family systems approach to their work), in an attempt to clarify matters have argued convincingly, albeit controversially (see Davis 1985), that in contrast to the adversarial system, conciliation

1 attempts to 'reduce acrimony and conflict and defuse crises rather than exacerbate them'.
2 is 'in keeping with the general ideological move away from allocation of blame in divorce towards a concern with the resolution of practical consequences' of marital breakdown.
3 at least partially acknowledges that the intervention of the legal system is limited and is not intended to resolve all the issues, particularly where the relationships are highly charged.
4 attempts to reach agreement rather than secure by court orders in order to achieve lasting results, for the sake of likely continuing relationships between parties concerned.
5 implies the recognition that the disputes are family ones rather than legal problems and therefore require family solutions.
6 'enables the parties to retain more control both over the way the situation is handled and its outcome'.
7 'gives the parties at least some opportunity to regain some degree of [both] autonomy . . . and self respect', as divorce involves many other losses as well as that of a partner's status, self-esteem and possibly also loss of the home and children.
8 facilitates the development of patterns of communication which could enable more constructive future negotiations between the parties.
9 facilitates change towards considering family interests as a whole rather than a preoccupation with winning or losing.
10 provides emotional support at a time when the individuals are vulnerable.
11 assists in promoting the welfare of the children.
12 saves court costs and time.

Drawing on the evidence from Davis' survey of in court mediation clients (see above), Howard and Shepherd point out that the presence of the court exerts a powerful pressure on the conciliator and parties alike to 'get a solution'; that this places conciliators in something of a dilemma between the expectations of the court and

the wish to allow the parties to control the outcome themselves; als
that the parties themselves feel 'stampeded' as well as feeling a lac
of control and participation in the proceedings. They outline thre
principles for practice: *parental decisions, presumption of parentu
competence*, and *parental responsibility*. Many of their subsequen
suggestions for the practice of conciliation based on a family system
approach are similar to those which have already been outlined, th
major difference being that they prefer to start the process o
intervention by seeing the whole family together. This is, howevei
an arguable premise in that the Divorce Court welfare officer who i
asked to make an investigative report is usually required to do so i
order to assist the court to make a decision with regard to futur
arrangements for the children and therefore should commence th
process by focusing on the children in the family (though see 'Divorc
Court welfare officers', page 221). However, this also seems to b
contrary both to the general principles on which conciliation is base
and those put forward by Howard and Shepherd, in that the paren
should be presumed competent, responsible and able to make thei
own decisions unless proved to be otherwise. In fact this seems likel
to be the case after the implementation of the Children Act (1989) i
1991 (see Chapter 12, 'The enterprise culture and the family', pag
277).

Some critics, notably Davis (1985) and Roberts (1990), hav
argued that there is a basic incompatibility between conciliation (o
mediation) as a method of intervention (particularly that based on
family systems approach) and the task of welfare investigation a
requested by the court. This has also included discouragement fror
among the judiciary, indeed in a particular judgement – Re H. (
Minor) (1986) 1 FLR 476 – Mr Justice Ewbank stated that becaus
'conciliation and welfare reporting are quite different functions an
should be carried out by different people in any particular case'. Thi
was subsequently endorsed by the (then) President of the Famil
Division (Sir John Arnold). As James (1988) states, 'this has create
further confusion' as some areas have responded by changing th
nomenclature rather than the practice, referring to such method
as 'family meetings' when preparing reports, instead of conciliation
According to Davis (1988),

> [the] 'really important distinction . . . is that between . . . interven
> tion by professional third parties in the context of legal proceed
> ings; and . . . non statutory mediation offered to the parties as
> service quite independent of any litigation which they may b

contemplating. ... [O]nce the parties enter the legal arena they lose control over the conduct of their own case.

A further recent article by Hayles (1988), takes an even more radical position, arguing that

> state intervention in the private domain of the family cannot be justified solely on the ground of divorce, first, because there is no genuine attempt to apply principles of child protection systematically and secondly because the 'at risk' premise upon which state intervention is justified is insufficiently tenable.

Most recently an article by Fricker and Coates (1989) describes what they call a 'consecutive approach' through which the same probation officer, while initially attempting conciliation which fails, may move to an investigatory role. They outline guidelines and safeguards, among which is the opportunity for the clients to move to another Divorce Court welfare officer, should they so choose, and propose that this should be put in writing to both clients and their solicitors. The implication would be that the clients would thus waive their privilege for the confidentiality of conciliation, and the matters discussed in their previous conciliation meetings with the Divorce Court welfare officer might then be included in the welfare report. There, as is frequently said, for the present 'the matter rests' (though future proposals and possibilities will be explored in Chapter 12).

A COMPARISON OF THE OCCUPATIONS INVOLVED WITH PARTNERS IN SEPARATION AND DIVORCE

Drawing on Huntington's research (1981) on the collaboration between social work and general medical practice, it might be of interest to speculate on the findings if some similar research comparing the implications of the differences between lawyers and conciliators (or mediators) were to be conducted.

In extrapolating the major differences between family lawyers and conciliators, it will be immediately noticed that because the latter have only so recently emerged as practitioners within the divorce scene (whatever their original professional orientation), the long-established and highly respected family lawyers might well have some doubts about collaboration with them. Indeed, a number of solicitors regard conciliators and mediators with some suspicion, fearing that they will compete for their clientele. While family lawyers are easily accessible in almost every town throughout the country, there are, as yet, many areas where family conciliation services are not yet

	Lawyers in divorce	Conciliators/mediators
Age of occupation	Long established, one of the oldest professions	Very new, have emerged in response to concern about rising divorce rate, includes Civil Unit Divorce Court welfare officers (probation officers) marriage guidance and social workers, some lawyers
Age of membership	Full age range	Mostly 30s to 50s
Size	Approx. 50,000	Approx. 700 Civil Unit officers and 342 conciliators in NFCC-affiliated services
Location and distribution	National	Increasing steadily but not yet national
Sex	More men but numbers of women increasing	More women in independent services, more men in Civil Units
Marital status	Probably most married; some divorced, some remarried	Mostly married; some divorced, some remarried
Class of origin	Predominantly middle class	Mostly middle class
Educational attainment	Law or other degree plus Law Society examinations and articled apprenticeship (2–5 years)	Some graduates, all professional qualifications, and conciliators have further training
Work setting	Legal practice usually in towns, locality of courts	Civil Units (in court) or in independent service (out of court)

(Continue

	Lawyers in divorce	*Conciliators/mediators*
		though office may be in court building
Income size	High when established, comparable to other senior professions	Probation salary, low professional, voluntary or low sessional fee
Clientele	Client choice, as s/he instructs solicitor	Client choice, or referred from court
Mission, aims, tasks	Achieve settlement in substantive issues	Achieve settlement Encourages agreement Promotes cooperation
	Negotiator and champion	Reduces conflict Creates options
	To assess client's legal his/her advantages in law	
	Translate into legal solutions	
	Should court appearance prove necessary, to win case for client	
Focus and orientation	Individual, legal	Couple or family
Knowledge	General and family law	Family systems theory Attachment theory
	Courts and court procedures	Psychodynamic theory Child development
	Negotiation theory	Negotiation theory
	Agreements which are probably acceptable to the court	
Techniques	Single interviews Advice giving Bipartisan negotiation through or	Joint interviews with both parties (usually) Engagement skills Conflict management

(Continued)

	Lawyers in divorce	*Conciliators/mediators*
	alongside legal colleague	Manages process not outcome
	Legal strategies	Explores suggestions
	Presents choices ultimately acceptable to court	If necessary, balances power more equally
	Arranges affidavits	
	If necessary, advocacy in court	
Language and terminology	Legal or related to law language	Use couple's own, though need to understand legal and psychological language
		Positive reframing
Ideology	Social Darwinism: individual rights and freedom produce society best for all	Varies, primarily interactional view family relationships either positivist or humanist
	Individual orientation	Family orientation
Identity	Respected, established independent professional, often in partnership but changing especially in family law	Barely established, gaining in confidence Usually work from within team base
Status and prestige	Long-standing, high	Slowly gaining respect
Relational orientation practitioner–client	Client instructs solicitor, so can change if dissatisfied	Client choice, so can discontinue, except Civil Unit when referred by court
Relational orientation inter-occupational	Wary of inter-occupational collaboration, unless under auspices of legal system	Works in confidence unless investigative report required by court

(Continued)

Lawyers in divorce	Conciliators/mediators
Wishes to retain control of case in order to protect client rights and manage court procedures	

Source: Based on Huntington (1981)

Figure 10.1 A comparison of the occupations involved with separation and divorce

available, or even known to exist! The educational attainments of lawyers, like their status, are long-established and still rising (with the requirements of the Law Society for post-qualification training). The National Family Conciliation Council (NFCC) is now establishing a basic training and accreditation, and discussing further advanced training, although the first introductory training courses of the Family Mediators' Association have only recently been completed. However, there is, as yet no generally recognised qualification in conciliation and/or mediation.

The issue of income is an important one, as lawyers have long been able to look forward to a high standard of living and thus to taking their place among the professional elite. In the independent services, many conciliators are paid a small sessional fee, given an honorarium or are in essence volunteers, which may well account for the preponderance of middle-class women among the practitioners. The mission, aims and tasks of matrimonial lawyers and conciliators may in some ways be similar; after all, they are both involved with the resolution or settlement of disputes. Yet ultimately they differ primarily because lawyers focus on the issue of their clients' legal rights, while the conciliators emphasise the clients' autonomy and self-respect. Their current knowledge base may be broadly similar, in that each is expected to know enough about that of the other if they are to work alongside each other, whether collaboratively or collaterally. Yet, inevitably as matrimonial lawyers and conciliators they will each draw primarily on their own original professional knowledge base and this is likely to lead to differing emphases. While both kinds of practitioner use interviewing skills with their clients, it is only very recently that lawyers have been expected to have training in developing such skills, which will have been part of the original basic professional training of conciliators, although they may be used with a different emphasis. Divorce lawyers usually have single interviews with their individual clients, giving advice and working through or alongside their colleagues, using legal strategies. Conciliators, on the other hand, while they may initially interview clients singly, ultimately have joint interviews with both of the partners who are their clients, using their engagement and conflict management skills. Lawyers conduct bipartisan negotiation for their clients, for whom they are ultimately advocates, while conciliators expect to manage the process, not the outcome. The law has its own language, and an important aspect of the work of the matrimonial lawyer is to assess and 'translate' the client's legal position into the legal framework. While it may be arguable that the conciliator's own language should approximate that of the clients as nearly as is possible, it is important that the conciliator clarifies the issues into language which both can understand.

The ideology of the law is based on individual rights, while that of conciliators is interactional. As was indicated earlier (see page 213), the lawyer can choose from a variety of stances, while one of the current major issues for mediation (on pages 195 ff.) is the choice of position to take on a continuum ranging from a minimalist, negotiation model to a therapeutic one. The lawyers' clientele instruct them and they can theoretically change their lawyer should they wish, and some certainly do. Clients of independent conciliation services can also request a change of conciliator, if one should be available; but the voluntary or involuntary clients of the Divorce Court welfare officers usually cannot change, although if the mediation is (semi)-voluntary and the partners fail to reach agreement, they are required to change their welfare officer, which sometimes neither party wishes to do, nor is an alternative easily available. Lawyers are naturally cautious of inter-occupational collaboration, unless this is under the auspices of the legal system, as they prefer to retain control of the case in order to protect their client's rights and to manage the court process. Conciliators work in the strictest confidence and with an explicit contract in order to maintain the autonomy of their clients, although they respect the status of the legal process and, as far as possible, ensure that the lawyers of both parties are kept informed of any agreements reached. The implications of such inter-occupational relational orientations have already been briefly touched upon, but these and many other issues are likely to become a preoccupation for both occupations in the future.

REFLECTION PROCESS AND/OR GREEK CHORUS?

This section is purely speculative. It is based on the hypothesis that certain methods of marital therapy in which the underlying theory is that of the object relations model of psychoanalytic theory, and/or some models of family therapy, might be adapted and used as an aid to understanding some of the conflict, which (it could be said) is already mirrored among the services and interventive practitioners who are involved with partners in conflict during the divorce and remarriage processes (see Johnston and Campbell 1988).

The reflection process

Mattinson (formerly the Director of the Institute of Marital Studies) first described the way in which marital conflict can be both mirrored and also played out between colleagues who are working with a particular client (1975). Drawing on the work of Winnicott (1960) and quoting Guntrip (1973), she wrote, 'it is the *personal relationship*' (author's italics) which 'is therapeutic, not something called the "technique of interpretation"'. She noted that Greenson (1967) described the transference as the 'experiencing of feelings, drives, attitudes, fantasies and defences towards a person in the present which do not befit that person, but are a repetition of reactions originating in regard to significant persons of early childhood, unconsciously displaced on to figures in the present'. While originally the practitioner's reaction to the transference had been considered as suspect, after Winnicott (1939) referred to 'the worker's love and hate reaction to the actual personality and behaviour of the patient', countertransference came to be seen 'as an innate and inevitable ingredient, which is sometimes a conscious reaction to the observed behaviour of the client' and 'sometimes an unconscious reaction to the felt and not consciously understood behaviour of the client'; and that this 'can be used for increasing understanding of the client'.

Mattinson goes on to describe the countertransference as the practitioner's 'response to the client's transference which itself is characterised by an inappropriate reaction and a need to make the present relationship fit into the psychodynamic structure of a previous relationship'. Some of the practitioner's responses are straight identification, but others seem to be unconscious to client and therapist alike and may be left with the latter, who unconsciously identifies with the client and experiences stirring up of comparable personal anxiety. The therapist in turn seems unconsciously to cope with this anxiety either by the defence which the client is using, or resorting to one which is complementary' to it.

Mattinson originally found the reflective process between clie and practitioner to be mirrored in the supervisory relationsh between the worker and the supervisor. Subsequently, she and I co-workers began to notice that the marital therapists often mirror the conflict of the marital couple with whom they were working their colleagal relationship. Clulow and Vincent (1987), in writing the verbal violence evident among the clients of the Divorce Co welfare unit, describe how their initial surprise at 'hearing t firm raised voices of our colleagues used with parents over t telephone was later replaced by an appreciation of the justification behaving in that way', found their own 'interviewing and telepho manners gradually overtaken by a wariness and directness which w unusual for them'. They go on to comment, 'we became more acti and assertive than we were before the project began', and refer Mattinson's concept of 'mirroring behaviour between clients a workers and the unconscious purposes served by such reflection Does this reflective process perhaps account for some of the findir of Davis (1988) and also the general stress which is frequen experienced by those working with couples in conflict?

The Greek chorus

It was Bateson (1956) who first distinguished the idea of the 'doul bind', the general characteristics of which have been described Jenkins as follows:

(a) When the individual is involved in an intense relationship; th is a relationship in which he feels it is vitally important that discriminates accurately what sort of message is being commu cated so that he may respond appropriately;
(b) and the individual is caught in a situation in which the oth person in the relationship is expressing two orders of message a one of these denies the other;
(c) and the individual is unable to comment on the message bei expressed to correct his discrimination of what order of message respond to, (that is) he cannot make a metacommunicative stat ment [that is, a statement about what the message being express means to him].

(Jenkins 198

In certain types of family therapy (particularly the strategic mode one therapist works together with the family, while behind a one-way screen is a consultation team, who are presented to the family as a special resource and as experts in the field who are authorities on their kind of problem (Papp 1983 and others). The group are introduced to the family members if they wish; and, as with the chorus in a Greek play, which comments on the progress and process, the group regularly send messages that provide a running commentary between the dilemma of change and the relationship between the family and the therapist. As Papp describes it: 'the group remain at a distance, an invisible eye, a prophetic voice: unapproachable, unimpeachable, and unnegotiable'. Group messages are formed in collaboration with the therapist, who has the final say as to their content and who decides on what position to take in relation to them. At the therapist's discretion, the group may be used to support, confront, confuse, challenge or provoke, with the therapist free to agree or disagree with its position. When working within such strategic models the therapist excuses the family for a break and consults with the team; and, after reconvening the family, gives them a message from the group who usually take a position of antagonists of change as distinct from the therapist, who is in the position of protagonist and defender of the family's ability to change.

The family is thus put in the position of agreeing with the therapist or the group as they struggle to make sense of the message, thereby putting them in a 'double bind' regarding their ability to change. 'This triangle shifts the therapeutic contest from the dyadic struggle between the therapist and family into a three-way bargaining operation between family, therapist and group'. There are variations of this intervention, many of them paradoxical, and indeed one of the major criticisms of this way of working is that as the therapist covertly retains the power to shift the family towards change, this is manipulation which implicitly denies the autonomy of the clients.

Could the description of the double bind situation be applied to partners in conflict who are engaged in a legal, adversarial process with affidavits winging backwards and forwards between their solicitors, leading to a possible appearance in the Divorce Court, when both protagonists are represented by their partisans and publicly they are not expected to comment? Might it be regarded as too far-fetched to compare this concept of the Greek chorus with the panoply of the law courts in matters of divorce, with the judge 'unapproachable and unimpeachable' and all negotiation conducted by the lawyers rather than the partners themselves?

A more recent adaptation of the Greek chorus, and one which

was briefly mentioned earlier when discussing constructivist fam
therapy, is that of the 'reflecting team' (Andersen 1987). Using
method the family is asked if they would like to view the team (w
are introduced as helpful colleagues rather than experts) as tl
spontaneously discuss the family's problem (in the everyday langua
of the family), and the therapist in turn invites the family to comm
on the team discussion. This seems to be much more respectful of
family who are given an open and clear choice to accept the var
comments of the team. It also gives them the opportunity to 't
back' to the team. The conciliation team at the Institute of Fam
Therapy use a variant of this model, in which (usually) only c
conciliator sees the parties, but explains that there is a team (wh
they can meet if they wish) who will see neutrality and ev
handedness is maintained by the conciliator, which, as the cou
know, is not always easy to achieve in a situation such as theirs. Th
methods can be used without a one-way screen, although admittec
they are more cumbersome, and sensitive care has to be taken
explain the situation to the family and to distinguish the differ
roles of the practitioners. Such a model is demonstrated by Smith a
Kingston's (1980) discussion of 'live supervision', in which a secc
practitioner is in the room, whose primary task is supervision of
therapist rather than engaging with the family (for example,
pointing out problems and processes not recognised by the therapi:
Both these and other similar methods have been found to
successful, although they are not yet adequately researched.

Given the strength of feelings which lie within and between
partners in many families during the divorce process, especially th
in conflict and particularly because of the adversarial nature of
legal phase, it is not unlikely that the mirroring processes descrit
above are operative. These may be reflected not only as betwe
clients and their welfare officers (as Clulow and Vincent 1!
describe), but also within the Divorce Court welfare unit, betwe
colleagues who are co-working as conciliators. It would be interest
to explore how these mirroring processes might be revealed betwe
conciliators and lawyers who are co-mediating, where the mirror
of clients' conflicts by the co-mediators is likely to be highlighted
their differing styles. The traditions of the legal practitioners' o
professional discipline are structured so as to differentiate betwe
their roles as colleagues and those of adversaries in their partisans!
of their clients, and in this way enable them to contain and man:
the conflict which may arise because of this. Thus the management
the impact of the client conflict on the practitioner reflects

knowledge base on which they each draw. One way of handling this during conjoint interviews with clients might be to adapt the 'live supervision' model (perhaps especially during training) so that the lawyers would comment on the legal implications of a particular stance or proposal, while the conciliator would comment on the psychological ones. This would not only be more empowering and participative for the clients but would also ensure that they would have the opportunity to reflect (either in or outside the interview) on the psychological and legal implications. The practitioners, too, would have more time to manage their own reactions, thus going some way to dealing with the stress which is inevitable when working with couples in conflict. The availability of an experienced conciliator who is also a marital counsellor who could act as consultant to both co-mediators would be helpful; such a person might also, and with their consent, assist them to reflect on their own professional interactions within their co-mediating relationship.

At another level, that of the Divorce Court itself, where the justice model (Parsloe 1976) is operative and the balance of needs and rights must be structured, it could possibly be argued that the incorporation of some of the more participative elements characterised by the 'reflecting team' could also bring more participant justice to the clients in civil proceedings where the parties are in dispute. As things are at present they are playing a primarily passive and dependent role in a decision-making process, the results of which will completely change the future not only of the rest of their lives, but also of the whole of the future lives of their children.

11 Can re-formed extended families become 'good enough'?

What we call the beginning is often the end
And to make an end is to make a beginning.
The end is where we start from.

We shall not cease from exploration
And the end of all our exploring
Will be to arrive where we started
And to know the place for the first time.

T.S. Eliot (1888–1965), 'Little Giddin▮

It is important to point out that there are problems and difficulties ▮
the family life of every family, and that these also give both 'challen▮
and promise' (Wald 1981) to the development of stepfamily life. F▮
many reasons (some perhaps related to the guilt about the beginnir
of their relationship as well as stepfamily folklore), the parents ar
stepparents in remarried families have a tendency to attribute ar
developmental difficulties to their being a stepfamily. This somewh▮
facile conclusion is often also drawn by others, not least those in th
interventionist professions. At the time of writing (1989) the▮
appears to be what amounts to a 'moral panic' regarding the future ▮
marriage and the family (see Mount 1982 and others), and the fir
part of this chapter therefore attempts to draw together and highlig▮
some of the more positive findings from academic and empiric▮
research.

Because the research and clinical findings are often somewhat ▮
variance with one another, it is also important to realise tha
clinicians are apt to develop a somewhat skewed picture of the worl▮
because they draw their conclusions from the families who come t
them seeking help for their difficulties. Because the current positio
regarding joint custody and access gives a particularly confuse▮

picture, whether it is based on academic or clinical research, or the received wisdom of judicial decisions from the courts, these sections will attempt to present the situation as it at present appears to be. It is evident that more research is necessary, and especially collaborative research between academics and clinicians in this important field of family research.

Despite the fact that we all consider ourselves to be 'experts' in family life (after all, most of us were brought up in some type of family), there is nevertheless little practical guidance easily available to parents going through the transformation of divorce and re-marriage. The last section of this chapter therefore sets out some brief practical guidelines during the divorce process for parents, both for themselves and with regard to their children. Inevitably these will reflect the current beliefs and practices of the author, although these may well change in future as more research is undertaken and the results become available. Finally, as an epilogue, some conclusions are drawn and tentative guidelines set out which may prove useful as signposts for the families of the future. Some useful addresses to contact for help and advice are given in the appendix.

THE HIERARCHY OF NEEDS

The basis of Maslow's (1970) hierarchy of needs of the individual is that of physical survival. It is only when this need, together with those of protection, are safely met that the individual can focus attention on social needs, such as those of acceptance and of belonging. If the individual is protected while experiencing a sense of being cared about, then each needs to experience the confidence and self-esteem which comes from an ability to care for the self. Only then can the individual contemplate and pursue a course which leads towards self-fulfilment.

Terkelson (1980) both builds upon and extends this hierarchy of Maslow's when he states that unless the survival needs of family members are adequately met, then the family is unable to meet their developmental needs. According to him, 'the purpose of the family is to provide a context that supports need attainment for all its individual members'. In distinguishing the concept of the 'good enough family' he developed Winnicott's (1975) original idea of the 'good enough environment', or 'good enough mother'. Terkelson broadens the concept to include the interactions of each family member upon one another and their impact on the developmental welfare of the whole family. He stresses the importance of the

structure of the family, and how this corresponds to the combin
developmental and interactional primary needs at any given point
its history; adding that a family is sufficient (that is, good enough)
the extent that it is matching specific elements of structure to
specific needs'. Thus the appearance of primary needs in one memb
sets in motion new need attainment sequences which in turn lead
the processes of change in the family life cycle (see Chapter 2, 'T
family life cycle', page 35).

In discussing family sufficiency he proposes three levels of g(
attainment. In the first place is the family's ability to recapture
capacity adequately to promote need attainment in all its membe
which may of course happen spontaneously but can also be as a res
of the various forms of intervention already discussed, and whi
Terkelson describes as *therapeutic*. Second, the family may ne
supplementation in order to attain sufficiency, such as in the ma
situations in which the whole family or various members are giv
long-term supports of a kind which allow the family to maintair
semi-autonomous status. Third, there are families from whom t
much is missing, and in such situations *replacement* is necessary – :
for instance, when children from neglectful and abusing families m
ultimately need to be placed for long-term fostering with a view
adoption. The families where (in Terkelson's terms) long-term supp
mentation and/or replacement are needed have not been especia
the focus of this book, although they often form the greater part
the day-to-day work of social workers (see Chapter 12, 'The Childr
Act, 1989, page 282). Nor, as he primarily concentrates on t
nuclear family, has his idea of the 'good enough family' be
extended to include the binuclear family (Ahrons and Rodgers 198
or the re-formed extended family which may link across two or mc
households, consisting of stepfamilies and single-parent famili(
although this is the basic theme of this chapter.

In the first place, the divorcing couple need to complete the stag
of the divorce process before embarking on a remarriage, or at le:
recognise that there is still more work to be done – as, for instance,
complete the retrieval of those aspects of themselves which we
invested in the marriage and each other. Kressel (1985) describes
constructive divorce as

> one in which the process of psychic divorce has been successfu
> completed. . . [A] consensus that psychic divorce has occurred [
> when certain conditions prevail with regard to the attitudes a1
> behaviour of the former spouses toward one another, the welfa

of the children, and the level of functioning of each of the former partners as a newly single person.

The life-cycle processes involved in becoming a stepfamily (see Chapters 6 and 7) demonstrated that while stepfamilies cannot ever become nuclear families, yet nevertheless a stepfamily is still a family, as was described in the model of a re-formed and extended family (see Chapter 2, 'The marital system', page 38). One of the primary tasks of a stepfamily, therefore, is to accept and come to terms with this reality and to regard their situation as a challenge which is positive, rather than negative. The summary of research on children of divorce and in stepfamilies also indicated some of the developmental tasks which stepchildren need to address (see Chapter 8).

While recognising the need to describe re-formed extended families as living between two (or even more) households, it becomes cumbersome to describe them except in terms of stepfamilies and the households in which they primarily reside, although this does not explicitly recognise the household of the 'other' parents, nor do justice to the complexities of such family systems. Thus each household of the re-formed extended family gradually begins to establish belief systems and patterns of behaviour, which are uniquely characteristic to the members of the stepfamily unit who share their day-to-day lives together. Whether or not the children and stepchildren spend the greater part of their lives in that household, they need to know what the family rules are, and that they belong to and have a part to play in that stepfamily unit as well as that of their other biological parent. One of the distinctive features of the re-formed extended family is the need for permeable boundaries between the households. As the result of their US study, Ahrons and Rodgers (1988) consider that functional binuclear family systems also 'need to have permeable boundaries which permit children and adults to continue prior family relationships while slowly integrating the new remarried subsystem'. This chapter therefore focuses on some of the issues about structures, roles and relatedness which seem to be functional for re-formed extended families following divorce and remarriage and which allow the re-formed extended family to rebuild a family life in which the households are autonomous yet interconnected.

SINGLE-PARENT HOUSEHOLDS

After the separation and divorce the now binuclear family usually lives within and between two separate and autonomous one-parent households, one of them consisting of the parent (usually the mother) with whom the children primarily live, and the other of the parent (usually the father) to which they may become welcome and frequent visitors (see Chapter 6). However, initially at least, this is more difficult to achieve, as many noncustodial parents do not have a household within which the children can easily be accommodated. The boundaries between the two households are necessarily ambiguous and necessitate the negotiation of agreements regarding the movement of the children and contact between the two households. These will obviously depend on the geographical distance between them, the age and stage of development of the children, and other factors. Indeed many parents seriously underestimate how much each household needs to take into account the day-to-day living arrangements of the other (Jacobson 1987). However, there are other forms of contact than visits, such as regular telephone calls and letters from the nonresidential parent to the children.

It is often helpful for separated or divorced parents to separate the access visits or telephone calls between the parent and the children from the negotiations regarding their children and financial matters, which are also necessary and which could happen at a different time. Such a situation becomes both more controversial and complicated if one or both of the parents have ended their marriage in order to share their lives and home with someone else; then in at least one household, there is a potential or actual stepparent, if not one waiting in the wings. Many divorced parents agree that until the children become used to their separation and adjust to the new form of relationship with each parent and the access arrangements, the new partner of their father or mother should be kept in the background. Obviously, if such a partnership is intended to be permanent, this cannot continue indefinitely, but for a few months this may make things more manageable for everybody. If this is not done, the children may be faced with further confusion and, in the case of adolescents, the possible arousal of their own sexual anxieties by being made aware of their parent's renewed sexual energies.

It has already been indicated that most men remarry quite soon after divorce, as do many young women, though not as quickly. Thus the single-parent household often becomes a temporary stage on the way to becoming a stepfamily. When this happens the re-formed extended family begins to move into the early stages of stepfamily development (see Chapters 7 and 8). However, for many, and particularly older women, the single-parent household becomes a more or less permanent way of life, one which, while it may be overburdened with responsibilities, also in time allows many women freedoms they have not previously enjoyed as well as the opportunity to develop strengths they have not hitherto possessed.

REMARRIAGE/COHABITATION

Unless specified otherwise, the terms 'remarriage', 're-formed family' or 'stepfamily' are used to indicate both families where the partners are married or in a committed cohabitation, which is intended to be long term. In the separate households of the re-formed extended family, whether one is a single-parent household and the other is a stepfamily household, or whether both involve remarried parents, the viability of the new relationship becomes crucial. When one or both parents remarry, then unless their new relationship is allowed the time and support to develop solid bonds and become stabilised, further problems are likely to ensue. In the early stages of stepfamily life, the newest and most vulnerable relationship is therefore that between the parent and his or her new partner, and a parent who is anxious that their new relationship will founder is not likely to be able to give thought and time to his or her parenting role as regards the children. As well as dealing with the losses and changes made necessary by the divorce and remarriage, the adults in the situation need to negotiate regarding the differential needs of parents, step-parents, children and stepchildren and begin to establish new and distinct traditions for each household of the binuclear family (Visher and Visher 1988). As Perkins and Kahan (1979) state, 'remarriage calls for the welding of two systems ... with different histories, memories and values – a type of assimilation which is very difficult'. Indeed, this is usually the time when the conflicting needs of parents and children are highlighted, as has already been indicated in Chapters 6,7 and 8.

SHARING THE PARENTING IN STEPFAMILIES

As was discussed in Chapter 6, parental remarriage creates a new relationship in a family where there is already a shared history of parent–child relationships, and the new partnership is therefore the only relationship which is not rooted in a shared family history. While both partners will need to create both psychological and physical space in order to develop their own relationship, for the partner who has not previously been a parent, the demands of parenthood (not to mention stepparenthood) will be a completely new experience. This partner needs the time and the opportunity to create some kind of parenting coalition (Visher and Visher 1989), and this needs to be one which recognises and accepts the continuing co-parental relationship between the biological parents of the children. As Solomon (1989) writes, 'Marriage embraces two individual subsystems that combine to form a new family system. The task of the spouses is to devise, consciously and unconsciously, a mutual working system that allows them to function comfortably without completely sacrificing the values and ideals they brought into the marriage' (see Chapter 2, 'The development of behaviour which is problematic for the family', page 34; Feldman 1979; Willi 1984, 1987; and Wynne 1984).

In reassembled stepfamilies (in which one of the partners has not previously been married), not only will the stepparent be facing many of the initial experiences involved in trying to develop such a close relationship, but also in developing for the first time individualised relationships with the stepchildren. Furthermore, such a remarriage immediately involves the couple in a test of their communicative and joint problem-solving capacities. The previously unmarried partner becomes husband or wife and a stepparent (that is, some kind of parental figure) at one and the same time. Partners who have previously been married are likely to bring to their remarriage some of the disillusionments and disappointments from their first marriage which they may or may not have faced sufficiently, nor perhaps consequently reflected upon their own contribution to its failure. But they will have had some experience of what it is like to live with another person and in a family situation. In other words, both partners are at different stages in the family life cycle, even though they may be virtually the same age. The partner who has previously been married but has not yet become a parent has experience of marriage, and their remarriage brings instantaneous stepparenthood, whatever that may entail.

Until recently there has been surprisingly little research in the field of remarriage, although there is now a small but steady stream, mostly from the US (see Chapters 6, 7 and 8 and later in this chapter). For example, Kvanli and Jennings (1987) have carried out a small exploratory in-depth study of ten remarried partners following remarriage 7.8 (average) years after divorce. Their findings indicated that, as individuals, the couples had experienced both increased differentiation and extended family support during the divorce/remarriage family life cycle. They described stages of courting and early remarriage as developmental sequences, and as the tasks of the initial period of remarriage were completed each of the spouses experienced a recoupling process of emotional bonding. 'The satisfactions of the remarried couples centred around general feelings of contentment, a stage of blending, [and] a closeness [which] was maintained as they experienced the frequent individual changes and couple challenges through the transitions of the remarriage.'

As has already been indicated Burgoyne and Clark in their 1984 study of forty stepfamilies in Sheffield (see Chapter 5, 'The post-divorce family', page 113), carried out several interviews with their remarried couples, in which they examined the relationships between the individuals' personal troubles and the legal and economic structures which shaped them. Although they did not interview the children, in the final interview they explored the parenting in the stepfamily, subsequently constructing a factual life history, focusing on the field of marriage and family interpersonal relations. These life histories they interpreted, describing them both in terms of the private troubles of the couple and those in the public sphere, which they concluded often seemed contradictory. What emerged in general was that the younger the children were at time of the remarriage, the more likely they were to be absorbed into the remarried family, thus making it possible for the stepfamily to think of themselves as an ordinary family, which was what a significant proportion of them wanted (sixteen out of the forty). When the remarried couple have both previously been married and are also parents, both are therefore familiar with the demands and expectations of parenthood, although they, too, have to build their own partnership relationship with each other. The issues in such combination stepfamilies are then often concerned with how to make sufficient space for their own relationship while simultaneously trying to parent their own children, often managing to create both a more or less full-time (usually her children) and a part-time (usually his children) stepfamily as well as presiding over the attempts of all the children to create stepsibling relationships!

In summary, therefore, the remarried or cohabiting couple in a stepfamily are pitched headlong into a family situation, within which there is considerable pressure for them quickly to renegotiate both a new marital and a family belief system which suits both of the partners and the new situation, but with neither the time nor sufficient privacy to do so. We know that about half of second marriages end in a further divorce; but because of the lack of research we have insufficient knowledge about the other half, those whose second marriages do survive. By all accounts many of these second marriages are considered successful, and while for some it seems that this may be at the cost of the need fulfilment of one or more children, for others this will be achieved at the cost of a virtual cut-off of parental (usually paternal) contact with the children of the first marriage (Wallerstein 1989). It seems that there are, nevertheless, many good enough remarriages and stepfamilies though there is no general consensus as to how long this might take to achieve. For instance, Papernow (1984) indicates that this usually takes a minimum of from three to five years; while Mills (1984) proposes that in a custodial stepfamily the stepparent may expect to achieve a functional role (though not that equivalent to a parent) in as many years as that of the age of the child when the family forms. On the other hand, Hodges (1986) points out that the older the child, the less likely it will be that bonding will develop between stepchild and stepparent; indeed that some adolescents may need permission to avoid bonding.

STEPFATHER FAMILY HOUSEHOLDS

Since after divorce most children live in mother custody families, it is likely that most of the stepfamily households of primary residence are stepfather households; indeed, it is estimated that there are three times the number of children living in stepfather households as there are in stepmother households. The research into custody decisions shows that in the six studies which have been conducted some 70 per cent of mothers are awarded custody of their children on divorce. What we do not know is how many of these remain single-parent households, though we do know that the younger the custodial mother, the more likely she is to cohabit or remarry. In so far as there has been comparative research, much of it has been in stepfather family households.

When considering the research on stepfamilies it is necessary to recognise the perspective from which the research has been conducted, as the same family can be perceived very differently from the viewpoint of the parent or parents and the stepchildren. A more reliable picture is therefore obtained if more than one member of the stepfamily are interviewed (Pasley and Ihinger-Tallman 1987). It is also known that perceptions of stepfamily life differ according to the distance of the timespan as perceived by those interviewed. In Duberman's (1975) study (see Chapter 8), in which she interviewed couples together and separately, she found that, while family integration was better if the stepfather had previously been divorced rather than a bachelor, men who had left their own children behind on remarriage related less well to their stepchildren than did bachelors. Perkins and Kahan's (1979) study (see also Chapter 8, 'Children living in stepfamilies', page 175) examined the differences between forty natural father families and stepfather families, where the mothers had initiated a divorce and had been remarried for an average of three years. The study examined dimensions of psychological adjustment, satisfaction with the family, reciprocal understanding and perceived goodness. They interviewed family triads of husband, wife and a child (aged between 12 and 15), using various instrumental tests. Their findings led them to conclude that if there are children, divorce does not end the adult's relationship,

> it merely ends one set of roles. When a remarriage occurs a new set of husband and wife roles come into being. New parental roles are not created, a new role is merely added, with the possibility of creating as much confusion for all the members of the family if the roles are not explicitly well defined.

This view was supported by the majority of family members who wished that the family could be different, yet they also indicated that the dysfunction was perceived as residing within the family rather than in any one individual. They found that the primary difficulty for stepfathers was due to the perception of them as outsiders; indeed, in only four of the twenty stepfather families did the stepchild go to the stepfather with personal difficulties. At the same time they found that the mothers in stepfamilies rated their children similarly to those in nuclear families, while the children's ratings of their biological fathers were not affected by whether or not he occupied the father role at home. Perkins and Kahan conclude from their findings that mothers and fathers and mothers and children are able to understand each other's views of the family, regardless of family type, because they have access to one another's interpersonal systems. They interpreted their findings to conclude that a dual family system exists, which in systemic terms they described as the stepchildren relegating their stepfathers to the intraspace between the current family unit and their original interpersonal subsystem which makes it difficult for each to understand the other's perspectives.

Another more recent US study, by Anderson and White (1986), also compared a total of sixty-three family triads (mother, father or stepfather) for at least two years, and one child (thirty-two male children and thirty-one female children). Through using five instrumental tests to test various hypotheses, they were able to identify the key variables which distinguish functional nuclear families and stepfamilies from those which are dysfunctional. They found that functional stepfamilies had many similarities with functional nuclear families, in that they demonstrate good marital adjustment and strong bonds between the biological parent and child. Such families do not generally exclude family members and are able to make 'mutually compromised family decisions'. They found two key differences: first, that there was less intense interpersonal involvement between stepfathers and their stepchild; and, second, that there was a stronger tendency towards parent–child coalitions. In dysfunctional families they also found similarities in that within both nuclear and stepfamilies there were stronger parent–child coalitions and a lack of mutual decision-making skills. Unexpectedly, they also found that the marital adjustment in the dysfunctional stepfamilies was better than in the dysfunctional nuclear families. The implications of Anderson and White's findings confirm that although, in some aspects, well functioning stepfamilies are similar to functional nuclear families, relationships in others, such as the stepfather–child relationship show that the patterns need to be perceived from a different perspective where overall acceptance is more important than closeness. Hetherington's longitudinal comparative study (1987), discussed earlier (see Chapter 8, 'Children living in stepfamilies', page 175), of remarried mother and stepfather households indicated that if the remarriage relationship was satisfactory then, over time, the relationship between stepfathers and their stepsons improved.

STEPMOTHER HOUSEHOLDS

Perhaps one of the best known books on stepparenting is Maddox (1975) who not only writes vividly of her own experience, but also draws on a long literary tradition, particularly of stepfamilies created by the remarriage of the biological parent after the death of their spouse. As already indicated, this kind of 'revitalised' stepfamily (Robinson 1980) has not been the subject of this book, which has focused primarily on stepfamilies after divorce. While there are similarites, however, there are also differences. Although the parent who has died cannot return to 'haunt' the re-formed family in actuality, they can remain alive in phantasy, and often do, because many are idealised. For stepfamilies where the deceased parent has died as the result of suicide or murder, there is a legacy of fear and anger which usually requires psychiatric assessment and therapy – at least for the children.

Although exact numbers are not known, it seems that there are far fewer stepmother *households*, as there are only a small number of custodial fathers, even though the numbers are increasing. For instance, as has already been indicated (see Chapter 8, 'Children of divorce and the school', page 178), the small number of research studies which have been conducted show that an approximate average of father custody stepfamilies has risen from 3.4 per cent of 58 families in 1975 (Maidment) to 18.1 per cent of 12,771 families in 1985 (Eekelaar et al.); but there are almost no studies of re-formed extended families in which the children live permanently with father and stepmother (though see Santrock and Sitterle 1987). There are, however, stepfamilies in which both remarried partners bring children of their first marriage into the 'combination' stepfamily created by their remarriage. Nevertheless, there are many part-time stepmother households where the children, who are primarily living with their mother, spend weekends and holidays with their father and step-mother. Generally, it seems, that as with folklore, so research also shows that stepmothers have the hardest time in establishing a recognised position in the stepfamily household, and that unless the stepchildren are very young, it takes much longer to develop a positive stepmother relationship which is good enough for the whole family (Visher and Visher (1988), Smith (1990) and others).

It is worth drawing attention to a small Canadian research study by Morrison and Thompson-Guppy (1985), based on two clinical studies of women presenting as depressed which led to the discovery that the symptoms demonstrated were remarkably uniform. The women were seen either at a mental health clinic or in a private practice and included both those whose stepchildren lived with them full-time and those who were part-time stepmothers. The twenty-two stepmothers had between them a total of eighty-two children, half boys and half girls, the majority of whom (forty-four) were in the 11 to 18 age range. While 90 per cent of them worked outside the home many had traditional expectations of themselves as wives and mothers; indeed, many already had children of their own. Most of the stepmothers experienced identity confusion regarding their role and feelings of helplessness and inexperience in their home. None of them was severely depressed, though half demonstrated mild sadness, anxiety, anger and low self esteem. Many felt rejected by their stepchildren towards whom they felt hostility and guilt, and which they attempted to manage by over-compensating. They seemed unable to resolve the difficulties of their stepmother role with their husbands and fathers of the stepchildren, which led to marital tensions and fear of rejection in the marital relationship. Morrison and Thompson-Guppy (1985) in concluding that these stepmothers functioned well in their other life roles, including marriage, mothering their own children and social relationships, distinguished the symptomatology described above as Cinderella's Stepmother Syndrome. As the numbers of father custody families increase there will be even more need for research on such families.

RE-FORMED EXTENDED FAMILIES WHERE THERE IS 'CUT-OFF' FROM ONE BIOLOGICAL PARENT (USUALLY THE FATHER)

As the research shows (see Chapter 7), the stepfamilies in which the children have no contact with their biological parent following divorce are those at most risk (see Visher and Visher 1988, and others). However, if the children are very young at the time of the remarriage, the stepparent is most likely to become the psychological parent, so that such a family becomes the stepfamily which has the closest similarities to an adoptive family, where the children were adopted as babies. However, this does not mean that such psychologically (if not legally) adopted stepchildren do not want to know about their biological parent and to understand how what happened in the past between their parents led to their present family situation. They may want to know about their absent parent, even to meet them; and like some adopted children may well feel betrayed by their parents if they are not told the truth about what is after all *their* family history. This needs to be done with the care and sensitivity appropriate to the age and stage of development of the child; and may need to be repeated over the years so that the child can make his or her own sense of what happened.

STEPSIBLINGS AND HALF SIBLINGS

Recently there has been some research into the arrival of siblings (Dunn and Kendrick 1982) and into the bonding between siblings (Bank and Kahn 1982 in the US), both of which stress the powerful feelings of love, envy, loyalty and understanding as well as the influence on sexual identity. Bank and Kahn stress that sibling bonds are likely to be strong when there is insufficient parental influence; the siblings have high access to one another, have shared common experiences and where they meet each other's needs. It is important to point out that children have little or no power over their biological parent's remarriage, indeed are often not consulted at all. We know that, initially at least, there is very often hostility between stepsiblings. While at least some of this may be due to the sequelae of the divorce, some may be due to a natural wariness of strangers in a new situation. It may also be partly the result of sibling rivalries, and partly because of jealousy of the stepsiblings' claim on parental attention, as well as the lack of physical space in many stepfamily households. One study of the relationships between stepsiblings who are brought into the same re-formed extended family by the remarriages of their parents, and between siblings and their half siblings (who are the children of their parent and stepparent) is that of Ihinger-Tallman (1987) who draws on the earlier study (amongst others) of Bank and Kahn, concluding that 'in an environment that necessitates siblings meeting each other's needs when parents fail to meet them, [this] will increase their dependency upon one another, and consequently [they] will be more tightly bonded'. For instance, there is some evidence from research in child care which indicates that, in families where the children are orphaned or received into care following the death of a parent, the strength of the sibling bond sometimes partially compensates, though clinical evidence indicates that the usually somewhat overbearing parenting of older siblings fails to provide the individualised emotional nurturing which young children need.

In families of remarried mothers and stepfathers, the stepsiblings are likely to have different surnames, which emphasises what Ihinger-Tallman describes as the 'natural cleavage' between them, at least initially. She concludes that when stebsiblings perceive a mutual benefit of association and feel that they share equally or equitably with their changed circumstances and their new joint living arrangements, then strong emotional bonds will develop between them.

In view of the complexity of stepfamilies and the ambivalence towards them, it is hardly surprising that there is a good deal of confusion about the blood relationships with kin in stepfamilies, and about who is related to whom and how much, whether through affinal relationships as the result of marriage, or common law relationships. In those stepfamilies which result in a change in family ordinal order of the children, on the one hand this may result in a child who is the eldest or the youngest fearing or actually being displaced by a stepsibling who may take over that role, which can be both perplexing and distressing if it is not recognised and acknowledged. On the other the hand, advent of stepsiblings can fill new roles in the stepfamily which have previously not been available to a child. An example is the addition of a stepbrother or stepsister for a child who has not previously had a brother or a sister, being an only child or one of several children of the same sex. The arrival of a half sibling (the child of the remarriage) is generally considered to cement the bonding in the stepfamily, and there is some empirical evidence to support this (Duberman 1975). However, this is likely to depend on how long the stepfamily has been together and the age and stage of development of the children and stepchildren. Clinical experience over the years also indicates that much depends on the previous family history of the stepchildren, their ages on joining a stepfamily and the quality of relationships within the re-formed extended family. This would include the attitudes of the biological parent who is not living in the stepfamily household, which either negatively or positively are often very present in the minds of all who live there.

In general, stepfamilies allow the possibility of new insights into family patterns which may have become redundant and are therefore no longer beneficial to the family members, whose needs they no longer meet. In stepfamilies a greater flexibility of roles is also allowed, as well as the possibility of new ideas and values coming into the family, and, particularly for young families, the opportunity for each of the parents in binuclear family households to have a 'rest' from the exigencies of full-time parenting.

GENDER ISSUES

The gender roles in stepfamilies need particular consideration. Carter (1987) considers that stepfamilies can lead the way towards the redefinition of gender roles. She points out that traditional gender roles for women lead to the expectation that they will be responsible for the emotional life of the family. This leads to both pressures and confusion for the stepmother, as she is expected (and indeed often expects herself) to nurture the family relationships and manage the tensions in a stepfamily where the children do not love her – indeed, initially often hate her. It also puts the stepmother in competition with her stepchildren's natural mother, as she understandably resents her current interventions and past history with the man who is now her own partner.

In Western societies, men are generally expected to fill the role of family provider and to control the finances. There may therefore be money coming into the family from another father, and/or going out of the family for other children, though more often the expected maintenance, which might go some way towards mitigating the resentment and financial constraints which are typical of stepfamilies, fails to arrive. As Carter (1987) succinctly commented, there can be too many women trying to mother too few children and too few men failing to provide for too many children. Carter, in Walters et al. (1988), points out that such old assumptions about gender roles can almost inevitably lead to triangles in which the stepmother is perceived as 'wicked'. She gives a number of examples. In the first place, either the father or his new wife or both assume that she will care for and be in charge of his children, thus leading to resistance from both the children and their mother. A second is that a father may be so distant from his children that stepmother intervenes in an attempt to help them or him and gets caught in the middle. A third is when the father and stepmother implicitly or explicitly agree that the children's previous unhappiness or deprivation can only be compensated for by another woman, which leads to resentment on the part of the children and thus for the new wife who feels she has to provide nurturant affection for her stepchildren who are ungrateful. A fourth is when the father, while accepting responsibility for his own children, is too busy with his occupation, especially if it involves travel and the stepmother feels she must move into the vacuum. A fifth is when the father is in conflict with his ex-wife and therefore his new wife is obliged to manage arrangements for the sake of his children. Finally the new wife may feel that she takes second place to the children and thus competes with them for their father's attention.

Traditional family roles do not therefore fit the re-formed stepfamily system, and many writers suggest (see, for instance, Carter 1988, McGoldrick 1989) that each custodial parent should retain the primary responsibility for raising and disciplining their own children, and for their own finances, thus allowing the stepparent and stepchildren the time to work out their own roles and relationships with one another. For instance, the stepparent can have the freedom and the time to move at the family's own pace from stranger, to parent's lover, or intruder, towards becoming a friend, an additional 'aunt' or uncle', an extra parent, or even a kind of 'kissing cousin'. As has already been indicated, in remarried father households where there are young children the stepmother will almost inevitably move into a parental role, thus in all probability changing the role of the natural parent, who is therefore likely to become a more distant figure.

CUSTODY

There seems to be some confusion both within the UK and the US as regards what is the exact definition and meaning of joint custody. Allowing for the implications of the legal definitions, which are certainly different on both sides of the Atlantic, there is something to be gained by attempting a comparison of the similarities and differences.

In the United States

Since the early 1980s there has been a presumption or expectation of joint custody in many of the states in the US (Weitzman 1985) as, for instance, there is in California where much of the research has been conducted. There are differences in the definition of joint custody between states, although it is generally taken to mean that both parents have the right to participate in such major decision-making as religious upbringing, surgery and choice of school. On the other hand, joint physical custody means shared parenting, whereby both parents from their separate households participate in the day-to-day care and decision-making for their children.

Two studies which reviewed the research on joint custody as well as some of the case law concluded that although the children benefited from maintaining a relationship with both parents, there were both positive and negative aspects for them as well as for their parents, in that while it may prevent the loss of one parent, it may make it impossible for formerly married parents to conclude their marital relationship. It was also apparent that joint custody was becoming the legally preferred arrangement which eased the burden on the courts (Nehls and Morganbesser 1980 and Derdeyn and Scott 1984).

Two other studies, which compared children (aged 6–11, and 9–12) in mother custody, father custody and intact families of children in matched comparison groups, found that the status of custody alone did not predict the post-divorce adjustment of the children. However, they did find that the children living with the parent of the same sex were better adjusted than those living with the parent of the opposite sex (Warshak and Santrock 1983 and Camera 1985). A third small in-depth study of the parental perspectives of joint custody parents found that one of the pragmatic problems was the synchronising of the schedules of each of the parents and those of the children; geographical location was an issue, as was the development of parents' career paths (Rothberg 1983). A large majority thought that joint custody did not cause problems for their own social lives, and felt like parents regardless of whether their children were with them, while a minority did not like being part-time parents. Most of the women considered that joint custody gave them free time for their own lives, while the men felt that it both added structure and provided continuity for theirs; and a majority agreed that it was the mother who had more responsibility for the child-care tasks. A third of the sample, both men and women, were not satisfied with the financial arrangements; and while for half the sample the traditional payments were made by the fathers to the mothers, the other half calculated the costs and split them either evenly or proportionally between them.

Kelly (1987) emphasises the importance of weighing consistency of routine against stability of relationships between children and both their parents; and a further study (Schwartz 1987) distinguished between joint custody as seen judicially and as seen psychologically. Judicial consideration takes the proximity of the two parental homes into account as well the need to renegotiate in the event of major changes in parental circumstances. Psychological considerations pay particular attention to the age of the children – as, for instance, the need of young children to have a consistent and predictable routine, as well as the implications of curriculum differences, and the importance of friendship networks for children of school age. Schwartz points out that joint legal and physical custody is often taken to mean that the children spend almost equal time with each parent.

She outlines the arguments *for* joint legal and physical custody as follows:

1 Such an arrangement maintains the parent–child relationship in such a way as to approximate that in the intact family.
2 The parents will both feel involved with the children rather than having a sense of being deprived of their 'parental rights'.
3 Because the parents share legal and physical custody, the complexities of negotiating child-care arrangements are reduced and the tendency towards the 'Father Christmas' syndrome of the noncustodial parent is diminished.
4 There is some argument in the assertion that joint legal custody makes it more likely that child maintenance will be paid, as fathers will feel more involved with their children, but this has been questioned by Weitzman (1985) and others.
5 The parents' joint responsibilities are emphasised, and thus there

is the possibility that this promotes collaborative co-parenting relationships and the need for contact with both extended families.

6 The chances of child kidnapping are reduced.

Schwarz's arguments *against* joint custody include the following:

7 It is unlikely that couples who could not agree when married could manage to co-parent in a harmonious fashion, at least until they are able to differentiate between their spousal and parental functions.

8 It is not always easy to clarify which are day-to-day decisions and which are major decisions.

9 The burden of such arrangements falls upon the children, as it is usually the child who moves every three or four days, although in a few families the parents move in and out of the former family home.

10 Difficulties are likely to arise when one parent's career involves a move to a different locality.

11 There is a question of fairness in relation to the developmental needs of several children as well as individual children's needs at different ages.

12 There are particular problems if one parent has abused their spouse and/or been a child abuser.

Wallerstein (1989) was once an advocate of joint physical custody, but since her latest ten- and fifteen-year follow-up of some of the families from the original research study, conducted with Kelly (1980), now seems to have changed her mind. Noting a tendency towards the interchangeability of men's and women's roles both in the workplace and the family, she points out that the central argument for joint custody rests on the importance for the child to maintain relationships with both father and mother post-divorce so as to try to soften the losses which research shows that children experience as the result of parental divorce. From 1981 to 1984 she followed parents and children between the ages of 3 and 14, of whom one-third were living in joint custody households, while the remainder were in sole custody households. Although she found that in the joint custody families none of the fathers had stopped visiting their children and were more committed to them, they also discovered that the children in joint custody households were no better adjusted than those in sole parent households, and neither did they show better social adjustment or less disturbance than the sole custody children.

In 1985 Wallerstein and her research team invited twenty-five couples who had joint physical custody to take part in a pilot study, and over a period of six months met monthly to discuss their experiences and those of their children. The most common pattern was three days with one parent and four with the other. On the positive side, where it worked well, joint custody enhanced the positive regard which the former partners had for each other in their roles as father and mother. However, on the more negative side in some cases such custody resulted from the fact that neither parent was willing to take full responsibility for the children, while in other cases parents chose it as a way of maintaining frequent contact with an ex-spouse. Joint custody calls for a considerable degree of collaboration and communication between parents, and while it increases cooperation it does not diminish the anger. ·

Schedules seemed to become inflexible once they had been made; and the change-over days were hard for both children and their parents, the constant transitions taking their emotional toll on them. There were several thorny issues which seemed to arise frequently, one being that in most households bedtime was not only different but non-negotiable, resulting in adjustment difficulties for the children and irritation and concern for their parents. In some households the children had their own beds, while in others the parent shared their beds with their children and, perhaps not surprisingly, did not wish to discuss this. The children and their parents were also seen individually every three to six months for four more years, the children being seen individually in the playroom, as children often behave differently in different contexts.

Wallerstein found that the children compared with children being raised in sole custody households rather than with those in intact families. Rather than solving their problems themselves or turning to their peers, the children were more likely to turn to adults. Somewhat to her surprise she found that the younger children (the 1- and 2-year-olds) showed less troubled behaviour than those of nursery school age (4- and 5-year-olds), which they attributed to them making their first steps away from the family. While Wallestein considered that her research and that of others indicates that 'children in primary school may be better equipped to adapt to joint custody arrangements. . . . [n]evertheless in a recent joint custody study, one third . . . were troubled and unhappy'. She acknowledges that this is a small study, but points out that joint custody 'succeeds or fails on the bedrock of "little" issues'. At best, it enables children to maintain their attachments to both parents and enrich their lives through membership of two well-functioning households. At worst, it can 'lock children into a destructive relationship with a violent or otherwise inadequate parent or into continuing bitter struggles between angry parents, so that the child runs the gauntlet in both homes – and feels that he or she has no home anywhere'.

There has also been some research on joint physical custody, which Kelly (1988) reports as being considered as highly satisfactory to the parents, after an initial period of adjustment in which to work out what are essentially very complex arrangements, although she points out that to date there has been little comparative research between joint physical custody and sole custody. Emery (1988b), who has himself conducted research on children's adjustment post-divorce, stresses the symbolic importance of joint legal custody, but is more guarded about the success of joint physical custody although he applauds those parents who seem able to make this work. He considers that the comparative research on children in joint and sole custody arrangement carried out so far (Leupnitz 1982) indicates that 'the parents with joint custody are an unusual group, they are older, more wealthy and better educated than sole custody parents and it may be that they also have a particularly cooperative relationship'. He goes on to point out that 'policy makers need to be careful in using research into negotiated joint custody to draw inferences about court imposed joint custody' (see Isaacs, Leon and Kline 1987, and Johnston and Campbell 1988).

Children's definitions of who is in the family are dependent on three factors: the frequency of access, the child's perceptions of the parents ability to get on, and the custody arrangements. Leupnitz (1982) argues that children in joint custody arrangements maintain filial relationships with both parents, whereas children in sole custody arrangements are more likely to have avuncular relationships with the noncustodial parent. In her most recent research, however, Isaacs (1988) indicates that it is not so much the type of custody which shapes the child's perceptions of family as the nature of the relationships within the custody arrangements. Furthermore, she indicates that those children who do best are those for whom there is an access arrangement during the first year post-separation and also one in the third year.

In the United Kingdom

In the UK there are apparently very few cases of shared physical custody, and indeed there are some judicial decisions which have overturned parental agreements to do so. 'In England and Wales Joint Custody commonly means that legal responsibility for taking "strategic" decisions as to the child's upbringing is shared, while one parent has day to day care and control and the other has access' (Law Commission Paper 96). There is a relatively small but steadily rising number of joint custody orders, especially among the middle classes and in the South. However, there is some clinical indication that a small but growing number of separating or divorced parents, often of young children, who live within the same area (or intend to do so), and have a reasonably cordial relationship are either considering or voluntarily embarking on an arrangement which resembles joint physical custody. A present perception of joint custody at present is that it is considered to diminish the 'winning and losing' aspects of the adversarial nature of divorce law and reinforces the importance of both parents, who in many cases are able to cooperate over decision-making in relation to their children. It also has an important symbolic meaning for the family in that it indicates the intention of both parents to continue to be interested and involved with their children. It may be significant that a recent programme on TV showed an hour-long American programme in which parents, stepparents and children spoke favourably of joint custody (Channel 4, 6 February 1990)

Thus there is an increasing recognition that the task of bringing up children is a shared responsibility and that continued qualitative contact with both parents is usually best for the welfare of the children; also that the arrangements regarding the children's access to the parent with whom they will not primarily be residing should be established as early as possible after the separation. The arguments outlined above are therefore likely to have increasing relevance in the future, perhaps especially when the new child-care legislation is enacted. The Children Act (1989) replaces custody and access orders with Section 8 orders, which specify residence, contact, prohibited steps and specific issues (see Chapter 12, 'The Children Act 1989', page 282).

Conclusions

The advantages and disadvantages of joint physical custody have been outlined by Schwartz and research remains inconclusive, though it seems clear that in order for joint physical custody to be workable, the two households need to be geographically proximal and carefully linked; and the post-divorce relationship between the parents needs to be a sufficiently cooperative one.

There are clear advantages of joint legal custody and especially its meaning to both parents and children alike, though there appears to be more doubt about how it works out in practice. Since shared parental responsibility for children is the basis of the Children Act, 1989, it is likely that in the immediate future joint custody will inevitably become the subject of considerable legal and psychological debate (see Chapter 12, 'The Children Act, 1989', page 282).

ACCESS

Maidment (1975), in reviewing the legal literature on access conditions in custody orders, points out that as 'the welfare of the child is the first and paramount consideration ... any right of access by the parent would always take second place to the child's interests'. She goes on to quote the decisions taken in two cases, which both reiterated the above and also indicated that access was to be the basic right of the child: '(T)hus Latey J. said "where one finds ... a reference to the basic right of a parent to access to the child, I do not accept that the meaning conveyed is that a parent should have access to the child although such access is contrary to the child's interests"'. Note also the elaboration by Mr Justice Wrangham in the case of *M.v. M.* (1980).

(T)he companionship of a parent is in any ordinary circumstances of such immense value to the child that there is a basic right in him to such companionship. I for my part would prefer to call it a basic right in the child rather than a basic right in the parent. That only means this, that no court should deprive a child of access to either parent unless it is wholly satisfied that it is in the interests of that child that access should cease, and that is a conclusion at which a court should be extremely slow to arrive.

For the children there are many advantages and functions of access:

1 It maintains the continuity of attachment so that the child does not experience the rejection, sense of abandonment, and damage to self-esteem which the loss of the noncustodial parent would entail.
2 It minimises the phantasies that the fears of such a loss would entail, as well as allowing the possibility of managing their phantasies about their noncustodial parent.
3 It helps to decrease child's feelings of responsibility for the separation.
4 It provides the child with a living example of paternal and maternal role models and potential examples of alternative 'good enough

parenting', as well as the examples of the ability to end intimate relationships in a responsible manner.

5 A continuing relationship with the noncustodial parent acts as a safeguard against possible future recriminations that the custodial parent has caused a 'cut-off' in relationships with the noncustodial parent and extended family. It also affords the custodial parent some parenting relief, with probable resultant benefits for the child.

6 The child is able to keep in touch with his or her genetic identity (Stone 1989) and thus with both sides of the re-formed extended family as well as with their family history.

7 Although the evidence for financial advantages of access seems to be contradictory, it is clear that this allows the potential availability of an alternative home, should a change of domicile become appropriate or even necessary, as may later be the case.

Eekelaar et al. (1977) carried out a study of 855 divorces in England and Wales and found that in the first twelve months following separation there was an increasing failure to exercise access and that this led to increasingly infrequent access. James and Wilson's (1984) exploratory study collected data from probation officers during a twelve-month period on a sample of cases in which the custody was disputed. The children ranged in age from 0 to 5 (thirty-four), 6 to 8 (thirty-eight), 9 to 12 (thirty-nine), 13 to 18 (twenty-three). About a quarter of the total number of children (sixty-five, of which thirty-five had custody disputed) in the study in each age group. In twenty cases the parents had been separated for twelve months or less when contacted by the Divorce Court welfare officer and in the remainder they had been separated for up to two years. In twenty cases the children were living with their father, while their mother was contesting custody in seventeen of them. While in thirty-nine (62 per cent) of the cases the parents had mutually agreed where their children should live, in only twenty (31 per cent) of the cases had the children been consulted about the decision by one or both parents. Among their findings was the suggestion that the involvement of the probation officer (or other third party who is not partisan) was beneficial to the discussion leading up to crucial decisions; and yet in 50 per cent of the cases the probation officer received no request for a report until six months after the petition had been filed.

As in many other similar studies, they found that the children, particularly the boys aged 9 to 12, revealed a high level of behaviour difficulties. There were also indications that the sex of the custodial parent and that of the oldest child are related to access difficulties. Their conclusions pointed to the lack of empirical evidence, which results in decisions being made by judges, lawyers and social workers offering advice and making decisions based on little more than their own views. They also found that conflict between the parents which effectively excludes their children from consideration is more likely to lead to disturbed behaviour among them. Their study also tended to confirm that access gradually tails off as time passes, as well as its generally problematic nature. In the light of their findings they suggest that there should be further explorations into the role and contribution of children in such negotiations and decision-making processes.

The subsequent review of law in relation to children (1986) found that of the 150,000 children whose parents divorce each year, half of them lose touch with their noncustodial parent within two years; and it is in the light of such findings that the 1989 Children Act proposes radical changes in policy relating to access.

Weir's (1985) study for the Family Court of Australia into access patterns and conflict distinguished different basic styles of access:

1 *Free access*, where the arrangements occur in response to the child's needs and are often instigated by the child, particularly an older one.
2 *Flexible regular access*, where there is an understanding between the parents about it and it can be modified by negotiation as necessary.
3 *Rigid regular access*, where there is a regular arrangement, but little scope for renegotiation.
4 *Irregular access*, where access takes place on an occasional basis, but usually at the instigation of the noncustodial parent and to suit his or her convenience. This includes occasional contact by letter or telephone.
5 *No access*.

Weir compared the parental perceptions of access both as regards parental conflict and in relation to their children and distinguished meaningful access in terms of hourly access either weekly or more than once a week, and all day or overnight fortnightly. However, she pointed out that while a fair relationship between parents indicated a higher probability of meaningful access, it may be the very existence of access that makes it difficult for parents to achieve a good enough relationship with each other. She also found that there were several factors which influenced the arrangement of meaningful access, such as the support available to the couple, the impact of the separation and their current adjustment to it, as well as the degree of conflict, the last two having the greatest influence.

In the US Jacobson (1987) carried out an exploratory study, eventually interviewing 288 families, where both partners agreed to take part in the study. The parents in both households were interviewed, as well as the child (aged between 8 and 14) who linked both households, who had been living in the same place for at least one year and who had seen his or her noncustodial parent at least once during the past year. Both partners had high school education and lived within 150 miles of each other, and at least one partner had previously been married. The families were divided into a sixfold typology, the first three where the child was in a mother custody family, either one (living with a single mother and visiting a remarried father), two (living with a remarried mother and visiting a remarried father), or three (living with a remarried mother and visiting a single father). In family types four, five and six the child was living with the father and visiting the mother in parallel types of families. The children in type two families (that is, where both parents were remarried) spent most time visiting the noncustodial parent, while those living in type four (that is, those with single fathers) spent significantly less time. The children in type four families also had the highest level of behaviour problems, while those in type two had the least. Although it was found that the children of divorce and remarriage were somewhat more stressed than those in the general population, as a group they were not regarded as being in need of treatment. However, the children in the father custody families were found to have significantly higher behaviour problems than children in two of the three mother custody families. Like Wallerstein, Jacobson found that in many instances the families had had to take into account almost daily decision-making in planning visiting (access) schedules, weekends, holidays and so on much more than they had anticipated, so that some of them virtually lived 'in tandem'. She concludes that any inclination to draw a boundary around the custodial household needs to be reconsidered in the light of these findings.

Isaacs (1988) studied the visitation (access) schedules in mother custody families (103) who were interviewed when the parents had recently parted and again in the third year of separation. In the early months of separation 44 per cent of the parents reported that they did not argue, 32 per cent said that they did sometimes, and 24 per cent said that they were always arguing. Three-quarters of the families who had a schedule in the first few months still had it two years later, while 75 per cent who had not, still had no schedule two years later. Isaacs found that the regularity rather than the frequency of the visiting was more relevant to the outcome; and that as the parents consolidated their visitation procedures, the impact became apparent. The relationship which the parents managed to set up in the first year was crucial to their ability both to set up and maintain the visiting arrangements. She concluded that the first year emerges as a critical period, and points to early intervention in the divorce process. Even though a conflictual relationship between the parents cannot be altered early on, if they can be helped to maintain a stable schedule then their children can still be helped.

GRANDPARENTS AND STEPGRANDPARENTS

Although there seems to have been virtually no research into the role of grandparents during the divorce and remarriage process, it is well known that during family breakdown the grandparents often play a very significant role in providing a supportive family network, particularly in relation to their grandchildren. Indeed, during the most tempestuous stages of the divorce process, grandparents can provide them with a supportive stability that their parents may be unable to manage. Although attitudes towards divorce have changed considerably during the past twenty years, it is nevertheless possible that grandparental attitudes towards the divorce of their adult children is likely to be more traditional, especially where this is against the teachings of their religious beliefs. Many grandparents, perhaps particularly those who have moved closer to their grandchildren during the divorce process, also find it difficult to adapt and allow space for the new stepparent. Others remain firmly attached to the previous partners of their own children and find it difficult to manage their own feelings related to the divorce and remarriage sufficiently to embrace the new and vulnerable, developing stepfamily, thus attenuating the relationships with their grandchildren.

However, as has already been stated, and as Ahrons and Bowman (1981) confirm, divorce also requires a major reorganisation of the extended family. They quote some US research which seems to indicate that while relationships with consanguinial kin (namely, blood relations) continue much as before, relationships with affinal kin (that is, by marriage) are more likely to suffer. Research carried out in Wisconsin following a change in the divorce law which recognised grandparental rights for visitation (access) after divorce indicated that mothers continue to be an important source of support for their divorced adult children, particularly immediately after the legal divorce. In the UK the Children Act (1989) gives grandparents the right of legal representation in certain circumstances and also enables them to apply to the court for contact and residence orders (see Chapter 12, 'The Children Act 1989', page 282), the welfare of the children being paramount.

Stepgrandparents may often demonstrate ambivalence towards the newly formed stepfamily, some resentful of the addition of step-grandchildren who are not blood relations to their extended family. Others find the complexity and sheer size of the stepfamily somewhat overwhelming and feel themselves unable to adapt sufficiently to promote bonding with their stepgrandchildren.

REWARDS OF STEPPARENTING

The rewards of stepfamilies are rarely mentioned and yet, where the relationships between the formerly married spouses are both flexible and reasonably amicable, it is possible for both households to have some relief from being full-time parents.

Ihinger-Tallman and Pasley (1987) mention the possibility of several benefits. In the first place, because they are neither affected directly by the past family history nor so emotionally attached to the child, stepparents can bring a degree of objectivity, particularly as regards the child's behaviour, which is not usually possible for biological parents. Second, because of this, a stepparent who be-friends a stepchild can be used as a sounding board, or a source of information on subjects which the child may be embarrassed to discuss with biological parents. Third, stepparents can bring new opportunities and ideas and values into the family – as for instance a stepparent who is musical, artistic or particularly interested in some sporting activities, which are not characteristic of either biological parent. Finally, but perhaps most importantly, the children can have the opportunity of day-to-day living with different family units, thus having an alternative place to go, and further models of family life.

EPILOGUE: SOME GUIDELINES FOR DIVORCING PARENTS AND STEPFAMILY FORMATION IN RE-FORMED EXTENDED FAMILIES

Terkelson (1980), writing of the processes of change in families during the life cycle and under normal conditions, describes three phases, which he describes as insertion, destabilisation and resolution. When a new need becomes manifest in the family and it is recognised and validated by other family members this sets in motion sequences of behaviour which permits its fulfilment through insertion. Perturbations occur in the family system as attempts are made to assimilate the new behaviours within the ongoing family structure, and the behavioural sequences clash with some existing elements but integrate with others. The behaviour of the whole family becomes more conflictual and some needs go unmet as the family becomes destabilised. A compromise structure gradually takes shape, through the emergence of trial sequences which consist of integrated elements of new and pre-existing structures, which allow for a resolution in which one of the sequences is eventually accepted as permanent structure. At the same time, there is a parallel process through which obsolete behavioural sequences of need attainment gradually fall away through deletion. Terkelson primarily focuses on changing family structures rather than change in family belief systems, though clearly the family belief systems at the levels of family myths, life scripting and relationships must also experience corresponding changes in meaning for the family (see Cronen and Pearce 1985; Chapter 2, 'Advantages and disadvantages of a family systems model', page 27). The previous discussions on the processes of divorce and becoming a stepfamily (in Chapters 3, 4 and 5) have shown just how problematic and complex these processes can be, usually taking from three to five years or longer.

The guidelines suggested which are outlined below have been developed from empirical research as well from the research studies already discussed, or (as in those for parents and children of divorce) based on the parental guidelines prepared by a family conciliation service (the Institute of Family Therapy, London). They may be of use for divorcing parents, stepfamily members and interventionist practitioners alike.

Guidelines for parents of children of divorce

First, children need to be told what is happening, and the explanation provided, should be direct, honest and consistent with their age and understanding. It is important to reassure them that their parents are doing their best to consider them and their needs and that they are not responsible for the separation of their parents or any possible divorce. If at all possible parents should attempt to sit down together with the children and provide them with an explanation of what is going to happen. If this proves too difficult, they should agree, as individual parents, on what each might say to the children, who should say this and what reply the other is likely to make when the children come for a response from the other parent.

Second, children will want to know where they are going to live and where the parent who is leaving will be living; they will also want to know when they will see him or her again. They need to be reassured that their parents still love them. Many younger children are worried that they are going to be abandoned and that if one parent can leave so can the other.

Third, children need to be helped to make an explanation for themselves which is relevant to their own age and stage of development. This implies that they need to return to the divorce process from time to time in order to update their own explanation according to the development of their cognitive abilities and psychological understanding.

Fourth, the time of the actual separation is a crucial one for the children's relationship with the parent who is leaving the family home. It is usually best to start with fixed, clear-cut arrangements, as children, particularly young ones, need a consistent and predictable schedule when they can look forward to seeing a parent. As the family situation improves and becomes clearer, these can become more flexible.

Fifth, the actual transition of leaving one parent to stay with the other can be stressful for any child and needs to be made as easy and comfortable as possible. This is not the time to discuss any disagreements parents may have. Children need to be reassured that the parent with whom they are primarily living approves of their stay with the other parent and is actively encouraging them to enjoy their time with them.

Sixth, if the child seems sad or angry around these times this is not necessarily indicative of a problem with either parent but may reflect the child's level of stress and concern regarding the changes in the family. This situation generally settles down once a routine is established which both parents support.

Seventh, parents are responsible for arranging time for their children with each of them so that the children feel a part of their lives.

When problems arise they should discuss these together and not involve the children. Communicating through the children can place them in the middle of a parental conflict which makes them stressed and unhappy.

Eighth, children are intensely loyal. Young children should not be asked with which parent they want to live. Older children should be consulted about their views, but it is the parents' responsibility to make the final decision. Children should not be encouraged to take sides when their parents disagree.

Ninth, extended visits during the school holidays can provide an opportunity for children to spend a longer period of time with the parent they usually see only on brief visits. This can allow a parent–child relationship to develop in a realistic manner. When such visits are arranged, the children should feel comfortable with the length of time and know what the plans are for their stay.

Tenth, if, for whatever reason, there is a long gap between meetings of a child and a parent it is a good idea to keep the relationship going with telephone calls, letters or cards. Even very young children appreciate the fact that a parent is thinking of them and that they are valued.

Eleventh, parents do need to show mutual respect for each other's privacy, and interrogating children about their time with the other parent can make them resentful and angry. If they do have problems they should always be encouraged to take them up with the parent involved.

Twelfth, when the divorce process generates feelings of deep anger parents may find themselves or other family members making negative comments about the absent parent. This can only heighten a child's sense of divided loyalties and lead to confusion and anxiety. Children have a great need to love and respect both their parents.

Thirteenth, stopping a child seeing a parent should never be a weapon in an adult battle. All the evidence shows that children can adapt to the separation of their parents. What can cause long-term damage is losing contact with a parent. Children have a great need to feel that both their parents love them and want them to be part of their lives. On this rests a great deal of their self-confidence and self-esteem.

The remarriage/cohabitation partnership

As the relationship of the marital pair (or partnership) will become another element in the architectural basis of the stepfamily system

(Mills 1984, Kvanli and Jennings 1987), the new partners need to allow time and space (both psychological and physical) for the creation of their relationship, and especially for the growth of a mutual trust between them (Visher and Visher 1988). While encouraging the development of a shared approach, they also need to allow for the recognition and acceptance of differences between themselves – as, for instance, regarding the disciplining of children. They each need to accept each another's past history and the present commitments, including the advantages of a collaborative parental relationship between former partners and the financial commitments entailed in previous marriage(s).

The stepfamily household

The new stepfamily living in the same household needs to allow for a separateness between the parents and children or stepchildren which recognises and accepts the necessity for intergenerational boundaries. These are especially important regarding behaviour which may be experienced as sexually provocative (for example children bathing or sleeping with parents). As only infants are likely to have the same developmental needs as the stepfamily (Mills 1984), it is often useful to assess which stage of the stepfamily life cycle the stepfamily has reached; and also to try to distinguish the different life-cycle tracks of family members (Sager et al. 1983). While young children who have lived with a custodial parent are likely to become assimilated within a few years into a family which now includes a stepparent, those who are adolescent are unlikely to do so. Many older children want to live with their 'other' parent during their adolescence and, providing the parent and new partner accept this, often settle down reasonably well in such a stepfamily, whose expectations may match their own emerging adulthood.

As the stepfamily begins to attempt to settle down together, it becomes necessary to negotiate or renegotiate the household rules, particularly those which take into account both crowding and strong feelings about territorial issues. It is helpful in the long run if both the adults and, as appropriate to age and understanding, also the children are able to confront the lack of clarity about the role of the stepparent and to begin to negotiate and build one which neither competes with nor usurps that of the natural parent. One aspect of the building of this stepparent role is the necessity to be straightforward and open about both negative and positive feelings. As has already been discussed, it is useful to consider the gender implications for the parent–child and stepparent–stepchildren in the household.

The re-formed extended family

As far as possible it is helpful to negotiate flexible boundaries between households, which allow respectful autonomy between the adults and their household management, but relative and appropriate freedom for the children. It is also necessary to build realistic expectations of stepfamily life and rules for behaviour, while recognising that these may be different for each household. The psychological and territorial space between the stepsiblings, and also stepsiblings and half siblings, needs both recognition and protection. Arrangements for access should be negotiated and communicated directly parent to parent, and should be based on the needs and interests of the children, while allowing for flexibility, especially for older children.

The children should not be used as go-betweens or spies between the households. Younger children need arrangements for visits to be made for them; and, while older children may need some support initially, they can gradually be helped to make their own arrangements. The adults should recognise their responsibilities towards maintaining attachments and also the need for individual contacts between children and each parent. If uncertainties are faced honestly and questions are answered truthfully, even if the answers are unknown, then it becomes possible to develop a network of relationships which are experienced as reliable and relatively trustworthy.

It is important to recognise that the family history has been interrupted and to allow for review and reinterpretation of events (Visher and Visher 1979, 1988). Providing that attachments do not undermine the development of the stepfamily, their maintenance between grandparents and grandchildren can also be supportive during the period of transition. If at all possible grandparents and stepgrandparents should be encouraged to treat all the children as they do those that are their own kin.

Gender issues

Stepmothers need to inform themselves sufficiently as to the developmental stages and individual history of their stepchild and, together with their partner, to assess whether the child now seems to be at a level which is age- and stage-appropriate. They should begin by relating to the child as a friendly adult, rather than as the partner of their stepchild's father, and move steadily and cautiously towards a more intimate relationship. Stepfathers, many of whom may not have previously been parents, or, as indicated earlier (in Chapters 6, 7 and 8) may themselves still be grieving from the part-time or total loss of contact with their own children, also need to be sensitive and cautious, perhaps particularly as to any intimate contact with the children, such as bathing or dressing them. Both stepfathers and stepmothers will need to move towards a greater intimacy at each child's pace, rather than their own, and to develop an individual relationship with their stepchildren as well as a paired relationship with their spouse, particularly as regards household rules.

Continuing disagreements

If parents cannot resolve their differences regarding arrangements, whether as regards their children or in relation to financial matters, as often the two are intertwined, then it is likely that outside assistance will be useful. Despite the fact that in such a situation each of the parents have a great need for someone who is on their side, in the long run it is best to go together to discuss their differences with someone who is impartial before their positions become too entrenched. Parents in dispute can seek the assistance of a conciliation service (affiliated to the NFCC or through the Family Mediators' Association) where they can be helped to explore their differences, isolate their genuine disagreements and try to reach at least some agreements which are the most appropriate for themselves and their own children according to the stage of family transformation which they have reached (see Chapter 3, 'The mediation model of intervention during the divorce process', page 53, and Chapter 9, 'Comparison between mediation, psychotherapy and family therapy', page 57). For instance, in families where the children are still relatively young it is as well to recognise the possibility of change of custody in future, and to prepare to be flexible as different needs arise for children (such as at adolescence) and parent (for example, when there is a change of job necessitating a move of home). If parents are unable to resolve their disputes in relation to their children, then at the time the petition for divorce is being considered by the courts they may be referred to the court welfare officer, who may also help them to resolve their differences through a conciliatory approach.

It is usually both advisable and reassuring for separating and divorcing parents to consult lawyers to clarify their own legal position, both prior to the eventual decision to separate, for legal scrutiny of any agreements reached and subsequently, if they cannot reach agreements together. Should the need for litigation ultimately become necessary, where possible those involved in legal disputes are advised to choose non-adversarial lawyers who are also specialists in family law (for instance, members of the Solicitors Family Law Association). In the long run it is best if parents instruct their own lawyer to negotiate for the most appropriate option within the legal framework which is relevant to the current situation and stage of the family life cycle (as, for instance joint custody and regular access). Contested proceedings in court are best avoided, unless they become necessary to protect the immediate, short- or long-term welfare of children. However well conducted, there are emotional as well as financial costs for both parents and children which follow from contested proceedings, and they should never be embarked upon without a full consideration of the possible consequences. There are no real winners from such proceedings, as, to a large extent, all are losers.

12 Afterword

The reformation of family policy – a second chance for families in transition?

I hold it indisputable, that the first duty of a State is to see that every child born therein shall be well housed, clothed, fed and educated, till it attain years of discretion. But in order to effect this the Government must have an authority over the people of which we now do not so much as dream.

John Ruskin (1819–1900), *Time and Tide*, Letter xiii

The Family is the natural and fundamental group unit of society and is entitled to protection by society and the state.

Article 16 (3), UN Charter of Human Rights, 1948

THE ENTERPRISE CULTURE AND THE FAMILY

We are now fast approaching the twenty-first century and also, but more slowly and uncertainly, attempting to make the necessary plans and policies which will take us into the future in a world which is becoming increasingly ecologically and economically unstable. In this book until now there has been no attempt made to address the sociopolitical level directly, but this can no longer be ignored, and therefore this last chapter will attempt to consider, albeit briefly, the role of the state in relation to divorcing families, and, though to a lesser extent, those re-formed extended families whose difficulties eventually lead to some state intervention.

Because there is a reciprocal interplay between families and the society in which they live, some attention must be paid to the cognitive dissonance which presently exists in our society. For the past few years each of the political parties has expressed its concerns regarding the state of family life, and yet our record for family and social policy in the seventies and eighties has led to serious questioning as to whether indeed we have had any coherent policies relating to the family at all! The present government has made much of its claims to be the upholder of family values, Margaret Thatcher extolling the virtues of 'the family as the building block of society . . . as the preparation for the rest of our lives [and of] the women who run it'. More recently she condemned the present position in which

> one out of every five children experience the break-up of their parents' marriage before they are 16; and one in every four children are now born outside marriage . . . children are in danger of seeing life without father, not as the exception but as the rule . . . This is a new kind of threat to our whole way of life, the long term implications of which we can barely grasp.
>
> (*Independent*, 18 January 1990)

Yet it is only now in late-term that any attempts appear to be being made to consider ways in which real assistance can be given to family support. As Wicks (1989) pointed out, 'there is a contradiction where there should be a strategy', the Government picture of the family being one of 'marriage, rock permanent and durable; man, the breadwinner, woman the keeper of hearth and home and children secure within the nuclear family'; yet social trends, particularly over the last decade, have challenged this traditional, and often idealised, iconographic view.

Seabrook (1989) also considers that there is a contradiction at the heart of the enterprise culture of Thatcherism, which extols economic success at the cost of human relationships. The savage cuts in the welfare state and health service, frequently imposed on the pretext of efficiency, are accompanied by entrepreneurial activities which uncover fresh needs and 'goad people into desiring whatever commodity appears to answer it'. He considers that 'the real disrupters of human closeness are the forces of invasive individualism [as] egotism and self interest are now prized as the most powerful motors of human endeavour'. This double message, whereby the rhetoric of the right exhorts the responsibilities of parenthood, also brings about the subversion and rearrangement of human relationships and the materialism which results in the feminisation of poverty, and causes children to become the victims of the failure of their parents' ability to live up to the iconography of the 'happy family'.

The majority of women who petition and are eventually divorced initially did not wish to end their marriage, although they might have wanted to improve it. As it is, they find themselves on their own with their children, virtually abandoned by their husbands, struggling to make ends meet on half their original income, 75 per cent of the husbands and fathers making no contribution to the household. Many of the mothers in single-parent households find themselves caught in the child-care poverty trap, in that the costs of child minders or day care for their children are so high that they would be worse off if they returned to work, as they are exhorted and increasingly will be needed to do.

The costs of divorce and its sequelae are soaring. These include not only those costs for legal aid, but also those related to welfare benefits and the health service. According to Dr Dominian (Director of One plus One) divorce costs this country £1.4 billion a year (*The Times*, 2 June 1990). In a recent television programme (*Panorama*, BBC 2, 18 September 1989) Toynbee pointed out the £3.4 billion cost per annum for social security to support (usually) mothers coping alone with their children. The state provision for child care facilities is negligible and yet at a cost of £70 subsidy per week, many of these women could return to the labour market, where jobs may well await them. There is much talk of, though little evidence for, what is known as the 'perverse incentive', whereby state provision is alleged to encourage young women to become pregnant as a way of obtaining state-subsidised housing. Yet for many of these young women becoming mothers may be their only chance of getting away from home, to have someone to love who also loves and needs them, thus acquiring a sense of purpose; and perhaps also because they believe that society's idealisation of motherhood will reward them with some appreciative recognition. Frank Field, MP, in a recent article points out that 'what is required is a change in the atmosphere in which young people make major decisions. Crucial to this change is that young men become aware of the financial responsibilities which fatherhood brings, and young women appreciate the full range of choice that is open to them' (*Independent*, 24 October 1989).

Concern about the financial costs of single-parent households has led to the setting up of an interdepartmental committee to consider the question of nonpayment of maintenance, a matter now high on the agenda of the Government (*Independent*, 20 June 1990). A recent article by Garlick points out that 'Maintenance payments will always rest on the payer's ability to pay and many fathers have pressing financial commitments in the form of a new family'. On the other hand, the present system 'puts the entire burden on mothers to chase fathers through the courts, four out of five of them receiving no maintenance whatever from the fathers of their children'. There is considerable interest in a new Australian scheme recently introduced in two stages, in which the Child Support Scheme initially set up a new branch of the tax office to collect the payments at source.

Since 1989 either parent, following the breakdown of their relationship (whether married or not), can apply to the Child Support Agency for maintenance at the level already agreed by parents or laid down by the courts. This has had a considerable success rate in tracing fathers. In the second stage (recently implemented), the Child Support Agency assesses maintenance levels, and arranges for deductions from the paying parent's wages, using a formula which sets child maintenance at a percentage of the noncustodial parent's taxable income above a threshold intended to cover adequate living expenses (assessed at the equivalent of a five-weekly period). Maintenance for the children of the first family is given preference over subsequent children born of new relationships (Mrs Justice Emery Murray of the Family Court of Australia 1990).

Pressured by financial necessity, and encouraged by the availability of jobs for women, more than half of all mothers return to work after childbirth (56 per cent in 1988). For some of these women the return to work allows them the psychological and (some) financial freedom which prompts them to review their own lives, as the result of which they seek to emerge from the shackles of an unhappy marriage and house-bound family life to a new form of independence, but over-responsibility. Many of them do not go off to set up home with other men, but prefer to live alone with their children, rather than in families to which their husbands contribute very little, either in terms of household assistance or financial help, yet use their power to continue to make demands on them (Clulow and Vincent 1987).

Despite the rising costs of income support, family credit, housing benefit (including loans available from the Social Fund which have to be repaid out of social security benefit) and legal aid, as well as the numbers of children that need to be received into care as the result of family breakdown, there is still too little cooperation across the departments of government. Hard pressed and often vilified social workers are trying to undertake preventive work with families in order to keep parents (or at least mothers) and children appropriately housed and together as a family unit. Many such families are living below the poverty level and are therefore unable to function at a level which allows attention to be given to sufficient need fulfilment for either parent(s) or children. The fact that many of them are also single-parent households does not necessarily mean that if their standard of living could be improved and supports provided for them, they could not become 'good enough' families.

At the same time, among the professional and blue-collar groups more and more couples, in an attempt to prevent their partnerships breaking down, are seeking individual, marital, or couple counselling or therapy, as the waiting lists for agencies which specialise in this form of intervention demonstrate. There is a growth in telephone counselling services and self-help groups, for example the number of callers to the Stepfamily Telephone Counselling Service has doubled in the last two years and the support groups run by the Stepfamily Association have risen in response to local need. Many conciliation services and civil units of the probation service are providing Divorce Experience courses for their clients, so that they can not only learn for themselves about the divorce process, but also that there are others in the same situation; yet there is still a great need for Access Centres, where children and their noncustodial parents (usually fathers) can rebuild (or even build) their relationships with one another.

This paradoxical situation is also reflected by the media, which on the one hand reports the moral panic over the rising divorce rate; children born out of wedlock, especially to young single women, single-parent families arising from divorce and desertion by the fathers of the children, yet also the plight of fathers who cannot see their children; child sexual abuse (particularly by stepfathers and cohabitees). On the other hand, the media sometimes reflect an almost desperate preoccupation and search for ways of relating which promote personal fulfilment and preserve some form of traditional family life. An apparently endless stream of articles of social interest in the press and programmes on television, which seek to explore human relationships (such as *Desert Island Discs* on BBC radio and *The Session* (BBC2), shown at peak viewing time), demonstrates this paradoxical search for mutuality and intimacy within a family unit, coupled with a preoccupation with individualistic materialism which the enterprise society encourages if not actively promotes.

At the national level there are a number of 'second chance' possibilities which the government could promote. Moreover, through the allocation of adequate funding and departmental coordination and cooperation it could also provide the necessary support at various key stages and at different levels in the various systems which become involved with families in transition during the process of divorce and remarriage. The first of these is the Children Act (1989) which, although it is on the statute-book, awaits a number of directions and procedures before its implementation, planned for October 1991. The language in which the Act is framed, together with pamphlets and explanatory leaflets which are to be made available, should help to bring about a new culture in which ideas about parental responsibilities post-divorce will be more accessible to the general population. Second, are the Law Commission's proposals related to changes in the divorce law which are imminently due to be presented to the Lord Chancellor. Although these proposals could not rectify the failure of a marriage, nor prevent the inevitable short term distress which marital breakdown brings to a family, they could recognise its ending and provide some protection of the rights of the more vulnerable family members, especially the children. They could also make some provision for the possibility of reconciliation and promote parental entry into a process of conciliation. As things stand at present the invocation of the divorce law actively encourages the mutual allocation of blame between the parties. Third is the report of the Conciliation Project Unit of Newcastle University, which proposes a national Family Advisory Counselling and Conciliation Bureau. Finally, there are a number of recommendations which are emerging from a series of research studies carried out at the Socio-Legal Centre for Family Studies at the University of Bristol.

THE CHILDREN ACT 1989: IMPLICATIONS FOR FAMILIES IN SEPARATION AND DIVORCE

The Children Act of 1989 is revolutionary in that for the first time, almost all the law (both public and private) relating to children is brought together in uniform structure in that all the statutory remedies available to determine the upbringing of children will be available in all courts and all proceedings. Hoggett points out that

> such a comprehensive revision only became possible because of the unlikely coincidence of three events. In the first place, the Government's review of Child Care Law (1985, 1987) resulted in a commitment to legislate, but no Parliamentary time until the 1988/9 session. Second, the Law Commission's Complementary review of the private law relating to the upbringing of children (Working Papers No. 91 (1985) on guardianship, No. 96 (1986) on custody, and No. 101 (1987) on wardship) was completed in time for integrated legislation to be prepared. Third, the Cleveland Report (1988) made it essential that action should be taken as soon as possible.
>
> (Hoggett 1989)

The Act, which is based on three major principles, is also revolutionary in that, for the first time in British legal history, the concept of parental responsibility is introduced. This principle replaces the more traditional idea of parental rights, which implies that unless they are considered to be at some specified risk, children are still considered to be the possessions of their parents. While reiterating that the welfare of the child is the paramount consideration, the Act also introduces an entirely new and consistent philosophy whereby, in addition to setting out principles for children who may need protection, it also seeks to involve parents by emphasising parental responsibilities, duties and authority, as well as their rights and powers. Furthermore, the Act also introduces a second principle which stresses the state's role as being to help rather than hinder parents, and places a duty on the courts *not* to make an order *unless it would be better for the child than making no order at all.* Under Section 31 it specifies that a court may only make an order if it is satisfied that:

1 that the child concerned has suffered significant harm, or is likely to suffer such harm;
2 and that the harm or likelihood of harm is attributable to –
   (a) the standard of care given to the child, or likely to be given to the child if the order were not made, being below that which it would reasonable to expect the parent of a similar child to give him; or
   (b) the child's being beyond parental control.

The third principle, on which the Act is based, is the requirement that the court must have regard to the fact that delay in decision-making related to the child is likely to prejudice the welfare of that child (Section 10). The court is therefore empowered to set a timetable and to give directions which ensure that (so far as is practicable) it is adhered to. This includes specifying periods within which specific steps must be taken in relation to the proceedings and to ensure that such questions are determined without delay. This section would give the courts the power to set a timetable, which would prevent the delaying legal tactics of some parents, who are involved in disputes relating to custody or access and who seek to delay decision-making in order to gain legal advantage. Nor will the court be legally bound by the original application or solutions asked for.

The Act, which is described as an enabling one, will be implemented in the autumn of 1991. From that time onwards not only should the child's welfare be paramount in deciding all questions about upbringing, but it will also be ensured that parental authority is shared between both parents, though they may act independently of each other. Parental authority also includes, by agreement or through application to the court, those not married to each other, although there is no presumption that an unmarried father shares such authority. There will be the *presumption* of shared parental responsibility for married couples, and that this will continue should the parents separate or divorce. However, there will still be court scrutiny, probably by Registrars, regarding the children, and this is likely to be at an earlier stage than the present Conciliation Appointments, under Section 41 (see page 95). It is hoped that this will both encourage and empower fathers who want to take an active role in the lives of their children after divorce. While there is at present an expectation that fathers will carry out their paternal duties, for instance as regards maintenance, the intransigence of many separated or divorced mothers as regards paternal access for their children often offers little encouragement for them to do so. In such situations the courts are frequently helpless, as their only ultimate remedy is imprisonment which they are understandably reluctant to enforce as it would be likely to lead to the further distress and impoverishment of all concerned. It seems likely that in the future there will be an expectation that divorcing parents will voluntarily make agreements which allow the children regular access to their out-of-house parent (at present usually the father) and which will thus promote a continuing shared parental responsibility.

The second part of the Act outlines a number of orders. Those which may have particular relevance to children of families where the parents are divorcing are included those under Section 8:

1 *Residence orders* – which set out the arrangements to be made as to the person with whom the child is to live. As is the case at present under a custody order, the child may not be known by a new surname, nor may any person remove the child from the United Kingdom.
2 *Contact orders* – which require the person with whom the child is living to allow the child to visit or have contact with the person named in the order, or for that person and the child otherwise to have contact with each other. Such orders will not only replace the defined access orders, which are at present sometimes made by courts where the parents cannot agree arrangements for access, but will also recognise contacts by telephone or letter, which at present are often subverted by custodial parents reluctant to allow any contact at all.
3 *Specific issue orders* – which give directions for the purpose of defining a specific issue which has arisen or may arise in connection

with any aspect of parental responsibility for the child concerned. Such orders will give the court a wide range of enabling options – as, for instance, supervised contact (which will replace supervised access), and visits to grandparents.

4 *Prohibited steps orders* – in which particular steps spelled out in the order may not be taken by a parent in meeting parental responsibility for the child (as specified in the order) without the consent of the court. These orders too will allow for a wide range of negative injunctions to be specified, as for instance allowing an abusing stepparent or cohabitee to return to the household where a child who was the recipient of the abuse is now living; or a custodial parent allowing a young child to believe that a stepparent is a biological parent. Courts will also be able to make a combination of two or more orders.

Another order which may have particular relevance for divorcing families is a Family Assistance Order (Section 16), under which a local authority social worker or a probation officer will be made available to give advice and assistance to a person named in the order (who may be either the child, a parent, guardian or other person with whom the child lives, or in whose favour a contact order may be in force). Such an order would be for six months only and is intended to provide such expert help as may be necessary for families during a difficult period of transition (due, for example, to divorce).

When the circumstances are such that the court is considering whether to make, vary or discharge any order, and the making of the order is opposed by any party to the proceedings, then the Act, under Section 1 (2), outlines what is virtually a checklist to which the court is directed when seeking to determine any question with regard to the upbringing of a child (which has been altered so as to indicate a child of either sex):

(a) the ascertainable wishes and feelings of the child concerned (considered in the light of his/her age and understanding);
(b) his/her physical, emotional and educational needs;
(c) the likely effect on him/her of any change in his/her circumstances;
(d) his/her age, sex, background and any characteristics of his/hers which the court considers relevant;
(e) any harm which s/he has suffered or is at risk of suffering;
(f) how capable each of his/her parents, and any other person in relation to whom the court considers the question to be relevant, is of meeting his/her needs;

(g) the range of powers available to the court under this Act in the proceedings in question.

Much of the Act specifically relates to children who are considered to be at risk, and although one aspect of that risk may well be indirectly related to the marital or partnership breakdown of their parents, such children have not directly been the focus of this book. However, the changes as regards parental responsibilities which are envisaged in the Children Act may well lead to a greater focus on the marital and partnership relationships of children at risk of significant harm than has hitherto often been the case.

The Act also specifies that where a residence order is made in favour of two or more persons who do not themselves live together, the order may specify the periods during which the child is to live in the different households concerned. This *seems* to give legal recognition to those families where the parents have agreed to share the children in physical as well as legal joint custody. But, where such a residence order has been made specifying that the child lives (or is to live with) with one of two parents who each have parental responsibility for him, it will cease to have effect if the parents live together for a continuous period of more than six months. Similarly, a contact order would cease to have effect if the parents resumed cohabitation.

As regards families during separation and divorce, one of the aims of Part II of the Act is to assist parents after separation not only to continue to retain shared parental responsibility for their children, but also to encourage them to try to resolve any disputes between themselves. Indeed, as Fisher (1989) writes, research findings indicate the importance of maintaining the bonding between children and their parents after divorce and that therefore such encouragement of joint parenting reinforces already held professional opinion. However, the Act is also proactive for public opinion. Certainly, the philosophy of shared parental responsibility may well discourage the 'winner take all' custody battles which some couples wage, in which one partner is awarded the custody of the child while the loser is given access as a consolation prize. But it remains to be seen whether such a change in parental attitudes could be achieved by those couples whose bitter and entrenched anger seems to require fuelling and some kind of negative fulfilment through acrimonious legal proceedings. Nevertheless, the promotion of parental responsibility, coupled with the increased clarity as regards the arrangements, should diminish the tendency to stake out battle lines when there is disagreement. The Act also implicitly allows opportunities for voluntary mediation, and it seems possible (if not probable) that the courts will encourage welfare officers to refer couples in dispute to the Out of Court independent services (where available), not least because this would save court time and public money.

Fisher (1989) also points out the importance of the language employed to do the task which is required of it. While the word 'custody' coming from the Latin root to do with 'guarding' generates emotion and conflict, will the use of the word 'residence' prove more benign? 'Access' means coming or going, even yielding, while 'contact' means touching. Will such a term prevent more parents from withholding their children from one another? She goes on to indicate that 'bond breaking and bond maintaining set off deep cultural and instinctual processes whatever the words used', and while some manage the process more easily than others, it will be necessary for such changes relating to attachment and bonding to have cultural support if parents are to be able to grasp the concept of shared responsibility. This indicates more than the change of emphasis which is the underlying philosophy of the Act; one which will require considerable changes of attitude, particularly within the legal profession.

Unless additional resources are available to provide welfare assistance (whether for 'in court' or 'out of court' – see the next section of this chapter), for parents who are in dispute as regards the future plans for their children, to work this out without weakening their bonds to their children, the intentions of the Act are unlikely to be realised. It will clearly be important for families during separation and divorce that such changes should both be encouraged and supported by more family-oriented organisational structures or the new philosophy of shared parental responsibility may never see the light of day. As will be discussed in the next section of this chapter, an important part of such reinforcement will be changes in the divorce laws so that they too may provide further basic support for shared parenting. Without such changes it may well prove too difficult for many parents to break their own attachment as husband and wife, while maintaining the bonds between their children and also with each of them as father and mother. Indeed, Lyon (1989) considers it is unfortunate that the basic principle of parental responsibility is not explicitly stated as continuing following divorce. While it may be implicit, she considers that the Act does not specifically declare the intention of the Law Commission that parents should be encouraged to sort out the arrangements for their children without going to court. She also points out that the duties which the Lord Chancellor and the Secretary of State have under the Act to make regulations give considerable executive power and are the cause of some concern to the legal profession. Finally, there is also considerable doubt that sufficient resources will be made available in order to ensure that the changes can be properly accommodated.

FACING THE FUTURE: IMPLICATIONS OF THE PROPOSED CHANGES IN THE LAW IN RELATION TO DIVORCE

Hoggett (1989) points out that the Law Commission's discussion paper, 'Facing the future – on the grounds for divorce', demonstrated that the existing divorce law fails to live up to its original aims. First, because it does little to deter hasty and acrimonious divorce, nor encourages reconciliation or negotiation as regards the future of the family, it fails to buttress the stability of marriage. Second, it does not enable marriages which have become an 'empty shell' within which lies a dead marriage to be buried with minimum bitterness, distress and humiliation, yet with maximum fairness. As discussed (in Chapter 1, 'The legal framework: grounds for the dissolution of marriage', page 4) the mixture of fault and no fault cannot attribute the blame for the breakdown of the marriage either accurately or fairly. Whether or not this should be a justiciable issue, is it practicable to dispute whether or not the marriage has irretrievably broken down? As various research studies have made clear (see Murch 1980; Davis and Murch 1988; Davis 1988) and has already been discussed (see Chapter 9) the present law has resulted in considerable bitterness amongst those who have felt they were treated unfairly. Third, although the law purports to safeguard the welfare of children, by obliging the couple to concentrate on the grounds rather than the effects of divorce, by making hostile allegations or separating for a prolonged period of uncertainty before a divorce can be obtained, it often has the opposite effect. Such criticisms have been widely supported by respondents to the paper, and in particular those who have professional experience of the divorce process (the interventionist practitioners).

Various possible solutions were canvassed in the paper, some of which are clearly not acceptable, and an analysis of the respondents is indicated as follows:

1 There is a body of opinion which would prefer a wholly fault-based system; but for most it would be both unacceptable and impracticable to turn the clock back in such a way. Even the retention of some fault based facts would fail to resolve some of the major problems which have been identified within the present law.

2 There is also a body of opinion, particularly within the Church of England (which originally suggested it), which considers that there should be a full inquiry into whether or not the marriage has indeed irretrievably broken down. Although most think such steps to be both impracticable and unacceptable for similar reasons to those discussed above in that it would encourage recriminations without a realistic focus and consideration of future options.
3 As expected, immediate unilateral demand proved unacceptable.
4 Divorce by consent while honest and humane, seems to be attractive to many, but clearly could not be the sole ground as there may be no consent in some of the most deserving cases. A small minority view would favour a combination of divorce by consent for those who wish it, and fault-based divorce where one party is opposed to it. While such a proposal has a conceptual logic, it would be inconsistent with the principle of irretrievable breakdown for divorce.

The two options which are considered most realistic by the Law Commission are divorce following a fixed period of separation and divorce as a process over time. While there are obvious and strong arguments for the former option, most respondents shared the Law Commission's concern that this would make divorce too difficult for those who are unable to bring about a separation, especially where housing is in short supply. It would discriminate too greatly between rich and poor, as between men and women and, in particular, against poorer women with children. It is such women, in particular who have the most difficulty in bringing about a separation and who use the fault procedures. Such grounds, might therefore lead to a duplication of proceedings, if only for the right to live in the matrimonial home.

The option of divorce as a process over time would not require any adjudication as to whether or not the marriage had indeed broken down; it would also envisage a fixed or minimum period, possibly nine to twelve months. During this period there would be the expectation or even requirement that the parties would consider and resolve all the the issues related to their children, the matrimonial home, their assets and financial arrangements for the future; as well as other potential and practical problems which result from the breakdown of the marriage, At the end of such a period, if one or both still wanted a divorce, this should be granted though an extension might be granted if practical problems still remain unresolved. It is now generally accepted that while the law cannot buttress marriage, what is becoming known as 'process divorce' has a number of benefits. Among these are that the divorcing couple would have the opportunity to concentrate on the implications that would accrue from a possible divorce. This would allow the possibility of reconciliation, and if the petition for divorce still goes ahead, the couple themselves would have more control over the pace of the process within the specified period and the necessary decisions might be made in an atmosphere of greater calm, though not necessarily less hostility. It would also avoid the present unrealistic attempts to allocate blame between them for the breakdown of their marriage.

The practical problems related to the outcome of the divorce would therefore become apparent to the couple before the final steps were taken. Each would then have to face up to these, to their responsibilities to each other and to those related to their children. It would be hoped that by such a time, whatever the time limit agreed under the law, the couple would be calmer and more able to come to the necessary decisions than is possible under the present system which encourages allegations of behaviour. Hoggett points out that it would be important that the process should not be rushed, especially where one wants a divorce and the other does not. Depending on the period chosen, and the present favoured length of time, being one year from the date at which one (or both partners) files a notice stating they want a divorce, such a proposal would make the period of the divorce process shorter for some and longer for others. At every stage of the process, advice and encouragement should be made available to the couple, so as to assist in working out the problems. This would clearly allow scope for conciliation and mediation, but as indicated below, whether or not this should be a formal part of the court process the Law Commission considered to be a matter for debate.

While originally expected during the summer of 1990, because of difficulties in framing the legislation, the final proposals from the Law Commission and their accompanying bill are likely to be presented to the Lord Chancellor towards the end of 1990 (*The Times*, 31 May 1990). The present Lord Chancellor has made it clear that divorce should not be made easier and that under a reformed divorce law, conciliation has an important role to play. However, it now seems unlikely that there will be any change in the divorce laws during the life of the present Parliament.

THE IMPLICATIONS OF THE CONCILIATION PROJECT UNIT'S PROPOSALS FOR A NEW STRUCTURAL MODEL FOR THE PRACTICE OF CONCILIATION

The research findings of the Conciliation Project Unit at Newcastle University (Ogus, Walker and Jones-Lee 1989), see also Walker (in preparation) have only recently been presented to the Lord Chancellor's Department, and it remains to be seen whether the Government will act upon them, though it seems likely that this will be linked with the proposals for the reform of the divorce laws. It may have come as a disappointment – though perhaps not a surprise – to those in the independent services who are member organisations of the National Family Conciliation Council – to learn that the net impact of conciliation in the independent services is to add £250 to the cost of settling a child related dispute, some £40 being met by the parties themselves, while the net impact in the court based services is £150. However, it should be pointed out in a contested divorce which results in a court hearing, the legal costs alone, which fall to the family, whoever pays the bill, are likely to be far in excess of these sums.

The research team distinguished four models of conciliation service:

Court-based with high judicial control;
Court-based with low judicial control;
Independent with probation control;
Independent with no probation control.

Their finding that court-based conciliation with a high degree of judicial control was less effective than court-based conciliation with low judicial control, or independent conciliation with probation control, may well prove controversial among the judiciary, some of whose members are known to prefer judicial control of matters which have generally been regarded as within the law, while others have been strongly in favour of independent conciliation. The largest reduction in the number of issues over which the parties involved disagreed were found to be in the two services with some degree of probation control (that is, court-based services with low judicial control, or independent services with probation control). However, it was the broader therapeutic goals of the independent conciliation services which were generally regarded by the parties themselves as being the most successful in providing counselling and dealing with personal feelings in such disputes.

In considering the effectiveness of conciliation Ogus et al. found the method to be at least as effective as other procedures in generating satisfactory settlements, and in the case of independent services, also to promote improvement in psychological well-being. They distinguished five factors which influenced the effectiveness of conciliation.

1 The disputes which were most likely to be referred to the court based services, particularly those with high judicial control, were those which were most entrenched and perhaps therefore not appropriate for the intervention of conciliation.

2 Couples were unlikely to be in dispute about only one issue, and therefore those who were in conflict about their children were also likely to be in dispute about other issues. Thus when one dispute was apparently settled, others emerged and the agreements which related to only one issue were likely to prove unstable.

3 The court-based services are only able to allocate a relatively brief amount of time to each case, while independent services do have more time to explore the issues relating to the dispute and, according to the pace and emotional state of the parties, to reach settlements. The court-based services also usually carry out their conciliation on court premises, which are often perceived as bringing the pressure of the court on the parties to reach quick settlements. It was also found that the probation officers who staffed the civil units experienced a tension between their duties as agents of the court and their wish to offer a service which was client-focused.

4 The general confusion which relates to conciliation was also shown to apply to the divorcing couples who were the clientele, who misunderstood conciliation to mean reconciliation; nor were they usually well prepared for conciliation before attending the services. In fact there was a lack of information, which was exacerbated by the fact that the one intervention that was usual formed part of a series of both legal and welfare processes.

5 The overlapping of legal and judicial procedures with those of welfare and conciliation processes, especially for clients who attended the court-based services, exacerbated their confusions regarding the terminology. They found it difficult to comprehend the differences between the issues and it was difficult for them to make the necessary switches between them, perhaps especially when they were expected to be conciliatory on matters relating to their children, while other issues were being dealt with through negotiation between solicitors or adjudication.

As the result of distinguishing the factors which they considered limited the effectiveness of the present services, Ogus et al. recommended that conciliation should not be mandatory for all couples, neither should it focus exclusively on issues relating to the children, nor overlap with other legal and welfare processes, nor should it be surrounded by ambiguous terminology. In order to maximise its effectiveness, they stated their belief that conciliation

> should be recognised as an alternative mechanism to legal, adjudicatory procedures for the resolution of disputes and be identifiable as a discrete, unambiguous process; [that] its distinguishing feature should be to enable couples to retain control of the decision making process consequent on separation and divorce, encouraging them to reach their own agreements; and the arena in which it takes place should be conducive to civilised discussion with an appropriate degree of informality.
>
> (Ogus et al. 1989)

After considering the current four models (described on page 291) and also a mixed model of court based and independent services such as currently operates in New Zealand (see Hipgrave 1988), the research team proposed the setting up of a local network of services which are independent of both the court and the Probation Service, which they suggest should be called the Family Advisory Counselling and Conciliation Bureaux. This would overcome the boundaries which currently exist between marriage guidance and the conciliation services and thus provide a range of services, which would include advice, counselling and also conciliation for individuals, couples and families with relationship difficulties, who after a brief assessment interview would be referred to the appropriate 'service'. The bureaux would also fulfil an educative function by providing the centres at which would be available a range of advice and information relating to marriage, divorce, children and the legal system.

They also proposed that at an early stage of the legal proceedings, all couples (together with their solicitors if they so wish) should be requested to attend a conference with a registrar and a court welfare officer. The objective of such a conference would be to investigate the nature of the disagreements, and to explore the potential for a negotiated settlement, while also providing information about the options available for the resolution of the disputes. It should *not* slide into conciliation, but with the free agreement of the couple might result in a referral to a Conciliation Bureau and the suspension of legal proceedings. If one or both of the couple should decide not to enter the conciliation process, then the court would deal with the dispute through the present traditional procedures, which, if a child related dispute were the issue, might involve referral to the divorce court welfare unit of the probation service, for the preparation of an investigative report.

The court welfare officer conducting the enquiries would have a *clear duty* to consider the best interests of the *child* as well as to provide a sufficiently comprehensive report so as to allow the judge to make an informed decision. Although the research team considered that the court welfare officers should continue to use the range of social work skills, they should *not* undertake conciliation, and under no circumstances should this be provided on court premises. If during the course of the investigative enquiry, the couple decided they would prefer to attempt to settle their dispute through conciliation, then they could be referred to the conciliation agency, and until this was concluded the preparation of the report would be suspended. Should a settlement be reached, the court welfare officer would only present a short report to the court. This proposal makes quite clear to client couples the statutory nature of providing an investigative report and also removes the tension for the court welfare officers which, at present, exists between their accountability to the court and the provision of client-focused services. They would thus be freed from the specific task of conciliation and would be able to focus on providing family-focused help and, in providing a welfare report for the court, would continue to have access to the necessary case documentation as at present.

The research team also made recommendations regarding the staffing and organisational structure of the Family Advisory Counselling and Conciliation Bureaux by proposing some kind of partnership or amalgamation of the National Family Conciliation Council and Relate (Marriage Guidance) Council. They suggest that such an agency should be be professionally managed, with clear lines of accountability, and should be run on a full-time basis independent of the courts and the Probation Service (though probation officers might be seconded to it) and away from court premises and probation offices. They point out that, despite the acknowledged stress of the task, at present many conciliators receive neither regular supervision nor consultative support, and they emphasise the importance of the provision of training for the staff, including the need to extend this to enable the conciliators to deal with the other issues of marital breakdown. Because of their implications for funding, these proposals for a new model for a National Family Advisory Counselling and Conciliation Service are likely to find broad acceptance with the counselling-oriented agencies, but also because they seem to propose the best use of such expertise and resources which are at present available. Indeed, many of those connected with various organisations within the divorce lobby are already engaged in discussions about both these sets of proposals and those of the Law Commmission.

Although the proposal to allow secondment of probation officers to the proposed Service may be welcome, it may, however, also prove disappointing for those probation services which have put resources into the civil units and built up expertise in conciliation (see Chapter 10, 'Divorce court welfare officers', page 221). The confusion which can arise in the court based services as regards confidentiality and privilege would be obviated if conciliation were to be restricted to the independent sector, although exceptions would need to be made for allegations of child abuse, as they are under the current practice.

As Ogus et al. found no evidence that suggested that conciliation was any more effective when solicitors were present (as they are sometimes in court based services), they would not wish to encourage the attendance of solicitors, as this would not only increase the costs but also tend to blur the boundaries between conciliation and adjudication. However, where there are issues other than child related ones, they did concede that a stronger case for the presence of solicitors might be made. The research revealed differences in conciliator preferences as regards the need to have prior knowledge of the history of a case, some regarding it as inefficient, while some clients found it unhelpful. As the problem of this lack of context was particularly acute in the court-based services, partly because of lack of time and partly because many clients seemed to expect the court welfare officers to have access to the case files, this would be resolved.

The proposal for independent conciliation would allow conciliators to proceed at the clients' pace and to explore past history if it seemed relevant. The team did not find any one technique of conciliation more helpful or unhelpful than others, nor was there evidence that the co-working favoured by many services was more effective than working with only one conciliator; though it does not appear that they considered the issue of conciliator stress, which co-working seems to be of some assistance in ameliorating. They did, however, suggest that the advantage of cross-gender co-working would be more likely both to balance power between the couple and also avoid gender bias. While they suggest that further research might study practice style at greater depth on the basis of their findings, they were only able to conclude that the conciliation process should be clearly defined and that practitioners should have the freedom to adopt a range of styles adapted to the needs of their clients.

REPRESENTATION OF THE CHILD IN CIVIL PROCEEDINGS

Murch's (Murch et al. 1990) most recent research has been into the representation of the child in civil proceedings, and it concentrated on cases in which adults claimed the care and custody of children, in care proceedings and in matrimonial and other civil proceedings. This entailed exploring the roles of the guardians *ad litem* (in care proceedings) and of the court welfare officers (usually in matrimonial proceedings); these, while in some ways overlapping at present, are also different, in that while both are independent investigators and advisers to the court, the guardian is also expected to take a position regarding the best outcome for the child. While it is possible for the court to order that the child should be made party to matrimonial proceedings and therefore be separately represented, Murch found that this rarely happened in practice. Their findings, which predominantly relate to the role of guardians *ad litem* in care proceedings at the present time, are not strictly relevant to the issues on which this book focuses. It is however, important to state that in the relatively short time they have become operative (since 1984) they have gained considerable credibility, with the courts in general and especially with solicitors, and to some extent with the parents (Murch et al. 1990).

While acknowledging that 'intervention by the state is different in kind from choosing between two parents' and that 'denial of the parents' right to represent their children is an intrusion into family autonomy which may be hard to justify when there is no question of parental capacity to care', they nevertheless point out that Clause 9 (Children Act 1989) does give the child the right to apply to take custody and access proceedings ' if he has sufficient understanding to make the proposed application.'

Murch et al. (1990) (see Chapter 10, 'Solicitors and children') have proposed that the courts should be able to make the child party to the proceedings in some divorce cases, as this would allow the court the option of ordering the provision of a welfare report only (as at present), a report plus the legal representation of the child, or a guardian *ad litem* and a solicitor. They also suggest that the child's position could be strengthened by three possible alterations to the role of the court welfare officer: first, 'that there should be a formal requirement that the officer convey to the court the ascertainable wishes and feelings of the child, unless to do so would be detrimental to the child's interests or the child himself [or herself] objects'; and second that the court welfare officer should be granted the right to give evidence and, if he so wishes, to address the court on behalf of the child. A third, but more tentative suggestion is that the officer, in his own right, might be able to make application to the court for representation.

Murch et al. point out that during the last twenty years there has been a gradual evolution towards a radically different view, in which children's interests are no longer seen as necessarily identical with those of their parents (or those adults who have responsibility for them) and therefore that their own opinions have been increasingly recognised as relevant. They set out the arguments for and against a separation of the civil court welfare units from the probation service as well as for and against their inclusions of the panels of guardians *ad litem*, which are, at present, administered by the local Social Services departments, though independent of them. They themselves would prefer the establishment of a separate and distinct Children's Advocacy Service, whose title would reflect this change of attitude towards children's rights, rather than seeing them as the objects of need, and which would include both guardians *ad litem* panels and the present court welfare services, as well as lawyers, as members of a core team as part of the infrastructure for family jurisdiction. Such a service would advise the court, in addition to services already provided by the court welfare service and the guardians *ad litem* panels, would be regionally organised as well as separate from both the Probation Service and the local authority Social Services departments. They also set out arguments as to the organisational structure of such a service, pointing out the professional credibility which has been achieved in such a relatively short time by the social workers who are, at present, the independent members of the guardians *ad litem* panels.

In recommending such changes Murch et al. stress the necessity for a new and more flexible approach to the conduct of civil proceedings related to children. They point out that it is important to retain effective judicial models, although the courts seem to be moving towards a 'problem resolution' model which involves a more settlement-seeking approach and is one which includes the associated conciliation/mediation mechanisms (namely, interventions). Their arguments are in line with some of those expressed in this book that 'many of the family problems with which family jurisdictions are called upon to deal with arise from ... "the making and breaking of affectional bonds"' as described by Bowlby (1979), 'and it is these ... which give the practice of family law much of its particular poignancy' (Murch et al. 1990).

These proposals could be seen as complementary to those of the Newcastle Conciliation Project Unit, in that the Civil Unit welfare officers could still carry out the filtering role proposed for them, as well as the investigative one, should conciliation prove inappropriate or fail to achieve agreement.

CROSS-DISCIPLINARY TRAINING

As the result of Murch's enquiries into support services for the family jurisdictions (with Hooper 1989), and into representation of the child in civil proceedings (Murch et al. 1990) he stresses the need for cross-disciplinary training, especially as between the judiciary, lawyers and social workers who now form the staff of both the civil units of the Probation Service and the panels of guardians *ad litem*, though they may have distinct post qualification training and expertise. Arguing for such cross-disciplinary training for all those working within the ambit of family jurisdiction (including conciliators working in out-of-court services, the police, child psychiatrists, paediatricians, health visitors and educational psychologists), they stress the different world view of each of these occupational groups. As has previously been argued as regards lawyers and conciliators (see Chapter 10, 'A comparison of the occupations involved with partners in separation and divorce', page 234), each of these occupations has its own perspective, and what is needed are educational and training programmes in a neutral setting, which 'monoprofessional training appears unable to accomplish'. Experience of interdisciplinary training would suggest that, while basic professional training should include the introduction of cross-disciplinary collaboration, this should primarily be provided at a post-professional level.

Hooper and Murch are now embarking on the second stage of their proposals, in which located initially in two out of a possible six judicial 'circuits', they will explore specific issues with respect to cross-disciplinary studies. Among these are the scope of action, the principal groups of practitioners to include, what the training should comprise, what matters need to be dealt with in a cross-disciplinary way and which require specialist intervention, as well as various ways related to location and linking with existing services and resources (Second Phase of Inquiry 1989–90).

CONCLUSION

The number of families with dependent children who live in one-parent households has risen from 6 to 16 per cent since 1961. There has been a threefold increase in the number of single women cohabiting between 1979 and 1987 (Kiernan and Wicks 1990); 20 per cent of unmarried women aged 18–49 are now cohabiting, as are 28 per cent of those divorced and 16 per cent of those separated, a rise of 2 per cent since 1987 (OPCS 1988). This total includes the increases in various groupings as follows: unmarried mothers rose from 4 to 5 per cent; divorced mothers increased from 5 to 6 per cent and separated mothers from 2 to 3 per cent while the percentage of widowed mothers remains at 1 per cent. On further examination, it appears that the number of so-called illegitimate births has risen (in 1987 25 per cent of the total), yet seven out of ten are jointly registered by two parents living at the same address, indicating that their parents are apparently steadily cohabiting couples (Roberts 1989; Brindle 1989). This considerable rise in the number of couples cohabiting, some as a prelude to marriage, but others who remain in stable cohabitations, from which there are children, would seem to indicate that in future this will become an inceasingly common type of family (Richards 1990). In over half (52 per cent) of the married couples with children, both parents are working (Kiernan and Wicks 1990). The divorce rate which had fallen in 1986 and 1987 rose again in 1988 to 152,633, thirteen divorces per thousand couples. One in three present-day marriages are likely to end in divorce, and from one-fifth to one-quarter of children will have parents who divorce or whose cohabitation will split up (Kiernan and Wicks 1990). A substantial proportion of divorced people eventually remarry (36 per cent) or cohabit, and about half of these relationships are likely to end in a further separation. Nevertheless these would seem to indicate that couples entering new partnerships, if not marriages, demonstrate that their hopes and expectations of family life are as lively and optimistic as ever. While approximately half of these remarriages apparently end in a subsequent separation and divorce, the other half of them not only appear to endure, but also manage to make a go of it (see Burgoyne and Clark 1984; Clark and Haldane 1990), though we know relatively little about them. For those (mostly women) who do not remarry and for all those whose remarriage results in a second, third or more divorce or break-up of partnerships, there is a strong indication that in addition to the lack of guidelines and signposts for stepfamily living, the lack of state support has been an important factor in the demise of their re-formed extended family.

Few second wives or husbands or partners (other than those in the media and show business) reveal what they have learned from their first-time failure, nor do they make a public song and dance about the positive aspects of their present relationship, which may be an exceptionally mutual and fulfilling one, which those forged in adversity often are. Research seems to show that while (usually only) one of their parents (mostly the men and the younger women) do have a second chance of marital success, many if not most of the *children* of divorce suffer at least short-term distress and disruption of their lives, for many their social competence is affected and they have a higher incidence of the more serious behavioural problems. The recent research evidence indicates according to Kelly (1990) that the significant factors for longer term adjustment are the conflict and cooperation between the divorced parents, the post-divorce adjustment of the custodial parent, the type of custodial arrangements, the economic standing of the family (according to Richards (1990), all post-divorce families move down one class), and finally that of remarriage. For those children (one in nine by 1985, now certainly higher) whose parents remarry or cohabit, although they may come to terms with their position in their stepfamilies, many would have preferred their parents to stay together. There are those whose early experiences give them a robust independence and determination to succeed in their relationships, in parenthood and in life; but while we may meet them as individuals, as a group we know almost nothing about them. We need to find out because, according to present trends, by the twenty-first century approximately 25 per cent of children will have parents who have divorced. About 50 per cent of children will not grow up in what has been seen as a 'traditional' family life (Kiernan and Wicks 1990). We also hear a great deal about lone parents, particularly those with young children and the older women who are left poverty-stricken and overburdened, alone and isolated. Yet again we know very little about those who *do* make a success of single parenthood or those who build new and fulfilling lives for themselves.

The fact that two out of three marriages do endure would indicate that we need not give up hope for the nuclear family, which is still a viable family unit. However, we now know that there are many different types of families – that one in seven are single parent households (some albeit temporarily) and that such families are often living below the poverty line; and that about one in nine families is a stepfamily, and it is perhaps partly because of societal attitudes towards stepfamilies that until recently we knew relatively little about them. As this book has tried to show, we now need to change not only the ways in which we think about families but also our attitudes towards some of them, and also to stop stigmatising those who do not conform to the traditional view of what constitutes a 'good enough family'. We must find ways of recognising realistically that all family life is hard work which deserves both recognition and support, which should be regardless of whether the families are among the two-thirds who are nuclear families, or among the third who are reformed extended families, whether or not they live in unmarried partnerships, single-parent households or in stepfamilies. We now often need to think in terms of linked households, so that we can begin to perceive that some of the so-called one-parent families do in fact have two parents who live separately, whether or not they have remarried and have further children. Some of them indeed continue to share the parenting of their children and with some success, and we need to learn more about them. We should provide family life education, for children and young people, both within the education system and perhaps even in the workplace. In particular we need to find ways to support, encourage (and, if appropriate, even compel) those apparently absent fathers to play their paternal part in the shared parental responsibility for their children. One of the ways to do so is to ensure that they remain in touch with their children. Much more research is needed to ask the right questions, and to provide some of the answers which can guide the family policies for the twenty-first century.

The Lord Chancellor in his address to the President of the Family Division's Conference (October 1989) stated,

> The bedrock of a free society lies in the independence and integrity of the family. That view is founded on the belief that, save where there is a demonstrable and recognised neglect or abuse, it is for the parents to decide how to bring up their children, not the organs of the state, be they legislative, executive or judicial.

We cannot turn the clock back – as a society we have now moved beyond the nuclear family and we must find new ways of providing both appropriate financial and interventionist support, particularly at the crisis points of the family life cycle. In order to do so we have to regard such support as an investment in the lives of every family, regardless of the household in which they might live, for their children will be the architects of the future of society.

Some useful addresses

Consult the local Citizens Advice Bureau or telephone directory for information about services in the locality.

Catholic Marriage Advisory
Council,
15, Lansdowne Road,
London W11 3AJ.
Tel.: 071–371 1341

Families Need Fathers,
37, Garden Road,
London SE15.
(send s.a.e.)

Gingerbread,
35, Wellington Street,
London WC2.
Tel.: 071–240 0953

Institute of Family Therapy,
43, New Cavendish Street,
London W1.
Tel.: 071–935 1651

Jewish Marriage Council,
529b, Finchley Road,
London NW3 7BG.
Tel.: 081–203 5207

National Family Conciliation
Council,
Shaftesbury Centre,
Percy Street,
Swindon SN2 2AZ.
Tel.: 0793–514055

National Council for One Parent
Families,
225, Kentish Town Road,
London NW5 2LX.
Tel.: 071–267 1361

National Marriage Guidance
Council,
Herbert Grey College,
Little Church Street,
Rugby CV21 3AP.
Tel.: 0788–573241

London Marriage Guidance,
76a, New Cavendish Street,
London W1.
Tel 071–586 2681

Scottish Family Conciliation Service,
40, Shandwick Place,
Edinburgh EH2 4RT.
Tel.: 031–220 1610

Solicitors' Family Law Association,
24, Croydon Road,
Keston,
Kent BR2 6EJ.

Stepfamily,
72, Willesden Lane,
London NW6.
Tel.: 071–371 0844

Counselling Service
Tel.: 071–372 0846

References

1 INTRODUCTION: THE POST-NUCLEAR FAMILY

Ahrons, Constance (1980) 'Redefining the divorced family: a conceptual framework', *Social Work* (Nov.): 437–41.

Ambrose, Peter, Harper, John and Pemberton, Richard (1983) *Surviving Divorce: Men beyond Marriage*, Brighton: Harvester Press.

Association of Directors of Social Services (1985) *Children Still in Trouble*, London: Association of Directors of Social Services.

Barrett, Michele and McIntosh, Mary (1982) *The Anti-social Family*, London: Verso.

Berger, Brigitte and Berger, Peter (1983) *The War over the Family: Capturing the Middle Ground*, London: Pelican.

Booth, The Hon. Mrs Justice (1985) *Report on the Matrimonial Causes Procedure Committee*, London: Lord Chancellor's Department.

British Agencies for Adoption and Fostering (1986) *Family Justice: a Structure for the Family Court*, London: British Association for Adoption and Fostering.

British Association of Social Workers (1985) *Family Courts*, London: British Association of Social Workers.

Browne v. *Browne* (1988) IFLR 291.

Chester, Robert (1983) 'A social agenda: policy issues relating to the family', in *The Family*, British Society for Population Studies, Conference Papers, OPCS Occasional Paper no. 31.

Davis, Gwynn and Murch, Mervyn (1988) *Grounds for Divorce*, Oxford: Clarendon Press.

Dicks, H. V. (1967) *Marital Tensions*, London: Routledge & Kegan Paul.

Divorce Law Reform Act (1969), implemented 1971, London: HMSO.

Dominian, J. (1985) 'Patterns of marital breakdown', in W. Dryden (ed.), *Marital Therapy in Britain*, vol. 1, London: Harper & Row.

Donzelot, Jacques (1979) *The Policing of Families; Welfare versus the State*, London: Hutchinson's University Library.

Eekelaar, John and Clive, Eric, with Clarke, Karen and Raikes, Susan (1977) *Custody after Divorce*, Centre for Socio-Legal Studies, Wolfson College, Oxford.

Eekelaar, John and Maclean, Mavis (1986) *Maintenance after Divorce*, Oxford: Centre for Socio-Legal Studies.

Family Policy Studies Centre (1983) 'Divorce: 1983 Matrimonial and Family Proceedings Bill', briefing paper, London: Family Policy Studies Centre.
—— (1986) 'One parent families', Fact Sheet 3, London: Family Policy Studies Centre.
Ferri, Elsa (1984) *Stepchildren: a National Study*, London: National Foundation for Educational Research / Nelson.
Field, Frank (1989) 'Missing fathers called to account', *Sunday Times*, 5 March 1989.
Finer, Mr Justice (1974) *Report of the Committee on One Parent Families*, London: Department of Health and Social Security.
Goode, William J. (1956) *After Divorce*, New York: Free Press.
Haskey, J. (1986) 'Secular changes in divorce in England and Wales by class of decree – a socio-legal analysis', *Biology and Society*, 3.
—— (1989) 'One-parent families and their children in Great Britain, numbers and characteristics', *Population Trends*, 55: 27–33.
Interdepartmental Review of Family and Domestic Jurisdiction (1986), Lord Chancellor's Department.
Justices' Clerks Society, *Resolving Family Conflict in the Eighties: a Unified Family Court*, Bristol: Justices' Clerks Society.
Lasch, Christopher (1977) *Haven in a Heartless World*, New York: Basic Books.
Law Commission (1981) *The Financial Consequences of Divorce*, London: HMSO.
—— (1986) *150,000 Children Divorced a Year: Who Cares?* London: HMSO.
—— (1988) *Facing the Future? A Summary of the Issues Arising from the Law Commission's Discussion Paper on the Ground for Divorce*, London: HMSO.
Law Society (1979) *A Better Way Out*, London: Law Society.
Leete, R. and Anthony, S. (1979) *Divorce and Remarriage*, Population Trends 16, London: HMSO.
Marriage Matters: a Consultative Document on Marriage and Divorce (1979) Home Office in Consultation with the Department of Health and Social Security, London: HMSO.
Matrimonial and Family Proceedings Act (1984) London: HMSO.
Matrimonial Causes Act (1973) London: HMSO.
Mattinson, Janet (1988) *Work, Love and Marriage: the Impact of Unemployment*, London: Duckworth.
Mesher v. *Mesher* (1980) 1 All ER 126n 85 153.
Mount, Ferdinand (1982) *The Subversive Family: an Alternative History of Love and Marriage*, London: Counterpoint.
Murch, Mervyn (1980) *Justice and Welfare in Divorce*, London: Sweet & Maxwell.
Parkinson, Lisa (1986) *Conciliation in Separation and Divorce*, London: Croom Helm.
Parsons, Talcott (1964) *The Social System*, London: Routledge & Kegan Paul.
Poster, Mark (1978) *Critical Theory of the Family*, London: Pluto Press.
Rimmer, Lesley (1981) *Families in Focus: Marriage, Divorce and Family Patterns*, Study Commission on the Family, London:
Shorter, Edward (1975) *The Making of the Modern Family*, New York: Basic Books.

Skynner, A. C. R. (1976) *One Flesh: Separate Persons*, London: Constable.
Smart, Carol (1984) *The Ties that Bind: Law, Marriage and the Reproduction of Patriarchal Relations*, London: Routledge & Kegan Paul.
Social Trends (1986) No. 16. Central Statistical Office.
—— (1989) No. 19. Central Statistical Office.
Stepfamily (1984) Information Sheet No. 1, Erica De'Ath, National Children's Bureau.
Stone, Lawrence (1977) *The Family, Sex and Marriage in England 1500–1800*, London: Weidenfeld and Nicolson.
Thornes, Barbara and Collard, Jean (1979) *Who Divorces?* London: Routledge & Kegan Paul.
Toynbee, Polly (1987) 'Happy families', *Guardian* 12 Jan. 1987.
Wachtel v. *Wachtel* (1973) Fam 72 1AER/89.
Weitzman, Lenore (1985) *The Divorce Revolution: the Unexpected Social and Economic Consequences for Women and Children in America*, New York: Free Press.

2 THE FAMILY AS A SYSTEM

Adcock, Margaret, (1988) *Some Thoughts on the Cleveland Report*. Newsletter, Association of Family Therapy, 21–3.
Ahrons, Constance and Rodgers, Roy H. (1988) *Divorced Families: a Multidisciplinary Developmental View*, New York: Norton.
Anderson, Harlene and Goolishian, Harold (1988) 'Human systems as linguistic systems: preliminary and evolving ideas about the implications for clinical theory', *Family Process*, 27 (4) (Sept.): 371–93.
Anderson, Harlene, Goolishian, Harold and Winderman, L. (1986) 'Problem determined systems: towards transformation in family therapy', *Journal of Strategic and Systemic Therapies*, 5: 1–13.
Bateson, Gregory (1967) 'Cybernetic explanation', *American Behavioral Scientist*, 10: 29–32.
—— (1973) *Steps to an Ecology of Mind*, London: Paladin.
—— (1979) *Mind and Nature*, New York: E. P. Dutton.
Birtchnall, John (1986) 'The imperfect attainment of intimacy: a key concept in marital therapy', *Journal of Family Therapy*, 8 (2): 173–77.
Bowen, Murray (1972) 'On the differentiation of self', in J. Framo (ed.), *Family Interaction: Dialogue between Family Researchers and Family Therapists*, New York: Springer.
Bowlby, J. (1969) *Separation Anxiety and Anger: Vol. 1 of Attachment and Loss*, London: Hogarth/Institute of Psychoanalysis.
—— (1973) *Separation Anxiety and Anger: Vol. 2 of Attachment and Loss*, London: Hogarth/Institute of Psychoanalysis.
—— (1980) *Loss, Sadness and Depression: Vol. 3 of Attachment and Loss*, London: Hogarth/Institute of Psychoanalysis.
Burnham, John (1986) *Family Therapy; First Steps towards a Systemic Approach*, London: Tavistock Library of Social Work Practice.
Byng-Hall, John (1980) 'The symptom bearer as distance regulator: clinical implications', *Family Process*, 19: 355–65.
—— (1986) '*Resolving distance conflicts*', in Alan Gurman (ed.), *Casebook of Marital Therapy*, New York: Guilford.

Campbell, D. and Draper, R. (1985) *Applications of Systemic Family Therapy: The Milan Approach*, London: Grune & Stratton.

Carter, Elizabeth and McGoldrick, Monica (1980) *The Family Life Cycle: Framework for Family Therapy*, New York: Gardner Press.

Combrick-Graham, L. (1985) 'A developmental model for family systems', *Family Process*, 24 (4) (June): 139-50.

Compton, Beulah Roberts and Galaway, Burt (1979) *Social Work Processes*, Homewood, IL: Dorsey Press.

Cronen, Vernon E. and Pearce, W. Barnett (1985) 'Toward an explanation of how the Milan method works: an invitation to a systemic epistomology and the evolution of family systems', in David Campbell and Rosalind Draper (eds), *Applications of Systemic Therapy: the Milan Approach*, London: Grune & Stratton.

Dare, Christopher (1979) 'Psychoanalysis and family therapy', *Journal of Family Therapy*, 1 (3): 137–53.

Dell, Paul (1985) 'Understanding Bateson and Maturana', *Journal of Marital and Family Therapy*, 11: 1–20.

Dicks, Henry (1967) *Marital Tensions: Clinical Studies towards a Theory of Interaction*, London: Routledge & Kegan Paul.

Epstein, Eugene and Loos, Victor (1989) 'Thoughts on the limits of family therapy', *Journal of Family Psychology*, 2 (4) (June) 405–21.

Erikson, Erik (1950) *Childhood and Society*, New York: Norton.

Feldman, L. (1979) 'Marital conflict and marital intimacy: an integrative-psychodynamic-behavioural-systemic model', *Family Process*, 18 (1): 69–78.

Gorell Barnes, Gill (1984) *Working with Families*, Practical Social Work Series, London: Macmillan.

Haley, Jay (1987) *Problem Solving Therapy*, 2nd edn, San Francisco: Jossey Bass.

Hart, Nicky (1976) *When Marriage Ends: a Study in Status Passage*, London: Tavistock.

Hoffman, Lynn (1980) 'The family life cycle and discontinuous change', in E. Carter and M. McGoldrick (eds), *The Family Life Cycle: Framework for Family Therapy*, New York: Gardner Press.

—— (1981) *Foundations of Family Therapy*, New York: Basic Books.

—— (1988) 'A constructivist position for family therapy', in V. Kenny, *Radical Constructivism, Autopoiesis and Psychotherapy*, *The Irish Journal of Psychology*, a Special Issue, 9 (1).

—— (1990) 'Constructing realities: an art of lenses', *Family Process* 29 (Jan): 1–12.

Keeney, Brad (1983) *Aesthetics of Change*, New York: Guilford Press.

Kohut, H. (1977) *Restoration of the Self*, New York: International Universities Press.

Lask, Brian (1982) 'Illness in the family', in A. Bentovim, G. Gorell Barnes and A. Cooklin (eds), *Family Therapy: Complementary Frameworks of Theory and Practice*, London: Academic Press.

Lawson, Annette (1988) *Adultery: an Analysis of Love and Betrayal*, Oxford: Blackwell.

McGoldrick, Monica, Anderson, Carol and Walsh, Froma (1989) *Women in Families: a Framework for Family Therapy*, New York and London: Norton.

Mansfield, Penny and Collard, Jean (1988) *The Beginning of the Rest of your Life: a Portrait of Newly-wed Marriage*, London: Macmillan.

Maturana, H. R. and Varela, F. J. (1980) *Autopoiesis and Cognition*, Dordrecht: D. Reidel.

Minuchin, Salvador (1974) *Families and Family Therapy*, Cambridge, MA: Harvard University Press.

Minuchin, Salvador, Rosman, Bernice L. and Baker, Lester (1978) *Psychosomatic Families: Anorexia Nervosa in Context*, Cambridge, MA: Harvard University Press.

Mitchell, Ann (1985) *Children in the Middle*, London: Tavistock Publications.

Morgan, D. H. J. (1985) *The Family, Politics and Social Theory*, London: Routledge & Kegan Paul.

Morley, R. (1982) 'Separate but together – the essential dichotomy of marriage', in *Change in Marriage*, a collection of papers presented at the National Marriage Guidance Council.

Parsons, Talcott (1964) *The Social System*, London: Routledge & Kegan Paul.

Reiss, David (1981) *The Family's Construction of Reality*, Cambridge, MA: Harvard University Press.

Rice, Joy K. and Rice, David (1986) *Living Through Divorce: a Developmental Approach to Divorce Therapy*, New York: Guilford Press.

Robinson, M. (1986) 'The search for intimacy', unpublished paper.

Sluzki, Carlos (1983) 'Process, structure and world views: towards an integrated view of systemic models in family therapy', *Family Process*, 22: 469–76.

Solomon, Marion (1989) *Narcissism and Intimacy: Love and Marriage in an Age of Confusion*, New York and London: Norton.

Terkelson, Kenneth (1980) 'Towards a theory of the family life cycle', in Elizabeth Carter and Monica McGoldrick *The Family Life Cycle: Framework for Family Therapy*, New York: Gardner Press.

Varela, F. (1979) *Principles of Biological Autonomy*, Holland and New York: Elsever.

Von Foerster, H. (1981) *Observing Systems*, Seaside, CA: Intersystems.

Von Glaserfield, E. (1984) *An Introduction to Radical Constructivism in the Invented Reality*, Paul Watzlawick (ed.), New York: Norton.

Wallerstein, Judith and Kelly, Joan (1980) *Surviving the Break-up: How Parents and Children Cope with Divorce*, London: Grant McIntyre.

Walrond-Skinner, Sue and Watson, David (1987) *Ethical Issues in Family Therapy*, London: Routledge & Kegan Paul.

Watzlawick, Paul (ed.) (1984) *The Invented Reality*, New York: Norton.

Watzlawick, Paul, Weakland, John and Fisch, Richard (1974) *Change: Principles of Problem Formation and Problem Resolution*, New York: Norton.

Will, David and Wrate, Rob (1985) *Integrated Family Therapy: a Problem Centred Psychodynamic Approach*, London: Tavistock.

Willi, Jurg (1984) 'The concept of collusion: a combined systemic– psychodynamic approach to marital therapy', *Family Process*, 23 (2): 177–85.

—— (1987) 'Some principles of an ecological model of the person as a consequence of the therapeutic experience with systems', *Family Process*, 26 (Dec.): 429–36.

Winnicott, Donald (1965) *The Maturational Process and the Facilitating Environment*, London: The Hogarth Press and the Institute of Psychoanalysis.

Wynne, Lyman (1984) 'The epigenesis of relational systems: a model for understanding family development', *Family Process*, 23 (Sept.): 297–318.

Wynne, Lyman, McDaniel, Susan and Weber, Timothy (eds) (1986) *Systems Consultation: a New Perspective for Family Therapy*, New York: Guilford.

3 THE FAMILY AS A SYSTEM: MODELS OF INTERVENTION

Andersen, Tom (1987) 'The reflecting team: dialogue and meta-dialogue', *Family Process*, 26 (4) (Dec.): 425–28.

Anderson, Harlene and Goolishian, Harold (1988) 'Human systems as linguistic systems: preliminary and evolving ideas about the implications for clinical theory', *Family Process* 27 (4) (Sept.): 371–93.

Anderson, Harlene, Goolishian, Harold and Winderman, L. (1986) 'Problem determined systems: toward transformation in family therapy', *Journal of Strategic and Systemic Therapies*, 5: 1–13.

Cecchin, Gianfranco (1987) 'Hypothesizing, circularity, and neutrality revisited: an invitation to curiosity', *Family Process*, 26 (4): 405–13.

—— (1988) Speaking on an intensive course on *The Practice of Systemic Therapy*, Williamstown, MA.

Clulow, Christopher and Vincent, Christopher (1987) *In the Child's Best Interests?: Divorce Court Welfare and the Search for a Settlement*, London: Tavistock Publications, Sweet & Maxwell.

Dell, P. (1985) 'Understanding Bateson and Maturana', *Journal of Marital and Family Therapy*, 11: 1–20.

Epstein, E. and Loos, V. (1989) 'Thoughts on the limits of family therapy', *Journal of Family Psychology*, 2: 405–21.

Folberg, Jay and Milne, Ann (eds) (1988) *Divorce Mediation: Theory and Practice*, New York: Guilford.

Folberg, Jay and Taylor, Alison (1984) *Mediation: a comprehensive Guide to Resolving Conflicts Without Litigation*, San Francisco: Jossey Bass.

Haley, J. (1987) *Problem-Solving Therapy*, San Francisco: Jossey Bass.

Haynes, John (1981) *Divorce Mediation*, New York: Springer.

—— (1982) 'A conceptual model of the process of family mediation: implications for training', *American Journal of Family Therapy*, 104: 5–16.

Haynes, John and Haynes, Gretchen (1989) *Mediating Divorce: Casebook of Strategies for Successful Family Negotiations*, San Francisco: Jossey Bass.

Hoffman, Lynn (1980) *Foundations of Family Therapy*, New York: Basic Books.

—— (1988) 'A constructivist position for family therapy', in Kenny Vincent, *Radical Constructivism, Autopoiesis and Psychotherapy*, The Irish Journal of Psychology, special issue, 9 (1).

—— (1990) 'Constructing realities: an art of lenses', *Family Process* 29 (Jan): 1–12.

Holmes, Jeremy and Lindley, Richard (1989) *The Values of Psychotherapy*, Oxford: Oxford University Press.

Keeney, B. (1983) *Aesthetics of Change*, New York: Guilford Press.

Kelly, Joan (1983) 'Mediation and psychotherapy: distinguishing the differences,' *Mediation Quarterly*, 1 (1) (Sept.): 33–44.

McGoldrick, Monica, Anderson, Carol and Walsh, Froma (1989) *Women in Families: a Framework for Family Therapy*, New York and London: Norton.

Minuchin, S. (1974) *Families and Family Therapy*, Cambridge, Mass.: Harvard University Press.

Mnookin, R. H. and Kornhauser, L. (1979) 'Bargaining in the shadow of the law: the case of divorce', *Yale Law Journal*, 88 (5): 950–97.

Papp, Peggy (1983) *The Process of Change*, New York: Guilford.

Parkinson, Lisa (1988) *Separation, Divorce and Families*, London: Macmillan Education.

—— (1989) 'Co-mediation with a lawyer mediator', *Family Law*, 19 (April): 135–39.

Penn, Peggy (1982) 'Circular questioning', *Family Process*, 21 (3): 267–79.

—— (1985) 'Feed forward: future questions, future maps', *Family Process*, 24 (3): 299–311.

Roberts, Marian (1990) 'Systems or selves? some ethical issues in family mediation', *Journal of Family Welfare Law*, 1: 6–17.

Robinson, Margaret (1986a) 'The search for intimacy – marital therapy with couples: a strategic use of family sessions', unpublished paper.

—— (1986b) 'Conciliation in divorce: stages in conflict management', unpublished lecture given at the Institute of Family Therapy, London.

—— (1988) 'Mediation with families in separation and divorce in the United Kingdom: links with family therapy', *American Journal of Family Therapy*, 16 (1) (New York: Brunner Mazel): 60–72.

Robinson, Margaret and Parkinson, Lisa (1985) 'Family systems approach to conciliation in separation and divorce', *Journal of Family Therapy*, 7: 357–77.

Saposnek, Donald (1983) *Mediating Child Custody Disputes: a Systematic Guide for Family Therapists, Court Counsellors, Attorneys and Judges*, San Francisco: Jossey Bass.

Storr, A. (1972) *The Dynamics of Creation*, New York: Atheneum.

Tomm, Karl (1987a) 'Interventive interviewing: Part 1, Strategizing as a fourth guideline for the therapist', *Family Process*, 25 (March): 4–13.

—— (1987b) 'Interventive interviewing: Part II, Reflexive questioning as a means to enable self-healing', *Family Process*, 26 (June): 167–83.

—— (1988) 'Interventive interviewing: Part III, Intending to ask, linear, circular, strategic, or reflexive questions', *Family Process*, 27 (March): 1–15.

Varela, F. (1979) *Principles of Biological Autonomy*, Holland and New York: Elsever.

Walker, Janet (1988) 'Divorce and conciliation: a family therapy perspective', in Eddy Street and Windy Dryden (eds), *Family Therapy in Britain*, Milton Keynes: Open University Press.

Walters, Marianne, Carter, Betty, Papp, Peggy and Silverstein, Olga (1988) *The Invisible Web: Gender Patterns in Family Relationships*, New York: Guilford.

Watzlawick, Paul (ed.) (1984) *The Invented Reality*, New York: Norton.

White, Michael (1986) 'Negative explanation, restraint, and double description: a template for family therapy', *Family Process*, 25 (2): 169–84.

—— (1988) 'The process of questioning: a therapy of literary merit', Dulwich Centre Newsletter (Winter), pp. 8–14.

Wynne, Lyman (1984) 'The epigenesis of relational systems: a model for understanding family development', *Family Process*, 23 (Sept.): 297–318.

4 FAMILIES THROUGH THE DIVORCE PROCESS: DIVORCE AS A PRIVATE SORROW

Ahrons, Constance (1980a) 'Redefining the divorced family: a conceptual framework', *Social Work* (Nov.): 437–41.

—— (1980b) 'Divorce: a crisis of family transition and change', *Family Relations*: 533–80.

Ahrons, Constance and Bowman, Madonna (1982) 'Changes in family relationships following the divorce of adult child: grandmothers' perceptions', *Journal of Divorce*, 5: 49–68.

Ahrons, Constance and Rodgers, Roy H. (1987) *Divorced Families: a Multidisciplinary, Developmental View*, New York: Norton.

Ahrons, Constance and Wallisch, Lynn (1987) 'The relationship between former spouses', in Daniel Perlman and Steve Duck (eds), *Intimate Relationships: Development, Dynamics and Deterioration*, London: Sage.

Ainsworth, M. D. S. (1973) 'The development of infant–mother attachment', in B. M. Caldwell and H. N. Ricciuiti (eds), *Review of Child Development Research*, 3, Chicago: University of Chicago Press.

Berman, William (1988) 'The role of attachment in the post divorce experience', *Journal of Personality and Social Psychology* 1(3): 496–503.

Bernard, Jessie (1975) *The Future of Parenthood: the New Role of Mothers*, London: Calder and Boyars.

Bohannon, Paul (1970) *Divorce and After*, New York: Doubleday.

Booth, Mrs J. (1985) *Report on the Matrimonial Causes Procedure Committee*, London: HMSO.

Bowlby, John (1969, 1973, 1980) *Attachment and Loss*, vols 1–3, London: Hogarth Press.

—— (1979) *The Making and Breaking of Affectional Bonds*, London: Tavistock; Sweet & Maxwell.

Carter, Elizabeth and McGoldrick, Monica (1979) *The Family Life Cycle*, New York: Gardner Press.

Davis, Gwynn, Macleod, A. and Murch, M. (1982) 'Divorce and the resolution of conflict', *The Law Society's Gazette*, pp. 40–1.

—— (1987) 'Public issues and private troubles', *Family Law*, 17 (Sept.): 299–308.

Davis, Gwynn and Murch, Mervyn (1988) *Grounds for Divorce*, Oxford: Clarendon Press.

Gold, Judith (1988) *Divorce as a Developmental Process*, Washington: American Psychiatric Press.

Goldstein, Sol (1987) *Divorced Parenting: How to Make it Work*, London: Methuen.

Hart, Nicky (1976) *When Marriage Ends: a Study in Status Passage*, London: Tavistock.

Haynes, John (1981) *Divorce Mediation: a Practical Guide for Therapists and Counselors*, New York: Springer.

Hetherington, E. M., Cox, M. and Cox, R. (1981) 'Children and divorce', in

R. W. Henderson (ed.), *Parent–Child Interaction: Theory, Research and Prospects*, New York: Academic Press.

—— (1982) 'Effects of divorce on parents and children', in M. E. Lamb (ed.), *Non-traditional Families Parenting and Child Development*, Hillsdale, NJ: Lawrence Erlbaum Associates.

Hetherington, Mavis and Tryon, Adeline (1989) 'His and hers divorces', *The Family Therapy Networker* (Nov.–Dec.): 58–61.

Isaacs, Marla Beth, Montalvo, Braulio and Abelsohn, David (1986) *The Difficult Divorce*, New York: Basic Books.

Johnston, Janet and Campbell, Linda (1988) *Impasses of Divorce*, New York: Free Press.

Kaslow, Florence and Schwartz, Lita (1987) *The Dynamics of Divorce*, New York: Brunner Mazel.

Kelly, Joan (1986) Personal communication.

—— (1988) 'Adjustment in children of divorce', *Journal of Family Psychology*, 2 (2) (Dec.): 119–40.

Kitson, Gay (1982) 'Attachment to the spouse in divorce: a scale and its application', *Journal of Marriage and the Family* (May): 379–93.

Kressel, Kenneth (1985) *The Process of Divorce: How Professionals and Couples Negotiate Settlements*, New York: Basic Books.

—— (1988) 'Parental conflict', *Journal of Family Psychology*, 2 (2) (Dec.): 145–49.

Kressel, Kenneth, Deutsch, M., Jaffe, N., Tuchman, B. and Watson, C. (1980) 'A typology of divorcing couples', *Family Process*, 19 (2): 101–16.

Lund, Mary (1984) 'Research on divorce and children', *Family Law*, 14 (Sept.): 198–201.

Mitchell, Ann (1983) 'Adolescents' experiences of parental separation and divorce', *Journal of Adolescence*, 6: 175–87.

—— (1985) *Children in the Middle: Living through Divorce*, London: Tavistock Publications.

Richards, Martin (1982) 'Post divorce arrangements for children – a psychological perspective', *Journal of Social Welfare Law*, p. 133.

Robinson, Margaret (1986) 'Families During the Divorce Process', unpublished lecture at the Institute of Family Therapy, London.

Rosenthal, K. M. and Keshet, H. F. (1981) *Fathers Without Partners*, NJ: Rowman and Littlefield.

Solomon, Marion F. (1989) *Narcissism: Love and Marriage in an Age of Confusion*, New York: Norton.

Vaughan, Diane (1987) *Uncoupling: Turning Points in Intimate Relationships*, London: Methuen.

Wallerstein, Judith and Kelly, Joan (1980) *Surviving the Breakup: How Parents and Children Cope with Divorce*, London: Grant McIntyre.

Wallerstein, Judith, with Blakeslee, Sandra (1989) *Second Chances: Men, Women and Children a Decade After Divorce*, London: Bantam Press.

Walczak, Yvette with Burns, Sheila (1984) *Divorce: the Child's Point of View*, London: Harper & Row.

Weiss, Robert (1975) *Marital Separation: Coping with the End of a Marriage and the Transition to Being Single Again*, New York: Basic Books.

Willi, Jurg (1984) 'The concept of collusion: a combined systemic psychodynamic approach to marital therapy', *Family Process*, 23 (2): 177–85.

Wright Mills, C. (1959) *The Sociological Imagination*, Harmondsworth: Penguin.

Wynne, Lyman (1984) 'The epigenesis of relational systems: a model for understanding family development', *Family Process*, 23 (Sept.): 297–318.

5 FAMILIES THROUGH THE DIVORCE PROCESS: WHEN DIVORCE BECOMES A PUBLIC ISSUE

Ahrons, Constance (1980) 'Redefining the divorced family: a conceptual framework', *Social Work*, 25 (Nov.): 437–41.

Ahrons, Constance and Wallisch, Lynn (1987) 'The relationships between former spouses', in D. Perlman and S. Duck (eds), *Intimate Relationships: Development, Dynamics and Deterioration*, London: Sage.

Ainsworth, M. D. S. (1973) 'The development of infant–mother attachment', in B. M. Caldwell and H. N. Ricciuiti (eds), *Review of Child Development Research*, vol. 3, Chicago: University of Chicago Press.

Ambrose, Peter, Harper, John and Pemberton, Richard (1983) *Surviving Divorce: Men Beyond Marriage*, Brighton: Harvester Press.

Berman, William H. (1988) 'The relationship of the ex-spouse attachment to adjustment following divorce', *Journal of Family Psychology*, 1 (3): 312–28.

Bernard, Jessie (1975) *The Future of Marriage*, Harmondsworth: Penguin.

Booth, Mrs Justice (1985) *Report on the Matrimonial Causes Procedure Committee*, Lord Chancellor's Department.

Bowlby, John (1969, 1973, 1980) *Attachment and Loss*, vols 1–3, London: Hogarth Press.

—— (1979) *The Making and Breaking of Affectional Bonds*, London: Tavistock.

Cretney, Stephen (1984) *Principles of Family Law*, 4th edn, London: Sweet & Maxwell.

Davis, Gwynn (1987) 'Public issues and private troubles', *Family Law*, 17 (Sept.): 299–308.

Davis, Gwynn, Macleod, A., and Murch, M. (1982) 'Divorce and the resolution of conflict', *The Law Society's Gazette*, pp. 40–1.

Davis, Gwynn and Murch, Mervyn (1988) *Grounds for Divorce*, Oxford: Clarendon Press.

Eekelaar, John (1984) *Family Law and Social Policy*, 2nd edn, London: Weidenfeld & Nicolson.

—— (1986) 'Divorce English style – a new way forward', *Journal of Social Welfare Law* (July) (Sweet & Maxwell), pp. 226–36.

Eekelaar, John and Maclean, Mavis (1986) *Maintenance After Divorce*, Oxford: Socio-legal Studies.

Finer, Mr Justice (1974) *Report of the Committee on One Parent Families*, London: HMSO.

Gersick, K. E. (1979) 'Fathers by choice: divorced men who receive custody of their children', in G. Levinger and O. C. Miles (eds) *Divorce and Separation*, New York: Basic Books.

Herz Brown, Fredda (1989) 'The post divorce family', in Betty Carter, and Monica McGoldrick (eds), *The Changing Family Life Cycle*, 2nd edn, London: Allen, Unwin & Bacon.

Hetherington, E. M., Cox, M. and Cox, R., (1979) 'Stress and coping in divorce: a focus on women', in J. E. Gullahorn (ed.) *Psychology and Women: in Transition*, New York: John Wiley.

—— (1981) 'Children and divorce', in R. W. Henderson (ed.), *Parent–Child Interaction: Theory, Research and Prospects*, New York: Academic Press.

—— (1982) 'Effects of divorce on parents and children', in M. E. Lamb (ed.), *Nontraditional Families, Parenting and Child Development*, Hillsdale, NJ: Lawrence Erlbaum Associates.

Hetherington, Mavis and Tryon, Adeline (1989) 'His and hers divorces', *The Family Therapy Networker* (Nov.–Dec.): 58–61.

Huntington, Dorothy (1986) 'Fathers: the forgotten figures in divorce', in John Jacobs (ed.), *Divorce and Fatherhood: the Struggle for Parental Identity*, Washington, DC: American Psychiatric Press.

Jones, Tim (1990) *A Survey of 500 men and women following Separation and Divorce since 1980*, carried out by the Universities of Brunel, Alaska and Michigan and reported in Personnel Management (*The Times*, 2 Feb. 1990).

Kaslow, F. and Schwartz, L. L. (1987) *The Dynamics of Divorce: A Life Cycle Perspective*, New York: Brunner Mazel.

Kelly, Joan (1986) Personal communication.

—— (1988) 'Adjustment in children of divorce', *Journal of Family Psychology*, 2 (2) (Dec.): 119–40.

Keshet, Harry F. and Rosenthal, Kristine (1978) 'Fathering after marital separation', *Social Work*, 23 (Jan.): 11–18.

Kitson, G. (1982) 'Attachment to the spouse in divorce: a scale and its application', *Journal of Marriage and the Family* 44: 379–93.

Matrimonial Causes Act (1969), London: HMSO.

O'Brien, M. (1982) 'Becoming a lone father: differential patterns and experiences', in L. McKee and M. O'Brien (eds) *The Father Figure*, London: Tavistock.

Parkinson, Lisa (1988) *Separation, Divorce and Families,* Practical Social Work Series, London: Macmillan Education.

Pearson, Jessica and Thoennes, Nancy (1982) 'Custody mediation in Denver: short and longer term effects', in John Eekelaar and Sanford Katz (eds), *The Resolution of Family Conflict: Comparative Legal Perspectives*, Toronto: Butterworth.

Robinson, Margaret (1986) 'The search for intimacy', unpublished paper.

—— (1988) 'Mediation with families in separation and divorce in the United Kingdom: links with family therapy', *American Journal of Family Therapy*, 16 (1): 60–72.

Rosenthal, Kristine, M. and Keshet, Harry F. (1981) *Fathers without Partners: a Study of Fathers and the Family after Marital Separation*, Totowa, New Jersey: Rowman & Littlewood.

Santrock, J. W., Warshak, R. A. and Elliott. G. L. (1982) 'Social development and parent–child interaction in father-custody and stepmother families', in M. Lamb (ed), *Non-traditional Families; Parenting and Child Development*, Hillsdale, NJ: Lawrence Erlbaum Associates.

Wallerstein, Judith with Blakeslee, Sandra (1989) *Second Chances: Men, Women and Children a Decade After Divorce*, London: Bantam Press.

Wallerstein, Judith and Kelly, Joan (1980) *Surviving the Breakup: How Parents and Children Cope with Divorce,* London: Grant McIntyre.

Weiss, Robert (1975) *Marital Separation: Coping with the End of a Marriage*, New York: Basic Books.

Weitzman, Lenore (1985) *The Divorce Revolution: the Unexpected Social and Economic Consequences for Women and Children in America*, New York: Free Press.

Whybrow, Jonathon and Priest, Jacqueline (1986) *Custody Law in Practice in the Divorce and Domestic Courts*, London: Law Commission.

6 BECOMING A STEPFAMILY: STARTING OUT

Ahrons, Constance and Rodgers, Roy H. (1988) *Divorced Families: a Multidisciplinary, Development View*, New York: Norton.

Boszormenyi, Nagy and Spark, Geraldine (1973) *Invisible Loyalties*, London: Harper & Row.

Burgoyne, Jacqueline and Clark, David (1984) *Making-a-Go-of-It*, London: Routledge & Kegan Paul.

Carter, B. and McGoldrick, M. (1980) *The Family Life Cycle: A Framework for Family Therapy*, New York: Gardner Press.

Cherlin, Andrew (1978) 'Remarriage as an incomplete institution', *American Journal of Sociology*, 84: 634–49.

A Child in Trust (1985) The report of the panel of inquiry into the circumstances surrounding the death of Jasmine Beckford presented to Brent Borough Council and to Brent Area Health Authority.

Clingempeel, W., Glenn, Brand, Eulalee and Segal, Sion (1987) 'A multilevel–multivariable–developmental perspective for future research on stepfamilies', in Kay Pasley and Marilyn Ihinger-Tallman, *Remarriage and Stepparenting: Current Research and Theory*, New York: Guilford.

Coleman, Marilyn and Ganong, Lawrence (1987) The cultural stereotpying of stepfamilies', in Kay Pasley and Marilyn Ihinger-Tallman (eds), *Remarriage and Stepparenting: Current Research and Theory*, New York: Guilford Press.

Draughon, Margaret (1975) 'Step-mother's model of identification in relation to mourning in the child', *Psychological Reports*, 36: 183–89.

Duberman, Lucile (1975) *The Reconstituted Family: a Study of Remarried Couples and Their Children*, Chicago: Nelson Hall.

Furstenberg, Frank and Spanier, Graham (1984) *Recycling the Family: Remarriage after Divorce*, Beverly Hills and London: Sage.

Ganong, Lawrence and Coleman, Marilyn (1987) 'Effects of parental remarriage on children: an updated comparison of theories, methods and findings from clinical and empirical research', in Kay Pasley and Marilyn Ihinger-Tallman (eds), *Remarriage and Stepparenting: Current Research and Theory*, New York: Guilford.

Goldstein, Sol (1987) *Divorced Parenting: How to Make it Work*, London: Methuen.

Hetherington, E. M. (1987) 'Family relations six years after divorce', in Kay Pasley and Marilyn Ihinger-Tallman (eds), *Remarriage and Stepparenting: Current Research and Theory*, New York: Guilford.

Hetherington E. M., Cox, M. and Cox R. (1978) 'The aftermath of divorce', in J. H. Stevens and M. Matthews (eds), *Mother–child, father–child relations*, Washington, DC: National Association for the Education of Young Children.

Hodges, William F. (1986) *Interventions for Children of Divorce: Custody, Access, and Psychotherapy*, New York: Wiley Interscience.

Ihinger-Tallman, Marilyn and Pasley, Kay (1987) 'Divorce and remarriage in the American family', in Kay Pasley and Marilyn Ihinger-Tallman (eds), *Remarriage and Stepparenting: Current Research and Theory*, New York: Guilford.

McGoldrick, Monica and Carter, Elizabeth (1980) 'Forming a remarried family', in Elizabeth Carter and Monica McGoldrick (eds), *The Family Life Cycle: a Framework for Family Therapy*, New York: Gardner Press.

Maddox, Brenda (1975) *The Half-parent: Living with Other People's Children*, London: André Deutsch.

Mills, David (1984) 'A model for stepfamily development', *Family Relations*, 33 (July): 365–68.

Mitchell, Ann (1983) 'Adolescents' experiences of parental separation and divorce', *Journal of Adolescence*, 6: 175–87.

—— (1985) *Children in the Middle*, London: Tavistock.

Papernow, Patricia (1984) 'The stepfamily cycle: an experiential model of stepfamily development', *Family Relations*, 33 (July): 355–63.

Pasley, Kay (1987) 'Family boundary ambiguity: perceptions of adult members', in Kay Pasley and Marilyn Ihinger-Tallman (eds), *Remarriage and Stepparenting: Current Research and Theory*, New York: Guilford.

Pasley, Kay and Ihinger-Tallman, Marilyn (1987) *Remarriage and Stepparenting: Current Research and Theory*, New York: Guilford.

Report of the Committee of Inquiry into the Care and Supervision Provided in Relation to Maria Colwell (1974), Department of Health and Social Security.

Report of the Inquiry into Child Abuse in Cleveland, 1987. Presented to the Secretary of State for Social Services.

Rimmer, L. (1981) *Families in Focus*, London: Study Commission on the Family.

Robinson, Margaret (1980) 'Step-families: a reconstituted family system', *Journal of Family Therapy*, 2: 49–53.

—— (1986) 'Reconstituted families: some implications for the family therapist', in Arnon Bentovim, Alan Cooklin and Gill Gorell Barnes (eds), *Family Therapy: Complementary Frameworks of Theory and Practice*, London: Academic Press/Grune & Stratton.

Sager, Clifford J., Brown, Hollis Steer, Crohn, Helen, Engel, Tamara, Rodstein, Evelyn and Walker, Libby (1983) *Treating the Remarried Family*, New York: Bruner Mazel.

Santrock, J. W. and Sitterle, Karen A. (1987) 'Parent–child relationships in stepmother families', in Kay Pasley and Marilyn Ihinger-Tallman, *Remarriage and Stepparenting: Current Research and Theory*, New York: Guilford.

Santrock, J. W., Warshak, R. A. and Elliott, G. W. (1982) 'Social development and parent–child interaction in father custody and stepmother families', in M. E. Lamb (ed.), *Nontraditional Families: Parenting and Child Development*, Hillsdale, NJ: Erlbaum.

Shulman, Gerda (1972) 'Myths that intrude on the adaptation of the stepfamily', *Social Casework*, 49: 131–39.

—— (1981) 'Divorce, single parenthood and stepfamilies: structural implications of these transactions', *International Journal of Family Therapy* (Summer): 87–112.

Skynner, Robin (1989) *Institutes and How to Survive Them*, London: Methuen.

Smith, Donna (1990) *Stepmothering*, Brighton: Harvester Press.

Terkelson, Kenneth (1980) 'Towards a theory of the family life cycle', in Elizabeth Carter and Monica McGoldrick (eds), *The Family Life Cycle: a Framework for Family Therapy*, New York: Gardner Press.

Visher, Emily and Visher, John (1979) *Step-families: a Guide to Working with Stepparents and Children*, New York: Brunner Mazel.

—— (1988) *Old Loyalties, New Ties: Therapeutic Strategies with Stepfamilies*, New York: Brunner Mazel.

Walczak, Yvette with Burns, Sheila (1984) *Divorce: the Child's Point of View*, New York: Harper & Row.

Wald, Esther (1981) *The Remarried Family: Challenge and Promise*, New York: Family Services Association of America.

Wallerstein, Judy and Kelly, Joan (1980) *Surviving the Break-up: How Parents and Children Cope with Divorce*, London: Grant McIntyre.

Watzlawick, P., Weakland, J. H. and Fisch, R. (1974) *Change: Principles of Problem Formation and Problem Resolution*, New York: Norton.

Wayne, Brewer (1977) *Report of the Review Panel*, Somerset Area Review Committee for Non-accidental Injury to Children.

7 BECOMING A STEPFAMILY: GETTING IT TOGETHER

Ahrons, Constance (1980) 'Redefining the divorced family: a conceptual framework', *Social Work* (Nov.): 437–41.

Bentovim, Arnon, Elton, Anne, Hildebrand, Judy, Tranter, Marian and Vizard, Eileen (eds) (1988) *Child Sexual Abuse within the Family*. London: Butterworth.

Burgoyne, J. and Clark, D. (1984) *Making-A-Go-Of-It: a Study of Step-families in Sheffield.* London: Routledge & Kegan Paul.

Carter, Elizabeth (1987) 'Gender issues in marriage and remarriage', paper given at the International Family Therapy Conference, Rome.

Carter, Elizabeth and McGoldrick, Monica (1980) *The Family Life Cycle: a Framework for Family Therapy*, New York: Gardner Press.

—— (1989) *The Changing Family Life Cycle*, 2nd edn, Allen, Unwin & Bacon.

Cherlin, Andrew (1978) 'Remarriage as an incomplete institution', *American Journal of Sociology*, 84: 634–49.

Ephron, Delia (1988) *Funny Sauce,* Harmondsworth: Penguin.

Finkelhor, David (1984) *Child Sexual Abuse: New Theory and Research,* New York: Free Press.

—— (1988) 'The nature and scope of child sexual abuse: intervening in child sexual abuse', paper given at Conference at Glasgow University.

Finkelhor, David, with Araji, Sharon, Baron, Larry, Browne, Angela, Peters, Stefanie Doyle, Wyatt, Gail Elisabeth (1986) *A Sourcebook of Child Sexual Abuse,* Beverly Hills: Sage.

Gersick, K. E. (1979) 'Fathers by choice: divorced men who receive custody of their children', in G. Levinger and O. C. Miles (eds), *Divorce and Separation*, New York: Basic Books.

Giles-Sims, Jean (1987) 'Social exchange in remarried families', in Kay Pasley and Marilyn Ihinger-Tallman (eds), *Remarriage and Stepparenting: Current Research and Theory*, New York: Guilford.

Glaser, Danya and Frosh, Stephen (1988) *Child Sexual Abuse,* London: Macmillan.

Hetherington, E. M., (1987) 'Family relations six years after divorce', in Kay Pasley and Marilyn Ihinger-Tallman (eds), *Remarriage and Stepparenting: Current Research and Theory*, New York: Guilford.

Hobbs, Christopher (1989) 'Child sexual abuse: paediatric and child health aspects', paper given at Association of Child Psychiatry and Psychology, London.

Hodges, William F. (1986) *Interventions for Children of Divorce: Custody, Access, and Psychotherapy,* New York: Wiley Interscience.

Ihinger-Tallman, Marilyn and Pasley, Kay (1987) 'Divorce and Remarriage in the American Family', in Kay Pasley and Marilyn Ihinger-Tallman (eds) *Remarriage and Stepparenting: Current Research and Theory*, New York: Guilford.

La Fontaine, Jeanne (1988), 'Child sexual abuse', Educational and Social Research Council briefing.

McGoldrick, Monica and Carter, Elizabeth (1980) 'Forming a Remarried Family', in Elizabeth Carter and Monica McGoldrick (eds) *The Family Life Cycle: A Framework for Family Therapy*, New York: Gardner Press.

Mills, David (1984) 'A model for stepfamily development', *Family Relations* 33 (July): 365–68.

National Society for the Prevention of Cruelty to Children (1988) 'Child abuse 1987: initial findings from the NSPCC'S Register research', *Child Abuse Review*, 2(3) (Winter): 15–16.

Papernow, Patricia (1984) 'The stepfamily cycle: an experiential model of stepfamily development', *Family Relations* 33 (July): 355–63.

Parker, H. and Parker, S. (1986) 'Father–daughter sexual abuse: an emerging perspective', *American Journal of Orthopsychiatry*, 54 (4): 531–48.

Pasley, Kay (1987) 'Family boundary ambiguity: perceptions of adult members', in Kay Pasley and Marilyn Ihinger-Tallman (eds) *Remarriage and Stepparenting: Current Research and Theory*, New York: Guilford.

Pasley, Kay and Ihinger-Tallman, Marilyn (1987) *Remarriage and Stepparenting: Current Research and Theory*, New York: Guilford.

Report of the Inquiry into Child Abuse in Cleveland, 1987, London: HMSO.

Robinson, Margaret (1980) 'Step-families: a reconstituted family system', *Journal of Family Therapy*, 2: 49–53.

—— (1986) 'Reconstituted families: some implications for the family therapist', in Arnon Bentovim, Alan Cooklin, and Gill Gorell Barnes (eds) *Family Therapy: Complementary Frameworks of Theory and Practice*, London: Academic Press/Grune & Stratton.

Sager, Clifford, J., Brown, Hollis Steer, Crohn, Helen, Engel, Tamara, Rodstein, Evelyn and Walker, Libby (1983) *Treating the Remarried Family,* New York: Brunner Mazel.

Wald, Esther (1981) *The Remarried Family: Challenge and Promise*, New York: FSAA.

Wallerstein, Judy and Kelly, Joan (1980) *Surviving the Break-up: How Parents and Children Cope with Divorce,* London: Grant McIntyre.

8 CHILDREN DURING DIVORCE AND REMARRIAGE

Beals, Edward W. (1979) 'Children of divorce: a family systems perspective', *Journal of Social Issues*, 4: 141–69.

Cox, Kathleen M. and Desforges, Martin (1987) *Divorce and the School*, London: Methuen.

Chethik, Morton, Dolin, Nancy, Davies, Douglas, Lohr, Rebecca and Darrow, Susan (1987) 'Children and divorce: the "negative identification"', *Journal of Divorce*, 10: 121–37.

Child Abduction Act (1984), London: HMSO.

Children's Legal Centre, Information Sheet on Child Abduction.

Emery, Robert (1988) *Marriage, Divorce and Children's Adjustment*, London: Sage.

Ferri, Elsa (1984) *Stepchildren: A National Study,* National Foundation for Educational Research/Nelson.

Guidubaldi, J., Cleminshaw, H., Perry, J. and McLaughlin, C. (1983) 'The impact of parental divorce on children: report of nationwide NASP Study', *School Psychology Review* 12: 300–23.

Guidubaldi, J, and Perry , J. D., (1984) 'Divorce, socioeconomic status and children's cognitive-social competence at school entry', *American Journal of Orthopsychiatry*, 54(3): 459–68.

—— (1985) 'Divorce and mental health sequelae for children: a two year follow-up of a nationwide sample', *Journal of American Academy of Child Psychiatry,* 24: 531–37.

Haley, J. (1980) *Leaving Home*, New York: McGraw-Hill.

Herr, Robert D. and Camara, Kathleen A. (1979) 'Post-divorce family relationships as mediating factors in the consequences of divorce for children', *The Journal of Social Issues*, 35(4): 79–96.

Hetherington, E. M. (1987) 'Family relations six years after divorce', in K. Pasley and M. Ihinger-Tallman (eds) *Remarriage and Stepparenting*, New York: Guilford.

Hetherington, E. M., Cox, M. and Cox, R. (1979a) 'The aftermath of divorce', in J. H. Stevens and M. Mathews (eds) *Mother–child, father–child relations*, Washington, DC: National Association for the Education of Young Children.

—— (1979b) 'Play and social interaction in children following divorce', *Journal of Social Issues*, 25 (4): 26–49.

—— (1985) 'Long-term effects of divorce and remarriage on the adjustment of children', *Journal of the American Academy of Child Psychiatry*, 24: 518–30.

Hetherington, E. M. and Furstenberg, Frank Jr (1989) 'Sounding the alarm: a review of second chances', in Judith Wallerstein and Sandra Blakeslee, *Second Chances*, London: Bantam Press; in *Journal of the American Orthopsychiatric Association*, 4 (2) (June): 4–8.

Hildebrand, Judy (1986) *Helping the Young Child Survive Marital Breakdown*, Institute of Child Health.

Hodges, William F. (1986) *Interventions for Children of Divorce: Custody Access and Psychotherapy*, Chichester: John Wiley & Sons.

Isaacs, Marla B., Leon, George and Donohue, Ann Marie (1987) 'Who are the "normal children" of divorce? On the need to specify population', *Journal of Divorce* 10: 107–19.

Isaacs, Marla B., Leon, George and Kline, Marsha (1987) 'When is the parent out of the picture? Different custody, different perceptions', *Family Process*, 26 (March): 101–9.

Jacobson, Doris (1978) 'The impact of marital separation/divorce on children: II Interparent hostility and child adjustment', *Journal of Divorce*, 2(1) (Fall): 3–19.

Johnston, J. and Campbell, L. E. G. (1988) *Impasses of Divorce: The Dynamics and Resolution of Family Conflict*, New York: Free Press.

Kaslow, Florence W. and Schwartz, Lita Linzer (1987) *The Dynamics of Divorce*, New York: Brunner Mazel.

Kelly, Joan (1987) Personal communication.

—— (1988) 'Adjustment in children of divorce', *Journal of Family Psychology*, 2 (2) (Dec): 119–40.

Kelly, Joan and Emery, Robert (1989) 'Review of second chances', in *Family and Conciliation Courts Review*, 27 (1): 81–3.

Kurdek, Lawrence and Siesky, Albert (1980) 'Children's perceptions of their parents' divorce', *Journal of Divorce*, 3 (4): 339–76.

Leupnitz, D. (1982) *Child custody: a Study of Families After Divorce*, Lexington, MA: Lexington Books.

Lund, Mary and Riley, Jenny (1984) 'Schools caught in the middle: educating the children of divorce', *Journal of the National Association of Primary Education.*

McCredie, Gillian and Horrox, Alan (1985) *Voices in the Dark,* London: Unwin (paperback).

McGurk, Harry and Glashan, Martin (1987) 'Children's conception of the continuity of parenthood following divorce', *Journal of Child Psychology and Psychiatry*, 28 (May): 427–36.

Maclean, Mavis and Wadsworth, Michael (1988) 'The interests of children after parental divorce: a long term perspective', *International Journal of Law and the Family*, 2: 155–66.

Mitchell, Ann (1983) 'Adolescents' experiences of parental separation and divorce', *Journal of Adolescence*, 6: 175–87.

—— (1985) *Children in the Middle,* London: Tavistock.

Morawetz, Anita and Walker, Gillian (1987) *Brief Therapy with Single-parent Families,* New York: Brunner Mazel.

Nord, Kristin (1989) 'Charting rough waters', *Family Therapy Networker* (Nov.–Dec.): 23–9.

Perkins, T. F. and Kahan, J. P. (1979) 'An empirical comparison of natural fathers and stepfathers systems', *Family Process*, 18: 175–83.

Richards, Martin and Dyson, Maureen (1982) 'Separation, divorce and the development of children: a review for the DHSS', unpublished.

Rodgers, Rick (1982) 'Children, separation and divorce', in *Where?*, 174: 23–9, London: ACE.

Rutter, Michael (1972) *Maternal Deprivation Reassessed,* London: Penguin.

Santrock, John W. and Warshak, Richard A. (1979) 'Father custody and social development in boys and girls', *Journal of Social Issues*, 35: 112–25.

Santrock, John and Sitterle, Karen A. (1987) 'Parent–child relationships in stepmother families', in Kay Pasley and Marilyn Ihinger-Tallman (eds) *Remarriage and Stepparenting: Current Research and Theory*, New York: Guilford.

Saposnek, Donald (1983) *Mediating Child Custody Disputes*, San Francisco: Jossey Bass.

Schlesinger, B. (1982) 'Children's viewpoints of living in a one-parent family', *Journal of Divorce*, 5: 1–23.

Stirtzinger, Ruth (1987) '"Where is my daddy's house?" preschool-age children of divorce and transitional phenomena – a study', *Journal of Divorce*, 10: 139–51.

Visher, Emily and Visher, John (1978) *Stepfamilies: a guide to working with stepparents and stepchildren*, New York: Brunner Mazel.

—— (1989) *Old Loyalties, New Ties: Therapeutic Struggles with Stepfamilies*, New York: Brunner Mazel.

Wadsworth, Michael (1979) *The Roots of Delinquency*, Oxford: Martin Robertson.

Walczak, Yvette with Burns, Sheila (1984) *Divorce: the Child's Point of View*, New York: Harper & Row.

Wallerstein, Judith (1984) 'Children of divorce: preliminary report of a ten-year follow-up of young children', *American Journal of Orthopsychiatry*, 54(3): 444–58.

Wallerstein, Judith and Blakeslee, Sandra (1989) *Second Chances: Men, Women and Children a Decade Afterwards*, London: Bantam Press.

Wallerstein, Judith and Kelly, Joan (1980) *Surviving the Break-up*, London: Grant McIntyre.

Warshak, R. A. and Santrock, J. W., (1983) 'The impact of divorce in father-custody and mother-custody homes: the child's perspective', in L. A. Kurdek (ed.) *Children and Divorce*, San Francisco: Jossey Bass.

Weiss, Robert (1979) 'Growing up a little faster: the experience of growing up in a single-parent household', *Journal of Social Issues*, 35: 97–111.

Zill, N. (1983) *Happy, Healthy and Insecure*, New York: Doubleday.

9 WAYS AND MEANS OF INTERVENING DURING DIVORCE AND REMARRIAGE: OUTSIDE THE COURTS

Ahrons, Constance and Wallisch, Lynn (1987) 'Parenting in the binuclear family: relationships between biological and stepparents', in Kay Pasley and Marilyn Ihinger-Tallman (eds) *Remarriage and Stepparenting: Current Research and Theory*, New York: Guilford.

Ambrose, Peter, Harper, John and Pemberton, Richard (1983) *Surviving Divorce: Men Beyond Marriage*, Brighton: Harvester.

Barnard, Jessie (1972) *The Future of Marriage*, Harmondsworth: Penguin.

Davis, Gwynn (1988) *Partisans and Mediators: the Resolution of Divorce Disputes*, Oxford: Oxford University Press.

Davis, Gwynn and Roberts, Marian (1988) *Access to Agreement: a Consumer Study of Mediation in Family Disputes*, Milton Keynes: Open University Press.

Domestic Proceedings and Magistrates' Courts Act (1978).

Feldman, L. (1979) 'Marital conflict and marital intimacy: an integrative psychodynamic-behavioural-systemic model', *Family Process*, 18 (1): 69–78.

Finkelhor, David (1988) 'The nature and scope of child sexual abuse: intervening in child sexual abuse', paper given at conference at Glasgow University.

Haynes, John (1981) *Divorce Mediation: A Practical Guide for Therapists and Counsellors*, New York: Springer.

—— (1988) 'Power balancing', in Jay Fohlberg and Ann Milne (eds), *Divorce Mediation*, New York: Guilford Press.

Haynes, John and Haynes, Gretchen (1989) *Mediating Divorce: Casebook of Strategies for Successful Family Negotiations*, New York: Jossey Bass.

Hipgrave, Tony (1989) 'The way forward', *Family Law*, 19; 264–66.

Holmes, Jeremy and Lindley, Richard (1989) *The Values of Psychotherapy*, Oxford: Oxford University Press.

Howard, John and Shepherd, Graham (1987) *Conciliation, Children and Divorce: a Family Systems Approach*, London: British Association for Adoption and Fostering/Batsford.

Jackson, Christopher (1986) 'Mediation is not Conciliation', *Family Law* 16 Dec.: 353–84.

Johnston, Janet and Campbell, Linda (1988) *The Impasse of Divorce: the Dynamics of Family Conflict*, New York: Free Press.

Kaslow, Florence and Schwartz, Lita Linzer (1987) *The Dynamics of Divorce*, New York: Brunner Mazel.

Keshet, Harry Finkelstein, and Rosenthal, Kristine (1978) 'Fathering after marital separation', *Social Work* (Jan.): 11–18.

Matrimonial Causes Act (1973).

Milne, Ann (1983) 'Divorce mediation: the state of the art', *Mediation Quarterly*, 1 (Sept.): 15–32.

Mnookin, R. and Kornhauser, L. (1979) 'Bargaining in the shadow of the law: the case of divorce', *Yale Law Journal*, 950.

Murch, Mervyn (1980) *Justice and Welfare in Divorce*, London: Sweet & Maxwell.

O'Brien, Margaret (1987) 'Men and fathers in therapy', paper presented at the British Psychological Association Annual Conference, April.

Parker, Diana (1989) paper given at the Conciliation Project Unit Conference, University of Newcastle.

Parkinson, Lisa (1986) *Conciliation in Separation and Divorce: Finding Common Ground*, London: Croom Helm.

—— (1988) *Separation, Divorce and Families*, London: Macmillan.

Roberts, Marian (1988) *Mediation in Family Disputes*. Community Care Practice Handbook, Aldershot: Wildwood Press.

—— (1990) 'Systems or selves? Some ethical issues in family mediation', in *The Journal of Social Welfare Law*, 1: 6–17.

Roberts, Simon (1988) 'Three models of family mediation', in Robert Dingwall and John Eekelaar (eds), *Divorce Mediation and the Legal Process*, Oxford: Clarendon Press.

Robinson, Margaret (1976) *Schools and Social Work*, London: Routledge & Kegan Paul.

—— (1988) 'Mediation with families in separation and divorce in the United Kingdom: links with family therapy', *American Journal of Family Therapy*, 16, 1: 60–72.

—— (forthcoming) 'A family systems approach in conciliation during the divorce process', in Andy Treacher and John Carpenter (eds), *Using Family Therapy*, 2nd edn, Oxford: Blackwell.

Robinson, Margaret and Parkinson, Lisa (1985) 'A systems spproach to conciliation in separation and divorce', *Journal of Family Therapy*, 7: 357–77.

Saposnek, Donald T. (1983) *Mediating Child Custody Disputes*, New York: Jossey Bass.

Walker, Janet (1988) 'Divorce concilation: a family therapy perspective', in Eddy Street and Windy Dryden, *Family Therapy in Britain*, Milton Keynes: Open University.

Walker, Janet and Robinson, Margaret (1990) 'Conciliation and family therapy', in Thelma Fisher (ed.) *Ten Years of Family Conciliation, National Family Conciliation Council and Family Law within the UK: Policy and Practice*, Bristol: Jordan.

10 WAYS AND MEANS OF INTERVENING DURING THE DIVORCE PROCESS: 'WITHIN THE SHADOW OF THE LAW'

Andersen, T. (1987) 'The reflecting team: dialogue and meta-dialogue in clinical work', *Family Process* 26: 415–28.

Bateson, Gregory (1956) *Steps to an Ecology of Mind*, London: Paladin.

Cain, Maureen (1979) 'The general practice lawyer and the client', *International Journal of the Sociology of Law* 7: 331–54.

Clulow, Christopher and Vincent, Christopher (1987) *In the Child's Best Interests? Divorce Court Welfare and the Search for a Settlement*, London: Tavistock.

Conciliation Project Unit (1989) *Report to the Lord Chancellor on the Costs and Effectiveness of Conciliation in England and Wales*, University of Newcastle upon Tyne.

Coogler, O. J. (1979) *Structured Mediation in Divorce Settlements*, Lexington, MA: Lexington Books.

Davis, Gwynn (1985) 'The theft of conciliation', *Probation Journal* 32 (March): 7–10.

—— (1988) *Partisans and Mediators: the Resolution of Divorce Disputes*, Oxford: Clarendon Press.

Davis, Gwynn and Murch, Mervyn (1988) *Grounds for Divorce*, Oxford: Oxford University Press.

Davis, Gwynn and Roberts, Marion (1988) *Access to Agreement: a Consumer Study of Mediation in Family Disputes*, Milton Keynes: Open University Press.

Dingwall, Robert and Eekelaar, John (1988) *Divorce Mediation and the Legal Process*, Oxford: Clarendon Press.

Erickson, Steve and Erickson, Marylin McKnight (1988) *Family Mediation Casebook: Theory and Process*, New York: Brunner Mazel.

Ewbank, Mr Justice, Re H (a Minor) (1986), 1 FLR 476.

Fisher, Mitchell S. and Fisher, Esther O. (1982) 'Towards understanding working relationships between lawyers and therapists in guiding divorcing spouses', *Journal of Divorce*, 6: 1–38.

Foden, Ann and Wells, Tony (1989) 'Unresolved attachment', *Family Law* 20: 189–91.

Folberg, Jay and Taylor, Alison (1984) *Mediation: a Comprehensive Guide to Resolving Conflicts Without Litigation*, San Francisco: Jossey Bass.

Fricker, Judge Nigel and Coates, Laurence (1989) 'Conciliation and a conciliatory approach in welfare reporting', *Family Law* 19: 56–60.

Greenson, Ralph (1967) *The Technique and Practice of Psychoanalysis*, London: The Hogarth Press and the Institute of Psycho-analysis.

Guntrip, H. (1973) 'Psychotherapy and psycho-analysis', lecture given at the Tavistock Clinic, June.

Hayles, Michelle (1988) 'State intervention and the role of the court welfare officer', *Family Law* 18 (May): 174–77.

Howard, John and Shepherd, Graham (1987) *Conciliation, Children and Divorce: a Family Systems Approach*, London: British Association of Adoption and Fostering/Batsford.

Huntington, June (1981) *Social Work and General Medical Practice Collaboration or Conflict?* London: George Allen & Unwin.

Jackson, Christopher (1986) 'Mediation is not Conciliation', Family Law 16 Dec.: 353–84.

James, Adrian (1988) '"Civil work" in the Probation Service', in Robert Dingwall and John Eekelaar (eds), *Divorce, Mediation and the Legal Process*, Oxford: Clarendon Press.

James, Adrian and Dingwall, Robert (1989) 'Social work ideologies in the Probation Service: the case of civil work', *Journal of Welfare Law*, 6: 323–38.

James, Adrian and Wilson, Kate (1986) *Couples, Conflict and Change*, London: Tavistock.

—— (1988) 'When the bough breaks . . . Matrimonial Supervision Orders?' *The Journal of Social Welfare Law*, 4: 240–49, London: Sweet & Maxwell.

Jenkins, Hugh (1980) 'Paradox: a pivotal point in therapy', *Journal of Family Therapy*, 2 (4) (Nov.): 339–56.

Johnston, Janet and Campbell, Linda (1988) *The Impasse of Divorce: the Dynamics and Resolution of Family Conflict*, New York: Free Press.

Kressel, Kenneth (1985) *The Process of Divorce: How Professionals and Couples Negotiate Settlements*, New York: Basic Books.

Law Report (1990) *Evans* v. *Evans*, Family Division, Mrs Justice Booth, *Independent* 6 Feb.

Matrimonial Causes Act (1973), London: HMSO.

Mattinson, Janet (1975) 'The reflection process in casework supervision', Institute of Marital Studies.

Melamed, James (1989) 'Attorneys and mediation: from threat to opportunity', in Steve Erickson (ed.), *Legal Issues Affecting the Practice of Mediation, Mediation Quarterly*, 23 (Spring), San Francisco: Jossey Bass.

Mills, Heather (1989) 'Divorce role of probation service "to be removed"', *Independent* 27 Nov.

Mitchell, Ann (1981) *Someone to Turn to: Experiences of Help before Divorce*, Aberdeen University Press.

Mnookin, R. H. and Kornhauser, L. (1979) 'Bargaining in the shadow of the law: the case of divorce', *Harvard Law Journal*, 88 (5): 950–97.

Murch, Mervyn (1980) *Justice and Welfare in Divorce*, London: Sweet & Maxwell.

Murch, Mervyn and Hooper, Douglas (1989) 'Developing support services for the family jurisdictions', Discussion document, Socio-Legal Centre for Family Studies, University of Bristol.

Murch, Mervyn, Hunt, Joan and McLeod, Alison (1989) *The Representation of the Child in Civil Proceedings*. Report of the Research Project, Socio-Legal Centre for Family Studies, University of Bristol.

Papp, Peggy (1983) *The Process of Change*, New York: Guilford.

Parkinson, Lisa (1986) *Conciliation in Separation and Divorce*, Beckenham: Croom Helm.

—— (1988) *Separation, Divorce and Families*, London: Macmillan.

—— (1989) 'Co-mediation with a lawyer mediator', *Family Law*, 19 (April): 135–39.

Parsloe, Phyllida (1976) 'Social work and the justice model', *The British Journal of Social Work*, 6 (1) (Spring): 71–89.

Priest, J. A. and Whybrow, J. C. (1986) 'Custody law in practice in the divorce and domestic courts', The Law Commission Supplement to Working Paper No. 96, London: HMSO.

Report of the Matrimonial Causes Procedure Committee (1985) Chair, the Hon. Mrs Justice Booth, London: HMSO.

Roberts, Marian (1990) 'Systems or selves? Some ethical issues in family mediation', *Journal of Social Welfare Law* 1: 6–17.

Robinson, Margaret (1988) 'Mediation with families in separation and divorce in the UK: links with family therapy', *American Journal of Family Therapy* 16 (1): 60–72.

Smith, Donna and Kingston, Philip (1980) 'Live supervision without a one-way screen', *Journal of Family Therapy*, 2 (4): 379–87.

Solicitors Family Law Association (1982) 'Code of practice', *Family Law*, 14: 156–57.

Summary Procedure (Domestic Proceedings Act) (1976), London: HMSO.

Winnicott, Donald (1949) 'Hate in the countertransference', *International Journal of Psycho-Analysis*, 30.

—— (1960) 'Ego distortion in terms of true and false self', in *Maturational Processes and the Facilitating Environment*, London: The Hogarth Press and the Institute of Psycho-analysis.

11 CAN RE-FORMED EXTENDED FAMILIES BECOME 'GOOD ENOUGH'?

Ahrons, Constance and Bowman, Madonna (1981) 'Changes in family relationships following divorce of adult child: Grandmother's Perceptions', *Journal of Divorce*, 5: 49–68, Haworth Press.

Ahrons, Constance and Rodgers, Roy H. (1988) *Divorced Families: a Multidisciplinary Developmental View*, New York: Norton.

Anderson, Judith Zucker and White, Geoffry D. (1986) 'An empirical investigation of interaction and relationship patterns in functional and dysfunctional nuclear families and stepfamilies', *Family Process*, 25 (Sept.): 407–21.

Bank, Stephen P. and Kahn, Michael (1982) *The Sibling Bond*, New York: Basic Books.

Burgoyne, Jacqueline and Clark, David (1984) *Making-a-Go-of-It: a study of Stepfamilies in Sheffield*, London: Routledge & Kegan Paul.

Camera, K. (1985) 'Social knowledge and behaviour of children in single-parent and two-parent households', Paper presented at 62nd Annual

Meeting of the American Orthopsychiatric Association, New York; reviewed in Joan Kelly (1988) 'Adjustments in children of divorce', *Journal of Family Psychology*, 2 (2) (Dec.): 119–40.

Carter, Betty (1987) 'Gender issues in marriage and remarriage', paper presented at the International Conference on Couples in Conflict, Rome.

—— (1988) 'Remarried families: creating a new paradigm', in Marianne Walters, Betty Carter, Peggy Papp and Olga Silverstein, *The Invisible Web: Gender Patterns in Family Relationships*, New York: Guilford.

Children Act 1989, London: HMSO.

Children and Divorce: Guidelines for Parents (1988) Family Conciliation Services, Institute of Family Therapy, London.

Clingempeel, W. Glenn, Ievoli, Richard and Brand, Eulalee (1984) 'Structural complexity and the quality of step-father–stepchild relationships', *Family Process*, 23 (Dec.): 547–59.

Cronen, Vernon, E. and Pearce, W. Barnett (1985) 'Toward an explanation of how the Milan method works: an invitation to a systemic epistemology and the evolution of family systems', in David Campbell and Rosalind Draper (eds) *Applications of Systemic Therapy: the Milan Approach*, London: Grune & Stratton.

Derdeyn, André P. and Scott, Elizabeth J. (1984) 'Joint custody: a critical analysis and appraisal', *Journal of the American Orthopsychiatry Association*, 54 (2): 199–209.

Duberman, Lucile (1975) *The Reconstituted Family: a Study of Remarried Couples and their Children*, Chicago: Nelson Hall.

Dunn, Judy and Kendrick, Carol (1982) *Siblings: Love, Envy and Understanding*, London: Grant McIntyre.

Eekelaar, John and Clive, Eric, with Clarke, Karen and Raikes, Susan (1977) *Custody After Divorce,* Oxford: Centre for Socio-Legal Studies, Wolfson College.

—— (1985) updated 1977 Wolfson College study quoted in R. Priest and J. Whybrow (1986) *Custody Law in Practice in the Divorce and Domestic Courts*. London: Law Commission/HMSO.

Emery, Robert (1988a) 'Comment: children in the divorce process', *Journal of Family Psychology*, 2 (2) (Dec.): 141–44.

—— (1988b) 'Marriage, divorce, and children's adjustment', London: Sage.

Family Law, Working Paper no. 96 (1986) *The Review of Child Law: Custody*, London: Law Commission.

Feldman, L. (1979) 'Marital conflict and marital intimacy: an integrative, psychodynamic-behavioural-systemic model', *Family Process*, 18 (1): 68–9.

Hetherington, E. M. (1987) 'Family relations six years after divorce', in Kay Pasley and Marilyn Ihinger-Tallman (eds) *Remarriage and Stepparenting: Current Research and Theory*, New York: Guilford.

Hodges, William F. (1986) *Interventions for Children of Divorce: Custody, Access, and Psychotherapy*, New York: Wiley.

Ihinger-Tallman, Marilyn (1987) 'Sibling and stepsibling bonding in stepfamilies', in Kay Pasley and Marilyn Ihinger-Tallman (eds), *Remarriage and Stepparenting: Current Research and Theory*, New York: Guilford.

Ihinger-Tallman, Marilyn and Pasley, Kay (1987) *Remarriage*, Beverly Hills: Sage.

Isaacs, Marla Beth (1988) 'The visitation schedule and child adjustment: a three year study', *Family Process*, 27 (June): 251–56.

Isaacs, Marla Beth, Leon, G. H., and Kline, M. (1987) 'When is a parent out of the picture? Different custody different perceptions', *Family Process*, 26: 101–10.

Jacobson, Doris (1987) 'Family type, visiting patterns, and children's behaviour in the stepfamily: a linked family system', in Kay Pasley and Marilyn Ihinger-Tallman, *Remarriage and Stepparenting: Current Research and Theory*, New York: Guilford.

James, Adrian and Wilson, Kate (1984) 'The trouble with access: a study of divorcing families', *British Journal of Social Work*, 14 (5): 487–506.

Kelly, Joan (1987) Personal communication.

—— (1988) 'Adjustment in children of divorce', *Journal of Family Psychology*, 2 (2) (Dec.): 119–40.

Kvanli, Judith A. and Jennings, Glen (1987) 'Recoupling: development and establishment of the spousal system in remarriage', *Journal of Divorce*, 36: 198–203.

Kressel, Kenneth (1985) *The Process of Divorce: How Professionals and Couples Negotiate Settlements*, New York: Basic Books.

The Law Commission, London: HMSO.

Leupnitz, D. (1982) *Child Custody: a Study of Families after Divorce*, Lexington, MA: Lexington Books.

McGoldrick, Monica (1989) 'Women through the family life cycle', in Carol Anderson and Froma Walsh (eds) *Women in Families: a Framework for Family Therapy*, New York: Norton.

Maddox, Brenda (1975) *The Half-parent: Living with Other People's Children*, London: André Deutsch.

Maidment, Susan (1975) 'Access conditions in custody orders', *British Journal of Law and Society*, 2 (2): 182–200.

Maslow, A. (1970) *Motivation and Personality*, New York: Harper.

Mills, David A. (1984) 'A model for stepfamily development', in *Family Relations*, 33 (July): 365–72.

Morrison, Katalin and Thompson-Guppy, Airdrie (1985) 'Cinderella's stepmother syndrome', *Canadian Journal of Psychiatry*, 30 (Nov.): 521–29.

Mount, Ferdinand (1982) *The Subversive Family: an Alternative History of Love and Marriage*, London: Counterpoint, Unwin Paperbacks.

Nehls, N. and Morganbesser, M. (1980) 'Joint custody: an exploration of the issues', *Family Process*, 19 (June): 117–25.

Papernow, Patricia (1984) 'The stepfamily cycle: an experiential model of stepfamily development', *Family Relations*, 33: 355–63.

Pasley, Kay and Ihinger-Tallman, Marilyn (1987) 'The evolution of a field of Investigation', in Kay Pasley and Marilyn Ihinger-Tallman (eds), *Remarriage and Stepparenting: Current Research and Theory*, New York: Guilford.

Perkins, Terry F. and Kahan, James P. (1979) 'An empirical comparison of natural-father and stepfather family systems', *Family Process*, 8 (June): 175–83.

Priest, J. A. and Whybrow, J. C. (1986) 'Custody law and practice in the divorce and domestic courts', Supplement to Working Paper No. 96, The Law Commission, London: HMSO.

'Review of child law: custody', Working Paper No. 96, London: HMSO.

Robinson, Margaret (1980) 'Step-families: a reconstituted family system', *Journal of Family Therapy*, 2: 49–53.

Rothberg, Barbara (1983) 'Joint custody: parental problems and satisfactions', *Family Process*, 22 (March): 32–53.

Sager, Clifford J., Brown, Hollis Steer, Crohn, Helen, Engel, Tamara, Rodstein, Evelyn and Walker, Libby (1983) *Treating the Remarried Family*, New York: Brunner Mazel.

Santrock, J. and Sitterle, Karen (1987) 'Parent-child relationships in stepmother families', in Kay Pasley and Marilyn Ihinger-Tallman (eds) *Remarriage and Stepparenting: Current Research and Theory*, New York: Guilford.

Santrock, J., Warshak, R. and Elliot, G. (1982) 'Social development and parent-child interaction of father-custody and stepmother families', in M. Lamb (ed.), *Non-traditional Families: Parenting and Child Development*, San Francisco: Jossey Bass.

Schulman, Gerda (1981) 'Divorce, single parenthood and stepfamilies: structural implications of these transactions', *International Journal of Family Therapy*, 3: 87–112.

Schwartz, Lita Linzer (1987) 'Joint custody: is it right for all children?', *Journal of Family Psychology*, 1 (1) (Sept.): 120–24.

Smith, Donna (1990) *Stepmothering*, Brighton: Harvester Wheatsheaf.

Solomon, Marion (1989) *Narcissism and Intimacy: Love and Marriage in an Age of Confusion*, New York: Norton.

Stone, Nigel (1989) 'The case of the naked blood tie', *Family Law*, 19: 74–6.

Terkelson, Kenneth (1980) 'Towards a theory of the family life cycle', in E. Carter and M. McGoldrick, *The Family Life Cycle: a Framework for Family Therapy*, New York: Gardner Press.

Visher, Emily and Visher, John (1988) *Old Loyalties, New Ties: Therapeutic Strategies with Stepfamilies*, New York: Brunner Mazel.

Visher, John and Visher, Emily (1979) *Stepfamilies: a Guide to Working with Stepparents and Stepchildren*, New York: Brunner Mazel.

Wald, Esther (1981) *The Remarried Family: Challenge and Promise*, New York: Family Service Association of America.

Wallerstein, Judith (1989) *Second Chances: Men, Women and Children a Decade after Divorce*, London: Bantam.

Walters, M., Carter, B., Papp, P. and Silverstein, O. (1988) *The Invisible Web: Gender Patterns in Family Relationships*, New York: Guilford.

Warshak, R. A. and Santrock, J. W. (1983) 'The impact of divorce in father-custody and mother-custody homes: the child's perspective', in L. A. Kurdek (ed) *Children and Divorce*, San Francisco: Jossey Bass.

Weir, Robyn (1985) 'Access patterns and conflict', Research Report No. 7, Family Court of Australia.

Weitzman, Lenore J. (1985) *The Divorce Revolution: the Unexpected Social and Economic Consequences for Women and Children in America*, New York: Free Press.

Willi, Jurg (1984) 'The concept of collusion: a combined systemic-psychodynamic approach to marital therapy', *Family Process*, 33: 177–85.

—— (1987) 'Some principles of an ecological model of the person as a consequence of the therapeutic experience with systems', *Family Process*, 26 (Dec.): 429–36.

Winnicott, D. W. (1975) 'Aggression in relation to emotional development', in *Through Paediatrics to Psychoanalysis*, New York: Basic Books.

Wynne, Lyman (1984) 'The epigenesis of relational systems: a model for understanding family development', *Family Process*, 23 (3) (Sept.).

12   THE REFORMATION OF FAMILY POLICY – A SECOND CHANCE FOR FAMILIES IN TRANSITION?

Bowlby, John (1979) *The Making and Breaking of Affectional Bonds*, London: Tavistock.

Brindle, David (1989) 'Breaking up, not breaking down', *Guardian*, 6 Sept. 1989.

Burgoyne, Jacqueline and Clark, David (1984) *Making a-Go-of-It: a Study of Stepfamilies in Sheffield*, London: Routledge & Kegan Paul.

Children Act 1989, London: HMSO.

Clark, David and Haldane, Douglas (1990) *Wedlocked*? Cambridge: Polity Press.

Clulow, Christopher and Vincent, Christopher (1987) *In the Child's Best Interests*, London: Tavistock.

Davis, Gwynn (1988) *Partisans and Mediators: The Resolution of Divorce Disputes*, Oxford: Clarendon Press.

Davis, Gwynn and Murch, Mervyn (1988) *Grounds for Divorce*, Oxford: Clarendon Press.

Davis, Gwynn and Roberts, Marion (1988) *Access to Agreeement: a Consumer Study of Mediation in Family Disputes*, Milton Keynes: Open University Press.

Facing the Future: a Discussion Paper on the Ground for Divorce (1988), Law Commission No. 170, London: HMSO.

Field, Frank (1989) 'A springboard to freedom for single parents', *Independent*, 24 Oct.

Fisher, Thelma (1989) 'The Children Bill: the challenge to out-of-court conciliation', *Family Law*, 19 (June): 222–23.

Garlick, Helen (1990) 'A sordid game of cat and mouse', *Independent*, 26 Jan. 1990.

Hipgrave, Tony (1988) 'Family courts: New Zealand's other anti-nuclear policy', *Family Law*, 18 (March): 109–12.

Hoggett, Brenda (1989) 'Family law into the 1990s', *Family Law*, 19 (June): 177–80.

Hooper, Douglas and Murch, Mervyn (1989) 'Developing support services for the family jurisdictions: a discussion document', Socio-Legal Centre for Family Studies, Unimersity of Bristol.

Kelly, Joan (1990) 'Family Research, past, present and future. North American and British perspectives', paper given at the conference 'From Rights to Responsibilities for Parents – the emancipation of children', York.

Kierman, Kathleen and Wicks, Malcolm (1990) *Family Change and Future Policy*, London: Family Policy Studies/Rowntree Trust.

Law Commission Working Papers: Family Law, 'Review of Child Law', London: HMSO. No. 91 (1985) 'Guardianship'; No. 96 (1986) 'Custody'; No. 101 (1987) 'Wardship'.

Law Commission (1988) 'Facing the future – a discussion paper on the ground for divorce', London: HMSO.

Lyon, Christina (1989) 'Redefinition of parental rights – recent English developments relating to joint custody, custodianship and adoption in England', *The Journal of Social Welfare Law*, 3: 138–48.

Murch, Mervyn (1980) *Justice and Welfare in Divorce*, Sweet & Maxwell.

Murch, Mervyn and Hooper, Douglas (1989) 'Developing support services for the family jurisdictions', discussion document, Bristol: Socio-Legal Centre for Family Studies, University of Bristol.

Murch Mervyn, Hunt, Joan and McLeod, Alison (1990) 'The representation of the child in civil proceedings', report of the research project for the Ministry of Health, 1985–89, Bristol: Socio-Legal Centre for Family Studies, University of Bristol.

Office of Population Censuses and Surveys (1988) General Household Survey, London: HMSO.

Ogus, Anthony, Walker, Janet and Jones-Lee, Michael (1989) *The Costs and Effectiveness of Family Conciliation*, London: The Lord Chancellor's Department, Law Commission.

Report of the Inquiry into Child Abuse in Cleveland 1987 (1988), Cmnd. 412, London: HMSO.

Review of Child Care Law (Consultative Document) (1985), London: HMSO.

Richards, Martin (1990) 'Family research, past, present and future. North American and British perspectives', paper given at the conference 'From Rights to Responsibilities for Parents – the emancipation of children', York.

Roberts, Yvonne (1989) 'Time to end the slander of the innocents', *Observer*, 1 Oct.

Seabrook, Jeremy (1989) 'The enterprise culture that makes blood thinner than water', *Independent*, 19 Aug.

Social Trends (1989) 19, London: HMSO.

Toynbee, Polly (1989a) 'Divorce today', *Observer*, 3 Sept. and 10 Sept.

—— (1989b) *Happy Families* (Panorama Programme, BBC 1) 18 Sept. 1989.

Wicks, Malcolm (1989) 'A contradiction where there should be a strategy', *Independent*, 28 Sept.

Name index

Subject index